Divine Madness

(Theia Mania)

For Funda,
My Light.

Avenue Winston Churchill, 28/10
(B)1180 Uccle
www.ederneditions.com
info@ederneditions.com

1st edition

Layout and art direction: Jack Durieux
Cover llustration:
Pıtırak, Lutfiye Batukan

Printed by BOD (Germany)

Dépôt légal : D/2025/10.807/63

ESİN
ÖZMEN

Divine Madness
(Theia Mania)

◆

novel

Asmodée Edern

The young are permanently
in a state resembling intoxication

Aristotle

1

Plekia Village, between Iconium and Constantinople, 1143

BASIL had his share of pain in life. I was the second child. My elder brother, four then, had fallen asleep clutching a sesame-honey sweet in his hand only to wake up to a horrific scene. Our mother up on her feet, blood trickling down her legs, a baby covered in blood, still connected to her lay on the floor. Yes, my mother gave birth to me while standing. The poor boy screamed in terror as she, still reeling, tried to explain what had just happened. It did not take him long to compose himself; the boy approached the gory sight innocently and offered his sweet to the newborn.

Apparently when my mother went into labour, in the throes of birth pangs, she urged Basil to go and fetch the midwife of the village. The ever-shy Basil begged her not to make him go. "Can't you wait till the morning?" he pleaded. "I implore you – please. You come from a virtuous family. Surely you can wait; I cannot wake the midwife in the middle of the night." My mother could not wait, of course. Basil had to go. By the time they came back, I had slid out of her womb and landed headfirst on the floor. I fell on my head and survived. The boy died a few months later.

The motif of 'headfirst' – that is to say, 'headlong' – lingered. My puppy, whom I named 'Dog,' and even allowed inside the house, caused something of a scandal in Plekia:

"Theia, ever heedless, shares her dishes with her dog, just like the Latins. That dog of hers licks the bowl clean, and then she has her own dinner from the same bowl without so much as rinsing it. Can you believe it? And they fall asleep curled up together."

Our neighbour Gabras gave him to me when he was a pup. There were two in the litter. I wanted the black one, but my crying and beseeching fell on deaf ears. He gave the black pup to his son Nikepheros, who had actually wanted the white one. Scrunching up his face, Gabras looked down at his son Nikepheros who was too scared to cry, though his lips trembled – and said, *"Nothing will ever be exactly as you would like it to be, nor will it ever be exactly what you don't want it to be."*

The black pup now lives the honourable life of an honourable hunting dog at the Gabras manor, keeping watch over it.

Mine follows me everywhere – which is to say, he loafs about without a care in the world. I was careful not to give him too much attention at first, fearing my donkey Pegasus might feel betrayed, but Dog finally won me over.

When he rested his muzzle on my knee – which was something he did whenever he felt comfortable – he was remarkably human-like, and that was, I believe, ironically, the very reason why we insult people using words referring to dogs and not to wolves or foxes: dogs were like us and not like us at the same time. That afternoon Dog was particularly lovable, though I couldn't feel a thing as his muzzle had been resting on my leg so long it had fallen asleep.

It was finally quiet, time for me to come out from my hiding place. The dust cloud kicked up by the Turkish horses as they had crossed the courtyard had finally fallen and settled. From where I was crouched, I hadn't heard any sound that might indicate a murder had taken place. That meant Basil and Anna were still alive. The question flashed through my mind: why hadn't they come looking for me after all this time? Then again, if Basil were still alive, indulging in such frivolous, trivial thoughts was unacceptable, I told myself. Besides, if they had truly been in danger, the fact that had I had run off to hide like this was something they could both use against me. But Thank God, Basil would never ever mention such a detail.

I stood, dusted myself off, and slowly opened the stable door. Peeking out, I saw no one in the courtyard. A dog barked somewhere in the distance, but Dog remained silent. This was a good sign; the coast was clear. When Pegasus looked me straight in the eye, I was sure the danger had passed – because that look also meant he wanted a treat. Not long ago, before they got to me and Dog, the gossip mill of the town was churning out rumours about Pegasus and me. The word was that I smelled of donkey. Of course, like all the other gossip, it was groundless. The strongest odour a donkey carries is dust, and, as everyone knows, dust doesn't really smell like anything. After all, how else could they ever ask the Emperor to carry the *akakia*, a silken bag filled with dust, if it smelled that bad? That soft, light, purple pouch was intended to remind the Emperor, and his entourage, that one day we will all return to dust.

Pegasus was an albino, hence a special donkey, and the very reason I'd wanted the black pup. Black and white, day and night, good and evil, sun and rain, war and peace, cruelty and kindness, a sage and a fool, sorrow and joy, and on and on the list went… Wasn't this life's modus operandi? Didn't we always ply between extremes?

And so, my *akakia*, the bag of dust designed to intimidate the emperor concerning the frivolity and fatality of life would take the colours of my two animals, a symbol not as threatening as his but more mature and less discreet and even slightly friendly. A cue to life's mysteries. Perhaps it would even relieve the sense of awe and guilt of being caught between opposites, for life is composed of traveling between the extremes. Life is made up of duality and separation. Mind you, there are, indeed, crueller symbols – take the sword of Damocles, for instance. Suspended by a single hair from a horse›s tail, it hangs directly over your head, and you never know when it will fall. That, too, we knew well… just another of life's contraptions. And thereupon, just as Gabras had said: nothing will ever be as you want it to be.

By the way, I should add: Pegasus had a musky smell with berry nuances – a fragrance redolent of freshly cut wood. And when his hair was wet, it gave off the scent of damp soil after rain. The colour of his stare was purple – the purple of Sidon and Tyre. There are different tones of purple: lilac, hyacinth, rose, violet, blooms of marigold and thyme. The ribbon tapes used to secure and mark lands confiscated by the Emperor, or the ink he used to sign official decrees was purple, as well. On flowers it came for free, but not in ribbons and ink. So, should the people in our town ever have the chance to see that hue anywhere beyond a petal, it would most likely be in Pegasus's eyes. Now, needless to say, I considered such groundless gossip about my donkey and his purple eyes to be nothing short of rude, ungrateful and ignorant.

I found the stump of cucumber I had tossed aside when I raced off to hide, dusted it off, and gave it to Pegasus. He always looks me in the eye when given a treat, pausing after each swallow as if to ask what the occasion might be – it was not Sunday, after all. I walked across the courtyard to the house leaving him in the barn alone with his cucumber. The entrance was filled with a snore that began small and palatal each time, then climbed higher and higher where tongue and the tonsil began to wrestle before the sound climaxed into a terrible bear's roar. From the living room, I hurried into the kitchen, where I found Anna, our veteran housemaid. Five bowls sat on the table. Her little hands were deftly plucking broad beans from one bowl, snapping the shells into another, and tossing the beans into a third. From the fourth bowl, she plucked a fresh green almond, tossed it in her mouth, chewed it, then spat the pip into the fifth. She moved in one swift motion, but when she sensed my presence in the room, she looked up and fixed a dark gaze on me.

"You have straw in your hair," she said. Lowering her head slowly, she went back to work.

Head thrown back awkwardly, mouth wide open, Basil was asleep in a chair. I marvelled that the grumble – still inhuman, but now less ursine and more metallic, clamorous, perhaps like something an automaton might let out – which pressured his throat and tormented his bulbous nose, did not wake him. It would surely strike fear in those who came knocking on our door. Eyewitnesses have spoken of a wooden replica of King Solomon's throne that sits in the Emperor's palace in Constantinople. Gold-plated lions stand guard beside it. This is no ordinary throne, this is an automaton, a machine. When the Emperor moves, the lions beat their tails on the floor, their heads turn, their tongues quiver and they roar so loudly that those in attendance cower in fear, cover their ears and vow never to show disrespect to New Rome and the Emperor's reign. I can tell you that, at the time, I had only rumours about such matters but later, I would hear a description from someone of the utmost reliability – the ultimate source. Indeed, most rumours prove groundless or flawed. In time, we come to learn that what passes for 'truth' can be at least as fallacious and deceptive as the idle chatter. However, I believe the description of the throne I had been given was accurate, for the most part – although, it should be noted that the throne was actually made of brass, and not wood. And when the Emperor sat upon it, someone would take hold of a secret lever and crank it up and down, causing such a racket that his audience nearly swallowed their tongues in surprise. Before the throne stood a gold-plated, bronze tree, with golden birds in its branches. When they came to life and began twittering, the audience would shriek. Precious stones set around the automaton reflected light, casting clouds of red and green. So, the atmosphere was softened and did not consist only of the intimidating effect of the lions. As everyone knows, we Romans are a people with a genius for masterfully combining the bitter with the sweet. This is what sets us apart from the barbarians. The Ruler of Eastern Rome is magnanimous; it is only natural he be seen as the height of refinement and worldliness.

Basil snuffled somewhere deep in his nasal cavity and let out a porcine grunt. His chest heaved. Closing his lips, he wiped the saliva from his chin with his sleeve and focused on me through one open eye.

To make myself busy, I began gathering up the empty wine glasses. Basil had been drinking with Ataman, the Turkoman tribe leader. I brought a glass to my nose and sniffed. No scent of cinnamon, mint, fennel or caraway seeds – so, the *eukration*, hot water flavoured with cumin had been spared. The mixture of water and herbs was never used in the fine wines. We reserved it for the lower-grade stuff. Clearly Basil had brought out two of the highest-quality bottles – one from Egypt and another from the island of Chios – which we kept for special guests. Obviously, just like the Latins, Ataman enjoyed his wine undiluted and without added cardamom resin; the glasses bore only the pungent aroma of pure wine. Interestingly enough, Basil – who normally preferred his wine with all the additions, had done the same, following Ataman's lead. Normally he drank the second- or third-rate bottles.

As I realised Basil was awake, I exclaimed, "So, what does the Turkoman want, father?"

He let out a startled yelp as he sat up. Apparently, he hadn't been awake after all.

"I didn't know you were here! What… what are you doing?" he stammered, opening both eyes and struggling to rouse himself.

"Why did the barbarian come? Something terrible's happened, hasn't it? Something to do with the fasting incident?! What was it about?"

A month ago, in April, a band of Turkomans sat down to eat with a few Greeks in the marketplace during Ramadan and they were flogged for it. The perpetrator was a short, fat man whom the Turks addressed as *bb*. I first thought that was his name, but later understood it referred to his rank: the Inspector or Emissary of the King of the Sultanate of Rhomanoi, stationed in our village of Plekia. Iconium was their chief city. Sultan Mesud belonged to the same dynasty that ruled another Muslim realm to the east: The Great Seljuk Empire, whose vast lands stretched from Persia to Central Asia in the north and from there to Hindustan in the south. Political and familial ties bound the two empires together.

The Greeks were moved aside but were obliged to stay and watch. The new Inspector, who had come from their capital Iconium, wore an exquisite kaftan that fell to his chubby ankles and fastened over his bulging chest with silver buttons and embroidery. Whenever things were not exactly as to his liking, his face would flush scarlet, sweat would trickle down the fat folds of his neck, and he'd begin to shriek at the top of his lungs. Anguished nomads would come scurrying, always managing to line up before him in a matter of seconds. First, they were made to hurl their red felt caps to the ground. Then they were stripped of their shirts, revealing bare shoulders and backs – olive-hued and unblemished. It was obvious these were men who had never suffered a flogging. Their skin bore no trace of pain, no blemish to betray their unspoiled animal like purity and integrity. That distinctive headgear they wore made of blood red felt had become fashionable in Latin countries after the crusade. So much so, in fact, that it was now banned, for it epitomised the unflinching daredevilry of these men and the blood that had been spilt in that unfortunate venture.

The *Muhtasib* always carried a whip with a silver handle, adorned with gems. He'd rattle the shiny silver balls attached to its leather thongs. The whip remained in mint condition, for though he screamed often, he rarely used it. That task fell to his underling, another short, fat man who would crack his own whip and then flog each offender three times. Their anguish served as a lesson to us all. After that, not a soul dared to eat in public during the holy month of Ramadan, not even a Christian. Still the *Muhtasib's* finely kept, jingling whip would still be brandished on behalf of Sultan Mesud of Iconium.

Once again, we heard through the grapevine that the Turkomans were having their sons baptised, as well as circumcised. Several Princes in Iconium, even the Sultan himself, along with various half-bred Princes, were doing the same, seeking the goodwill of both Allah and the Holy Trinity. Baptism was most certainly not a routine practise for them, but it happened more often than one might think. A Roman mother who had tried every Christian litany in vain to heal an ailing child might, as a last resort – and against the advice of her neighbours – go to a mosque and pray for a miracle. Such things were neither sanctioned or approved nor were they one-of-a-kind happenings. On the other hand, a Christian stricken with misfortune and forsaken by Christ, or the Virgin might decide to try their luck and appeal to the Prophet Mohammed, and if – lo and behold – they were to obtain a satisfactory result, they might convert. It was not unprecedented. We had even heard that Christians and Muslims alike prayed in the House of Judas on Straight Street in Damascus. If Muslim charms failed, Christian charms were the next best option.

It is doubtful the Turkomans knew anything about the Holy Trinity, but many were convinced that baptism could work wonders. It was a known cure for leprosy, for example, and it staved off the threat of witchcraft and wolves. The Turkomans had no fear of the latter; they had the blood of wolves in their veins – of a she-wolf, some said was blue, others, grey. The legend told of the ancient Sky Turks, a secluded tribe living in harmony to the west of the Caspian Sea, who were raided by a local enemy that killed every member of their tribe but one: a ten-year-old boy. When the enemy saw the scrawny little boy, they took pity on him – if you can call it that – by chopping off his feet and tossing him into a swamp. Out of nowhere came a she-wolf, who suckled him, licked his wounds, and later fed him. In time, he grew strong. He grew tall. When the enemy ruler later learned the boy still lived, he sent men to finish the job. Soon enough they found the blue-grey wolf with the footless boy in her care – but she seized him in her teeth and fled. She crossed the sea and came to a rich fertile plain in the southern foothills of the Altai mountains. Soon after, she gave birth to ten sons with dark brows, fiery lips and sky-like eyes. On that green plateau surrounded by cool waters, abundant fruit trees and grazing beasts, they grew up to be men. Each raised a blue flag with a grey wolf at the front of his tent. Each took wives from other tribes. Before long ten lineages had formed, with hundreds of families that working as blacksmiths.

Several weeks after the punishment of the Turkomans, the *Muhtasib*'s whip was found in the rubbish where the butcher would throw scraps of slaughtered animals. The leather thongs were burnt and nearly gone, the silver handle stained with smoke – but the gems remained untouched. And the whip was returned to the Inspector.

Basil humphed.

"Ataman had nothing to do with the flagellation, Theia. Would you please calm down," he said, waving his hand as though batting away a fly.

I snapped, "I am trying very hard, father. I am emulating you – though, I have to admit, it's really rather irritating to do that. But can't you just come out with it already and tell me: what has happened?"

"Ataman is disbanding the monastery."

"Oh! Disbanding? You mean, completely? Did he slay the monks?"

"By no means." He chuckled slightly. "He's having them deported to Constantinople." As my eyebrows rose he added, "At first he wanted to turn the church into a stable, then he came up with the idea of a weaving centre, but I managed to obtain the licence to keep it running – along with the Priest."

"How magnanimous of him!"

Ignoring my sarcasm, he went on, "Now, I just need to find some way inform Constantinople so they'll sustain the Priest's stipend, and, of course, cover the upkeep of the building. And most importantly…"

He puffed his chest slightly. "He's allowing our relics, the piece of the True Cross and the Holy Nail, to be sent to the capital! Instead of..."

Now, our village of Plekia happened to possess a chip from the True Cross and a rusty nail that had been pierced it. The story went that Helena, mother of the Emperor Constantine, stopped in Plekia – if indeed our little village even existed at the time – on her return from Jerusalem to Rome with the Cross and other relics. Basil's father, Zeno, claimed Helena was a Greek from Drepanon, not far from here, and that the relics were authentic. No one dared ask how he knew this, or how he got his hands on the splinter and the passion nail, or where they had been languishing for the past eight hundred years or so before they finally came to see the light of day. We simply took it to be true. When two great fragments of the True Cross, each as large a man's legs, were to be brought into the Hagia Sophia and placed beside the baptistry for blessing before being paraded about the city of Constantinople on the 30th of July, Zeno would be there too, with our relics, his hands tightly clutching the glass jar that sat atop a silk purple cushion. This meant that, perhaps, the foul air of Plekia might be made sweet. Perhaps, if anyone was ill, they might even be cured.

Basil now wore that endearing look that came over his face when we were in agreement, and he gushed, "Instead of ransoming them!"

"Oh! He does love his money, doesn't he?"

"Who doesn't?"

"What do those mouldy old relics mean to him, anyway? A scrap of worm-eaten wood and a rusty old nail, base materials at best."

"Without a doubt. But everything is in the eye of the beholder, my child. In the eye of the beholder."

I was far more annoyed at Basil than at Ataman. I feigned a smile.

"You should deliver the holy relics yourself. And, while you're in Constantinople, you might like to have a little chat with the Emperor and secure the Priest's salary!"

He sighed as I went on, "Who knows – considering your diplomatic skills, he might, God willing, give you a grand promotion. Maybe he'll appoint you Ambassador to the Barbarians!"

Basil rolled his eyes.

"Sarcasm," I said with a small shrug.

"I did notice, my dear. I will talk to the monks. I'm sure most will go, though I doubt Svoronos the bookbinder will – or Skleros. Svoronos will want to stay to support his son-in-law at his ceramic workshop, and Skleros will want to build that new oven for his breads. I've already lent him the money. You should record it in your ledger. I told him to take it slowly and give people time to trust his services." He sighed again. "And about that sarcasm of yours…" His brow now furrowed. "Since you wield it with such a sting – it really is wholly unattractive in a lady…"

"I'm attractive enough for Ataman to sell me as a slave to some stinky savage – and to kill you," I interrupted. "Don't you ever think…?"

Basil gave me a black look, as I knotted my brows in mock exaggeration. The sides of his fat lower lip drooped. I rolled my eyes in reply but held my tongue.

"Raising her voice like that and making such grotesque grimaces do not suit a decent girl, Theia. You should not take each emotion you feel so seriously. Just wait it out. A girl must smile at all times, even when she doesn't feel like it. If nothing else, she should not pull faces."

"So she must be either very strong – or very fake? I'm certainly not fake. And if I am a girl, why should I be strong then?"

He rolled his eyes again and ignored the question.

"By the way, he was telling me about the books in the monastery library, and I…"

"And you made him agree to grant them to us!" I burst in with sudden enthusiasm, then immediately flushed with embarrassment.

"Indeed I did." He chuckled. "Though he'll pick out what he wants first from the collection. Now then, what are we having for dinner this evening?"

A sudden urge to say something hurtful rose up in me, but nothing came to mind. I bit my tongue just to be sure.

"Dinner is Fava."

"Wonderful news!"

In the same pot was a dish of green almond fruits and broad beans. Anna, who was a meticulous cook, didn't normally experiment like this, trying out new combinations. Basil took a spoonful of the curious dish and slowly began to chew.

The monastery was to serve Turkish hopes from now on. Basil's dream of founding a convent in our village – and entrusting me to the nunnery, should I continue to refuse marriage – was not to be. Thus, the prospect of either holy marriage or sacred celibacy, which for me meant 'death' in the company of a man I did not treasure or 'life' entombed in a convent, was coming to an end.

Basil dipped his bread in olive oil, another errant ingredient which found its way into the dish as we had been fasting for Lent and seasoning was inappropriate if not sinful. He helped himself to another spoonful of broad beans with green almonds, then took a sip of hot water seasoned with cumin and fennel.

He beamed with pleasure.

2

I think of my fields, yearn for peace, curse city life and long for my village; no-one there shouted 'coal for sale' nor oil or vinegar either.

Aristophanes, *Acharnians*

OUR excursion led along Mese, a colonnaded street stretching the length of the entire city, one long line of marble flanked with mosaic-paved shop porticoes, artisan workshops, street traders, and taverns. Its width, only just greater than any street in our town, brought us to the farthermost destination, following sea bream patterns. Past the Milion into the Augustaion, we stood before its massive dome: The Holy Church of Wisdom reached up toward the sky, overshadowing all of God's other creations. In that respect, any wisdom Basil – or any other father, for that matter – might have hoped his child to have developed by then shrank in awe, and so did mine.

It was my thirteenth year in this world, when one is presumed to be either already wise or just wise enough to tell the difference between what is wise and what is unwise, and thus act accordingly. That is to say: when confused, one should adopt inconspicuous, preferably reticent, conduct – or, put another way, know better than to go looking for trouble.

Bands of dusky rose, cinnamon, rust-and copper-hued bricks enveloped and bound the building. Enormous buttresses with porphyry columns bore its immense bulk. Everything was immense – walls, arches, silences – and I felt myself dwindling beneath them.

My chaperone quoted the poet Geometres, saying: "Earth erected Athens, but heaven constructed Constantinople!"

He pointed to the bricks and said, "Some of them were stamped during the manufacturing process with the words, 'God is in the midst of her, and she shall not be moved; God shall always help her.'"

And then he added, "Bones of Saints are mixed into the mortar of the dome. They look after the structure."

I gaped at the alliance between the azure sky and the crimson of that Herculean structure. Behind it, at the Forum of Theodosius, where they sold pigs, above the columns of the Arch, stood a statue of Hercules himself, his colossal fingers sculpted as if gripping the pillars. A rope tied round his finger would be the size of a man's belt; the lower portion of its leg stood the height of a man. So not only was everything gigantic, but it was also God-meddled.

Inside that enormous column, they said, were stairs leading to the top. Whether it was God or angels or some saint who may have interfered in its construction, the idea of being shut in one of those confined, tubular spaces did not appeal to me. I felt a tightness in my chest. The swirling patterns on the pillars did not remind me so much of peacock eyes, as our guide insisted, but of tree rings – like vast logs an angry lumberjack might swing in a fight to bludgeon his assailant. And now something was clutching at my entrails, a stiffening uneasiness settled in my gut, and no number of pigs sold at the forums, or meek ox or cattle and their amicable familiarity would relieve it. My heart pounded. Panting, I fanned my face with my hand recalling:

"She shall not be moved; she will be guarded. God will always help her."

Somebody ought to have helped me, too, but in the end, I had to do it myself. And I did, by holding Basil accountable for this sudden shift from contentment to agitation. From that moment on, I imputed any perturbation I felt to Basil as well.

We had passed through the Forum of Constantine, circular and surrounded by a two-story colonnade, beamed with waxed timbers, and pierced by a monumental white-marble arch on each side, their keystones carved with fearsome Medusa heads. The legendary Emperor Constantine had erected a gilt bronze statue of himself there, crowned like the god Helios, with rays of sunlight on his column – a porphyry giant consisting of cylindrical drums joined together by a hoop, intended to resemble a laurel crown, concealing the joints.

The statue had glittered in the sun for eight hundred years, visible across the city and from the sea, until it was struck by lightning and later blown down by a great gale, killing many in the forum below. The chaperone's recounting of these events felt downright life-threatening, judging by the shortness of my breath and my physical discomfort. All the balderdash tales we attributed to the columns in the countryside – of which there were many – now seemed country-bumpkin brazen, even dull by comparison. Almost every significant column in the city had a tale to tell. For instance, Constantine had apparently incorporated a magical starling somewhere in this very, porphyry column. Once a year, the bird fluttered its wings and called out piercingly, in response to which all the birds of the world flew here, each carrying one olive in its beak and two in its talons and dropped them into the hole at the top of the dome, and the priests of the city partook of them. Yet another column had been fortified with holy nails, and for this reason, it is said that when the next flood arrives to end the world, this very column will survive, and the remaining few ships with survivors will moor themselves to it. A bronze wasp was allegedly encrusted on another column and buzzed constantly, keeping all other wasps from entering Constantinople. This I could not confirm. The philosopher Plato had built a column with the image of a mosquito, and thanks to this, mosquitoes did not enter Constantinople either. One could ask, of course, why Plato would concern himself with the mosquitos of Constantinople rather than graver matters? Apparently, Hippocrates the physician also raised one, and his functioned as an insect repellent. Socrates's column ensured that the city's cocks announced the dawning of a new day before those of any other city. Solomon's column allowed sheep to graze without a shepherd watching over them, for it was in the form of a wolf, and thus no real wolves dared hunt Constantinopolitan sheep. I recalled Basil again, to torment and harry him in my mind. "Father, all those fabled sights, and a prince who simply owns them all – the greatest minds of history labouring for him as insect and wolf repellers – why would you presume that he would be interested in me, when almost every girl in our village was engaged, and yet not a single suitor had ever come to ask for my hand?" Poor Basil. Even in my head, I gave him no peace. Perhaps, unbeknownst to me, my Basil was a visionary, who foresaw the return of 'rustic charm'. Maybe he assumed I would set a new fashion in Constantinople with my rural innocence, devoutness, and the fresh pastoral air I brought with me? Plekia had never sent a bride to Constantinople, only bickering couples.

One of the most marvellous taradiddles was that of Aristotle's column. The great philosopher had allegedly forged a bronze figure of a boy and a girl standing chest to chest, and when you visited it, love, peace and communion were restored to even the most ruinous marriage. If that failed, the couple would be dispatched once more to Constantinople, this time to the Virgin's Church in Blachernai. There, her cloak was on display. Visiting it was well-nigh impossible, for thousands wished to pose questions to the garment and there were extensive waiting lists. However, if you had the right connections in Constantinople, it could be arranged. The unhappy couple would address their inquiry to the dress, and if it moved in any way, the response was considered positive. Aside from us Romans, Turks and Latins also frequented the Virgin's robe. Everyone needs miracles, civilised and barbarous alike. Depending on the question – and what the couple desired – they would claim the dress had moved or not. At the foot of the city's sixth hill stood a holy spring, Mary's Hagiasma, their next stop on the marriage-saving circuit. Usually, the couple returned to Plekia in better spirits, and the villagers attributed this to the Marian relics; but once the novelty and excitement of their trip wore off, the quarrels resumed.

Another column contained, in a marble chamber, the body of the city founder Byzas's unhappy daughter – a malcontent, like myself. That one was said to ward off serpents and ants from the city. I had seen no cattle for sale there to remind me fondly of home, but the city teemed with ants, storks, mosquitoes, and probably many miserable couples, though I could not confirm any sightings of wolves or serpents. What I could confess was a growing contempt for rural fantasy and a touch of resentment for Basil. Why had I never detected a single trace of ambition in him? What was the sense of all this? Was he naïve, or merely too lazy to have prepared me for what lie ahead? And why had he employed such a backhanded and somewhat arrogant method like sending me to Constantinople with an olive in my mouth? What was I warding off?

From the Sphendon, near the lower edge of the Great Palace, a short, dead-end street descended towards the estate of My Lady, an exclusive path, bordered by plane trees, that led to no other building. Constantinopolitans liked turning their houses away from the sea. Through a modest iron gate in a plain stone wall – which offered no hint of what lay behind, or rather jealously concealed it, for, as we were to ferret out, what lay behind was not a house but a monument – we entered her property. Constructed of an opaque marble resembling moonstones rather than bricks, it was a two-storey mansion crowned with scalloped, pearly domes. Double-recessed archivolts, buttressed by twin columns, framed the entryway, where a monogram with a large 'K' was incised. The letter stood either for the initial of the family's name, which I did not know, or that of the Emperor John Komnenos, John the Beautiful, and his late father Alexios Komnenos. Below, a carved tablet read: "Hello, friend. May you receive twice that which you wish for me."

But the door of the house was barred by oak lattices arranged in a criss-cross pattern, concealing workmen but not the bustle and clamour of their passing. Servants in white silken tunics with golden cummerbunds rushed to us – a party of some thirty souls, the majority of whom cackled and tittered incessantly. As we were ushered unceremoniously round to the other side of the estate, I heard coarse words from behind and caught a glimpse of a man working at the rear, peeping through the filigree. I intended to turn back, but the servants had already steered us down the path to the house. It overlooked the terraced garden sloping gently away, and as our eyes followed the descent, the view that appeared before us forced us to stop in our tracks: The Propontis Sea! A magnificent view of the Princes's Islands stretched before us. Boats approached the Harbour of Julian, and little ferries sailed to and fro. We stood on a stretch of land between the Hippodrome and the sea, which widened out only to encompass another jewel, perhaps much smaller than Haghia Sophia but no less precious, the Church of Saints Sergius and Bacchus, its golden dome shimmering. This, too, testified to some sacred hand behind the city's creation. Once again I thought: Heaven is here – and so is hell, right in Constantinople. We were too far to glimpse the dolphins, but I knew they were there. The servants allowed us no time to revel in this grandeur and drove us inside.

Soon afterwards, girls formed into cliques and began casting looks at one another as if this were a chariot race to be won. A few threw glances and sniggers at me, but it did not take long before they flounced back to their infighting. It was a relief, for they left me alone for a while. Unnoticed, I observed the lustrous marble slabs, the vivid frescoes, and the refined silk wall coverings. My sense that our countryside home was the epitome of luxury made me smile, and that foolish smile stuck on my face for the rest of the day. After all, such a grin is the best armour for a juvenile overwhelmed with information.

The Lady of the house was nowhere to be seen. Servants offered fresh water in glass goblets to relieve us from the sweltering heat. At home we too brought out our glassware from the cabinets when visitors called, but our set, simple and thick, came nowhere near her gold-fused, rainbow-enamelled cups. Spun-glass pearls, arranged in bands, ornamented their surfaces; gold imbued the water with the colour of apricots. I forgot my thirst, wondering how generous and gentle the Lady of the Manor must be to let us use her special glassware – did she truly hold us in such high esteem, a bunch of dazed bird-brains, or was she simply counting on what we would say about her treasures when we returned home? With great care I lifted my goblet and moved to an icon I'd noticed on the far side of the room. There, on a stand, stood the Theophany – St John placing a hand on Jesus's head with an expression of deep affection. A human could not paint such an image so true to life. Surreptitiously, I rubbed my fingers along the blue of the Jordan River to see if it was wet.

A part of me knew that this was an example of outstanding workmanship unlike anything we saw in the countryside, and that it had not been crafted by angels but by a highly skilled artist, commissioned, no doubt, at great expense. The water would be dry. Remembering my thirst, I took a sip from my cup – and to my surprise it tasted brackish, rather disagreeable.

From my corner, I eyed the girls, respectable virgins, powerful magnates' daughters, a few even breathtakingly beautiful, able to readily conjure friendship and solidarity. They exulted in their newfound allegiances. It was pointless, though: in the end, only a few would be selected by My Lady and introduced to the Bride Show at the Palace. Finally, only one would be crowned Empress and reign over Constantinople. Hearing their incessant chatter, I doubted she was among them. The foolish damsels gathered here would conspire against her, grovel at her feet, or both. An Empress was bound to be alone. If these geese wished to be so haughty, they should first learn to be alone, by themselves. I, on the other hand, knew how to be alone; I fulfilled that requirement. I was alone. But I was lacking something else, something I could not quite put my finger on.

Murmurs were cut off abruptly when the Mistress entered the salon. Wearing a dashing, shamrock-green dalmatica, a gaunt, almost alabaster-skinned woman approached, taking us in with a jaded glance, as though we were not candidates for nomination and thus potential princesses but a nuisance to be dismissed as soon as possible. Aloof, yet in a rush, holding a parchment containing our names, she tilted her head back and, without a word of welcome, she said in an orotund tone:

"Ladies, we shall evaluate your qualities of beauty, piety, obeisance, servility, ladylike manners and social graces, respectively."

If you looked her in the eye, you would see her face was as plain as mine, but she moved in such an elegant manner, she appeared almost pretty. Was it accidental? Or had she discovered that if you perfect a sublime poise, people will believe you are God-sent, as a matter of fact? Perhaps green beseemed her, for it is a colour that imparts a certain power, it gives a person a slightly threatening air; It is not jovial like the marriage of red and blue, Haghia Sophia against the sky. Only a well-intentioned and prolific poet could envision flowers in connection with this woman though. Sulking snowdrops that need no water, only frosty soil. She resembled the snow of middle-spring, unwelcome and unwelcoming. And yes, bless our hearts, she did not give a fig about us.

With a nervous flick she swung the parchment upward. But how were social graces to be measured? Did the continual cackling of those present qualify? An attractive acrobat or a *danseuse* could manifest respectable manners if she practised hard enough. As for beauty, perhaps that lay within My Lady's power to assess – but beauty alone would not suffice. We all knew about Kassia. Even these darlings must have heard of her. She was a noble and exceptionally beautiful girl who lived some three hundred years ago. At the Bride Show organised by his stepmother, the Emperor Theophilos became fascinated by her good looks. Most likely in an effort to maintain decorum, he pompously declared,

"It is through a woman that sin came into this world."

To which she replied, "It was through a woman that mankind's redeemer was born, Your Imperial Majesty."

A shocked Theophilos then gave the golden apple not to Kassia, but to another girl.

In disgrace, she would now attract either aging men hoping to use her youth to cling to life, or – if she were slightly luckier – she would charm boys still smelling of their mothers' milk whose destitute parents sought a wealthy spinster to fund their needs. Kassia would need great powers of imagination to survive a life such as these. So cocksure, intelligent, and insightful, Kassia used that power to write aphorisms and compose hymns. Converting her calamity into strength, she spent her life as an abbess in a convent she founded. Times have changed, so we might now query: which is better? As for the question of being highborn – I did not know if I possessed a ladylike bearing, but I knew one thing for certain: I was not comely. An unpleasant twist of fortune impelled the Lady's taut voice to call out my name first – thus proving the veracity of my views on fate.

"Theia, great-granddaughter of Basil Malalas, founder of Plokia monastery, granddaughter of the late Zeno Malalas, daughter of Basil Malalas from Plokia."

"Here I am. Theia." Attempting to thrust out my chest I added, "And I am not from Plokia, My Lady. I hail from Plekia. It is a different town, you know? And my name is not…"

My voice died off as she drew near, and those chartreuse eyes raked me from head to toe. Perspiration ran down my sides. Although my body felt cold, my hands became clammy.

"…not Malalas but Maleinus."

She waved her hand. Re-announcing me properly – or better still, offering a simple apology – would have made a fine excuse to break the ice, far superior to even the most formal niceties. Neither was forthcoming. Instead, she launched straight into questioning. Tilting her chin, she asked in a strained tone,

"What is humility?"

Alas, her haste proved contagious, and the impulse to ingratiate myself with her was powerful. My words rang out: "Oh, Madam! Humility… Humility is just how it feels to be here."

And that was it. I stood aghast, nothing else coming to my mind.

The group drew in a collective breath. A few giggled at the rear. Her eyebrows rose, and I wanted the ground under my feet to open up and swallow me whole – or else devour those fatuous girls. Our noble Lady wasted no time indulging my wish to be punished. Rather austerely, she held up her palms and said in a high pitch:

"Humility is recognising our unworthiness before God! It is to fathom oneself, without the grace of God, as dust, as sinful and dead. Christ is humble because he associates with the lowly."

Clasping her hands, she frowned. While the irony of her words wasn't lost on me, I was stung by regret that I hadn't allied myself with a group here, and this gave birth to a new, unwelcome epiphany: discovering one's own triviality, and realising whither one's armpits can reek.

My Lady drew a deep breath and posed me a second question, in all likelihood for the sake of formality, for her eyes were steely and her voice void of sympathy:

"What does Jesus reveal in Mathew 7:13: 'Enter through the narrow gate. For wide is the gate and broad is the road that leads to destruction, and many enter through it'?"

As I collected myself, words flashed through my mind, almost screaming: "I know this one! The broad road and wide door symbolise what is easy to execute. If we want to reach the Lord's Kingdom and enter the Promised Land, we must struggle to merit it, hence the narrow doors. The test bridge leading to it is as narrow as a hair but probably not yours for it all seems quite luscious."

Proud of my answer, I grinned around me at the other girls. My urge to punish myself for my sycophantic state of mind was still strong, yet another feeling emerged: an intense need to provoke this woman. Unfortunately, the cure for my sickness was the same poison that had caused it in the first place. Emboldened, I returned to wiseacre flattery:

"Madam, as gentle and as lowly as you are, you are not dissimilar to the Son of Man, for He too came into this world to serve and not to be served. Your entrance gate is closed with narrow passageways between the lattice work – and behind it, we hear there is quite some destruction going on." I drew breath and gushed onwards, admiring my own artful insincerity even as the Lady stood impassively. "But your heart is wide and generous for we toured around this marvellous mansion and entered through a broad gate, which led us into this heaven. And appearance is indeed counter to mere reality – for the narrow upstairs is a broad downstairs and what seems to be the first floor is the second floor from here."

She narrowed her eyes. A hush fell. The girls stared at me again. For fear of catching anyone's eye, I turned my gaze to the drawing and spotted a peculiarity I had missed earlier. The marble statues – though they differed in posture, marble type, and technique – were all identical! Each represented Hygieia, Goddess of sanitation and healing. On some figures, snakes drank from her bowl, whereas on others she held them separately. A few smiled; others appeared stern. I regretted not having spotted the absence of a more convivial god earlier. The loving Aphrodite Basil had in his bedroom, for example, would be too permissive and flippant for My Lady, but the popular and hospitable Dionysus was also absent. Looking at her reddened face I felt my spirit of levity evaporate. A lump settled in my throat, and I lowered my gaze. She curled her lip and turned to the next applicant.

Later in the day I would reaffirm the saltiness of the drinking water and not only in My Lady's house but everywhere else in the city. I had forgotten the indignation I felt towards Basil. On the contrary, my heart was full of sympathy for him now. Looking back, I realised how reasonable his remarks could be at times. He always said, "light does not discriminate." He also averred that "nothing is perfect apart from God, the Holy Spirit and Jesus." I studied the icon of My Lady further. The dove descended upon Jesus' head, and he was cleansed in those holy waters, being born anew. God had touched my head too on that sunny day in the mighty capital which, surprisingly, was not free from defects such as its unsavoury water. Both Constantinople and My Lady were unapologetic, and each maintained a most natural manner, a manner both must have striven for years to perfect. That, I realised, was the style of the city and the city-dwellers.

I skulked away from the Lady's presence, traversed to the other side of the oak grill and stumbled across a labourer. He straightened up and grabbed the arm of his friend, who was appraising the girls through the grate. The man gave a bark of laughter and called out to others who were further off – at least a dozen, if not more men – all crouched, faces down, their backs turned to me. By screwing them into each other, they were laying ceramic and baked clay pipes into diversion canals dug beforehand in trenches along the steep side slope of My Lady's garden. They stopped and turned their heads in my direction. I began walking along the lattice rail fence towards the exit, pretending to be unaffected, but, serious-looking elderly man who had not crouched with the others approached, blocking my way. He first bowed and then, extending his arm toward my point of trespass, said:

"Pardon me, miss, you must be mistaken. The exit is on the other side. I shall guide you out."

I gave him a coy, doe-eyed glance and did precisely the opposite of what he advised, edging away towards the work site. On the second floor of the mansion, they were annexing an exterior cell and installing yet more statues of Hygieia. Pools hewn from pure-white crystal rock were scattered about – not dissimilar to the few we had in our garden at home, though ours were carved from ordinary stone. Basil had commanded birds to be sculpted on the rims of these artificial ponds, sparrows with their beaks dipped in water, seemingly ready to fly if anyone approached. Although most of our ponds were rudimentary, merely dug into the soil and lined with mortar to receive and hold the water, our plants were pleasing to the eye.

The foreman caught up with me again.

"Forgive my curiosity, master," I said. "What are you building here?"

The wrinkles around the man's eyes deepened as he smiled. "We're building a latrine exclusive to Madame, as well as bringing water from above, from the cistern up there."

"But how?"

"Well, there's someone up there in charge at all times during the day. He distributes the water through pipes – they run through hollow trunks and timber."

"But why? What's so special about this woman's house?"

Realising how I'd spat the word *this*, I felt my face burn and hastily corrected myself: "I mean, isn't rainwater collected from a roof gutter or downspout sufficient? Or isn't there a well here?"

He smiled again and kept silent. Taking my arm, he gently led me back to where I'd entered.

I never did find out whether Madame's latrine yielded better herbs than those fertilized with animal dung, for I was never invited back again to the mansion for the bride selection finals.

When I returned to Plekia, Madam Gabras was visiting Basil. I pressed my ear to the door of the room and tried to make out what they were saying, when behind me, I heard a harsh, angry whisper:

"One day the door will open in your face, and you'll be caught."

Anna had arrived at the crucial moment – as always.

I shrugged. "Is Nikephoros here too?"

"No. Only the mother."

"Why's she come? Showing off her new bones? Did her servants bring a box into the room?"

She shook her head. "A recently widowed Lady wouldn't come here to show bones. Of course."

Madam Gabras collected relics. In an attempt to appear sage – and not merely inane – she had assembled her reliquaries rather modestly. After the carpenter left for Constantinople, Svoronos the bookbinder took on the job of making chests for her: simple boxes of all sizes with no use of amber or coral or carving. In time, he improved at the trade. What made Svoronos invaluable was that he was absolutely terrified of Gabras, a trait she liked in people. She boasted about her divine skeleton collection which grew by the day. She accumulated hands, forearms, legs, thumbs and jaws of martyrs and saints imported from far and wide. Venerable Theodora of Caesarea had six legs and four arms in her collection. A poet once mocked a monk who hoarded relics in much the same way, saying he had "turned a martyred virgin into a bitch with innumerable nipples, and a holy warrior into an octopus." The same right arm of St. John the Baptist rested in the Church of the Virgin of the Pharos in Constantinople but also here in Plekia. The capital was lauded for being another Sinai, a Bethlehem, a Jerusalem, a Nazareth, a Bethany, a Galilee, a Tiberias with its vast collection of Passion Relics. Tomb raiders, paid handsomely by the gullible women of the village to conjure new glorified souls out of thin air, hailed Gabras as their new benefactor. Under her pioneering leadership, they organised newfangled gatherings where they bragged to each other about novelties: the more bones one had, the more pious and prestigious she became. None dared question, on the other hand, who these faux Saint Kilickos, Saint Maroulis, Saint Moustakas or Saint Karpouzis were.

By-passing Anna, I proceeded towards the hallway and stopped in front of the parlour, pricking up my ears. Gabras talked in her husky voice. I did not catch the entire sentence, only a few words. "Scandal… How dare… waited for him to die?"

I didn't hear Basil say anything. Anna appeared behind me, frowning, so I withdrew from the door, and headed for the stable. Peering out through the open door I began to spy. Gabras came blazing out. My eyes lit on a green dress not unlike that worn by My Lady in Constantinople – only shinier, perhaps too frilly for a mourning widow, and adorned with shimmering paillettes. Her servants rushed to the carriage and cleared off. I have disliked green on women ever since that day.

I came out and ran to the doorway where Basil stood. Crimson-faced, he was gazing off into the distance after Gabras.

3

You cannot teach a crab to walk straight.

Aristophanes, *Peace*

SYRUPY pancakes were laid out for the well-wishers, along with sherbets laced with cinnamon and clove meant not only to please the guests but to sweeten the mother's milk. A new boy. Anna had boiled lochozema with myrtle, galangal, pepper, muscat and honey – so sweet that my mother's heart would burn not only with love for the baby, but also with a craving to quench her thirst. A potion so deeply red that Gylou would dither in dread while the child suckled. But Gylou – the she-demon who feared only the colour red – and Medusa killed my mother and newborn brother on the day of his birth. Gylou eater of babies, born and unborn, of pregnant women and new mothers. It had taken my mother eight years to fall pregnant again after me, though I was told she had conceived both me and my first brother easily enough. The bereavement tore Basil's heart out; he hurled my mother's Medusa eagle-stone amulet to the floor smashing it and then stomped on the snake-like rays surrounding the head. The sight frightened me more than the loss of my mother, for it was against his nature to do such a thing. I had not yet grasped the gravity of my misfortune, and was, more sorrowful for him than for myself. During the delivery, Anna had lit two groups of candles, one for female saints, the other for male. The one that burnt longest would lend its name to the baby. Among the candles bearing the name of a woman, that of Saint Irene Chrysovolantou burnt the longest – Irene who levitated in the air while praying, and to whom the surrounding cypress trees bowed. To prove these miracles to her friends, one day when the trees were bent, a nun who spied upon Irene tied handkerchiefs to the tops of the trees. When later the trees stood straight again, other nuns were in awe, but Irene was annoyed.

One day she heard an invisible voice telling her that a sailor would bring her three apples from paradise, a gift from Saint John to gladden her soul. And, indeed, a sailor from Patinas did bring her three apples. For forty days, while those apples turned sweeter and more aromatic, she ate nothing but small pieces of them. They made her more youthful, and she became aware of countless radiant, angelic beings glorifying her. Irene died at the age of one hundred. Toward the end of her life, she began to exude the fragrance of myrrh.

But the baby was a boy and, ironically, among male saints' candles it was that of Saint Joseph, patron of a happy death, that burned the longest.

Madam Gabras observed that to make a courteous wife, a lady must be proficient in spinning and weaving, and not only spinning and weaving, but seaming and stitching, so after my mother's death, several neighbouring ladies took an interest in teaching me needlework and wore themselves out in the attempt.

Helena, widow of Musele, the banker, was the first to undertake the challenge. A band of maids trailed after her as she rode up on a horse with a silver bit in his mouth and a bridle embroidered in gold. The saddle's pomegranate-hued skirt, adorned with golden palmetto motifs, revived the blue of her brocaded frock. She was tall and angular, with a conspicuous aquiline nose latched on to a pasty countenance with no lips to atone for it. Basil blushed as he greeted her, while the servants led her into the drawing room. Assuming that only a sombre, stern character bore such features, I cursed destiny for putting me in her hands – her presumably dead-cold, bony-knuckled hands. But a voice warbling like a merry bird greeted me:

"Theia, my dear! How nice to meet you! You are so pretty! Are you prepared for our lesson today? Come, let me show you! First, I will demonstrate stitching, and if all goes well, hemming shall follow."

I rejoiced in my evident misconception and exclaimed, "Yes, Madam Musele, I am ready!"

"Dear girl," she looked gently into my eyes, "I am so sorry about the loss of your mother..."

Her words caught me off guard. Absorbed in my impressions of her, I had forgotten I was mourning. My eyes brimmed with tears. Perturbed, she reached out and hugged me.

"Shall we begin, darling? If you manage plain sewing and basting, we'll move on to for full backstitching. All right?"

She pointed to the wooden box her servant had brought. Taking out two pieces of cloth, two needles, and two spools of thread, she handed me one set and kept the other for herself. All afternoon we worked together. Sensing her regret in mentioning my mother, I had diligently tried to copy her examples, wishing to please her. She was gracious and patient, but my hands refused to obey. The cloth grew dirty, the lines crooked, and the result was far from decent. Helena persevered, visiting every other day for a while. We tried binding, shirring, seaming; chain, slip, and overcast stitching. We strove for honeycomb, full-and half-daisy patterns; we toiled to create pearl, herringbone, feather and capped feather stitches. All to no avail. One day, Helena married a widower, a landowner in a nearby town, and our time together came to an end.

Other dowagers followed in the years to come – some kind and forgiving, others rigid, even astringent. Basil always welcomed them with a complacent smile, and made sure Anna served cold sherbets or warm soups depending on the season. I shed tears for many, treated others with petulance, but I persisted. Still the copper thread was tangled, my golden plates and plaques twisted, and the motifs' contours swerved. Spangles and glass trinkets added to the designs cut my fingers. Where the fabric should have been crisscrossed by colourful silk threads, it was instead blotched crimson with my blood. My winged horses suggested donkeys, and my lions and tigers, alley cats. Flowers resembled thorns, and basilisks, lizards. My trees of life were passable, but Saint Peter had a hawkish nose and Saint Paul a skewed chin. Still, the majority of the ladies were cordial and lenient. That is, until I undertook a depiction of Jesus Christ.

Epiphania, widow of the honourable General Maurix, was my instructor that day. A significant landowner in our district, governor, and head of the regional Roman forces, Maurix had been one of the few generals loyal to his Emperor, but Constantinople, distracted by campaigns elsewhere, sent him only a ramshackle cohort of mercenaries. The Roman army and the vainglorious capital could never do justice to General Maurix's services. He had the idea of fastening small bushes to the horses' breast-straps and affixing little flags to the shoulders of their metal body armour, in order to strike fear into the hearts of the Turks. He fought bravely – but his soldiers, disloyal to their Byzantium, did not stand their ground. A number of them grumbled that their wages were not in keeping with the scale of the deed they were to undertake, while the majority, being Turks themselves, joined their brothers in the fight. Not to mention the fact that Ataman paid handsomely. Commissioned by the Sultan in Iconium, he exploited the low incomes of the townspeople, and in return provided military services with his garrison (though his relations with the central government remained blurry). Ataman demolished General Maurix's troops, and the bushes and tiny flags ended up beautifying Roman graves.

Epiphania sat grim-faced, silently watching me struggle. When I finished, I blurted out: "Look! My Jesus looks like Demitrios the butcher!"

The gawking eyes and rotund, obtuse face of my creation bore an uncanny resemblance to those of our obese town butcher. I burst into laughter.

Epiphania Maurix's mouth fell open. Her hand flew to her chest. Ashen, she collected her sewing kit, put it in a box, wrapped the fabrics in haste, summoned Anna for her horse and attendants, and left without saying goodbye.

I drew a deep breath.

Epiphania would never have been happy with Basil.

4

And lo, he draws near and his advance fills us with chilling fear,
Like a northern blast that falls on sailors unprepared.

Aeschylus, *Fragments*

FOREIGN voices shouted and horses neighed at our entrance once again, breaking the calm. The dog leaped up, ears pricked and neck craning forward. His muscles tensed as he took an attack position. He barked first and then lowered his head, pointed a foot, hackles rising – ready to pounce. He began to howl, howl like a wolf, something he does when he is anxious and desperate, a habit I find rather irritating when uncalled-for. Men on the other side who heard him started howling back, until the area outside the gate rang out with a chorus of howls. A fake hero, Dog was shocked by the defiance; tucking his tail between his legs, he fled to the barn. My insides twisting, I sallied to the gateway of the house, hollering along the way. The door was ajar. I pushed it open violently. It hit my father full in the face. Basil rubbed his reddening nose, and said, "Calm down, Theia. It's Ataman – I'm expecting him."

I hesitated, wondering whether I should hide Pegasus again in the back of the stable, but I realised he wouldn't appeal to a barbarian, not even one with such regal airs. I was in the field of this barbarian's interest, but he'd taken none the last time he visited, and that was precisely why he was now in the territory of my interest. Gylou ate mothers and babies in the house, but when we were children, in faraway places, it was the Barbarian Baboulas. His skin was quince yellow, his hair as long as a woman's. His squinting jet-black eyes would turn red and spew fire whenever he wanted to snatch a spoilt child. Disciplinary results were more than satisfactory – a single piercing glare from the corner of the eye was enough to subdue us. Basil never resorted to invoking the Barbarian Baboulas, but my grandfather Zeno and Anna both called upon him whenever I misbehaved. Nobody had ever seen Gylou in person, but Baboulas was real in the flesh, and now he was here.

Servants raced to the main gate in the garden and opened it as Ataman and his howling men burst into the courtyard. The men descended towards him in a flash to attend to him, but he had already sprung off his horse and dashed towards us. For an instant I lost my sense of reality, as if his slanting black eyes, distinctive cheekbones, his flavescent, wheat-toned skin – hairlessly smooth like a baby's bottom – were all images, and this man in front of me merely a delusion, some bizarre effigy. Or, perhaps, I, myself, was not here. I was a bird overhead, watching myself take in his sable fur cap, tapering to a point, his flat, shoulder-length, jet-black hair, his bright red lips, and his thin, bow-shaped moustache curling upwards at the ends. He wore high, fur-lined, crimson Moroccan leather boots, a silken tunic, and unusually tight britches.

I wasn't sure if he sported a curious earring in one ear, but alas, fear does not let you live dangerously. I didn't keep looking. I gave in to the urge to flee once again, cursing myself as I did. Following Dog, I scuttled to the stables and cowered again in the corner behind a hay bale. Ordinarily I would always look a new visitor in the eye, though Anna would then emerge, making signs with her eyes and brows, insinuating I should leave, but I often ignored her. She would then clutch her small arms to her large breasts, raise her otherwise songful, pleasant voice to a high, grating pitch and reprimand me, then grumble for the rest of the day. Basil, on the other hand, would frown to make himself appear furious, clear his throat to scold me, yet only utter a rather half-hearted, "Now, Theia, that was inappropriate"

Have you ever seen a Turkoman?

Light as a feather on his horse, as if amalgamated with the beast, he runs circles around himself while riding, shoots arrows in every direction – even backwards – and could hit a fly in its eye all at the same time. People say that by staring across endless, pristine fields of snow in their homeland for generations and generations, the Turk had lost his eyesight. Yet by being forever on the look-out he developed a third vision, similar to a Cyclops, invisible to a watcher yet able to see spirits, and demons too. His skin is not sensitive like ours is for the icy winds have flayed it. Our sun here is strict at times, in Bithynia, in Paphlagonia, in Optimatoi, in Opsikion, in far-flung places like that – in Anatolikoi, in Cappadocia, Chaldia, Charsianon and in Buccellarii, and she's merry at other times, akin to a loving mother wanting the best for her child, playing light games with shadows. But it's different for the Turks. The sun sears their wounds before they've healed; she scorches their senses without warming their bodies. Their ears don't hear our melodies; their music is the howling of winds and wolves. Their tongues don't taste the nectary flavour of our fruits – their mouths are lined with the dust of summer storms from Central Asia, their motherland, a place of vast wastelands, steppes and wilderness.

Zeno, my grandfather, knew it all. On his deathbed, after drawing a breath, his voice had strained as he said, "We have to accept the barbarians as punishment for our sins."

And those were his last words. His cheeks sunken, he clamped those thin, sinewy hands to his chest. His salient veins stood out like dregs of bitter wine against his pallid skin. When he was healthy, he had never shown concern that he would be punished for his sins, old belligerent Zeno. He must have been trying to impress God on his deathbed before leaving the stage. So long as he was dead, we were the sinful ones who would pay – not him. On that fateful day, I looked at Basil's pinkish face, the colour of a fool's paradise, and wondered how he could possibly protect me against the barbarians. We set the icon of gruff Zeno's favourite saint upon his arms: Theophilus of Adana who had made a pact with Satan. In exchange for his help in attaining a bishopric, Theophilus renounced Christ and the Virgin, signing a contract with his own blood. Later, terrified for his soul, he repented. He fasted and fasted and finally the Virgin appeared, granting absolution. Satan of course didn't go away so easily. Mighty Zeno didn't change. He always knew what to do. His final undertaking was to tint his body not with blue paint as the barbarians paint their faces, nor with pigment, but with the hue of sanctimony, purporting a dignified farewell.

Zeno's favourite dish was wild fowl, abounding with almonds, roasted on a spit with aromatic juices, and served with a nectar-like fragrant sauce which was the only sweet taste he ever tolerated. At his funeral supper, we served chicken baked in crispy pastry. Zeno drank local wine mulled with cumin or resin, or hot water brewed with cumin, pepper and anise, like monks. Basil offered neither. He bought sweet wine brought from Samos and Crete and served it undiluted, like the Latins.

I recall a fleshy stranger entering, a remarkably dispassionate figure among the mourners, half of whom were professionals hired by Basil. They wailed, tore hair from their heads, lacerated their cheeks with their nails, beat their breasts and ripped their garments. This scruffy peasant, with a ragged beard, presented Basil with a folded paper tied with waxed string and stamped with Zeno's insignia. He was claiming ownership of a single quince tree. Indeed, at the head of the text Zeno had drawn a sign of the cross, thus the bequest was authentic and valid. He had signed his name, declared his intent and described the tree's position, state, and age in detail. Basil did not inquire of the man the reason he was granted this inheritance. So, every year, at harvest time, the old peasant came, took the yield of this one particular tree, and left. Basil continued not to question who he was.

We laid Zeno out to be viewed in the reception room. Basil chose not to hire an orator to praise Zeno, so it was quiet. We lit candles and balsam oil lamps around his body, wrapped in a white linen winding sheet. We burned styrax and cassia incense even though he favoured acrid perfumes like myrrh or pine resin when alive. We served boiled wheat mixed with grains and dried fruits, though Zeno had loathed Kollyba. Relatives broke pots and plates to drive away evil spirits and sang dirges through their tears. I was dressed in black, conveniently; however, I did not wail or tear hair from my head, nor lacerate my cheeks with my nails, mostly for fear of damaging my already mediocre looks. Rumours spread. Apparently, the poor village folk were disturbed, for it was reported that I was uncaring about the loss of my grandfather. But believe me, I was the one most concerned. For days and days afterwards I repeated the question: what were we to do without Zeno now? Zeno, perceptive and admonitory – also scrawny, skeletal, dry, fat-free… I pondered whether I had caught a glimpse of a potbelly on Ataman. Somehow this helped me wrestle my cowardice into submission. I stood up, took a deep breath, exited the barn and returned to the courtyard.

A tall, slender horse stood in the courtyard, its delicate skin shimmering like foiled silver. A gold inlaid ox-rib and tail hung on the neck of the beast. Two men stood beside it. When they saw me, they bowed. One wore a hat topped with a wolf skull; the other, a pendant of a wolf tooth mounted by an iron wolf head, and a cap with a wolf tail. Both sported nose rings made of animal hair – likely wolf hair, I guessed. Basil and Ataman walked from the house toward the horse. Ataman was comically short, with a long torso, out of proportion to the rest of his body. His stocky legs looked powerful and had probably strangled or trampled many a neck. I expected him to avoid my eyes, so as not to offend Basil, though if he didn't, he would also fall afoul of his Mohammedan practice, but he met my gaze directly and nodded politely. His wolf tooth pendant was mounted with a silver wolf head and a leopard tail hung from his chunky wrist. His black, slanting Asian eyes didn't hint, in the slightest, that they might turn red – and verily, there indeed was the paunch I thought I had seen. Its confirmation gave me a small sense of relief. Still the concern persisted: we lived under a sword held by a single horse hair. He granted Basil a cordial smile; his cheekbones raised and widened as his slanting eyes squinted, and his pupils vanished. Firmly clasping hands, the two men leaned into each other to say farewell, evoking a mutual congeniality, which could almost qualify as friendship, albeit not in any conventional sense.

After all, when you eat a dish cooked with all the right ingredients save one, which is of dubious quality, the reaction of your stomach is not immediately evident. The flavour is palatable, the texture passable. We continued to gorge ourselves on the lush nourishment from a silver platter though under Ataman its name was 'uncertainty'. Had we chosen to dine on good old, safe stale bread – refusing to go along with, let alone collaborate with, the enemy – would he have let us live? We would never know. Dead people do not eat.

We put out the news that Zeno's clothes were to be donated. It is true that instead of calf-length fitted tunics with strong, contrasting colours, Zeno had worn ghastly, old-fashioned, wool mixes that hung baggily at floor length, dull and frayed. But several villagers were in dire need of clothing and these chlamyses could be altered.

The tunics' sleeves could be raised or cut off to make them work-ready. There was nothing to be done about the colours, though for dark madder paint was no longer tingible. Nobody came to take them, and so Anna parceled them up and set them aside.

5

Not even the gods fight against necessity.

Simonides,
quoted by Plato in the dialogue *Protagoras*

Rummaging through the tool cabinet in the barn, I found a chisel and a mallet, looked for a large auger but spotted only a paltry *terebra*. In the parlour, a disused door hidden behind silk wall-coverings led to a short, narrow corridor, conveniently located opposite the main entrance into the room, and I intended to bore a hole in the door and the samite hanging that hid it, which would allow me to peek in and listen to visitors from the security of the corridor. Basil had forced me to do this. When I asked him what he wanted this time, he gave an astonishing answer:

"Ataman wants to bring his son to Plekia to supervise the prisoner and take him to Iconium, to the Sultan Mesud."

"Who's that?"

"His son."

"I mean the prisoner?"

"Oh, that one? They kidnapped the Emperor's nephew."

"Who's that?" An imperial nephew, kidnapped? Here?

"Andronicus Komnenos. He is detained at the monastery and..."

"What? The notorious Andronicus is here? Here, in our village?"

"Yes indeed! Ataman..."

I interrupted again: "What has this got to do with us? Do we need to take fruits to him from the orchard? This must be why Ataman came all this way – mustn't it? It doesn't make any sense."

I screamed, "Trouble is coming! I knew it... Trouble!"

"Let me speak, Theia! Heckling is not the way a young lady should converse."

"Sorry… Go on."

"I told him his boy can lodge here."

"What? Oh, no."

"Naturally he accepted. He trusts me. He was glad. I felt the boy would be more comfortable here in a family atmosphere. I'll take care of him."

"Ah, I am sure he was beginning to broach the idea and you jumped at the chance, didn't you? Not that you'd have had any choice anyway…" He frowned.

"He absolutely did not! I do have a choice, and I chose this option."

Sneering I said.

"That's not true! You are most definitely obliged! And if you are denying that he was here to insinuate his son into your household, then tell me, why was he here at all? Haven't you ever heard what the famous commander, the greatest of the greatest commanders said?"

Basil grinning now, gasped:

"I don't know. I assume *you* do, and you will tell me whether I want to hear it or not."

"'Foreigners can never be friends,' That is what is what Kekaumenos said, 'their backgrounds make them incompatible.'" Pitching up my voice haughtily. "Do you know better than Kekaumenos?"

"Perhaps I know some things better than Kekaumenos does."

I snickered. He carried on.

"Ataman was here to inform me of the latest developments."

"How thoughtful of him!"

"Mockery is dreadful in a woman, Theia." Basil's face hung with an air of paternal hurt. "I would like to welcome his son with genuine compassion. I hope my daughter can be trusted to show respect?"

"So, you are imploring me to make a show of fake hospitality? You always pressure me to feign things."

"No. I am only asking that you not become prey to your own anger or any other type of excitement for that matter. Be patient."

I assumed a puffed up, upright posture. "Kekaumenos said another thing too: 'If a friend turns up in your hometown, never invite him to stay with you, lest he mock your domestic habits and try to seduce your wife. Have friends, certainly, but never get too involved.'"

"Well, I doubt he will try to seduce anyone. But if you are scared on your own behalf, my dear, it might be a good idea to make yourself as scarce as possible to our guest. I doubt you'll listen to reason, not even to your own, for you're prone to heeding fleeting thoughts. So please do not just go saying any old thing that comes into your head. And be discreet… and be fair! Can I trust you, Theia?"

He bent down and petted Dog.

"Wasn't it you, my girl, who wanted this house to be open to all the sacred creations of God?"

Dog wagged his tail and licked Basil's hands.

"How can you be fair with your enemy, Father?"

"Just by living – living, my child. For killing is an encumbrance on a soul, even on the soul of the enemy…"

"I don't understand. If you mean 'kind', I cannot promise unconditional deference." I could feel a familiar bluster coming on. "A person like me cannot plan such things in advance. And how unfair it is of you to request me to be fair, while you're busy trying to please that man Ataman. Your affections really are rather selective."

"My kindness is for everyone, Theia. As a matter of fact, I am neither a grand strategist nor an acclaimed commander. I judge others the way I would judge myself."

"So, we must flatter your new friend Ataman because we are alive – even though his men sacked half the village and slaughtered the Roman military garrison? Oh, and another thing Kekaumenos told his readers: 'many people whom he knew lost their property – or even their lives – because of friends.' He said, 'beware more your friends than your enemies.'"

"Well, what a life he had, your Kekaumenos! But let me tell you – we don't fully comprehend what Ataman's role is. We don't know. Maybe things are out of his control."

"In that case, who abducted the Emperor's cousin?"

"Now that you hold your Kekaumenos in such high regard, let me remind you that he also maintained: 'Your sons and daughters ought to honour you.' Ah, incidentally, he was afraid of mushrooms too. Strongly advised against them. Just in case you didn't know – since you seem to particularly enjoy devouring those white ones fried in olive oil." His voice lowered. His tone was serious now. "What I urge you to be is calmer. Restless actions and extreme unrest are the markings of a barbarian – or a rebel. As for your question: perhaps it was his tribe that abducted Andronicus. But this doesn't disprove his innocence in other matters, Theia."

A wave of heat rushed through my body.

"Well, if you're so sure this man is your friend, Basil – maybe you should go and ask him!"

And for fear of saying something even more insolent, I ran to the door and slammed it so hard behind me that a crack ran right through it.

Anna would scold me for that later.

6

Sweet for the thirsty in summer
is the cool drink of snow.

Asclepiades, *Epigram*

LEST Anna should show up, I said prayers. Fortunately, she did not make an appearance. The corridor leading to the secret door also led to the kitchen, which in due course would become my own entrance into the world of our parlour. At eye-level, using the mallet to drive it in, I made a puncture hole in the door and then placed the point of the terebra in it. Alas, the metal stick was rather feeble, so it took a while for the cutting edge to drill through the wood. Still, I crafted a beautiful peephole, clean through. Picking where to pierce a hole in the silk hanging, which vividly depicted a hunting scene, full of bright green trees, bounding deer, and athletic hunters, was more complex – and also a strategic moment: I had two alternatives: to use a stag's eye or a blue lagoon.

The eye seemed like the obvious option, but its suitability was debatable, for people tend to detect the eyes of living creatures, and guests would certainly notice any rapid eye movement. Yet determined to observe and not only hear, I chose to cut through the waters of the pond. Yes, I have blue eyes! But my reader should not mistakenly infer that I am attractive thanks to this singularity. As I have mentioned before: I am rather plain. How these oddities skip a generation or two remains hidden; my mother had hazel eyes, not blue. The family of Sophie, our village's amulet maker, was a similar case. Sophie's great-grandmother had eyes of different colours, one green, one brown. Sophie gave birth last year, and her daughter had one brown eye, and one green, just like her great-grandmother. In the olden days, this was thought to be the work of evil, but times have changed, nobody believes this condition is the foretoken of wickedness anymore. Mind you, the overall family's fatuous character also aided the relinquishment of this superstition as well. After all, even Satan needs a minimum amount of wit to settle in somewhere comfortably. With Sophie he would feel like a thief-tenant renting from a priest. God always moves in mysterious ways.

My eyes are a legacy from a Norseman, a Viking, who was a member of the Imperial Varangian Guards. Named Ivar, the young man had come to Constantinople with the king of the South Norwegians, Sigurd the pirate-turned-crusader. Sigurd was nineteen when he set forth with six vessels upon an expedition, and within the first two years he had plundered and laid waste to many lands in Europe. When he won victories over the Saracens of Portugal, he was so delighted to indulge his martial fervor while fulfilling his religious duty his uncouth exuberance transmuted into devout Christianity. These Nordics were known for their paroxysms of mad ferocity and wild savageries. The longer he travelled and the farther east he reached, the more restricted his bursts of fury became and the closer he got to Constantinople the more civilized – naturally – he grew. In their native land and tongue, these pirate sea-kings bore the epithet *Berserkr*, meaning "a hero that fought unclothed". As any sane person can easily conjecture, this sort of barbarous vulgarity could never be sustained in our Roman land.

Once the contact with refinement was established, the Nordics professed that their alleged obscenity was not well-deserved, for the idea of 'nakedness' did not mean being without clothes but rather without armour, but I personally doubt this. People tell all sorts of lies to impress Roman Emperors. Sigurd steered towards the Holy Land; on his return, he passed by Constantinople and there he sold his fleet to Emperor Alexios Komnenos. Subsequently he united all Norway under one sovereignty – his own – an act that was a far cry from his *Berserkr* past, but also a fine example of the refinement and statesmanship he learned in Constantinople.

And Ivar, my barbarian pirate-crusader grandfather, remained in Emperor Alexios's service, and made a considerable fortune in Constantinople. As one of his predecessors, Halvdan, had done about two centuries earlier, he carved his name in runic inscriptions into a white marble parapet in Haghia Sophia.

The veteran marked: *"Halvdan carved these, Halvdan was here."*

My Ivar also incised into the white marble of Haghia Sophia, but differently: *"Ivar carved these, Ivar stays here."*

Before visiting the great edifice in Constantinople, I was determined to examine its white marble and find Ivar's carvings – but the sheer awe that it inspired upon entering, and the overwhelming expanse of marble to inspect thwarted my plan at once. Halvdan's carvings were easy to reach, though: in open sight I saw the strange alphabets of the Nordics – the letters resembling dried, broken twigs – somewhat underachieving, pitiful when pit against its creators, the heavily built, strong Hyperboreans. Do not believe in the legend of Hyperborea, where inhabitants live forever, and commit suicide when life sates them. Do not believe the music of the lyres and flutes, and in eternal happiness. It's true that the summer sun never sets in those countries, but in winter it never rises, and it is cold – very cold. So Ivar, like the Turkoman who had left behind the slow-growing herbage of the frozen steppes and hay fields choked with shrubs, had understood: this Roman land was designed in Paradise. Goddess Mother Cybele made sure that fire, earth, air, and water knew their places well – here in Karia, in Ionia, in Cappadocia, Opsikion, Optimaton, Thraki, and Kibyrrhaioton. In place of being immortal in the cold, Ivar preferred to die here, where hot, freezing, dry and moist wait their turn patiently, though occasionally they do go insane. Ivar made the right decision. Still, the aftermath was not without drawbacks and constraints. However, remember the wise remark of Gabras?

"Things will never be as you want them to be."

People said Ivar's blood was frozen before he came to Rhomanoi and that it never melted until he reached the end of his life. Whispers alleged that he had left a wife and a child in his Nordic home. Notwithstanding this, he married my grandmother's mother – a woman half his age, who fell madly in love with him. For the first few years, life together was tolerable, but beware, a union with a Nordic spouse can be rather precarious for people like us who have a different mindset when it comes to expressing emotions and imparting money. But I shall elaborate on matrimony with Nordics later.

For now, I shall only tell you that a Roman woman prefers a troublesome, moderately attractive man – disregarding his half-presence – to an iced Adonis whose body is perhaps present while his soul is elsewhere.

It is said that when Ivar's fellow guards returned home and told his wife of Ivar's marriage to a Greek woman, she let out a shriek of damnation and lost her mind. One day, she loosed an imaginary arrow towards the southeast and walked out of her home. They later found her frozen body in a forest. Her arrow, though no more than a delusion, seemed to pierce the ice around Ivar's heart; from that moment, he grew restless, withdrawn, and ceased to love my grandmother – if indeed he ever had. He never returned to his old country.

Instead, this Hercules dug an underground vault using his bare hands, filling it with snow and ice in the wintertime. He would sit there all summer, unable to tolerate the heat. His skin reverted to its original pasty colour, his pupils and irises froze, and a layer of ice blurred his vision, rendering him blind. He never talked to anybody ever again, losing the vitality and zest of his old *Berserkr* days.

Regrettably, as generations passed, Ivar's chiselled face, Grecian nose, flowing golden hair, extraordinary height – I am told he was as tall as the trees – and the beauty of those eye-catching aspects, melted away like his ice and snow. And I, the last of his offspring, have inherited only one of his features: the blue eyes. This should not be surprising, for God had not been generous in granting Basil a particularly lavish share of physical endowments. Not unlike a tortoise, he had a barrel-like middle and thin arms and legs that stuck out from it, with a head bald and glossy like a gourd. His chest, in contrast, had more than its fair share of hair, even his back was hairy – so dense that his skin gave the illusion of being greyish. His nose looked like a large onion, but God is mighty, so his eyes, framed by long, thick eyelashes, were delicate and large and of a warm brown colour, as lovely as Pegasus's eyes and his smile, the smile of a donkey. It made you burst into laughter. And he was the only one who ever told me I was comely. Right after, he would either quote Sappho – *"What is beautiful is good, and who is good will soon be beautiful,"* – or he might say: *"Shapeliness is not always fortunate; it may be dangerous."* His statements contradicted each other, but he did not mind. Maybe the message he conveyed was that one must love me to find me good looking – and to forgive the defects in my character. Even in my old age, as I am now, I'm still not sure: was his an endeavour to console me or to console himself?

After making the peephole, I plugged it up with a wad of fabric, and placed the chairs at such an angle that the future guest would face me, and Basil would face him. Pleased with my work, I sat on the guest chair and waited.

7

What a heavy load a prosperous fool is!

Aeschylus, *Fragment 392*

NIKEPHOROS Gabras had the honour of being the first to inaugurate my peephole. This experience strengthened my conviction: I had been right to anticipate hazards. I congratulated myself on this small triumph of foresight. In fact, I was taking a stab at playing God, aware I was committing a sin by granting myself the superior status of 'viewer'. With one key difference: my victims were being watched without their knowledge.

We mortals, by contrast, never quite understood why we came into this world, though we were certain that we were being surveilled at all times. My callers, at least, knew the purpose of their visit. And since the next guest would probably be Ataman, or some other savage of Basil's choosing – in short, not the most exemplary mortal – I decided my trespass was pardonable.

As luck would have it, the second object of my inquisitive gaze was Pardos, our eunuch priest. That shook my confidence. However, the subsequent callers were Leo Roslinos, a *chartularios*, a high-rank chancery clerk recently arrived from Constantinople, and Michael, Basil's cousin, in whose house I had sojourned during the preselection of the bridal candidates at My Lady's house. Images of hanged men flitted across my mind, clouding it briefly, but their call restored my morale. A Roman officer dropping by might prompt Ataman to question my father's fidelity, but in fact, Leo, too, was also a distant cousin of Basil's, so the visit could be assumed to be personal. Still, Basil's boldness in receiving them under the circumstances was surprising. On the other hand, Nikephoros's stopover could have posed a far greater risk – had I not found an opportune moment to sabotage it.

Nikephoros, who had not shown his face for years, not even to attend his own father's funeral, had recently returned from Constantinople. Gabras had wanted his son admitted to one of the Empire's most prestigious guilds – the 'Twenty-Four Imperial Notaries' – or to become a court dignitary. A sound education being a crucial requirement, the boy had to learn rhetoric and arithmetic, and then law, philosophy and astronomy at the Patriarchal School in Constantinople. And yet, when we were younger, I remember Madam Gabras, in a rare moment of weakness, lifting her hands to the heavens and crying out, tears streaming down her cheeks:

"If he cannot even tell alphas from omegas, how will he ever learn Latin?"

She revealed that Nike's umbilical cord had been hidden in a chink in the wall of the Patriarchal Academy in Constantinople – an old Cappadocian custom meant to bless children's studies. Among her endless attempts, one was a combined Kakoskopos prayer arranged for both Nike and me. Kakoskopos prayers were supposed to help children who struggled learning their letters and, according to Madam Gabras, it also worked on the troublesome and tiresome.

So, she sought to kill two birds with one stone: hymns and prayers were chanted over our heads so that Nike might become a stronger pupil and I might desist from being naughty, disruptive, and difficult. In those days, Madam Gabras still had hopes for me, and she worked hard. I must give credit where credit is due – her tenacity was rather admirable.

For Nike, the rituals continued. They sponged off Justin the Philosopher's icon, squeezed out the water and made him drink it. They baked honey cakes shaped like the letters of the alphabet and made him eat them. They wrote magical prayers on a loaf of bread and made him swallow it. Last but not least, they scraped off the inked letters from the works of Saint John Chrysostom, dissolved the flakes in some obscure liquid, and obliged our priest to let it steep under the altar during Divine Liturgy. The poor child drank it. That's when he fell dreadfully ill and reverted to his usual gaunt self, having lost the little weight he'd gained from all the cakes and bread.

To introduce him into the right circles, Gabras sought to bribe some high functionaries and dignitaries who might recommend him to the guild. Whether these intercessions had borne fruit was unclear. He wasn't in Constantinople, after all, but here – in our drawing room – standing there like a beanpole, mumbling in his usual deadening, monotone.

We town children used to call him "The Nitwit," and played all sorts of inventive pranks on him. Yet this was a child who had once received a kiss on the forehead from the Emperor. On the Wednesday after Easter, six newly baptised children and six orphans would be brought to the Palace, where they would receive a kiss and a purse of coins as a gift from His Majesty. Gabras made the necessary arrangements – bribes, no doubt – and Nike got the royal kiss.

He'd had a privileged start, but I must admit he'd also become acquainted with barbarity earlier than the rest of us. We would grasp his forearm with both hands and twist it in opposite directions until it reddened and bruised. Or we wouldn't release him until we were finished playing the *Devil in Chains* game, and then we'd leave him behind, all alone. After tying him up to a tree and scaring him with a dead mouse, we subjected the wretched soul to a series of other brutal torments I do not wish to mention here. He would never protest – though his eyes filled with tears – never cry out, hit back, or complain to his parents. The next day, as if nothing had happened, he would come again and watch us quietly while we played five stones or pulled clay horses and birds on wheels.

My mother had given me a tiny-waisted ox-bone doll, with bitumen eyes and long, black hair glued with tar onto her head. She had a whole wardrobe of linen and cotton tunics. But I always left her at home – she wasn't built for the rough-and-tumble outdoors – much like Nike. We children believed him to be the dumbest creature on earth, and that to endure so much agony, he must be a nullity, a zero.

Years later, spying on him again, I saw no reason to change my mind.

One would expect that, having spent time in Constantinople and having received proper schooling, Nike might have gained a little vigour and zest, perhaps also a sprinkling of humour if that's not demanding too much. But no. The capital had given his skin a pale greenish-grey hue and layered him in a pedantic veneer, which I found to be most antipathetic. If anyone noticed and inquired why his skin was so pasty, studying indoors all daylong could constitute a good reason, but who cared enough about Nike to discern any subtle changes to his body and spirit? He was the sort of person who would remain forever unseen – unless his invisibility grated on someone's nerves. Hence his plight with me.

First impressions of people are the hardest to shake, and his had been worse than being invisible. If I didn't suspect that he and Basil were hatching a plan involving me, I would consign him to his destiny and his visit would pass unnoticed, but now the prospect of me in some way having to move in his prosaic ambit loomed. As soon as he left, I confronted Basil:

"Father, not on your life!"

"Theia, he's waiting for you. He somehow believes this was a betrothal made in the cradle – though for your sake, I've always taken an ambiguous stance."

"You mean you didn't want him either. And yet now you do? How lucky for me that you confess the truth. I like it when you're straightforward and honest."

"Suitors are not exactly lining up at our door. He seems to have forgotten about the fact that I sent you to attend the Bride Show selections behind their backs."

"Anthony Gabras wanted this marriage. Not you and not me."

"Nike is educated, well-off, modest and mature. A serious gentleman. Possibly he would make a good husband." Voice trailing off as I glared. "A very good husband… Possibly."

"Modest and mature?" I echoed, livid. "You mean dull and dry as a stick? The chair you are sitting on has more vitality than he does. Chickens think more interesting thoughts. And have you listened to that voice? Cows intonate better when mooing. The only thing statuesque about him is his stupid, eternally frozen expression. Even donkeys can laugh, so why can't he?"

"Respectful language, please."

"Why's he come back, anyway?"

"To take over the land," Basil said quietly.

"What? To come here, to this barbarian-infested district! From the ever glorious megapolis? He must have been a failure there. Nike goes to the metropolis to pursue his namesake, the Goddess of Victory, but returns defeated, empty-handed. Ha! How ironic!" I scoffed. "Constantinople still has its statue of Victory there, and we have ours here. Our very own Nike, here!"

"A cynical woman is not alluring, Theia," he muttered with a sigh and a shake of the head.

"Apparently, she is, though. Nike doesn't seem to mind, does he? Anyway, it's not going to happen, Father."

Leaving him gaping, I walked out. For a few seconds, I faltered, uncertain what to do. Then I thought of the books Ataman had sent from the monastery. These swift changes of thought, these movements between places had a soothing effect on anger and fear.

The box that contained the books, I thought, was one of one of the few Turkish 'entities' I was able to view close-up – apart from him, his men and the nomads who came to buy fruits or sold dairy produce at the market, of course. The box was as unusual as he was, its surfaces carved with interlocking patterns: octagonal stars across the facades, in strict geometrical conjunction with birds entwined among them – much like Basil and me, trapped in Ataman's ambition and in his cordiality.

Eleven books – worth more than eleven years of a peasant's wages – lined the interior, side-by-side, neatly wrapped in cotton fabric. A reluctant gratitude filled my heart. Were we in a shy collaboration sharing the bounty here, or did we do a heroic deed by rescuing a Roman treasure? When we heard death beyond the walls of our garden, fear crippled me, but had I ever wondered why we were spared? Or how? I had mastered numbing these apprehensions just as I numbed the shame of having been spared. One adapts to being alive rather quickly. Besides, why should I be more fickle than death itself?

I examined the first book – embellished with enamel and gilded in copper. I replaced it carefully and removed another – which had a gold jacket adorned with jewels. I put that one back and took a third, plainer than the others, though still delicate and fine. In the middle of its red leather cover a sunken panel was placed, made of engraved ivory, and illustrated with two warriors. Shivering, I opened it to the first page with the tip of my finger.

"*Timaeus*," Basil said.

I looked up. I felt my face burning. My ears rang. I curled my toes until they hurt, unable to bear the odd, tingling sensation – something between a tickle and a shiver, impossible to place. Something similar was happening in my tummy – a syrupy, sticky flood spreading through it, leaving behind a slow, oily tingle.

"Plato! Here, in this house! In my hands. Right now."

Basil chuckled "Ataman picked a few for himself and gave us the rest."

Tightening the muscles of my belly to keep the thrill in check, I grinned.

"That's curious! What did he choose?"

"Let's see… gospels, biblical and liturgical documents. Biographies of saints and theologians too. There was a lapidary, and a book of canon codes, and, of course, a work on medicine."

"What's he going to do with those?"

"He's sending them to the palace in Iconium."

"Intriguing. They might use the medical text – and the lapidary for stonework, I suppose. The law book, I understand. But Christian texts? What on earth will a barbarian do with Christian books?"

"The court is replete with Romans who defected to the Turks. And the reverse is also true. Not to mention, the Sultan and other leading figures in his retinue often take Greek wives."

"Look, there's *Achmet's Dream Interpretation*!" I cried. "How on earth did a book on dream interpretation end up in the library of a monastery—along with so many pagan works? Had grandfather Zeno known about this? He certainly would not have been happy." I laughed.

Basil stared at the floor and kept silent.

I was particularly delighted to have found this treasure, as thick as a Haghia Sophia brick! If someone named Achmet had gone to the trouble of sitting and writing down interpretations of mundane dreams, maybe there was indeed a sense to them? Maybe dreams deserved more attention? Could they possibly cast some light on the mysteries of life?

I sighed. I could never keep my thoughts collected, never hold a single thread for long. Never achieve that state of ultimate immersion…

"Obviously, Ataman isn't interested in dreams. For a man like him, it's life that counts, not the dreams, right?"

Basil shook his head. "He doesn't need it. His tribe practises its own dream work, under the auspices of a wise man or a magician."

Among the books, was a volume of Sappho's poetry. I clapped a hand over my mouth and shrieked.

Basil jerked upright, face crimson. "Don't touch that! It's not for you!"

"But – "

"Put it back. Now."

Against my better judgement, I obeyed. Sappho… She herself would confess, I would find out later:

Words More Naked Than Flesh

She went further still:

Now you are a broken seal:

A scarlet stain upon the earth….

It was not the right time to seek Sappho out, nor hunt her down. Only time would tell. As she rightly said:

"Someone will remember us, I say; even in another time."

Indeed, we were thinking of her now, and would continue to think of her later – more than we admitted. Evidently, Basil had plans for the forbidden poet's book. I couldn't help wondering again: had grandfather known there was a book of Sappho's poetry at the monastery?

As if the Sappho incident hadn't happened, I picked up where I'd left off, checking the other books. Histories by Herodotus, four classic plays – each adorned with elaborate ornaments – and three others that stood apart, with plain bindings and bare covers, as though trying to hide. *Hermetic Arcanum* and *Chaldean Oracles* had initials carved on their title pages: "MP." Whoever had owned them had marked them to make his claim clear yet seemed to want them to go unnoticed. Worthless, heathen texts, I thought.

A great pity: one labourer worked a whole year for the price of a single book. Here we had no less than a decade of books – and still no Homer. When I was separating the three plain volumes (which I had no intention of reading) from the embellished ones, a few small papyrus sheets slipped from between the pages of the *Hermetic Arcanum* onto the floor.

They were filled with disjointed, desultory thoughts:

For I am a man, a soul attached to a body. Therefore, I take pleasure in both thoughts and sensations. Should someone establish his soul above his body, he will be happy and blessed. Although I only half-live in the body, I must still love it.

Still shaken by Sappho, I found myself pondering the meaning. What could he mean? *'I half-live in the body....'* If not in the body, where then did we live? We were told to love the body, yet we were happier when the soul transcended it. Why own a body at all?

The second note read:

Soul is in one substance but has its own virtues and natural qualities. A particular pain would produce a different pain in a Scythian than in a compassionate man.

This made more sense. A certain Ataman and a Basil wouldn't experience pain the same way, would they? And you did not even have to be a barbarian to feel less. The likes of My Lady in Constantinople or our Madam Gabras here in Plekia – did they possess the same capacity to suffer as profoundly as, let's say as I, Theia did? I guffawed.

The final note revealed the identity of the books' owner:

Just as amorous people are impulsively affixed upon beautifully fashioned bodies, so also do most hang on my tongue.

The best educated Roman of them all. The grandest man of letters Constantinople had ever seen. The Consul of philosophers, Michael Psellos – whose lectures drew vast audiences from Babylonia, Persia, Egypt, and even the Latin West.

How had the private books of such a man ended up in the monastery library of my village some sixty years after his death? And his private notes – dangerous ones at that.

So, I decided to pass the ensuing days going over the books, beginning with *Timaeus*, followed closely by the strange writings of Psellos, rather than the classic plays or poems. I examined each page of every book repeatedly. I smelled and caressed the parchment, behind which a cow's heart once throbbed with joy at the sight of a deep green grass field. And when wounds pained the skin, calves had licked it. Not only the books but the poems and plays themselves were alive. The poems and plays knew Basil, Anna, Nike – even Ataman personally. Perhaps they knew me, too. But Plato's and Psellos's obscure books held knowledge one could not even imagine.

Thus, I discovered the Demiurge. But before that, I learned something else that pained me: one of the greatest calamities in life is to be intelligent, but not *very* intelligent. To be just intelligent enough to know that there existed a higher order of mind one can never reach. It was more comfortable to be the part of the flagpole stuck in the soil than the bit that fluttered in the wind.

How did the Demiurge fit into this? By *not* perceiving it.

Let me explain. According to the oracles:

The Father perfected all things and handed them over to the Second Intellect, which you - the entire human race -- call the First Intellect.

The Demiurge was an entity or deity, an auxiliary who "fashioned and shaped" the material world, a pupil, an apprentice or perhaps an errand boy of the true God. It was unreservedly benevolent and desired a world as good as possible. But the world remained imperfect, for the Demiurge had made it from chaos itself – shapeless, indeterminate, and not yet being.

But who was this Demiurge? A half-illiterate peasant? A monster – dim-witted and evil? Wasn't it naïve of us to think he meant well? How could the world be perfect if it was assembled from chaos? And why had God entrusted such an important task to a novice – an inferior one at that? What did Michael Psellos know? And what had he hidden?

It said:

In order that the All might continue to love for an infinite time, and the things woven, and the light of the Father might not collapse, the soul was filled with a deep love.

But wasn't love too significant to leave in novice hands? Was God betraying our love by refusing to take charge? What did Christ think? Did Michael Psellos share my doubts? I, a nobody in the countryside, could think whatever I wanted. But Psellos? Did he use only his initials because he was scared for his neck?

Because of Love, all things were suited to one another; with this Love, the elements of the world remained on course.

So – Love was the fabric of the cosmos. It held it together. The perfect foundation for an imperfect world, made by an imperfect deity.

Each day I read, rapture and melancholy swept over me, until my mind and soul alighted on the memory of a Turkish soup. I remembered the groups of nomadic Turkish women who sold it at the marketplace. Supple-limbed, and unadorned, sitting astride horses like men, they swung themselves down, red-cheeked babies peeking out of cradles strapped to the pommels of their saddles. Effortless and carefree, in men's leggings, they chattered to each other as they dismounted, set out pots and pans, boiled fermented milk, added wheat, flour, and eggs – stirring always in the same direction. Always.

If they got carried away with their chatter and forgot to stir, then started again in the wrong direction – widdershins – the soup would turn into an inedible mush. Fit only for pigs. Much like a mind after reading books.

Whenever this calamity occurred, the women just laughed – sometimes shrieking with mirth – every so often hugging and kissing their ruddy-faced infants as they poured the ruined batch aside and started afresh, still laughing.

8

To a father growing old nothing is dearer than a daughter.

Euripides, *Helen*

My plan was rather commonplace, resorted to more often than people realise – and even now, forty and six years later, it still is. Indeed, I have lived long – longer than anyone I know. Even Emperor Manuel – may God rest his soul – died a few years ago, and I am still here. The few people I knew who reached my age collapsed and could not stand up anymore. It was over for them then. When younger, I fell many times, but nowadays I do not even stumble, despite the twinges.

A Saracen once shared an aphorism with me: *"Don't be too hard, you'll break; don't be too soft, you'll be squashed."* The wise youngster had not yet realised that, with age, another curious circumstance presents itself: you become thin-skinned – figuratively and literally. You become both too soft and too hard at once, or find yourself oscillating between two opposing states of mind, either of which arrests you unpredictably – tearfully maudlin one moment, utterly heartless the next. And whichever takes hold in a given moment, in my modest experience, it is never the right one. Just as Anthony Gabras once said: it is never as you want it. Nothing is ever as we want in this life. This is the way this stage is crafted: a sob story grows into a drollery, and a funny farce turns into a tale of woe – by turns, in rotation, and all the time.

Moreover – and what is even worse – with old age your ears and nose grow larger, and that is also rather disturbing. When I was young, the moment you turned your face from mine, you would no longer remember my features; now if you look at me, you will never forget me, and that, too, is bothersome. Mysterious dreams that used to wake me shivering in the cold, soaked in hot sweat, would lead to musing throughout the day, visions that kept me marvelling and hoping until the next sleep. Now they have become transformed into mundane experiences – plucked ducks of dreams, inferior in quality, like second-hand pottery that has lost its glaze. The mists clear away faster these days. I wake and at once recognise that last night's angel, villain or monster's banal counterpart in real life – the friendly fisherman, the bizarre nomad or a beloved donkey. Options include either resisting these quagmires of undue self-discovery or resigning oneself to them by farming them out to the Divine in ultimate fatalism – this latter is preferred if one is to be considered a respectable elder. But neither option will change one fact: while you are waiting for your spirit to ascend, your parts and members will descend.

But let us return to my plan.

I was determined to travel to Constantinople, where on May 11 Emperor John was to stage the grandest of diversions at the Hippodrome to celebrate the city's foundation. So, on the eve of my Hair Covering ceremony – the formal threshold of womanhood – a year after my first time in the capital at My Lady's house, I resolved that my plan would not be thwarted by anyone or anything. First, I cut my hair. Then, with a coarse cotton band, I bound my breasts – not that they were noticeable then, and having fulfilled only half the duties assigned to them in my lifetime, they remain unremarkable in size. Nevertheless, leaving them unbound was a risk I could not afford to take.

When Basil saw me, he collapsed. When he finally came to, he refused to take me to Constantinople for the celebrations. And when I tried on his clothes – his tunic as big as a tent, the overall guise rather floppy and ludicrous – he became apoplectic with rage.

I suggested:

"Wouldn't it be more fitting to borrow a tunic from a boy my age then – Nike, for instance? We're going anyway, so what's the difference?"

He did not reply. He disappeared and showed up only at supper, pouting. He continued to pout until the moment of our departure.

I sent Anna to borrow garb from Nike. She protested, but I blackmailed her, saying that if she did not accept the task of requesting items from Madam Gabras's maid, I would demand them of her myself. Pressing her hands to her temples, Anna let out a primal scream and, fiery and red, ran to Nike's house.

Basil scowled and shook his head when he saw my new attire, and all throughout our journey to the metropolis he sulked and avoided eye contact with me. However, I did not let his ill-temper disturb my high spirits. A few times he muttered about our lunatic state of affairs. I shrugged my shoulders each time.

We stayed overnight at an inn, where Basil refrained from any conversation with me – or with anyone else for that matter. On the second day of travel, he repined a little in the morning, under his breath, but for the rest of the day, until late afternoon he said nothing. It took two to three days to reach the capital from Plekia. Our last post on the Asian side before traversing the strait was Chalcedon, and it was here that his glumness finally began to weigh on me – and actively anger me. But he conceded a sigh of admiration and offered a small smile when the city bestowed on us its first treat: the view of the Bosphorus, unfolding before us.

Do you know those rare instants where you are *in* the moment – without thinking about the past or mulling over the future? That is what happens when you watch the Bosphorus; the world stops.

But that was not the case for poor Io. According to the story, Zeus falls in love with Io, the daughter of the Argive King. After having Hermes kill her guardian Argus, he rapes her, and Io is transformed into a cow. Zeus's wife Hera, jealous of Io, sends a wretched gadfly to torment her, driving her from place to place. Fleeing, Io passes through Thrace and ultimately reaches the strait. She traverses it and eventually comes to the spot where the rivers Cydarus and Barbyses flow into a horn-shaped harbour, and there she gives birth to a girl called Ceroessa – the horned maiden – who gave her name to Ceras. Poseidon was Ceroessa's lover. She gave birth to a son, whom they named Byzas – the earliest founder of Byzantium. And remember Byzas's unhappy daughter and her snake-repelling column? This city produced both happy and unhappy daughters (and I contained both states that day, thanks to Basil) and it encountered both curses and blessings.

According to another legend, when Philip of Macedon besieged the city, he had a secret tunnel dug to stage a surprise attack. But on the night his troops emerged, the goddess Phosphorus lit up the sky with torches, exposing Philip and his soldiers to the citizens. A miracle was needed now to lift the weight of Basil's mood from my chest.

At the pier, Basil turned to me and for the first time after so many hours, addressed me in his usual modulated tone:

"When you were a child, you used to toss a handful of pebbles into the air and stand under them as they dropped on your head. You'd cheer as if they were raindrops."

Without waiting to see my reaction, he dismounted and walked towards the Venetian ferryman, deliberately avoiding the reconciliation I might otherwise have attempted. I was born bumping my head on the floor – was this a subtle reference to that incident? Was he suggesting I was trouble? Or implying I had a precious head? I could not tell.

The Latin suggested we enter the city from the Julian gate in the south, since Basil's cousin Michael – in whose house we would lodge – was nearer. But Basil cut him off at once. A hostile gleam appeared in his eyes and his voice deepened:

"The Barbara gate it shall be!"

The Latin's eyes widened at this abrupt outburst, but he said nothing, probably calculating the extra effort now required to detour from the northeast around to the level of Chrysopolis and dock at the Saint Barbara Gate. Indeed, he came up with an extortionate price to deliver us and our horses to the other side.

Basil haggled, but the Latin merely complained – about taxes, inflated quay fees, exorbitant boat costs. Boreas, the wind from the northeast, was blowing that day; it caressed my face, but the seaman gave a very different account. Boreas was said to come from heaven, while the other wind of Constantinople, Notus, which blows from the southwest, was supposed to come from hell. If heaven puffed a pleasant redolence, then hell's breath had arrived earlier and was already ubiquitous, I thought. Vast quantities of mackerel might have caused the stomachs of the city's poor to rejoice, for it cost next to nothing – but to visitors like us, it came at a price, for the reek that engulfed us was unbearable. Either the noses of the haughty Constantinopolitans had become impervious to it, or they no longer minded. Perhaps to them, the stench was a beauty mark – unsightly, but also a natural component of the whole countenance.

When Notus blew, some judges refused to hold court. The wind made people grumpy, silly, or sick – with bloodshot eyes and headaches. The Latin whined: yes, Boreas was lovely, but reaching the Saint Barbara gate was hard because of it. The current from the Black Sea was too strong; violent swirls and whirlpools abounded; deep cross-streams made the approach treacherous. To attempt it now, he claimed was to steer between Scylla and Charybdis – whichever route he took would be the wrong one. Currents rebounded off rocks, underwater shelves dropped off too sharply, and we risked crashing our prow into someone's house. And if we did – who would pay the damages?

Refusing to lower the price, he grumbled about the same conditions that, some five centuries ago, had instilled fear in the heart of a heroic Emperor – the mighty Heraclius, champion of seven campaigns against the Persians. Heraclius feared water; he dreaded crossing the Bosphorus. So his men constructed a bridge with their boats stretching from Phedalia to the Asiatic coast, concealing the view of the strait on either side with dense greenery and vegetation. Only then could Heraclius be persuaded to cross – on horseback, through the artificial thicket, as if he were still on solid ground. Such was the power of Constantinople, even over emperors. The city measured up to a Demiurge – not the unreservedly benevolent creator of Plato's imagining, but rather the one I envision: a trickster, complacent, and only questionably benign. It shifted at will between grandeur and pride, told you lies about yourself, made you empty promises so you'd finish your meal, go to bed, and grow wise. And if you stayed long enough, it blurred the lines between fact and fiction – until you no longer knew where one ended and the other began.

The Latin, ticking points off on his fingers, described each and every peril of his trade he might encounter, then, throwing his hands up, spoke of the actual fatalities and casualties suffered by his crew. Basil gave a long sigh, paid the fare and said no more. But once we were on board, his face turned sour, and he began to grumble about the Venetians.

They, along with other Italians, held special trading privileges in the city: not only did each own special quarters in the metropolis, but they also enjoyed countless advantages and exemptions over the locals, which we Romans deeply resented. Whenever things did not go their way, these Latins – mainly Pisans, Venetians and Genoese – rampaged through the streets, fighting one another and stirring up serious trouble, as if the city were neither conquered nor native ground to them. Their arrogance extended equally to Roman peasants and high officials alike. And the distant rulers of their homelands were no better.

Emperor Alexios had received Peter the Hermit, Godfrey of Bouillon, Bohemond and the other insolent leaders of the Crusades at the Blachernae Palace – out of prudence, not friendship. The Latins, brazen and pushy were never friends.

When Alexios's son, Emperor John, annulled some of their privileges, they didn't dare attack Constantinople directly. Instead, they set out in large fleets and attacked Roman islands – Rhodes, Kos, Lesbos and Chios from where the beloved "Tears of Chios" came, a gum with a seductive fragrance which the mastic trees of the island exuded. There was no warning, no protection; they destroyed the fortifications, stole relics, and took innocent people as slaves.

Helpless to stop their depredations, Emperor John would give in and renew their privileges. The idea that we Romans lacked the commercial acumen of the Latins naturally never occurred to Basil – though perhaps the Emperor knew it. Otherwise, why were we so dependent on them?

Basil smiled and murmured: "What would my father say now?"

I giggled, and in whispers we quoted Zeno together, mimicking his high-pitched voice: "Those Latins – rapacious vipers in our bosom…"

The ferry boat must have been built using the latest techniques, for it hovered over the water. The Venetian obviously knew the strait's temperament like the back of his hand and used its insane fluxes to his advantage, glancing off wharves and jetties, only barely avoiding them and making my heart race. I thought, my elation, akin to music moving the body and feet of a dancer, must have pushed the sails, lifting the boat forward. Isn't blue the most beautiful colour in this world?

Against the scarlet bandages that wrapped the white bulwarks, the Bosphorus's caprices produced thousands of different tones of blue. Purplish blue foams tossed, and the scarlet-painted yacht of the Emperor which was moored at the Boukoleon harbour of the Grand Palace, weltered. But he no longer resided there. His father, Alexios Komnenos, had moved the family to Blachernae district, on the northern slopes, in a new royal residence atop a hill with better protection. A chain – one that had consumed mountains and mountains of iron ore in its making – had been strung across the strait, blocking hostile ships at Megalos Pyrgos from entering the Chrysokeras. I scanned the distance for any flicker or movement of shadows on the walls of the city. A majestic vision of the Virgin Mary was said to appear over these walls to scare away ill-intentioned visitors; once, an Avar Khagan allegedly wet himself in horror at the sight and abandoned his siege. But though I may have erred in disguising myself as a man, the Virgin must not have found me threatening, for she did not appear. Still, I think I'd have preferred her company to My Lady's.

A marble terrace jutted from the city wall to the Acropolis Pier, where the Latin anchored his boat. Two large white marble towers flanked the Saint Barbara Gate, brought as a trophy from Tarsus by Phokas when he recaptured the city from the Arabs. While Basil was footing the bill, I galloped headlong to the gate. And instead of the Virgin, I was greeted by tax officials, stationed there to register goods and question arrivals such as this young, more effeminate-than-usual rider. One raised a hand. I came to a halt and dismounted. An elder officer – likely the superior – stepped forward from behind the others. Without saying a word, I pointed in Basil's direction, and we both watched the laggard bumping along on horseback at a dismal pace. Spotting our expressions, Basil quickened his pace. An incoming wine merchant and a Syrian cloth trader drew the attention of the junior officials, but the elder kept a close eye on both me and my father. By the time Basil caught up, he was panting and sweating copiously as if burning with fever.

He threw me a pained look and then bowed to the man. If he hadn't insisted so stubbornly on entering the city from the Saint Barbara Gate, I thought, he wouldn't be in this state. With an elusive, almost apologetic smile, the officer asked,

"Anything to declare?"

Then, without waiting, he added, "You are aware, I assume, that your sojourn in the city must not exceed three months. If you intend to stay longer, you must apply for permission – or else there will be penalties."

Basil's brow furrowed. Though we had no wares to sell and no intention of overstaying, his eyes became glossy, and I feared this would arouse the tax man's suspicion – and that a ransack of our belongings would follow, something Basil could scarcely endure in his present state. He was acting foolishly, so I stepped forward to answer, even at the risk of revealing my sex, but the officer smiled at me and hurried back to where his subordinates were standing. He murmured something to one of the others and then addressed the Syrian merchant with sharp authority:

"Your goods will be stored in designated quarters within the city. You will be confined there while conducting your sales. We will explain how to get there. Do not attempt to sell elsewhere, or…"

Indeed, the city had appointed public order officials commonly known as Catchers – Catchers of Egyptians and Catchers of Syrians – who targeted citizens of those provinces exclusively. Anyone unable to provide a valid reason for their presence in the capital was reprimanded and expelled.

As I debated whether to begin unloading our sacks, a jaded-looking official waved us through. We now stood upon the city's Acropolis, which led into the gardens of the Grand Palace. The gardens spread out into broad lawns and terraces, open to the public in the afternoons. From here, the road would take us all the way down to Haghia Sophia and the Hippodrome.

Insisting on entering through the Saint Barbara Gate brought us one unforgettable present: the Imperial Gardens. As we rode slowly through them, something came over Basil. His eyes seemed watery – but I could not be sure. We were, after all, exhausted. His shoulders hunched against the elements, his face down-turned, Basil suddenly broke into a gallop.

Despite being upset by his odd hastiness and his moroseness, I gave a squeal of joy when we passed the Eirene Church and reached the giant.

"Haghia Sophia!"

Music and fanfare echoed throughout the city as it celebrated its birthday. Still Basil did not cheer up. He acted like an unwelcome stork. Emperor Constantine had chosen neither the site nor the date of his New Rome by chance. His astrologers had proposed the location, at the confluence of the Cydarus and Barbyses rivers. The building site was encircled with rope and lined with small bells, set to ring at the Emperor's signal. When he gave the sign, the first foundation stones would be laid. But on May 11, 330, a silly stork was flying over the site far above and dropped a snake it had been carrying in its beak onto the rope. The bells rang, and the workers thinking Constantine had given the signal, broke ground. Constantine, enraged, cursed all storks:

"Storks, I damn you, your entrance to the new city is forbidden."

And since that day, it is said, storks no longer fly over Constantinople, nor build nests there. That same ill-omened spot, it was prophesied to Constantine, would be the very place from which the Ishmaelites would one day enter and take the city.

I cannot say whether storks enter the city or not, but I can tell you that Slavs, Italians, Russians, Spaniards, Lusitanians, and Celts from beyond the Alps – are all crammed into this place, alongside Venetians, Dacians, Jews, Arabs, Amalfitans, and heathen peoples, even Turks, all seeking heaven on earth while chattering in a hundred and one languages. On the Milion walls are carved the names and distances of cities – even some I've only heard of. Every obscure and minor place had sent its citizens here to New Rome, to the new Jerusalem, to the centre of the world.

Perhaps the Constantinopolitans were simply accustomed to it – so many dwellers from disparate worlds brushing past one another in their city that it scarcely gave them pause. But watching the endless stream of silken tunics and tattered rags rubbing shoulders in the streets, I felt a sudden sadness – not homesickness, but something closer to alienation. These people's paths might cross, but their stories never would. I became more stupefied than a Constantinopolitan struck by the Notus wind. How could they all walk around so calm and composed, immune to all these questions and surprises? Even our ever-phlegmatic Basil was struggling.

In days of yore, perfumers were placed closer to the entry of the old palace in an effort to mask the stink of mackerel and gratify the Emperor's nose as he approached home; perfumery stalls were set up between the milestone and the Brazen Gate. The Imperial Komnenos family moved the imperial household from the Grand Palace, which had been in the southeast, to the Blachernae Palace in the far northwest – free from the noise and smoke of the city centre, more remote but with easier access to their hunting grounds and, of course, more secure. The Grand Palace, with its thirty chapels and five hundred halls – said to all be connected – was far larger than the newer palace, which had only twenty chapels and three hundred halls. The Grand Palace was an intricate city unto itself and thus more vulnerable to attack. At the foot of the hill of the Blachernae Palace, stood the Church of the Mother of God, which housed the Virgin's robe – hoped by many to offer better protection against the approaching danger: the Turks.

The real reason for the Komnenos relocation was not the grime and vapours of the city centre but the Turks who, by the first decade of Alexios's reign, were already present on the shores of the Propontis. Their Sultan, Suleyman, had conquered a stretch of land that took a month to cross in length and ten days in breadth, and they were widening their martial activities under the auspices of their bigger brother, the Grand Seljuk Sultan of Persia. So, the eastern quarters of the city could no longer be considered secure.

Now that I was a man, I could spy on the Mohammedans at close range. These people were different than Turks – wearing turbans and long tunics, and sporting black beards. Their women, commendably more modest in dress than Roman women, would follow in the wake of their man like ducklings, their eyes fixed on his heels. For us, the bones of Saints mixed into the mortar protected Haghia Sophia – but Hagarenes too maintained their own legends about that mortar. According to them, Haghia Sophia's dome refused to hold and kept collapsing during construction. Then Saint George appeared to the architects in the guise of an old dervish and advised them to mix the Prophet Mohammed's saliva with Zam Zam water and Meccan soil in the mortar, and this would make it stand. The puzzled architects reported this to their priests, who, equally puzzled, travelled to Mecca. There they met the Prophet's uncle, Abu Talib, and explained to him their plight. Abu Talib fetched the Prophet. Foreknowing that Constantinople would one day become his Kingdom, Mohammed filled a bowl with his saliva. Seventy camels carried soil from Mecca, seventy more bore the Zam Zam water, and together they transported the sacred cargo to Constantinople. When the architects used the mixture, the dome finally stood.

A cramped semi-transparent window of veils was all these Saracen women had to see the world. I appreciated the degree of reliance these multiple wives placed in one man, trailing him in a half blind state and wondered what might have made him so special. What did they muse upon in the Queen of cities?

Their Qur'an said:

"And when We intend that We should destroy a township, We permit its luxury-loving people to commit wickedness therein. Then the word is proved true against it, and We destroy it utterly."

The Arabs' first siege of Constantinople was repelled by Greek fire; the second, by famine and winter. These defeats came centuries before the Turks arrived in Asia Minor. Mohammed, the Prophet of the Saracens, left his people with several messages about the Turks:

"The hour of resurrection shall not come until the Muslims win a decisive victory over the Atrak, Al Turk. These are people with faces resembling iron shields coated with leather, with small eyes, red faces and flat noses, who wear furs and shoes made of hair."

But he also said:

"Leave the Atrak, Al Turk, as long as they do not trouble you."

Even Aristotle warned Alexander the Great against them:

"Be careful not to hasten and attack the Turks, their lives depend totally on their beasts. They enjoy food, drinking and amusement and are satisfied with those; they do not like money and do not desire riches. Watch out, they are not scared of death nor fear being killed but they worry about imprisonment."

And yet today, among this motley crowd – diverse in race and creed – the Turks form part of the population of the Roman capital: at war elsewhere, perhaps, but here in the metropolis they roam freely, rubbing shoulders in peace, making it rather difficult for a young Roman – even a girl – not to feel a swell of pride.

Towers adorned with laurel garlands came into view as we progressed. Silk banners and pennants rippled from marble pillars. Myrtle and rosemary brocades festooned porphyry columns. The streets were lightly dusted in rosewater-scented sawdust, and fountains flowed with wine and almonds and pistachios. City guards manhandled unlicensed traders while countless other peddlers and vendors swarmed the forecourt, too many to check. Beneath the porticoes candle-makers, bronze workers, bakers, jewellers, blacksmiths, and weavers had set up small shops. Money changers, who also offered bank services, sat at iron tables with mounds of *tetarteron* and foreign copper coins, but stashed their precious gold *hyperpyra* and dinars in drawers. Taverns were scattered in between, while fishmongers, butchers and wine merchants were situated farther away.

The Mohammedans had a temple in the city. Even the North Africans had their own small mosque near the Forum of Constantinople. I wanted to stick around and watch these Muslims, go where they went and eventually, perhaps, even catch a glimpse of their church, but Basil hurried me along, never allowing me time to be with my thoughts. Wherever I paused, he urged me on – as if infected by the same haste that governed My Lady when she received us. Perhaps it was Constantinople itself that so exasperated and drove people onward?

An old man hawked and spat. A glob of red and yellow phlegm landed by our feet. I squealed, disgusted. He stared blankly and walked off without a word. Above us, an angry woman dumped foul water from her window onto a man below. He yelled and cursed, but didn't step out of the puddle. She reappeared with another pot and poured it over him again – this time, rotten pieces of fish and fishbone too, which I suspected were the remains of a failed garum sauce, splattered all around. The man flew into a rage and proceeded to bellow obscenities at her. Basil, his face flushed crimson, took my arm – in fact, yanked it – and pulled us away.

Ancients never founded cities by degrees; they came, chose a site and built it from scratch – and so did Byzas, Alexander the Great and Constantine. But behind these magnificent monuments lay squalid, fetid areas where the ground was overlaid with mud and people lived in cramped, sometimes five-storey tenement dwellings, where the rule that 'Balconies must be at least ten feet apart from the neighbour' was ignored – along with the ban on outdoor stairs leading from the street to the balconies. Even if you never set foot in these districts – especially in the northern Mese, where the ground was muddy and windows were slit-like – they came to you, and to where splendour abode, and they did so in a quiet, stubborn manner, typical of Constantinopolitans.

When we passed the Hippodrome, Basil shouted, "Don't gawk at them!" – meaning the prostitutes loitering beneath the Quadriga Horses at the outer façades of the Hippodrome boxes. A grinning constable raised his arm and drew an imaginary boundary in the air, motioning toward some far-off corner where he evidently thought the women should go. Laughing, they paid him no mind – one or two even jeered outright. His grin faded into a scowl. Advancing without humour now, he began to shove the harlots away. They shrieked and protested, but ultimately moved off, sullen and swearing. Yet the moment his back was turned, they returned – victoriously, heads high, strutting back to their spots beneath the Quadriga as though they'd never left.

I stared defiantly at Basil and said, "I am a man now, not a woman."

How ridiculous I found him. Had it never occurred to him, in his now overwrought state, that I might witness scenes like this when I came here without him? But Basil attached the greatest importance to whatever was immediately at hand. Glaring, he shoved me aside, looked up at the sky, and exclaimed:

"May God forgive these wretched souls!"

He lowered his gaze and glowered at me again, muttering something I couldn't make out.

9

The children, O billy-goat, have put purple reins on you and a muzzle on your bearded face, and they train you to race like a horse round the god's temple that he may look on their childish joy.

Anythe, *Epigram*

BASIL regained his composure when we took our seats on some marble benches resting on vaults – one of the finest vantage points on the long side of the track, directly across from the *Kathisma*, the Emperor's private box attached to the Hippodrome. The façade of the Hippodrome was built on arches, its position resembling a table leaning against the ridge of the steep hill. From cheaper but still acceptable seats one could enjoy the delectable view of the Propontis sea in much the same fashion as from My Lady's house. These seats, however, were not far enough from the common masses. The even cheaper seats of the hoi polloi in the *sphendone* were out of the question. I was quite certain Basil suspected I might enjoy myself too much among the plebs, and so he spent an exorbitant sum to ensure I neither made merry nor grew too intrigued.

The Latins occupied seats specially assigned to them. The Empress and her retinue sat far down the western side, in a chamber with latticed windows. Royal purple, porphyry pillars supported her private suit. My own pillar, I mused, was one hapless, shaky Basil – also purple now and then when my shenanigans irritated him – but I had a better view than hers. In the same way the valiant Empress Theodora had once dissuaded Justinian from fleeing Constantinople, I had found myself here simply by being bull-headed. Yes, I had succeeded, I had reached the Hippodrome. A certain brazenness and a compliant man accompanying you were always a prerequisite for such luxuries as female foolhardiness. Mine was mostly impervious to the city; now and then he grew cranky and grumpy but overall he was harmless.

The Empress Theodora and her male, Emperor Justinian, had once brought about noteworthy bloodshed at this very Hippodrome nearly seven centuries ago. The couple had stepped on many toes, unaware of the depravity of the political atmosphere and the magnitude of the uprising. When they realised, Emperor Justinian had intended to flee in horror. But Theodora refused to give up the purple. Once you've seen it, you cannot unsee it. Once you have tasted something, you cannot un-taste it. She too must have understood the old adage of our old Gabras, "Nothing will ever be exactly as you want it to be" So she said:

"My opinion then is that the present time, above all others, is inopportune for flight, even though it bring safety. For while it is impossible for a man who has seen the light not also to die, for one who has been an emperor, it is unendurable to be a fugitive. May I never be separated from this purple, and may I not live to see the day when those who meet me do not address me as Mistress."

The couple remained in Constantinople and crushed the Nika riots by slaying 30,000 insurgents in the Hippodrome, where the sporting competition between the Greens and the Blues became an outlet for popular rage and grievance. The anger of the rebels was quelled by the spilling of their own blood.

Nevertheless, who would expect a woman to be so manly nearly seven centuries ago? Mind you, in all likelihood her female vanity must have played a part in her risking death so foolishly. To relinquish the purple silk camisia, the gold-and pearl-embroidered mauve tunic, for a few purple tints of wildflowers while in exile in the countryside – that, in her mind, might have equalled death. The utmost she could expect would be purple ribbon tapes around some sequestered field, or the beautiful, purple eyes of an albino donkey, if they were really lucky. Whatever her impetus, it served its purpose: the sovereignty of the couple prevailed. Haghia Sophia took its final shape under Justinian's supremacy.

Basil steered me to my seat first first, then, daunted and tired, slumped into his own, shoulders so low that I all but pitied him for bearing such a burden. But soon my attention shifted to our surroundings. Organs blasted out hymns as the Emperor made his entrance through a passageway leading directly from the old Palace to the *Kathisma*. Thousands stood and hailed the standard bearers, who carried the great golden cross and dragon banners. I nudged the tall man in front of me aside and craned my neck to better see those across the way: the Emperor, and his four sons, sparkling in wisteria, lavender, plum, wine, eggplant, amethyst, berry, magenta and manifold other shades of purple I still cannot name. I could not make out their facial features, but the colours were incandescent.

What must have been a select group of ministers, functionaries, and superintendents, all dressed in vermillion, stood behind the Komnenos family. I thanked Basil for buying us good seats – only in my head, of course. How else would I have learned that purple could be woven into fabrics in so many different ways?

John wore the Imperial diadem on his head, an amaranthine mantle, and a gold *tablion* across his chest. The boy standing beside him must have been his eldest son, Alexios, promised the throne, and, according to rumour, already in red buskins, which only the Emperor and his heir were permitted to wear. A step behind the Emperor and the Prince stood his younger sons – Isaac, Manuel and Andronicus. The rest were likely nephews, cousins and other kin.

You may have gathered by now, that I was better informed this time. At the Bride Show, I was the one entertaining the big fish with my naïve provinciality. Now I was the one being entertained, a proper spectator, and those in Constantinople were performing for me. Smiling at the memory of My Lady's indignant face, I imagined that the most sublime man here – the Emperor, the divine Viceroy of God, not allowed to wipe his mouth or nose in public, nor spit nor turn his face this way or that, obliged to perform the ideal of a statue, to remain solemn at all times – must eventually return home to his wife, perhaps one recommended by the likes of My Lady. He would put his dust-filled silk purse on the table and listen to her complain – complaints about a toothache, or her mother-in-law.

After that, perhaps he must turn his back on her and answer an innocent call of nature, meet a bodily need. Even if a eunuch wiped him, he would still be subject to the vulgarity of defecation like anyone else in this world. God's design meant that if dignity was required, it was nearly always found within spitting distance of humility. Until discharged, faeces dwell in extreme proximity to us: in our very own body. Mortality had far more blatant ways of making itself known to an emperor than an elegantly symbolic silk purse.

The arena stood for earth, the *spina* with its water tanks for sea, and the Egyptian Obelisk of pink granite at its centre for sky. Emperor Constantine's ambition to embellish Constantinople with exotic objects knew no bounds. He wished to bring an obelisk from Thebes but found it would take too long, so he had his own built instead and had it covered with bronze plates that shone like gold. I always wondered why he did not attempt to import the Egyptian pyramids to the Hippodrome as well – where, we have heard, Joseph once stored and sold corn. Those pyramids were believed to be even more majestic than obelisks and, as I had heard, they contained Egyptian magic.

Perhaps bringing them would have posed an even greater challenge than the obelisk, especially considering what befell that one as it was being hauled from the port to the arena. Many years later, in the time of Emperor Theodosios, the obelisk that had been waiting at the port of Alexandria for at least fifty years – if not more – was finally shipped to Constantinople. Proclus was tasked with its transport, but the mission was only half-successful: part of the obelisk broke. To compensate for the lost height, a large marble base was prepared, and the remaining piece was erected at the port. A panel on the marble pedestal recorded the effort:

"It was only the Emperor Theodosios who undertook to raise the four-sided column which had ever lain a burden on the earth, and so great a column stood erect in thirty-two days."

Even without the addition of magical pyramids, there were other curious marvels at the Hippodrome. A bronzed eagle-clock with outstretched wings marked the hours as the sun shone through its feathers. Beside the colossal statue of Hercules, a giant woman held a life-size horse. Opposite the *Kathisma,* a three-headed serpent on a coiled bronze body formed a column dedicated to Apollo, the god who had defeated Python – the chaos-serpent, a fearsome creature.

That very column had once risen from the chasms of Delphi, gazing out toward three barbaric continents: Asia, Europe, and Libya and supporting a golden tripod atop its heads. Emperor Constantine brought it to Constantinople, though the golden tripod had been stolen – so they say – by the Phokaians.

Long before Constantine, Byzas – the son of Poseidon – had consulted the oracle about where to build his colony. As always, chewing laurel leaves, trembling, and salivating, the oracle answered sternly, with a riddle: "Opposite the blind." Upon reaching the magnificent Bosphorus, Byzas spotted the village of Chalcedon on the opposite shore. He understood: those settlers must have been blind not to recognize the splendour of the natural harbour before them, and the great advantages it presented. So he established his dominion exactly on that spot, a site so splendid that even General Megabazus of the Persian King Darius reaffirmed the blindness of the Chalcedonians when he learned their village predated that of Byzas.

Now the heart of the world was no longer Delphi, but Constantinople – born of Byzas' village. In Delphi, the serpent pillar represented the victory of order over chaos – Apollo over the gruesome Python and Greeks over the cunning Persians – whose captured bronze weapons and armour were instrumental in its casting. But here in the capital, where each citizen was a snake of minor importance, each equipped with more sophisticated methods than wielding bronze swords and stones, Constantine's serpent had to do more.

Have you ever heard the expression *similia similibus curantur*? It means: "like is cured by like": a disease may be cured by something that causes similar symptoms. That is to say, if venomous snakes are to be expelled, and serpent-like demons to be exorcised, then Romans must use a mirror image of the monster, much like the Brazen Serpent of Moses, fashioned during the Israelites' wanderings in the wilderness for years, when they cried out:

"Wherefore have ye brought us up out of Egypt to die in the wilderness? For there is no bread, neither is there any water; and our soul loatheth this light bread."

They meant the manna which God gave them daily, a miraculous, edible substance that fell daily from the skies. But it was not as good as bread. God raged, allowing fiery serpents to come among them and bite them. Then they came to Moses, confessing, "We have sinned… pray unto the Lord that He take away the serpents from us." Moses did so, and God told him to make a serpent of brass and to set it upon a pole, saying that all who looked upon it should live.

Two factions were competing today: The Blues and the Greens. Emperor John made the sign of the cross three times – once over the Blues, once over the Greens and once over the people. As the crowd acclaimed, *"Many upon many years!"* he dropped the *mappa*, and people went out of their minds, bawling so loud that I had to clap my hands over my ears.

Here there was something divine about the Emperor's power – but in this city, any power could be challenged by the streets. Today they lauded you, tomorrow they could revile you. The Emperor surely knew this – after all, even I, a child hailing from the provinces had grasped it. If these mean-spirited, quick-to-ignite Constantinopolitans couldn't do worse, they would at least teach their pet parrots to mock you. How many parrots hadn't learned to swear at the Patriarch, or mimic the Empress? In this city, both Constantinopolitans and their parrots could heckle if they were feeling cantankerous.

Twelve gates, each assigned to one of the twelve chariots, were raised simultaneously in one smooth gesture, provoking the horde to exclaim in awe. I stood up and applauded. Then I sat back and offered an idea:

"Father, listen – there was a Patriarch once who called the Hippodrome *Satanodrome*. Have you ever heard of that?"

Unwillingly turning towards me, Basil frowned slightly. "No, I have not."

I tittered. "Of course you haven't. I never told you – for fear you wouldn't bring me here. But look at this place! The ground has been impregnated for centuries with blood and sweat, pain and joy! Could it be that some sort of ancient dark hub of spirits has formed? Maybe that's what powers the gates, and the automata, and all the other strange things here?"

He gasped, gripped the sides of his head, and launched into a long explanation: there was no magic or spell involved in opening of the gates. Rather, two men were hidden on either end, he told me, and a mechanical device raised them together. But when I queried him about how the automata were operated, he sulked and went silent.

I supported the Blues – not because the Emperor did, but because I did not like the colour green on people. I shouted, while Basil, mortified, perched on his seat, resembling a bird, yet gaping like an open-mouthed sheep. Our neighbour, who seemed to approve of my enthusiasm, turned to him and said,

"Your son's enthusiasm is most remarkable!"

Basil grinned at that. He sat straight from then on, and even seemed to enjoy the spectacle more with each passing moment. At each extremity of the *Spina*, a seven-footed platform had been erected: seven fish lay on the northern platform, and seven ostrich eggs on the southern. The fish represented Neptune, god of the sea and creator of the horse, while the eggs stood for Castor and Pollux, the twin demigods who invented both chariots and races. Upon the completion of each circuit, a fish and an egg were removed, so the public could keep track of the laps.

At intervals there was wrestling, archery, and single-stick fencing. During a longer intermission, I demanded that Basil take me to the marble tables, so I could place a bet on the Blues. In response, he cradled his head in his hands. I begged, but he waved me away. A winsome smile served no purpose either. Scowling, I pestered him and accused him of being a killjoy. He told me to lower my voice, but I carried on complaining; I knew he would surrender – he feared drawing attention to us and revealing I was a girl. I was not wrong. He agreed, but only to watch the players, not to gamble, for betting was profanity.

We made our way to the tables, where gamblers launched green or blue marbles down carved tablets etched with winding, sloping tracks; the marbles rattled along the grooves before vanishing into a hole at random. The gamblers applauded when the Blues won, and I cried out with excitement. Glaring, Basil seized my arm and led me back to the races. Pretending not to see our neighbour – who smiled and nodded to greet us – he sat with his neck rigid, his eyes fixed ahead.

Everything competed in this city. Sycophants scrambled to rise in Imperial favour; officers clawed their way through administrative ranks, towers strained for greater grandeur. Caviar and fish roe travelled all the way from the Azov Sea to contest for rich clients. Garlic and bread mush lured sailors. Vendors vied to sell cabbage brine and medlar fruit to commoners, salted pork and flour gruel to poor folk. Taverns battled to serve fried fish and lentil soup, Cretan cheese, stinky tuna and bonito. Well-born ladies strove to become members of the court – and fallen women too fought just as fiercely for their trade. Even mighty gold was in competition to entice the buyer, running the risk of being kidnapped once it was moulded into something lovely. How did any customer not become giddy with the abundant supply in this city, much less bear the stress of selection and, when he finally chose something, how did he bear the sense of missing out on what he did not choose? Even the Emperor could never be certain that his choice was superior to that which he declined.

Daphne coronas on their heads, having received a gold seal, a helmet and a silk belt as prizes, the winners began to exchange horses with the losers for the next race. I had almost forgotten Basil's misery entirely, for my mind had become occupied by a new question: how did this city let us all partake in her glory, which we foolishly mistook as our own? Horse-swapping after each lap at the Hippodrome – a fair practice you might say, to ensure that victory depended on merit and not chance. So even *chance,* itself had to be hindered or worse quashed, unable to revel in its own luck here. We were clients of a young courtesan here who had already amassed great wealth and who dispensed her services as she wished – mostly, I suspected, for her own pleasure. Some of her clients were so exotic no interpreter could be found for them; languages spoken without being understood made this our Tower of Babel, a shared dialect of incomprehension.

And if you had no money to pay with, dignity and naivety were accepted currencies, too. In return, if she felt generous, you might receive a moment of bliss from her. But it would not last. Just like life, it never lasts, only transforms. We needed food to exist, but perhaps – unwittingly – were we not also food for someone or something else? Maybe we did not come into being as a gift of God but as an atonement for something we were unaware of, and that just by being and existing, we were repaying a debt. We copulated, reproduced and died – and in so doing, were we making amends to a mysterious power? And Constantinople too held a mysterious power. Verily, she fed you, but she also fed on you.

Sitting on seven hills, she was the Whore of Babylon – city of confusion, mother of prostitutes and of earth's abominations, beatitude and demise. Riding on her seven-headed beast, with no reservations she dared to rate herself with God:

"I am, and there is no-one besides me."

Arrayed in purple and scarlet, adorned with gold, jewels and pearls, she held in her hand a golden cup full of honey-dipped abominations and agreeable impurities. She either destroyed or subverted, eventually. She was lusted after. And she ruled Empires.

Constantinople was the cosmos. Constantinople was a whore. She was both the snake and the poison – and she was also the antidote, drawn from the snake's own venom.

In light of Basil's stony expression and his continued refusal to meet my eyes, I wondered whether he was indisposed by an unfortunate cramp. Or perhaps Constantinople's olive oil disagreed with his bowels? But I didn't ask. We would soon conclude our journey with a final visit to Haghia Sophia to touch its gates made with wood from Noah's Ark. That, I hoped, would make our journey back to Plekia untroubled and agreeable; we would drift home smoothly like a boat on still water.

10

Not even an ox would die but for a bad neighbour.

Hesiod, *Works and Days*

"He is a large man, exceptionally strong, you know, Ma'am? They feared he would struggle, fight back, yell, bark… yet, as if he'd foreseen the abduction and resigned himself to it, he stayed stolid, placid, when my brother and his friends jumped him in a narrow passage. His companions fled – unaware, of course, that the soldiers had already planned to let them go anyway. My brother tied Andronicus gently and carefully. After all, he's a nobleman born into the purple, isn't he?"

As he loaded his mules with fruit from our orchard in Plekia, and I balanced his account, the Turkoman chattered – speaking a Greek astonishingly rich in vocabulary, if faulty in syntax. I'd begun handling such transactions some time ago, when Basil had been ill, and I'd taken charge of urgent business with three Turkish nomads. My assuming such a responsibility would never have been possible in Zeno's times. Back then, Bulgarian slaves worked in the orchard – an unusual practice for two reasons. First, owning slaves was an urban custom: city households typically owned one or two slaves and utilised them mostly in craft shops or as domestic help.

Second, using them as an agricultural labour force in large numbers in the countryside was frowned upon – simply not done. But Zeno couldn't have cared less. Provincial aristocrats under the Komneni dynasty were gaining in strength; money equalled power, and Zeno was intent on exploiting it to the maximum. Strangely, under the same dynasty, and somewhat ironically, the development of human values was also encouraged. According to one edict, serfs had been granted the right – at the discretion of their owners – to retreat to a monastery, and this vocation was becoming increasingly popular.

Of their number, a particularly bold slave had heard of this and, convening with the others, discussed the matter: if they served Zeno Maleinus, who in turn served the Almighty by sending the Emperor dried fruits, then they too served both God and the Emperor – so why not cut out the middleman and thereby draw nearer to the Creator themselves? Surely the Emperor would be delighted if slaves were to retire to monasteries.

Proud of their initiative, and in joyful naïveté and wishful optimism, they presented the idea to my grandfather, only to be shocked when Zeno flew into a rage rather than welcoming their proposal.

"Whaaat?! Not until the vault of heaven falls on my head!"

Zeno was the only person I knew who believed the world was flat. In heated debates, he would rehash the description given by Cosmas the Indian, a traveling, monk and hermit, who claimed that the earth, being a rectangular plane, extended in length from east to west and in breadth from north to south – twice as long as it was wide – and was covered by a vaulted roof.

Basil and the priest of our village, a eunuch, both accepted Ptolemy's idea of a spherical world, but they kept quiet. They knew that contradicting Zeno would lead to public disgrace – and there were fates even less appealing than having the alleged vault come crashing down on one's head. Chief among them: witnessing a livid Zeno.

Yet inevitably, at every gathering, some naïve and foolishly brave youth would dare to challenge him. Zeno's eyes would bulge, his face would flush, he would spit and sputter, almost baring his teeth like a dog, before roaring:

"You heretics are at war with the divine Scripture!"

Pardos the priest was never spared from his damnation, even when he remained silent. Zeno would turn and address him directly, ignoring the goofy lad who had sparked the dispute.

"God modeled the world on the Tabernacle of Moses. Of all people, you, Pardos, should know this best. The world is not some queer bastard swinging in the middle of the universe, some sort of equivocal, shapeless thing!"

The typically hairless, pale and wrinkled eunuch face of the priest would turn red, appearing even more nondescript than usual. His oddly elongated limbs trembling, he would stammer in his high, unbroken voice:

"But... erm..."

Zeno would cut him off and continue:

"Heaven is God's throne, earth is His footstool, bearing upon its own steadfastness and balance."

Then he would turn to the lad and begin a tirade based on whatever he had heard about the boy's personal failings – past mistakes, missteps, family embarrassments. No doubt the parents, now cringing in their seats, regretted having revealed any of their son's shortcomings to Zeno in some friendly chat in the past while seeking his sympathy. Zeno always stored any and all information, about everything.

He would pound his fists on whatever furniture was nearby, take great, wide strides toward the door, storm out and slam it with all his might. I must confess I have adopted the habit of slamming door – and the power of the subsequent silence is something I learned from Zeno.

But if we return to the slaves who had infuriated Zeno: their mouths fell open, their upright postures slumped, pushed-back shoulders fell, in the end, they went back to work. Zeno was not just infuriated by the slaves' desire to leave – he was profoundly offended. After all these years, Zeno Maleinus' nature had been misunderstood.

They would pay for this foolishness. And so he informed the slaves they were free to go wherever they wished – once a certain amount had been paid. Elated, the poor souls whooped and capered about, but their glee was short-lived. When they calculated the cost, they saw that earning it would take until Doomsday.

Meanwhile, Zeno informed the priest that no monasteries could accommodate new arrivals. What could the priest do but comply? Now touchy and petulant, Zeno would prowl around the estate at the most unexpected hours, burst in on slaves as they rested or ate, and would conjure up farcical reasons to scold or whip them.

On rare occasions, he would go to the church the next day to confess, but that never erased the morose expression that had settled on his face since the slaves had dared voice their plan for manumission. Alas, the worm was now hatched in the apple, life would never be the same – neither for Zeno nor for the slaves.

Unaware yet that Basil intended to free them upon Zeno's death, the slaves' dream became a consuming disappointment. Some people are better off not exploring the full gamut of human emotions, especially toilers. Even for the freeborn, such variety can be agonising. At that time, it was the bodies that toiled; now minds laboured too, weighed down with sentiments they had not known existed. Now they were tired – very tired indeed.

As for me, the worm had hatched in my apple too, but I was the worm itself. This diverse array of clients had begun reveal to me the inscrutable connections between things, chains of events, knock-on and ripple effects. Unlike the slaves, I was not tired, but hungry and thirsty for more information, much more.

As I suspected the nomad before me would soon prove, the Turks transacted business in a carefree fashion, unbothered by a woman conducting such affairs so freely. Bowing and offering cordial farewells, they took their leave while my father, with his sallow complexion, slouched and plodded back to his bed. The temporary absence of a right-hand man or a secretary – someone to document the harvests, salaries, taxes, seasonal losses, and deliveries – and his eventual return could have ended this gratifying experience. But Basil employed no such person, and so the pleasure of helping him, though the conditions were humble and unconventional for a daughter, lasted for some time.

That is, until I began to suspect that his acquiescence was less about need and more about silent confirmation: that the path others pursued – matrimonial bliss and a guaranteed place in paradise would forever be uncertain for me. Thus, he was validating my inabilities, or as others saw it, my immaturity compared to that of my peers. In allowing me to keep the accounts, he was, perhaps unknowingly, reaffirming that *my* creations would never be flaunted in our church like theirs: those carefully embroidered cloaks, altarpieces and hangings.

At the same time, the nature of our income was shifting – from noble to vulgar, for while income from one's own estate was highly esteemed, involvement with commerce was not. So frowned upon, in fact, that in the year 829, Emperor Theophilus of Byzantium, having enquired about the owner of a beautiful merchant ship he'd watched sail into the Constantinople's harbour, was so enraged to learn it belonged to his wife that he had the merchandise on board burnt.

Still, if Basil ever blamed himself for any of this, it was in vain – for little did he realise that his influence over the matter was negligible. What once seemed to be the product of inadequate fatherly guidance, or a convenient excuse for Madam Gabras' tantrums, proved over the years to be nothing less than my true nature. I provided the ideal material for her tittle-tattle, an outlet for her cantankerousness. But I gained something valuable in the process: I learned how to feign maturity despite being incurably callow. Some wise souls claim that this action *is* maturity; in other words, if you are not mature, you cannot fake being mature. I never did find out what Basil thought about all this, and, in any case, I have forgiven him, whatever he may have thought.

Bouncing from foot to foot, the Turkoman opened his eyes wide and giggled in the manner of a child who has received sesame honey candy, and shouted:

"Andronicus tilted his head back, smirked and glared at the soldiers, Ma'am! Can you believe it? He was amused! My brother was really alarmed. He began to perspire – he couldn't prevent his hands from trembling. He swears that this man isn't a Prince of Constantinople, but Erlik, Prince of Darkness!"

Wandering merchants enlivened our uneventful countryside lives with urban gossip – vibrant with intricate, salacious details – and seldom did the news not pertain to Andronicus. Later in life, he grew into a bloodthirsty old man and exploited his exceptional intelligence and powers of imagination to devise inhumane crimes, so much so that the antics of his youth seemed almost innocent by comparison. One of his greatest transgressions was his shrewd observation of social behaviour; he could detect a weakness in character at a glance and stored each one for further use. Feeding on sycophants, slavish flatterers, and those who suffered delusions of grandeur – abundant in Constantinople – he would craft triangular relationships in which he always remained uppermost, forcing the other two beneath him, to love, hate, intrigue, or sometimes even kill one another, all to win his favour.

If he wanted something, he knew how to charm and present himself as deserving, and the world, he had learned would give it to him without question. My lady had mastered this same trick, in fact – it was a device all the clever folk of Constantinople mastered. He maintained several mistresses at a time, a few of them wives of eminent statesmen. Emperor John, a man of prowess on the battlefield and a resolute, accomplished statesman, overlooked Andronicus' endless intrigues and masterful lies. He indulged with a lenient smile each mischief committed by the prince. Aptly nicknamed, the Emperor was known as John the Beautiful: a good, prudent, cautious, and privately timid man. The disgraced, the bankrupt, the wounded, and the expelled – those victims left in Andronicus's wake-- told their stories, but John turned a deaf ear, which only fed Andronicus' arrogance.

To the Emperor, Andronicus' audacity was youthful impetuosity, his schemes a mark of his acumen, his so-called ignominious relations mere slander, his perversions the cost of sociability, and his sharp tongue a manifestation of his Komnenian wit. Blood, for some people, really is thicker than water – they forgive anything that comes from their family.

"Well, he certainly has a wicked reputation," I said to the Turkoman. "But who is Erlik?"

"I don't know about his reputation, Ma'am. But his eyes said enough. My brother himself is not a fellow to underestimate; as a child, he used to knock an adult out with one slap. We call him Bull. If he says Andronicus is Erlik, so must he be! He held his breath when tying him up for fear of inhaling his breath. Mother warned us about this sort of dangers, God bless her soul…"

"But who is Erlik?"

"Erlik lives under the ground in a palace built of black iron and black stone," the Turkoman began, inhaling deeply. "By day, he sits under a dim, scarlet sun; by night he sleeps on a bed of black beaver fur. His headquarters are by a river filled with people's tears. There is a black lake by his command post brimming with the blood of his ancestors and those who committed suicide. His sword is green iron, as are his shoulder blades." He gestured as though stabbing someone with a blade, then leaned close, savouring his words. "Blood smears his beard as he eats raw meat and drinks from a human skull-chalice filled with blood. His mealtime is when our sun is setting, and the sky is red. If you inhale Erlik's warm breath, you become paralysed, so to avoid opening your mouth when the welkin is crimson, and the wind blows is highly recommended. Erlik claims that the spirits of humans belong to him."

I gave a hoot of laughter at this heathen nonsense. Among respectable Roman circles, laughing oneself to tears was seen as 'female hysteria' and frowned upon. Luckily these nomads were a relaxed folk, prone to annoyance over completely different things than we did. His tale was not exactly funny by universal measures, but it made me fall into a fit of laughter. My cheeks ran with tears and the muscles of my abdomen ached, exactly the same marks of shame's manifestation and yet they were so carefree and pleasant that I let myself go, even at the risk of having those tears turning into real ones of sorrow. We were living on a knife's edge, under the sword of his leader, Ataman – and yet I laughed and laughed.

When the frenzy subsided, though still chuckling, I quickly threw a stare at him to see if there was any sign of reproach in his expression, but he was grinning like a donkey – a proud and jovial one at that, clearly interpreting my laughter as praise for his storytelling rather than a lapse of my self-control.

"Your Erlik drinks the blood of the dead?" I said. "Sounds like his is in misery on his own down there in the recesses. Isn't all this just imaginary peril? I mean he sounds like a naïve bully more than anything, but he is rather harmless in the end, isn't he?"

"Be careful, good Lady. One should not mock Erlik, he doesn't come aboveground himself – but sends spirits."

"Lo-and-behold! And what do you do then?"

"We must bargain with him."

"Ah! There you go! Now this Erlik is getting a bit more plausible. So how is that done?"

"We have special arbitrators assigned for that, Ma'am. How they do this, I do not know… but let's not talk too much about Erlik, I do not wish him to hear…"

"In any case, he seems to be in his right mind, not the type who beguiles people through wiles. No wonder you people are a rough-and-ready folk."

Smiling, the Turkoman riffled through his pockets. He pulled out something wrapped in cotton and handed it to me.

"Erlik fears this. I hope it will protect you, at least for a while, Ma'am."

He placed his hand on his chest, bowed, and took his leave.

I unwrapped the cloth. Inside was a huge thorn, thick and long.

11

The whole is more than the sum of its parts.

Aristotle, *Metaphysics*

A TALL, well-built, nimble body followed Basil into the house. Its head featured abundant, undulating sandy blond hair with golden highlights that reached below the ears, wild at the ends. It seemed a complete, polished, waxed icon, as if crafted by a master – the inspiration for which was Ataman. But Ataman's droll, droopy lines were here symmetrised, perfected. If it is true as Plotinus says, that "Beauty is when Divine Reason finds place in form," then his concept was made flesh in the youth before us. Ataman's olive skin, black eyes and even a few comical traits blended with the features of his Greek mother, and the mystery of what Plotinus said was made manifest in their son: "Only the whole will be beautiful; the several parts will have no beauty of their own but will be beautiful only as contributing to the beauty of the whole."

Naturally the rejuvenation of the colours in our freshly cleaned parlour only reinforced this impression. The sun-soaked alabaster slabs on walls revealed a new pinkish opalescent gleam, suggestive of a scene from paradise, with nacreous beige, white and vibrant clover green tones. I planned to insist that Anna maintain such high standards of hygiene at all times, not only for special occasions like a barbarians arrival. During the past few days under her supervision, the servants had scrubbed the house thoroughly, rubbing and polishing the floor with its spectacular mosaic: five wide mother-of-pearl leaves crowning a stem made of green glass. Tendrils, festoons, and foliage scattered around an inlaid flower, all encircled by an outer frame of stepped black marble squares.

Basil ordered the most luminous, spacious chamber to be prepared for the guest, a room I utilised as an extra sitting-room when the salon downstairs was occupied. I had resolved to make the boy pay for this arrogance, but now, gazing at that tall, rectangular forehead – like those of solemn men of high standing, I was no longer sure if I would stay loyal to my plan.

During the days leading up to today, Anna, too busy to listen to my complaints, had scampered around with her chubby, melon-shaped body, which bore comparison to a round wool hank in the paws of a cat. She had never expressed any worries about not having a waist, perhaps knowing no male arms would ever embrace it. Anna's husband had died after just one year of marriage, leaving her destitute, and so my parents took her in as a housekeeper, and she had remained ever since. My mother used to say it was as if Anna were a maid born in our house and that burying her man was just another errand she had to run – after which she came back home. She never removed the amulet she wore, which contained peony seeds mixed with mule earwax, meant to aid fertility – a small tribute to the memory of her husband. She now suffered from rheumatism and had lost her zest for housework.

Tensions had risen when she sent the servants to market to buy flat Turkish bread, so as not to upset His Serene Highness's sensitive stomach with our coarse durum wheat loaves. She did not go so far as to order oysters – the so-called food of angels – but only, I suspect, because she doubted a barbarian could appreciate them. Nonetheless she insisted on Egyptian rose marmalade, a fad brought to Plekia by Madam Gabras. Sellers claiming to import rose marmalade from Egypt sprang up like mushrooms all over the place after she had showed off a jar to her Lady friends, professing that it came from Egypt. Nobody knew the difference between the roses of Byzantium and those of Egypt, nor what made the latter more healthful or savoury? Not only in the capital but also in all the other Roman lands the flower abounded; even the hedges were made of them.

Crushing orchid tubers and mixing the resulting flour with rose water was a speciality of the city, a beverage the Emperor himself enjoyed. On hot summer days, a tumbler of rose extract and honey, cooled with a silver tube or shredded mountain ice if available was served to him. But Gabras knew better than the Emperor. The wide-eyed country bumpkin consumers of Plekia did not question why and by which means the wide-eyed country bumpkin vendors had such wide access to Egyptian marmalade exporters, and the affair became a success, one pot selling at triple the price of its local equivalents. Of all people, Anna, the best cook on earth, should never have fallen for such a scam, for she herself could make the best marmalades from any fruit. Yet even she had blindly followed Gabras's fad.

In keeping with Basil and Anna's determination to make the youth feel at home, the servants brought forth loaves of freshly baked white bread. The smell made my stomach growl. Worse still, Anna forbade Dog from entering the house and had him tied up in the barn. Discontented, he barked for a while, but when he heard the guest arrive, he began to howl.

Although I had enough time to run away, in a panic, I miscalculated and instead of rushing out of the parlour, I hurried to the wall, pulled aside the silk cover, opened the door with the peephole and crept into the corridor. My body had already reached the passageway, but my arm was still in the sitting room, trying to pull the samite hanging back into place – naturally to no avail. Wishful thinking bordered on idiocy: the door squeezed my arm, and it hurt. Anna burst in. She cast me a disapproving glance, one that made clear her rescue act was strictly to resolve the immediate problem, and that she would make me pay for it later. She shoved me into the hallway, closed the door, and pulled the fabric over it.

I shouted after her to ensure that the silk was drawn snug over the hole.

"What don't I have to do to save face for you?" she screamed at me and ran back to the vestibule.

My arm still throbbing with pain, I continued examining the half-breed. A strand of hair curled over that demure forehead like a kitten coiling up to sleep. His nose was a serious one--narrow and high-bridged, with a small upward nub on the tip that drew the eye to his lips, pink and plump.

Didn't everything that could exist already exist? The designer was not making new things. The Holy Book said, "Keep my decrees. Do not mate different kinds of animals. Do not plant your field with two kinds of seed. Do not wear clothing woven of two kinds of material." And didn't it also tell us: "and God said, 'Let the land sprout with vegetation – every sort of seed-bearing plant, and trees that grow seed-bearing fruit. These seeds will then produce the kinds of plants and trees from which they came.'" And it was so.

Didn't Fallen Angels lust after the daughters of men? And didn't their hybrid offspring, the giant Nephilim, corrupt the world by teaching people magic, evil and immorality? Didn't they begin to eat them eventually, causing the Grand Deluge?

God said, "be fruitful and multiply," and so we obey. Like must be grafted to like, so the fruit will look finer and taste better. It's very rare to graft apricot onto an almond tree. How would it taste if we managed to crossbreed apples and pears – and what would we call it? The Church would likely not disapprove of such meddling in God's work, but we would earn a fortune selling the fused fruit. The Emperor himself summon us to behold it, and the Maleinus estate would become legend.

You do not meddle in the business of nature, and yet that does not guarantee you reason for optimism either. The *Farm Book* instructs us not to plant different plants intermingled; variety may be attractive, but if you don't sort by type, the weaker plant will be overcome by the stronger and it will be deprived of nourishment. Only certain roses and lilies can be scattered together, and that is that.

There are good and bad hybrids. Bronze, for instance, is a good one: a blend of tin and copper, harder and stronger than either of its parents. But not all hybrids have been so fortunate. By eating meat, a centaur disgusted his horse side. Whenever he drank wine, the digestion went awry and drove the creature into a frenzy. Mules, being sterile, were unlikely to have been welcomed aboard Noah's Ark, but since they're more intelligent than their horse mothers and stronger than the donkey sires, I doubt it mattered.

I probably was not barren – but what did fertility mean without breeding anyway? The law forbade marriages between Romans and heathens. A Greek priest who blessed such a union would be excommunicated, suspended, and the fruit of such unions we called *gasmules* – meaning stupid bastards. Harpies – half-bird, half-woman – were the paradigm of evil, but lion-eagle griffins and lion-woman sphinxes, averted demons.

So what would the union of an angelic Greek and a barbarian tyrant yield? How did things that never existed before things come into existence?

Basil placed his hand on the boy's shoulder and said, "You are most welcome to our modest home, Ogan. I hope we shall make your stay here a comfortable one."

"I am honoured and thankful, Sir."

A deep, throaty voice – of not one or two, but of three or four men combined! Caught off guard, my chest tightened, just as a finger tapped my shoulder. I turned and naturally it was Anna whispering:

"You should stop, Theia. What if he notices?"

"Come on… Nobody would ever notice."

"How do you know?"

"Well, so what? Besides, their women greet guests. They even eat together." The corners of her mouth turned down.

"How on earth do you come up with such nonsense? Of course they don't."

"Yes, they do; they do! They even dance with men. Have you never seen them in the marketplace? They never ride side-saddle, and they scream and sing while their horses neigh, and they all go wild."

As Anna began to shake her head, I pressed on: "Their oxen low, their sheep bleat, ~~their pigs grunt~~ and their dogs bark! They are free spirits."

"You are not a nomad woman, young lady. Know your place. Please go to the kitchen and eat. I'll serve them."

I obeyed Anna this time. She may have ascribed my gracious compliance to deference, or to a newfound resolve to toe the line, but I gave in only because I had grown too excited watching that boy, his sheer perfection, calibration and finesse.

After eating, I passed into the women's quarters and stayed there till evening, when Anna's gruff voice broke the peace, giving a servant orders to bring fresh water from the well to the boy's room before he retired.

Dog howled a little, and then fell silent. I pressed my ear to the wall but heard nothing. The poor thing must have been exhausted and gone straight to bed.

12

One can be loved without knowing it, but one cannot love without knowing it.

Aristotle, *Eudemian Ethics*

In the late-morning quiet of the house, a sudden urge to go through Ogan's belongings arose in me. Making sure the corridor was clear, I cocked my ear to the noises downstairs and heard Anna ordering someone to bring in the laundry from the garden. Supplicating Divine Providence that nobody would find me out, I sneaked into the guest chamber.

In stark contrast to the elaborate coffer Ataman used to send the books in, an unembellished but rather large wooden chest stood in the corner. A filthy little drum leaned against it. I crouched to inspect it, and as I moved it, I caught a foul, smoky smell emanating from it. A thick stick hidden behind the drum fell with a clatter, and I let out a shriek. Scurrying to the hallway, I listened for footsteps – none came. I waited a few seconds to ensure no servant was looking for me. I heard only the mundane bustle and murmuring of the household from below; the continued silence in the corridor put me at ease. I returned to the drum.

The stick – likely used to beat the drum – was made of beech and had a leather head. The instrument's end was ornamented with nine iron hoops and tassels of feathers. A cross divided the oval-shaped drumhead into four spaces. Above the cross sat a circle; below, it bifurcated. It could not have been a Christian cross. One could think it the childlike drawing of a man who opens his arms or maybe a branchless tree with the sun above. I could not make sense of the pattern. In each upper quadrant was another round motif with lines around it, possibly representing the sun and moon with rays. Each section bore bizarre human and animal forms, and one peculiar wolf stood out. I suspected a particular horned figure with bloody eyes, sharp teeth, and a dagger might be Erlik himself. Seven red horses and seven crimson-clad men surrounded him. The same motif appeared again above, but this time with characters depicted in white.

Fixed to the back of the drum was a seven-holed bracket fitted with knobs, rattles, iron rings, and more feathers. Still baffled by the symbols, I set the drum aside and opened the chest.

A sweet perfume rose from among the neatly folded and arranged white shirts, tunics and leggings, sprinkled with rose petals. In a scarlet silk bag, I found dried apple blossoms. I studied the fabric, and though uncertain, I judged it to be a cotton-linen blend – confirming a question I'd long held: were Muslim men, just like the prostitutes of Constantinople, forbidden to wear silk?

A copper mirror, wrapped in red silk and polished to a brilliant lustre, shone amid the garments. I picked it up and looked at my face in it. At the sight of the pores and blemishes that generously marked my skin – a predicament of which I had been mercifully ignorant, thanks to the inferior quality of my own mirror – I let out a gasp, as if rather than his mirror it was the mirror's owner that saw me so close up and that this image would stay etched in his mind. Horrified, I threw it back in its place.

I briefly wondered if I should have taken the other girls more seriously when I listened in on them discussing remedies – washing the face with bean flour, or even applying spikenard oil, the same used by Mary at Christ's burial:

"Then Mary took a litra of very costly oil of spikenard, anointed the feet of Jesus, and wiped His feet with her hair. And the house was filled with the fragrance of the oil." (John 12)

But to use for my vanity what Mary had used to prepare Jesus for both life and death? I thought the better of it and did not. It never occurred to me to try such things – not to win Basil's approval of me or curry favour with Madam Gabras'. Well, even a mad cock who crows inopportunely was correct at some point – for there's always someone asleep who should be woken up. But wasn't a male withholding such a futile trinket more insane than an insane cock?

While I attempted to lift his clothes to see the underwear, an iron item placed by the side caught my eye, oblong in form and slightly pointed on one side. I picked up the curious object and turned it over. It was a rather heavy, ferrous item with a handle wrapped in cotton cloth.

"It's to press his garb."

I uttered a loud scream as it fell from my hand and chipped a stone from the mosaic floor. Anna, her face flushed, bent down and picked up the chipped piece of stone, and said through clenched teeth:

"Must I tell you something?"

"Well, you will anyway, so continue."

"You took a big risk."

"I know." There wasn't much else I could say.

She clicked her tongue, something she habitually did when preparing to harangue:

"I am so tired of your adventures, Theia."

"Don't be." My short reply was not the greatest riposte, but it would have to do. Under normal circumstances, I would never let her sanctimonious remarks pass without rebuttal, and we'd rant at each other loudly, but now my curiosity got the best of me; I had to retrieve as much as possible. "Anyway… Do you have any idea what he does with that squalid drum?"

"No, I don't. And it's none of our business."

I could see her peeking behind me. "Oh, so you claim you never, ever had a look at his personal items?" I did not wait for her reply. "Look at the weird symbols on it; they're like the gimmicks of a sorcerer."

Eyes averted again. "I prefer not to."

"Come on, have a look. Do you think this is something to do with the Mohammedan God – or something pagan?"

"I really don't want to."

I frowned. "Why are you here then?"

"To take the iron. I must press his tunics."

"Take what?"

"Nikephoros is here."

"Unannounced?"

"Well, I did not know he would come."

"Tell Father, then."

"He is not at home, and Nikephoros wants to see you."

"See me? That's strange. Whatever for? But tell me – how do you press the boy's clothing?"

She heaved a long sigh and held her palms up and out. Her posture sagged.

"He taught me. We place the iron on the fire grill; once its surface heats we rub it against the creases in the fabric so that they smooth."

"Why would a barbarian need to have his attire pressed? A barbarian who watches himself in a mirror, to boot?" Laughter seized me. How on earth did they think to invent such an apparatus? Effeminate – so incompatible with the mightiness they projected. Weren't the nomads the finest ironmongers, known for their exquisite swords? The creation of this defiled the craft…

"Theia!"

"Yes?"

"Nikephoros is waiting. And you ought not to cry each time you laugh."

I dried my tears smiling cynically.

"We always do. We always do…."

I ran to the ground floor, and breezed into the parlour yelling:

"Nike? What are you doing here?"

In a demeanour which did not bear its usual drooping quality, he stood by the silk drapery. A harsh light burned in those otherwise lifeless, downcast eyes. Pallid, the boy was clearly not himself. Basil came to my mind. Had something happened to him? Panicking, I shouted:

"What is wrong?"

He did not reply – seething like ground before an earthquake, a lonely, quiescent field ploughed season after season in silence, until a blow from deep within erupts with a deafening roar. That pitiable forehead of his puckered, and, pointing a finger at me, he blasted:

"The barbarian! It is reprehensible to have him here, yet you are falling about the place to welcome him?"

"What?"

"How can your father accept him into the house? The entire town is talking about this… scandal."

I did not fly into a rage at his impudence. On the contrary, he impressed me with his spirit. But despite this new costume of bravery, Nikephoros could never intimidate me. I shouted back:

"You mean your mother has been spreading calumnies, don't you?"

He winced. "It was she who told me. But…"

So much for the mighty tremor! The ground opens and instead of lava out pop dry worms. I sneered.

"Did you blow in here for this, Nike?"

"Yes. I did." The heat had gone out of him though.

Calmer after his unusual display of courage, I demanded:

"Did you know my father was not at home now?"

"Eh… yes. I waited for him to leave."

"So, you knew you'd be speaking to me?"

"Eh… yes."

"But you are querying me about his decision? A decision taken by my father?"

"I mean… yes. Me interrogating him would not be appropriate…"

"My Father's mind has its own particular workings," I said. "And as for the barbarians – I must admit they are full of surprises. Hence my chuckles."

"This is treachery!"

"Now, now. That's going too far…"

"I am sorry. I mean… eh… where is he now?"

"Who?"

"The barbarian. Are you alone with him in the house?"

"Your being here – and horning in on Basil's business, no less – is just as reckless, isn't it? And inflaming the matter by presuming to call us to account." He couldn't hold my gaze. "Nevertheless, out of courtesy, I'll tell you: I have no idea where the barbarian is. Besides, the house is replete with servants, and Anna is always here. He is not…"

The door clapped shut and Basil's chuckle rang out in the vestibule. Blood drained from Nike's face – first reverting to its normal pasty tone, then whitening as if he had swallowed some poisonous draught. His already prominent, unseemly Adam's apple protruded, while his eyes glistened with tears. Basil raised his eyebrows while entering the parlour:

"Ah, Nikephoros you're here? To what do we owe this honour?"

Nike slouched slightly. His voice trembled:

"Hello Mr. Maleinus, I…"

I exclaimed: "Nikephoros heard about the books – he'd like to borrow one, Father."

"Great! The more people benefit from this treasure, the happier I am. Let me introduce you to Ogan – Ataman's son."

Ogan bowed, his chiselled lips curving. I expected Nike to ogle him, but his eyes grew vacant. He neither bowed nor greeted him. He slipped back into his usual weary, withered self, and his failure to greet the guest seemed something more pitiable than rude.

Basil pointed at me. "And this is my daughter, Theia."

Aware that I stood aghast, Basil had taken a clever decision – to pretend my presence was permissible, thus saving appearances and precluding further disgrace. Politely, the boy bowed his head and greeted me. Baby dimples on his cheeks defied the virility of his angular jaw and strong chin. The interplay between this face's child-like delicacy and its manly features resembled a slobbering child tugging the tunic of his vexed but enamoured father – or an amicable wrestle between two brothers, each seeking victory but not daring to hurt the other.

My natural inclination was to blurt out a loud, overly cheerful "hello," fortunately my voice did not cooperate. I'd lost it. Anna brought sherbet on a tray with three glasses, then turned to me, making signs with her eyes and brows, insinuating I should leave. I saluted the guest with a more prudently enunciated "good day" and marched out of the room in an appropriate manner.

Silence prevailed after they all left. Had Nike just revealed an affection I certainly did not wish to be the recipient of? While standing there looking at me, had my father assumed the fondness was mutual between us? Whatever the clumsy boy had revealed, it did not honour or please me, it debased me. I felt clothed in rags and tatters – dirty and tainted.

13

So what if I am Syrian! Stranger, marvel not!
One is our country, one our world, all of us born of Chaos.

Meleager, *Greek Anthology*

Was Basil's choice random when he gave me the icon of Christ Pantocrator? Each half of his face was depicted differently, the left side being human, somewhat indignant, critical, the right-side being God, expressing divine tranquility and a sacred compassion. Basil said Christ is the mirror of the onlooker, exulted and loving if your heart is pure, gloomy and hostile if you are mischievous; he wanted to tame me. The room heated up, my head swam, I shivered and sweated. The left side of Christ's lip curled down, his brow frowned, and his nostril flared, becoming increasingly menacing. I began to turn and fell on my bed in an amorphous, sticky oblivion. I recollect a vague scene where servants are bringing herbal preparations and my father, distressed, is watching me. In another muddled picture, Anna changes my sweat-soaked clothes, and somebody puts leeches on my skin to let rotten blood out.

A strange-looking old woman with crazy eyes and Ogan are watching me. The woman is nervous. She is wearing a conical headdress made of white lambskin with feathers attached on top. Beads, snail shells and a string of small serpent heads hang over her forehead, half-obscuring her eyes. Leather plaits and ribbons sewn onto birds' tails and wings are suspended from her costume. She turns around my bed carrying an iron bar onto which a greasy-looking piece of cloth is attached. She sets it on fire and waves the burning stick over and around while singing a bizarre song with a tense, guttural articulation. I begin to cough with the smoke and my eyes burn but she doesn't care. She beats a drum which looks as strange as her costume, with its illegible symbols. She bends over me while mumbling abstruse words, then pricks thin golden needles into several places on my body. I become scared and try to scream in pain but do not feel her needles. She presses her head onto mine and blows on my brow; a wolf comes out of her mouth with a hare riding on its back. Though far away, I am still aware their visit is only a vivid, animated dream. The hare enters my head through my ears. The weight of my body lifts; my limbs loosen up, feather-light, vitality spreads like water falling from a cascade into a tiny bowl and overflowing; a burst of energy wakes me but not before the pot disappears into the blue.

When I opened my eyes, something was amiss, a cruel interruption had somehow impeded my presence at the inauguration of a glorious monument, my participation in a grand adventure. Famished, I arose from bed at once and stumbled out of my room, called for food and ate until I no longer could, but it did not fill me. After that, I barged into the parlour. Ogan and Basil raised their heads in astonishment, Basil doing a double-take before letting out a small cry:

"There you are!"

While he laughed joyously, Ogan smiled so broadly that his eyes evolved into a horizontal, almost comical black line, a jubilant toddler's first charcoal streak on a spar of limestone, gratifying and gratified: "How are you feeling?"

Taken aback by such affection, I tried to adopt an amicable tone but succumbed to awkward formality instead: "Much better, thank you."

I blathered about the mess Basil had made with my accounts while I was sick and raved on about the servants' trivial oversights, peppering them with minor gripes. Blood pounded in my head, my throat felt dry and still I talked, talked, talked until eventually noticing their consternated looks. When I realised I had just made a fool of myself with this tragi-comic tirade I rushed out of the room to my chamber pretending there were urgent matters to attend to and broke into tears without knowing why. That evening, I did not eat or sleep. The next morning, I knew, after the time lapse between the meeting with Nike and yesterday's hysterics that I needed either to go to the beautiful boy at once, tell him anything regardless of coherence, or always remain silent with him. The latter option, however dignified and noble, would inevitably entail silly embarrassment which would perturb me. I would then turn more hysterical and eventually grow desperate. So, I forced myself to take the first option and found him in the barn beside Pegasus, watching him. Slipping in any space unnoticed by these people was not possible, so it was better to do the exact opposite, to make an entrance with some panoply and fanfare. Keeping my chin up, forcing an orotund voice bordering on obtrusive I uttered:

"Pardon my intrusion!"

Of course, he knew I was there, even before I walked in; still I had a moment to admire the nobility of his nose from the side because he took his time to turn his head. A prominent, high bridge, long but shapely ridge, a sharp tip and fleshy wings, drawing the attention to pink, plump lips once again:

"My Lady!"

"Apparently, you've met Pegasus. He's my favourite." My voice feathery now…

"Is he? Is that because he's an albino?"

"It's more than that. He's special. He understands what you say – not to mention his royal purple eyes."

"Is he special because he understands everyone or because he understands you?"

I laughed: "Oh, so you know the right questions to ask."

Astonished: "How so?"

"Well, you must think I'm a bit troublesome. So wayward that only a donkey befriends me?"

He gave me an incredulous gaze. "No! I didn't think anything like that."

My voice not so feathery anymore:

"Oh, I'm sure you did. Everybody does."

Why was I telling him this?

I briskly shifted tone. "Anyway, would you care to see our orchard?"

"With pleasure!"

Dog howled at Ogan first; afterwards, his body loose, he wagged his tail, swishing back and forth, and followed us as we crossed the courtyard and exited through the rear door facing the apple trees. A writer should enchant even the non-existent readers with intricate descriptions of the landscape. However, this writer stops short of pleasing others, she does not possess the fine powers of observation and ability to admire the beauty of nature, in fact she takes nature's grace for granted as long as nature continues to grant it. She doubts whether the relatively few problems related to the dandelions, crabgrass, hemlock taking root, broad leaves emerging, and creeper plants strangling fruit trees – or wizened plums subsisting in her orchard and their elaborate depictions – would ever be of interest to any reader. Fields laid waste or burnt trees, on the other hand, would pique both her authorial interest and that of any curious readers, but Ataman was different from other Turkoman tribal leaders who now and then turned to this method as a weapon of war or means of advancing an invasion. Ataman did not cut the branch he sat on. In brief, our orchard was in perfect condition.

When the likes of Ataman walked in those traditional britches, one was tempted to avert one's gaze in abashment and give a sardonic smile at the same time, but in the case of his boy, as we strolled among the trees and his leg muscles contracted beneath the clinging leather, a strange sense of titillation arose in my belly. Was that the call of an unborn baby requiring to be conceived? But who was to hear it?

While leading him to the arbour to get a drink of water, I glimpsed something hanging from his belt. Realising it was a piece of fur and some teeth on a length of rope, I almost involuntarily asked what it was for and regretted my boldness at once. Heedless of my blunder, he smiled:

"This? This is the tail of a wolf. She watched over our clan for a while, a sort of guardian. One day my great-grandfather found her dead. He buried her, but kept her tail, and it was passed on to my grandmother, after her to my father, and now, obviously, it belongs to me."

"Funny that whenever you or your father make an appearance Dog jumps. Normally he's an indolent lump. He hardly ever reacts to anything. With you he jumps up at once. Did you notice? He tenses all his muscles and starts ululating like a wolf."

Amused, he said, "That's natural. We are descended from a wolf – he senses it."

I giggled. "So I've heard… a blue-gray wolf… The bad temper of a Turk comes from those ancestors who were given wolf's milk – I heard that too."

He smiled as I resumed:

"It is strange. What's even stranger is a dream I had last night. I saw a wolf carrying a hare on its back. And then you and an old woman were there too."

Was this sounding ridiculous? He didn't laugh, so I went on:

"She blew a hare into my head. Really. It came out of hers and entered into mine."

Surprised at first, his eyes narrowed to that jet-black line again – a strange sentence written between that noble forehead and the dainty mouth:

"Really? So, it worked. Good."

"What do you mean, it worked?"

"This means she succeeded. They always work at night. Dead or alive. The nighttime of this world constitutes the daytime of the other one, so she used to say."

"What are you talking about?"

"My *kam* sent those animal spirits to heal you." He smiled, as though revealing some simple fact to a small child. "The hare is your protector. He had left you, so she had to restore him back to you. Mine is the wolf; hers too. But we should not talk about guardian animals. Otherwise, we negate their powers; they might even get enraged and leave us."

"This is nonsense!" I tried not to scoff, but probably failed.

"Well, you were healed, no?"

"Healed? I got better. A coincidence. I would have recuperated sooner or later. This is ridiculous."

Sparks swarmed into his onyx eyes: "Absolutely not. You had lost your spirit and mine brought it back to you. And then you exchanged the vital force with your animal."

"Where did my spirit go? To Erlik?" I was trying to restrain my sceptical tone.

He gave me a disconcerted look. "You know about Erlik?"

He didn't appear to be joking. "Yes, I've heard about him, and his underground lake of blood and his river filled with people's tears."

Unsure whether I was being nosy again, or simply kind, or just sarcastic, I found myself simpering: "So, was he chasing me though I have a thorn? But before that, tell me, can he do things with infidels' tears and blood too?"

"After all, everybody and nobody is an infidel. Does someone who is starving anguish over which God a person who gives them bread believes in? Or does a maimed person care about what sect the person who stabbed them belongs to?"

So, he was taking my response seriously. I thought for a moment. "The answer to your first question is no, but to your second it is yes. People do consider the faith of those who hurt them. Not so much when they are being done favours. Human nature."

He appeared somewhat surprised and changed the subject.

"And how do you know that Erlik is scared of thorns?"

"The same way I know about him at all. Chit-chatting around."

"His river has a name. Do you know it?"

"No."

"Any idea?"

"Absolutely none. Who cares?"

"Erlik and the river do. It is called 'Toymadim'. This means 'I haven't had enough; I am still hungry.'"

"Aha! So, he was running after my blood and Basil's tears? Hmmm… The opposite would have been more intelligent I think: there's only Basil and a slight chance of Anna and no-one else to shed tears after me; perhaps my donkey would too. But you are saying Erlik and the river like human tears? They are in a way similar to the Church Fathers: "Woe unto you, laugh now for you shall mourn and weep," and there's a famous saying, "Tears are to the soul what food and drink are to the body." Have you heard that one?"

Before he could reply I was off again: "The only difference is Erlik and his river drink them themselves and leave you people carefree and happy. I saw your women at the marketplace. They indulge in loud laughter in public – they don't seem afraid of being stigmatised as lewd or obscene. As for my donkey, no matter how exceptional he is, crying is a long shot for him, for donkeys by nature are optimistic creatures, redolent of pagan gods. Have you ever observed a donkey peeling its lips away from its gums and a playful grin brightening its face?"

Overjoyed, he grinned, his eyes becoming invisible. Still without letting him answer, I pressed on:

"For Basil there certainly would be more sobbing. To start with, it would be me, then the Bishop and the priest, Anna, Svoronos, who's a bookbinder, and Skleros who borrowed money to build an oven. Madam Gabras for sure because who else would she have to reprimand now and then? And, of course, Basil's cousin Michael in Constantinople and a few distant relatives there would also cry. Mind you, Constantinopolitan tears are rather diluted, and have a quality just like their awful water. Maybe that's why you people haven't reached there yet; obviously Erlik has no interest in attenuated blood and tears. Well..."

Ogan looked unsure if he should speak now.

"Ah yes, I forgot to mention the debtors," I resumed. His chance was gone again. "Basil keeps on postponing their due payments, and he never demands interest on their debts, for he believes earning money on money is evil, but they know I might think differently if ever he perishes, so... And the tears of the Emperor of course, for no-one but my father can provide such high quality dried fruits. And who knows, maybe even your father Ataman would weep? But tell me, was he really coming after me?"

He paused, probably to make sure I was done, then nodded: "Perhaps."

"So, is humanity doomed to shed blood and tears?" I was in earnest now.

"In a way, yes. Things get better and worse in cycles don't you think? On the bright side, one is not alone. Blessings from ancestors can always be invoked."

"How?"

"A *kam* does that. Our ears are deaf to divine sounds, theirs are not. They hear them. They hear what water is babbling when it is flowing in the river. They understand animals, much like Pegasus understands you, but the other way round. They know what mountains utter when they resound back to you or what the wind whispers."

"And?"

He thought before he spoke. “Picture a cupboard filled with all that occurred in the past and all that will occur in the future; everything everyone who has ever lived – or will live – has undergone or will undergo, and how they handled it. Or a book where every incident concerning humanity is recorded and kept.”

“What does this have to do with the *kam*? Is she a Prophet?”

“No, she doesn’t keep the records, but she can talk to those who do. She can choose any page from the book or withdraw something from the cupboard concerning past or future.”

“Always?”

He smiled. “No, not always. She must endeavor. Sometimes it works, sometimes not. It’s her trade, as simple as that. As mundane as her profession is, what it proves is extraordinary.”

“And that is?”

“That there is more to our existence.” He sounded so certain. “If nothing, the *kam* brings the joy of life back, makes this life bearable. If there’s a loaf of bread up in the heavens, you are a portion of it here. When you die, you go back to the loaf; it is then mixed again. A new slice is formed which is to incarnate here anew.”

“I don’t understand you,” I groaned. “But I know you’re treading on dangerous grounds here.”

“Life is replete with infinite varieties and quandaries. The *kam* brings loose ends together and ties a knot, or when necessary, does the reverse: he opens entanglements.”

“Speak like this in Constantinople and they’ll do to you what they do to heretics.”

“But you are in Plekia, and you must know that this universe is a replica of the universe of the Gods. As above, so below. It shares sanctity; however, it remains far from perfect.”

I had to interrupt: “But this is what Plato says! Is that why your father didn’t take the Timaeus? Because you people have read it already?”

He smiled again: “My father did not take the book because Sultan Mesud already possesses anything written by Plato at the palace. In fact, people in Iconium believe the tomb of Plato is in the church of St. Amphilochius where a sacred oil still drips. Some believe it was brought about by Plato.”

As he talked, and I beheld yet again that tiny upward nub placed on the tip of his nose and the rosy plump lips it perfunctorily called attention to, I thought about the bread slices and Plato's claim: "Love is the longing of diversity for unity, the desire of parts to be brought together to form wholes, the instinctive urge of all creatures toward a perfect state." Ah Plato! How I envied his name and the lips that pronounced it:

"There is a spring named after Plato in Iconium as a memorial: by changing the course of a river, he is supposed to have prevented a flood and saved the city where a great part of the population perished in the grand deluge. He's a hero there. We call him 'Eflatun', which means violet." He smiled. "Just like the eyes of your Pegasus."

Indeed, this young man's mind was replete with oddities, and aberrations. Their exotic seasonings were certainly not lacking, and if he was a slice of something, I deemed it could only be a honey cake, unadulterated honey with no spices, no nuts and no zests added. There was a beautiful chaos in his words – multifariously formulated; utter purity within him: a wolf, a human, a Roman, and a Barbarian, crossbred in this chimera burning without the fire.

I remembered the only trip Basil, my mother and I had taken when I was a small child. When I realised that I was to remain at home with Zeno, Anna, and the servants, I howled like Dog; I wailed, shrieked, hollered and yelped so much that Basil had to agree to take me with them. In Lycia, I remember high mountains, rivers, and sheer drops, very steep slopes. While carrying me on his then young shoulders during a compelling half-hour walk up a steep rocky pathway, Basil told me the story of Bellerophon riding on the mythological Pegasus. We were on our way to encounter the Chimera, a mongrel breathing devastating fire. As I clapped along, he would laugh all the way up and say words full of admiration about my courage. When we arrived at the place, my mother – who I can hardly visualise today – Basil, soaked in sweat and out of breath, and I all shouted in awe of the flames that were spraying from vents in serpentine rocks. To my relief, he would say Bellerophon had defeated Chimera and sent him seven floors under the ground; the blazes the monster still spewed had been flowing out of these holes for hundreds and hundreds of years. In fact, Lycia at that time posed more palpable dangers than a monster made of a lion, dragon and goat all together, for Turks and Latins lurked all around. But, as you know by now, Basil would take what there was without mulling over what was not, unless the jeopardy was apparent. He would not speculate on the odds and chances of its occurrence, an attitude smart-aleck youngsters like myself might deem as 'chicken-heartedness'. When one sits and assesses this attitude with a clear head, one may come up with many other adjectives in addition to pusillanimity… I recall very old graves and semi-circular altars and basilicas abounding in coloured frescoes where both my parents prayed. It was different from our church, which was very sombre. There the colours were vibrant, resembling children holding hands; large circles were connected with knots, surrounded by red borders. I remember three branched yellow and four branched red flowers and green clovers also tied to each other in nodes, but hardly any human forms except a white-winged angel standing next to a figure wearing a tunic of blue, green, orange, and red, who extended his hand – I had taken for granted that it was intended for me. Too many vivid, happiness-inducing colours compacted into one limited place intoxicated the child that day. To this day, I have never forgotten the depictions and coloration of that church and the overwhelming effect it had induced in me corresponded so strongly to what this boy incited in me today, and yet that church was long gone. And my mother inside it too. Basil, happy to tread steep paths that day, was old now. If everything is in flux, I imagine it meanders around here and there and finally brings you back to the good things again. I extended my hand into the void like the angel in the basilica. But with the difference that my palm was open, so it was as if it wondered: "Is your father a *kam*?"

Ogan's expression tightened, frowning: "He refused."

"Oh. Why?"

He threw his hand up. "It is a profession. He did not want to engage in that."

I was somewhat taken aback. "So, traveling between universes and bringing aid, having access to Sky Gods and evil spirits… and benign ones in the celestial spheres, and the souls of ancestors, all of that is just a banal profession?"

"Yes, extraordinary in its nature, but equally tedious and customary."

"How entertaining. So, you do not take any responsibility for anything. A *kam* deals with everything, even the problems of conscience?"

"It's not as fanciful as it sounds. Nor as simple as you phrase it. Being a *kam* is a job like any other job, like a blacksmith. As for problems of conscience, no, that is not *kam's* occupation. That is between you and God."

"Hmm. Are you a *kam* then?"

"No. My grandmother was one. Probably the wolf that got impregnated by *the* wolf was a female *kam*. At will, a *kam* can appear as an animal or human."

"How do you become one?"

"Spirits select the right person. They make contact and demand the person accept the task. Mostly members of the same family are chosen."

An odd sort of profession indeed. "And do you become rich with this job?"

"No. You do not have a personal interest in pursuing the job. You cannot charge for any help you provide. Maybe a few symbolic presents can be accepted."

"Oh, and is that why your father turned it down?"

He let out a brief, humourless laugh: "No…"

He did not continue but gave a heavy sigh. For a second his eyes became vacant. He remained silent.

But I was still curious. "And your grandmother. I assume she's dead? Is she buried here in Plekia?"

"Yes, only her bones, not her flesh."

"What on earth does that mean?"

"Bones are the seat of the soul, to be re-used. God manifests through the marrow in the bones. We do not break the bones of the animals we hunt. Breaking a bone is forbidden."

"I see. But Plato says the soul is in the marrow too."

He smiled again: "A *kam* learns the profession in solitariness, in a tree. Their soul learns in the tree, a large, beautiful one that symbolises the Tree of Life, far from other trees. Hers was in Transoxiana. When she died, we wrapped her body in clothes and leather. We put it up on a wooden bedstead installed in a single, standing beech tree here in Plekia. Her face had to be turned to the west – that's the direction of the dead. We hid it within the tree branches and waited for the flesh to separate from the bones."

Noticing my slight wince, he explained: "While this happens the bones are getting washed of this life. *Kam* souls practice in the tree; it comes from a tree and goes back to a tree. A year later we bury the bones. What makes a *kam* a *kam* is the bones. A female spirit comes and mantles the bones with flesh again, so they're re-used from one generation to another. They pass on the soul of the *kam*."

"Awful! But Madam Gabras would love this! She collects bones."

"Madam Gabras?"

"The mother of the boy you met the other day. You should know he was really here to borrow a book. His father who passed away and my father were friends. . . Just a person I used to play with outside. And he…"

I almost let slip something nasty about Nike but managed to resist.

Ogan said, "I guess the signification of bones is different to her."

I giggled. "Once, a member of their family stole the Holy Lance only to be able to swear on it. Can you imagine? He ended up at loggerheads with the Emperor. Those Gabrases are also a weird bunch!"

For a second, I beheld his face to find out if he noticed my blunder. Quickly, I changed the subject. "So, your grandmother – you were saying?"

"Ah, yes. We hung her drum and rattle on the same tree because those are highly personal objects and re-using them is extremely dangerous, which is not the case for the mirror, so I kept it. She made a small drum for me to play with at the time, a replica of hers. I still have it too. I take them everywhere."

To me, the fact that I couldn't tell if he was a friend or foe – and that this intimacy escaped him was as odd as his stories. So, that fetid object in his room belonged to his sorcerer grandmother. No wonder something bothersome would crop up, just like dandelions, crabgrass hemlock, broad-leaves, and creeper plants. One can never anticipate what life will deliver. An elephant-faced boy was born in our village once upon a time: instead of limbs, he had lumps. The word spread in the middle of the night and people swarmed into the house of the unlucky couple to see the creature. The man was frozen, the woman weeping, prayers were said in unison. Next morning, the priest packed the lump and took it to an unknown monastery. The parents confessed their sins, their next child was born normal, and husband and wife reveled in a sinless, gratifying existence ever after. Nobody knew what happened to the elephant boy. Perhaps the new child made them pay a price, for we know a child may become good for nothing. Who paid for whose misdeeds in this life? Your Roman mother gave birth to a son and a sorcerer raised him. Was your mother atoning for her sins? How about me hanging on your plump lips which are speaking those innocuous words now? I find myself gladly at your beck and call to behold them forever and ever, ready to go to Hades or to the underground kingdom of Erlik.

"For your information," he added, "a *kam* is not a sorcerer."

I blanched. "Are you reading my mind?"

"Pardon?"

"Oh, nothing... So a *kam* isn't a sorcerer?"

"A *kam* does not manufacture, a *kam* calls. A priest talks to God, but God speaks to a *kam*. Incidentally, they have something peculiar about them. I'll show you."

"Really? I wonder what can be so curious, if the rest of this is commonplace?"

"No, this one will surprise you."

"Go ahead. I bet you can't."

He smiled, and his eyes again turned into that black line: "Bones again... Each *kam* has an extra bone in his body. Look at my thumb."

He extended his left hand to which I had paid no attention before. Verily the forefinger was exceptionally long, with four knuckles instead of three.

"Oh, how haven't I noticed that before? So unsightly!"

Evidently not offended by my insensitivity he continued to smile: "Do you know what this means?"

He crossed his arms and observed me. I shook my head in an exaggerated way and let my mouth fall open to please him: "Verily, it is rather unusual. What does that mean?"

He bit his cheek and said, "This is where the bone of a *kam* links with the bones of ancestors and the vocation is carried on. Bones are reused over and over again through the generations."

Somewhat irritated, I clenched my hands and frowned: "But you've just claimed that you're not a *kam*."

"True, I am not. Never been invited. One that does not respect and accept the request perishes."

"So your Father will perish because he turned it down. But after all, everybody must perish in the end."

"One who rejects is punished. In case he manages to elude a painful death, he gets either handicapped or goes mad alternatively."

His brow furrowed as he glanced down. I vanquished the urge to take his arm and simply lead him further into the orchard from the garden pavilion. Instead, I simply said, without taking his arm: "Come, let's leave the trellis and walk further into the orchard."

When he noticed the blossoms, he tipped his head back, turned his face to the sky, and beamed: "Apple blossoms!"

"No apples yet. If they were ripe, I would give you some and we could eat till our stomachs hurt."

"You would be obliged to request their permission first."

"Whose permission? Father does not care for such things; he has always been very generous with me I must admit…"

"I mean," he interrupted, "the most talented hunter cannot hunt an animal if it does not want to be hunted. One must ask for permission; same when you intend to pluck a fruit from a tree, you must also say sorry first."

"Sorry to whom?"

"To the apple here."

I stifled a snort. "Why do you say sorry to an apple, for God's sake?"

"Because when you eat it, you ingest its spirit."

"And… what if it does not want me to eat it?"

"If you chose it, then it must want to be eaten. You just plead for its acknowledgement, that is all. Nothing and nobody dies before it agrees to."

"If it wants to be devoured why then must I request its approval?" I asked. "And how," I went on, my tone not quite managing to remain serious, "is one expected to speak to an apple?"

His expression did not change. "The same substance is in fruits, animals, soil, rocks; it is everywhere. You ought not to talk; just think, acknowledge, then you will be rejoined. We eat, we grow, we age, we die, and we come back. We're a part of one whole, supreme being."

I winked: "Your grandmother again? If we had to get approval from all plants and all animals to take their lives, doing business for butchers and people like us would be, well, even more procedural and ceremonial than in Constantinople. People would starve."

I laughed lightly and went on: "In fact, Zeno, my late grandfather, would not fall short of your grandmother in oddities. He believed if an apple tree did not yield apples, a good way to encourage it was to approach it with an axe and threaten to cut it down."

He flapped his hand in dismissal. "One must hold apples dear and they will bloom, mellow and sweeten."

Day shone on his hair while he ranked nature as tantamount to God; night gleamed in those onyx eyes when he described creation as part of the Almighty. And after all, I supposed, he could be right. If I drew that carefree head gently towards my bosom, buried my nose in those golden, powdered locks, I could breathe in the perfume of the sun and of gold; if I pressed my lips to those black gems, I would, beyond doubt, learn the flavour of night. You were right, lovely boy, with you, paradise was not a promise, glimpses of which we seldom catch on this earth; with you, heaven was today: no nocturnal earthquakes, no barbarians to fear, no weeds to be irritated about, no evil omens, not even the hideous forefinger, but God's fragrances and flavours everywhere.

"Good!" I exclaimed. "Henceforth, we shall be rejoined with the apples. We'll be merged and united in one spirit!"

A melancholic expression passed over his countenance. He stared at the trees and said, "Yes, only blossoms for now and soon we are to reunite with the 'Apple'…"

14

It is equally wrong to send off a guest who wishes to stay,
and to keep back the one who is eager to go.

Homer, *The Odyssey*

With the intention of seeing the notorious prince in the flesh, I set out early and made it a fait accompli before any household member had the chance to object. I had schemed an unrequired delivery to the monastery with a clumsy convoy consisting of me, my horse, a few of our men, and two mules, one loaded with white mulberry, the other with green plums.

Dragging long wooden beams and iron rods, Ataman's men began work to transform the monastery into a commercial centre and inn. They fitted the inside walls with identical stalls; cleaned the surfaces of the arcades, the columns, and the fountain, all of which took on a fresh beige colour that added to the sense of being in a new place. New chambers were planned as annexes to the main body, and the building which Basil had dreamed of employing as a convent would operate as a prison. Monks' private cells were put to use as bedrooms for visitors. The round, domed treasury room was to resume its old function, but the library's new utility and the whereabouts of the silver chalices, incense burners, golden panels, and seals remained obscure. Sultan Mesud had ordered plans to construct a masterpiece, a vast mosque in their capital, Iconium. Our Ataman set about building a new mosque in the annex to a small chapel close to the inn, either because he didn't want to fall farther behind his Sultan in observable piousness, or to not miss out on sponsorship from the Caliph in Baghdad. Rumour circulated that around ten years ago, the Grand

Seljuk Sultan Sancar who ruled Persia and Asia had hired murderers from Hashshashin to kill the previous Caliph, Al-Rashid Billah and replace him with the present Caliph Al Muqtafi, to have the latter as a puppet in his hands, making perfect sense of the Turkish parlance:

"The mouse that scratches the cat's testicles is doomed to die."

The Hashashins were a mysterious order living in a Persian mountain fortress named the 'Eagle's Nest' specialising in taking down political and financial rivals. According to what we have heard from the crusaders, the order's leader, a mysterious man named Hasan Sabah, whom they claimed never left his mountain fortress, spent his days immersed in philosophical contemplation and writing, when not, of course, arranging for his rivals to be quietly eliminated. Rumour had it that he had even had his own sons murdered because one drank wine and the other murdered someone, both of which were forbidden by Islamic law. The castle was surrounded by lush gardens where beautiful women waited to give them a first taste of the pleasures of after life, just as promised by the Qur'an. But there was one firm condition: One had to kill in the name of God and religion. This was arranged easily. As I mentioned, Hasan Sabah was a philosopher, so reconciling murder with his conscience – and aligning of causes with outcomes – were, for him, nothing more than routine exercises in logic. So, he purified and legitimised the act of homicide and God complied. As you know, one must know how to talk to God; he may be convinced more easily than you can imagine. Naturally hashish and the flavours of the Garden of Eden also helped. The men were first intoxicated and then deployed. After all, hashish, too, was God's creation, was it not?

"Why get involved with these blood-curdling manslayers rather than simply having the opponent killed?" would be a legitimate question. I assume the faceless, nameless services they offered allowed no possibility of exposure, no likelihood for grudges to be held by particular citizens who might trace the origin of the sin, and thus they could continue 'Loving the Sinner, Hating the Sin' in happy ignorance. As you know, gossip first reaches the outermost circles; we knew all this, but did people in Baghdad know? The court of the Caliph whose official affirmation was essential for the legitimacy of every Muslim King would forever be under the shadow of Seljuk swords after the incident of Caliph al-Mustarshid's murder.

Ataman's mosque was a plain, rectangular stone structure with a dome adorned with turquoise-glazed tiles. Attached to the small derelict church, it began to grow at a steady pace.

Turks now called the complex a 'Caravanserai'. They employed a doctor, a veterinarian, a blacksmith and many servants who waited on lodgers. The barefooted were provided shoes a cobbler repaired for guests free of charge. Horses received barley and straw and, if necessary, horseshoes. Every Friday, butchers sacrificed a sheep for Allah, cooked the meat, and gave it away to people on flatbreads. In the evenings, the waiting staff served a honey sweet called *helva*. Regardless of their religion, travellers, merchants, dervishes passing by were all welcome. Shelter and food were complimentary for three days. Andronicus, on the other hand-- not merely a passing guest – needed to pay for his sojourn.

I entered through the gate. Above it, on an arch the Turks had embossed the stone slab with a double-headed eagle relief, with one head facing east and the other west, a symbol that people prized – Romans and pagans alike. Laying claim to the sun throughout history, both Romans and Turks chose this bird as a symbol due to the fact that an eagle can look directly into the sun.

A ruddy-faced, portly pantler did not object to my superfluous consignment, and from then onwards, being permanently immersed in the renowned vein of Turkish hospitality – on a personal as well as intuitional basis – he would accept the goods as if they were gifts. Out of breath, he would drag his feet, call someone to unload the mules, bring his ledger, and settle the account.

A restless crowd of cavaliers, archers and infantrymen dressed in tunics with lamellar cuirasses moved around the courtyard. Some were wearing turbans with aventails, and others conical helmets made of iron, and a few sported braided black hair and bandanas; all carried round shields, curved swords, and lances. Ogan made an entrance. While being led towards the door which I assumed was of Andronicus's room, he remained unimpressed by their reverence and salutations. He threw me a glance and gave me a vague bow. When I had told him at home that I wished to see, up close in the flesh, someone born in the purple, he'd seemed entirely indifferent. Even now, faced with the presence of a Prince in Plekia, he appeared just as unmoved. The door we stood in front of commanded attention alongside the others. A component of Ataman's monastery restoration project, it featured a ravishing carving of two creatures, half-human, half-animal, facing each other, adorned with a Tree of Life in between.

The door eventually opened and a tall, brawny man emerged. Standing in a vigorous, well-nigh offensive posture, and smirking, Andronicus was the tallest, most statuesque and majestic man I had ever seen in my life. Even in the streets of Constantinople I had never spotted such a stately and shapely person. He ceased smiling but deep laugh lines around the edge of his mouth remained and they suggested the continuation of a sardonic grin. The dark brown of his hair gave prominence to an odd eye colour: saffron and honey, amber-gold with orange, with almost red tints in it. Tanned like a peasant, he had an angular jawline, thin lips, a strong aquiline nose with narrow nostrils. His limbs, in perfect equilibrium, moved with an unusual ease. This was the figure of someone conscious of each organ, each flux, his capacity, power and competence, the body of someone who worshiped flesh, a corpus that was an ally to its owner and not a foe.

Heedless of the confidence the man radiated, Ogan gave him a firm handshake and delivered in a clear tone:

"Your Highness, I am Ogan, Ataman Bey's son. I serve as Ambassador to my tribe. I must inform you that on a campaign to Syria, during a hunt in Cilicia, your uncle, Emperor John, passed away. He has proclaimed your cousin Prince Manuel who was accompanying him on this expedition to be the new Emperor. He abandoned the campaign and is now marching back to Constantinople."

Andronicus' face became white. He turned back and walked into his room. One of the soldiers attempted to stop him but Ogan made a sign with his hand and the soldier let Andronicus go. The door stood open; I approached the threshold. Sitting on his chair Andronicus gazed at the floor. When he lifted his face, I could not say if his eyes were wet or not, but their frightening hue had become more distinct.

"Do you know? Those loathsome Latins can be wise at times. They say, '*a cane non magno saepe tenetur aper*'." Raising his shapely eyebrows affectedly, he added, "This means, 'a wild boar often falls prey to a teeny dog.' Did you savages kill him while hunting?"

I turned to the boy fearing he would get mad at this insolence, but, his composure prevailing, he replied: "No, he had a hunting accident. That wild boar made a counterattack when he thrust his javelin into the beast's breast. As the iron shaft penetrated its entrails, his hand was thrown back. It struck the quiver carrying a poisoned arrow, which hung by his side. He died the day we seized you."

Andronicus widened those orange eyes, and once the surprise sank in, he drew his head back, closed his lips, and sneered:

"Did they take Antioch from the Latin dogs?"

"No. He deemed it unwise to attack Antioch under the circumstances – his Latin mercenaries refused consent, supplies were lacking, and so on. He decided to return via Cilicia. He plundered the suburbs of Antioch, though."

"You, knowing all these details… Not to mention the admirable, well-planned operation you executed to catch me – ironically also while hunting. You, savages… you take the wind out of Komnenos's sails. What a way to end Eastern… Where is Manuel?"

"About to reach Constantinople."

"Does Manuel's elder brother know that his younger brother has been chosen Emperor instead of him?"

"No. John announced on his deathbed that he had decided that the younger Manuel and *not* the older Isaac was to be anointed Emperor. Upon his father's death, Manuel dispatched his commander Axouch to the capital while he himself took care of the obsequies and placed the body of his father aboard the ship that would bear it to the capital. Presently, Axouch is holding Isaac in check till Manuel reaches the capital – so he doesn't cause trouble."

Andronicus muttered something in Turkish and spat on the floor:

"Get the news from a barbarian! What a wide network of spies! I shall divulge their treacheries when the time comes. I'll expose their conspiracies and persecute these ignoble rats before the eyes of a myriad of spectators."

"I would like to inform you that I shall accompany you to Iconium where Sultan Mesud will receive your precious presence. We will demand a ransom for you once the new Emperor reaches his throne. Please rest assured – you shall not suffer any harm in the course of your stay here. We shall provide you with any assistance you may require."

Andronicus rolled his eyes: "Well, well… Perhaps Mesud wants to consort with civilised company for once. After all, he had a taste of it when he took my father and us children to his court when Emperor John betrayed us. We spent several years there."

He laughed and said something in Turkish to the boy, who blushed but kept silent. As Ogan turned to leave, Andronicus called out:

"By the way, isn't this a divine month – the month of staying home, sitting, and not fighting? Then again, you Turkomans do not even respect your own religion. It was Ramadan when they captured me."

The boy remained for a second where he was. His eyes did not blink, his muscles did not twitch. And then he said:

"Tomorrow is the first day of a sacred month and you shall do exactly what it mandates: stay, sit and not fight. I would suggest you refrain from making many plans about your future. In your situation, the present moment is all you have and all you will ever have during your layover here."

Andronicus smirked. "Ah! Your advice is most welcome. You have impressed me with your achievement; I am not easy to capture. However, you won't have the chance to deliver many such triumphs. I am confident my cousin will soon get me out of this catastrophe."

"Let's hope it happens that way."

"And with this occasion," he continued, his chin visibly jutting forward, "I await not only the reaffirmation of my significance and value, but also the Komnenian dynasty's enhanced appreciation of barbarian technique."

He turned to me and eyed me from head to toe.

"And you, curious Lady – who are you?"

"I distribute fruit to the inn."

He chuckled. "So, you are here to present me with your special fruit?"

A cloud passed over Ogan's brow; his face reddened.

Without time to blush myself, I said, "Majesty, the best fruit is reserved for the Emperor. You will have to make do with standard inn quality here."

His eyes widened. He took a wide stance, crossed his arms, and grinned.

"Very well, my Lady!"

He lay down on his bed with two hands behind his head, initiating an awkward silence that made are presence feel misplaced. Only then did I detect a slight expression of confusion on Ogan's face. But he got his bearings quickly, wiped the expression away, and we left Andronicus' room without offering a proper farewell.

I approached the boy while he waited for me to mount my horse. Unable to bear the weight of blunder, and angered by the insolence of Andronicus, I exclaimed.

"I am sorry!"

He looked perplexed. "You didn't do anything wrong. But now that you have satisfied your curiosity, perhaps you should no longer accompany me to the Caravanserai."

As he trotted towards the exit, clouds churned, and the sky grew grey, the acrid, dusty fragrance of a storm began wafting through the air.

15

Most beloved of those, we love most.

Aristotle, *Fragment*

SEEING Ogan from behind my spyhole – an earnest kid, I thought, the sort mothers and fathers wish to raise: reticent, with a dignified air, a person of substance, rarely or perhaps never stepping out of line – and when it happens, by accident, as must sometimes come to pass, parents overlook it. Whereas with my type, who must exert extraordinary effort to be silent at all times, parents lose patience rather rapidly; even Basil does on occasion. The detached conciseness Ogan had manifested in front of Andronicus the other day – had it signified his aplomb or a complete lack of it? And yet, when alone with me, he had been quite conversational.

Was he enjoying a position of contentment and rest in our house? This reflection prompted me to the calamitous epiphany: either I was finally beginning to 'grow up', or worse yet, I was turning into Basil. The voices in my head were nevertheless present, saying "spying is indecent; transgression is evil," but they were far enough away – and not me. My legs were in charge though, as if they had a mind of their own. They were at the monastery the other day and today they walked to the door with the hole. Nike's legs had brought him here yesterday though he knew they should not have. So, this was the way we became sick, demented, or in love – when our bodies ignore what our minds call for. If reason had to choose between being reasonable or being sick, demented, or in love, doubtless it would choose the first. But reason rarely gets to make the choice; I was invariably unreasonable.

Basil gestured toward the guest chair but remained standing, studying the boy with narrowed eyes before asking:

"Are you happy with your sojourn here Ogan? Is our house meeting your expectations? Are you comfortable?"

"Yes Sir, thank you very much. I am grateful."

"I hope my daughter does not intrude too much, and is not causing you disturbance? She can be slightly vexing at times…"

"No Sir, not at all. On the contrary, she is such a charming Lady. She reminds me of my mother when she speaks. Somehow, her intonation is similar."

"Your mother…"

"Did you know she was from Spori?"

Basil ensconced himself in his seat and said in a soft tone, "Yes, I know. I used to go there every week for business with my father. The journey would take two hours on horse; it passed in a flash on the way there and was endless on the way back."

"Did you make the acquaintance of my mother?"

Basil cleared his throat.

"Yes, I knew Barbara. Our fathers were friends."

"She died when I was nine."

Basil coughed. "I know. Did she die in peace? Did she suffer any pain?"

"I am not certain, Sir. She never mentioned anything about being in pain."

"How was she – lively, serene? Did she weep every so often?"

Ogan raised his eyebrows: "What do you mean, Sir?"

"Erm, was she a content mother, or… a sorrowful one? Had she…" Basil coughed again: "Had she been treated with compassion?"

Ogan, perplexed: "Well, never overjoyed… but I do not recall seeing her depressed either. My father was absent time and again, so we resided with my grandmother. The two women did not have anything in common, but I trust my grandmother behaved graciously toward her. Being the leader of the tribe, she was a wise person. My mother would speak Greek to her, and she would reply in Turkish. To what extent they understood one another was a mystery – perhaps even to themselves. Since I could understand both, I took advantage of it and mocked them occasionally… Overall, we were a happy family… The only thing that agonised her…"

Ogan lowered his gaze.

"What?"

"She was anxious about the prospect of her children stinking for the rest of their lives for she couldn't have us baptised. My father never objected to the idea; he even encouraged it – he'd heard it expels the innate foetor in blood. But my grandfather thought the ritual could clash with the spirits of the tribe and displease them… Therefore…" Ogan gave a little chuckle before continuing, "after Mother was gone, we paid the utmost attention to our personal hygiene – not to stink. Till today. To pay homage to her."

"Where are your siblings?"

"My brother is *Emir-i-Candar*, in charge of protecting Sultan Mesud in Iconium."

"And sisters?"

"One is married to a Seljuk Prince, the other to a Danishmendi Prince."

Basil smiled. "I see Ataman connected them well – though the two do not always get along with each other."

"They love each other, Sir!"

Basil laughed: "Oh, I meant the Seljuks and Danishmendis, Ogan. The rivalry between the two is sometimes fiercer than their struggle against the Romans. Do you ever see your sisters?"

"Rarely, Sir."

"You speak the Hellenic tongue exceptionally well."

"Thank you, Sir. I had chances to improve mine, whereas my sisters' Greek stayed rather rudimentary. When we were young, we inter-mixed Greek and Turkish without thinking about it and fabricated a private language of our own. On the rare occasions when we do meet, we still speak it. Not that we have anything else."

"You must miss them?"

A beam of something like joy lit his face and his lips revealed white, even teeth – indeed affirming his high standards of personal cleanliness.

"Yes… Certainly."

"You will also settle in Iconium and enter Mesud's service, I assume?"

Ogan raised his eyebrows. "Not at all, Sir. I shall leave statecraft to others. I seem to enjoy a life itinerant between high plateaus and plains – on the move. I prefer that way: to be dreaming summer in winter and winter in summer, listening to nature."

Basil mused, "I hope your obligations in life will comply with your desires."

Something clicked in the hallway. Not to be caught red-handed, I dashed out – only to ram into a servant bringing glassware on a tray. As we both fell, a violent, shrill tinkle rang out as jugs, goblets, pitchers and plates smashed to pieces. It did not take long for Anna to appear, placing her hands on her apple-shaped waist, her nostrils flaring as she shouted:

"How on earth did you manage that?"

While trying to get to my feet, I mimicked a mule's innocence and gawked at her black eyes. I had broken not the everyday pottery, but our expensive glassware.

"Sorry, Anna. God, I am so sorry!"

The tightened muscles of her plump face loosened. She lowered her voice and said in a weary tone:

"What is wrong with you, Theia?"

"Nothing Anna, nothing."

16

Oh, my lad, my son, what brings you here?
What blessed wind?

Sophocles, *Philoctetes*

THE courtyard quiet and still, sluggish guards waiting at his door, Andronicus took his time to open after we knocked. Chewing a mouthful of food, he gave a listless look, turned and trudged back into the room. In a tacit pact, we trailed after him; I pretended to ignore his boorishness, Ogan ignored it. While we stood, he sat on a stool and chewed his morsel unhurriedly. After swallowing, he allowed a silence to hang in the air. Finally, he asked: "Have you contacted Manuel?"

"Yes."

Without looking up: "Have you heard back from him?"

"No."

Almost in a murmur, he said, "He will respond. He must be preparing." Then a flash of those eyes towards Ogan. "Are you hoping to save your skin after this vile scandal? Is your tribe aware of the risk it has taken?"

"Surely."

"I assume Mesud is directly involved in this, or am I a surprise gift to him from your father?"

"I cannot answer that. You'll find out in due course."

Andronicus' face flushed, his lips disappeared and when they reappeared, there was a grisly twist to them. In a low tone, squinting and slowly clenching his fists, his voice was an intense hiss:

"You barbarians will pay for this. I shall fish and swim in pools filled with your blood and dry myself with clothes made of your skins."

It was as though Andronicus's body were hollow, filled not with organs but with liquid animus – a dense, hot bile, a yellow fluid tinted with orange that seemed to glow in his eyes whenever he erupted or hurled threats. Insanity may incite daredevilry, but something told me he was of sound mind, in so much as he was overtly self-centred, perfidious and consciously venturous. He was not a man to fail to fathom that his existence was at the mercy of his enemy and that a reluctant death is worse than death itself. Knowing the boy had not lied when he said they would not maim or wound him, Andronicus exploited the advantage to the fullest:

"After all, you stole me. Theft is punished by amputation in keeping with your religion, isn't it?"

Motionless, resembling a frosted rock under the dark shadow of a winter day, Ogan replied:

"You were not stolen. Booty from the infidel is not a crime in Islam if a part is donated to charity. The Sovereigns' faith upholds a practical stance towards these matters."

"Oh? You make a gift of my ransom and thereupon the whole thing is sin-free?"

"Exactly. One fifth of the amount is to be handed out. As such, you are a spoil of war, an indemnity."

Andronicus looked icily at him while the boy remained unmoved. "And you presume that to be true?"

"My personal opinion is irrelevant, I am not the chieftain."

"Someday you will be the chief, isn't that so? That is of course if you'll have the hap to escape my wrath."

"If you must know, I see no sense in dressing up your abduction or disguising it under a religious pretext – but I can neither assist you nor undo it. Who knows," he added, with what seemed to me a hint of mischief, "you might even relish the quiet, rural, lifestyle, as opposed to the turmoil of Constantinople. I shall give orders to my men to promenade with you every day in nature until the day we depart... If you'd like?"

Andronicus seemed puzzled, but he covered it quickly. He thrust out his chest and said:

"No, thank you. I happen to be fond of the hectic way of life in the capital. Especially the spectacles; one of which I am planning to organise with your assistance. It involves cutting off your right hand and pulling you on a cart through the streets… if that catches your fancy."

"It will be beneficial to be calm. Try to live in the moment; don't obsess over your appellation or what is forthcoming. It is a mental exercise which brings peace of mind, even a state of ecstasy if you succeed in emptying the mind fully."

Aghast, Andronicus sought for reply but came there none. Mouth open, he directed his stare at me, sizing me up in slow motion. I reckoned he must be considered an attractive man by a certain ilk of female – those unafraid of his melted snakeskin, honey topaz eyes, or else terrified, but clever enough to feign ease. In any case, his devotees would be ethereal houris, the likes of Aphrodite, Athena, Jezebel and Lilithe, mindful of their beauty; and not even Andronicus could distress those. Rare are the women who are unaware of their attractiveness and rarer still the plain ones who foolishly believe themselves alluring; but that variety would likely hold no interest for him.

The headstrongness that Basil so disliked in me might now come in handy, given the situation I had brought upon myself. I gathered my strength and waited for Andronicus' onslaught. To my surprise nothing came; he returned to the table to continue eating.

On the way home, I pleaded: "Forgive my curiosity, but how do you tolerate his audacity? He seems to test you to see how far he can go; he acts like he is an award from God presented on a golden platter."

"Are you disappointed in me?"

Taken aback, I exclaimed: "Oh, no. No… I am curious, that is all."

My face heated up. Basil observed my mood swings and never failed to communicate their mostly embarrassing consequences; therefore, I knew my revealing tics only too well. Hence, I rapidly hid my ears with my hair lest they should blush, and to prevent fidgeting I sought to introduce a new topic but could not come up with anything. Ogan came to my aid:

"Shall we race?"

Relieved, I shouted, "Yes, let's!"

He arrived home long before I did. Still on horseback, he beamed triumphantly.

I laughed: "Hey, I am not a barbarian born on a horse!"

17

Men regard it as their right to return evil for evil and if they cannot, feel they have lost their liberty.

Aristotle, *The Nicomachean Ethics*

Anna frowned. Jabbing her finger in the servant's face she yelled: "But *lavash* is not the same! I cannot use this. Too thin. And where is the horse milk?"

Not believing my ears, I first threw a piercing stare at Anna and then watched the servant, whose head drooped, his ears scarlet. *Kumis*, a filthy drink made from fermented mare's milk that renders nomads slightly drunk and makes them dance around fire. Mind you, I had great sympathy for mules and mares, but drinking their milk in this house?

"There was no nomad selling kumis, Ma'am. There were all sorts of barbarian sellers, but I saw no-one who sold flat bread either, so I bought this bread from an Armenian."

The servant turned his head downward. Anna planted her feet apart and, arms akimbo, and yelled:

"You, feckless dolt! This is too thin. It'll dry in a few hours."

She turned to me. "Theia, after the church service, can you go with this duffer back to the market and buy what I want, please?"

"Seriously? I thought the marketplace was not for respectable ladies?"

"You can dress decently. Bind your hair instead of sporting these straggly locks like a common maid. You can veil your face and stand away from the vendor. And don't look him directly in the eyes. Oh, and don't talk to him; just indicate to this idiot here what to buy and he'll do it."

I gave a loud laugh and said, "Thanks, your advice is much appreciated. I'll bear it in mind next time I go to the market, but I'm afraid I can't help just now."

Befuddled, she stepped back, opened her mouth, probably to give new orders to the servant, but nothing came out at first, then just some mumbles. She walked back to her kitchen and began whining at the maids as I veered into the barn. Pegasus, legs curled up, slept on his side. I crouched down and buried my nose in his neck. My impulse was to whine about Anna just like Anna, but seeing Pegasus exhausted, I decided he had already borne more than enough of a burden today and held my tongue. Basil's mellifluous voice calling my name resonated in the courtyard. Entering the barn, he squinted at us and smiled.

"Hello my Angel!"

"What is it this time, Father?"

"Please get ready. We should be leaving for the church soon."

"Tell me, Father, who is this Andronicus?"

"Him? He's the cousin of the new Emperor, Manuel, who is the son of the late Emperor John Komnenos. Andronicus's father is Isaac Komnenos, the older brother of John and thus the uncle of Manuel. Isaac has long coveted the throne. His conspiracies are endless. About thirteen years ago, Isaac became involved in a plot against John, and when the conspiracy was uncovered, Isaac fled to the Turks. As far as I know, Isaac wandered Asia Minor for eight years, trying to forge alliances against his brother John. Isaac provoked both Christians and Muslims, including Sultan Mesud. A few years ago, Isaac reconciled with John and returned to Constantinople. Andronicus is Isaac's younger son."

"And did Emperor John receive him with open arms?"

"Yes, he did. But history repeats, my child. We'll see what Andronicus will do to his cousin."

"You must admit Ataman is inconsistent and has bizarre ideas. Why should Manuel pay for his cousin who might eventually plot against him?"

"Love and hatred are two sides of a knife. Logic in a human being is a notional concept my child. We may never know the exact workings of another mind. Are you ready to leave?"

"And, Father…"

"Yes? We really must go."

"What did Ogan's mother look like?"

Taken aback, Basil turned. I saw his ears literally becoming red then a purplish unhealthy looking wine tone. He shifted his gaze around as if searching for help. His voice tremulous:

"Why do you ask that? I don't remember having told you I knew her."

"Ah, come on Father, Anna must have told you about my peephole? Don't pretend."

Annoyed, his face tightened. He snapped at me: "Theia, you may never ever end up in the bosom of Abraham but instead burn in hell if you persist in acting this way."

"Tell me; what did she look like?"

"She was an exceptional beauty. Never before seen…"

"Not even my mother?"

Basil gulped. "Well, your mother was a gracious spirit, most charming…"

"I'm glad to hear you say so."

He cooed like a dove. "Her eyes were emerald-coloured, almond-shaped."

"My mother had hazel eyes."

Sharply, he replied: "Ogan's mother had emerald eyes, but of course hazel eyes are also favourable."

"Well, I got blue, and that hasn't helped me much up to now, has it?"

"Beauty is in the eye of beholder, my dear."

A complacent expression bloomed on his face, and he continued:

"The entire village was infatuated with her pearly complexion… her blond hair with amber highlights… her beauty became a legend in neighbouring towns too."

Absorbed in his thoughts, he drifted into reverie. This time I interrupted him:

"Apparently beauty isn't only in the eye of the beholder. But it is time to set forth for prayer."

Startled, he nodded, and we left.

Our church was too small to relegate women to the upper gallery. I headed to the side aisle reserved for us and positioned myself on the verge of the nave where I could enjoy the best view of whoever made an entrance. Nicephorus and Madam Gabras turned up early. Throwing glances and grinning as if she was the first apple of the season or a piece of ice on a scalding day, she pranced in, her chin jutting, her arm fastened onto Nike's, who, in contrast to his mother, dipped his chin down as though he wanted to sink into the ground despite this sacred cargo he hauled. After all, he was intelligent enough to know that the villagers cared about him inasmuch as his many failures gave them a good enough reason to delight over and gossip about, in this case, renouncing the dream of the Grand Logothete's investiture in the capital. But just when you think things cannot be any worse, he had to get wise to his mother's dragon-like self-importance, which had to be fed endlessly as it burnt. Anything was powerless in the face of that: mind, wisdom, and even bitter actuality. Nike complied. Behind the automata in Constantinople, precious stones had been placed which when backlit by hidden oil lamps and candles, produced red and green clouds. Gabras was a genius manufacturer of such clouds without the automata, and I must confess, she did somewhat mitigate the customary lethargic solemnity of the service and foreshadowed God with her vigour.

They advanced towards the priest, an affable soul who stood at attention when Gabras began to talk to him, probably about Nike's studies. He listened to her as propriety demanded, posing the expected questions, with an air of genuine interest. After withdrawing from the altar, the lady liberated Nike's arm with a pained expression as if tearing it from hers and strutted to the women's section. To my greatest displeasure, her eyes found me and surveyed me from head to toe. Below her unusual sage-coloured veil a look of distaste appeared on her face, and I was struck forcibly by its similarity to that of My Lady in Constantinople to which I hadn't paid sufficient attention before. She wore almost the same dress as the other woman, the grass-green cuffs of her inner tunic flaunting gold-ornamented, dark green bands, while her open chlamys disclosed the fine golden decoration of the emerald-green outer tunic, made of silk from Thebes. In fact, the two women were well-nigh identical. Some instants passed before I recovered from this discovery, but once I did, I realised whither I despised these primitive women whose faces reveal all, especially when expressions disparage and belittle. I strode towards her and stopped right under her nose.

"Hello, Madam Gabras; how are you?"

She shot me a glance from her narrowed eyes, undoubtedly thinking I was being unctuous at the auspicious prospect of marrying her son. I assumed Basil had kept silent about how dreadful I found the prospect.

She managed a half-hearted, "Hello Theia."

"I see Nikephoros returned to the town. Is he in good health?"

Frostily, she raised her eyebrows.

"Of course. His health is splendid. Why should it not be?"

"Oh, I noticed he has rather a mildewy complexion nowadays," I innocently trilled. "Maybe his studies have exhausted him?"

She flapped her hand in dismissal: "He completed his curriculum, and he is perfectly fine, thank you very much."

I pressed on: "I assume he opted to emulate his late father – God bless his soul. Will he be counting fruit in the countryside instead of practising law in the Capital? How selfless of him to want to stay here with his family!"

She clenched her teeth and her jawline tightened. Raising her chin, she stared at a point far above my head, then her face broke into a broad grin: "Ah! Maria, there you are! I was looking for you."

And with that she scurried away.

Marveling at the agility of those facial muscles, how their contortions could alternate between expressing exact opposite feelings in an instant, I cast an eye over the other side of the nave. Nikephoros watched me with the same expression he always wore after the kids had tormented him in the playground: pained and embarrassed. He was not a maven like his mother – at least not as agile. He turned his eyes away, and the Service commenced. I apologised to God for my manner under his roof. I beseeched him for mercy, and do you know what? I truly meant it.

18

Some things you will think of yourself,
some things God will put into your mind.

Homer, *The Odyssey*

GRUNTING while walking beside his mules and complaining of ever-increasing pain in his feet, the Jewish merchant from Constantinople wiped the sweat from his forehead.

"Paper on which God's name is written cannot be destroyed," he puffed.

An arm of the sea shut the Jews in on one side in the capital and they were unable to go out except by way of the sea when they wanted to do business. Much despised, they were debarred from public and imperial functions and also from riding on horses. Years later, the physician of Emperor Manuel, a Jew, would be the first to be allowed to ride on a horse and his prestigious status would alleviate the miserable conditions of those people for whom beatings and insults were by no means unknown. The leather tanners of Constantinople throwing their dirty water at the doors of Jewish houses was ironic in view of the fact that it was Jews such as this pitiful trader who were the ones that endured all the hardship of bringing potash alum from Iconium. Jewish merchants walked all the way to Iconium to buy alum from the Venetians and Genoese living in the Turkish capital who dealt exclusively in that mineral so essential to textile dyers and tanners. I wished to tell him that here in Plekia he could ride on his mules with no worries and that nobody would care. Too engrossed in God, he said, "So, next to our synagogue, we build a chamber without doors or windows. We call it the *Geniza*, and we push manuscripts into it through a slot – papers that are no longer needed or are regretted, but where God's name happened to be written."

His eyes filled with tears while he held his aching foot. His mighty creed and cognates had invented a separate department to save the All Powerful from going to waste, a divine garbage pail for God alone – but not a cure against foot blisters. I wished to converse with the poor man but could not bring myself to detain him longer; documents could be disposed of, but what of the thoughts recorded on them?

The Lord planted desire into the hearts and ideas into the heads of scribes and he seemed not too discriminating in doing this. Anyone could scrawl – heathens, women, even barbarians; one could scribble on rocks, on sand, or on mighty parchment. God appointed messengers but he did not tell them how, what and why to write, and when he made someone like me write, he knew that the prose, laden with imperfections, would be inadequate, ungodly. So, what prompted the Almighty to make any individual write then?

Was it perhaps not about the story per se, but something about Him, simply echoing himself in whatever we were scribbling? Why did the Creator need to see his selfhood in such defects? Or was it true, as Plato had believed, that this world was engendered by an imperfect other God, a crafts-God who imitated the real God? Making himself in the image of the real, good God while using a different medium, a material one? If so, which God talked to the poets? The real one or his imitator? Why would the impulse to write not be decimated? Could we, after all, trust and believe a poet?

God would not look with favour on my sinful activity of writing. Precious paper had to be used for a noble purpose: to write something valuable on, but I did not have the talent of Kassia. Do you remember the girl who acted like a smart aleck at the Bride Show, the one who first fascinated Emperor Theophilos but later enraged him with her daredevilry when she praised the importance of women in life? After being eliminated at the show, she wrote the most beautiful hymns and the most spiritual poetry of history and composed the most heavenly music. I could never reach her glory and so I took the decision to learn how to make copies of the Gospels, hagiographical and liturgical works. Writing a story of martyrdom was preferable to duplicating, but to carry out that deed, one either had to possess grand powers of imagination or have actual experience of combat, and I was blessed with neither. I could not ever invent a martyr from thin air without injecting the much hated "impetus" into it. One had to stay still; inertia had to reign over action. A writer was required to speak about miracles – not about the expectation of miracles. The first was insurmountable, the latter impossible. I had no experience with miracles either. A writer was obliged to be unselfish, but I had noticed the very act of writing was selfish – yet benevolent as well. It was inhibiting my own perpetual state of being animated and vigorous, blunting the sharp ends, making me less barbaric and more civilised, sweeter, more lovable. In this way, I was inventing my own personal Geniza by penning what you are reading now – throwing my waste onto the paper. In the end, the Gospels, hagiographical texts and liturgical works were never copied. I have never managed to bring myself to duplicate anything in my life – but when I was young, the project gave me insight into myself. As you know, when young, the planning is more fun than the doing.

Today, forty and three years later, I know that life itself is a Geniza, a sacrilegious rubbish dump, and the one who has to be salvaged from it is not God or a crafts-God but humans, and one can never escape from herself – or from the Geniza. When the famous poet Tzetses mocked the literary ambience of our age, he was wrong: "Everybody is engaged in producing poems – women, toddlers, artisans, and even the wives of barbarians."

Tzetses did not know that if the tower wants to be built, it will be built by someone, and if the book wants to be written, somebody will write it. I intended to copy but ended up writing. Had these activities both been official, and Basil found out, he would have never said "Writing is not for a woman," instead he would have said, "two watermelons cannot be held under one arm," but I never told him anything about writing. I used my perpetual search for paper as an excuse to escape to the marketplace or to wander freely on any adventure of my choosing, on any day. The lack of results never caught Basil's attention. The promised copies of the Gospels, hagiographical and liturgical works never materialised, but this never overshadowed my apparent determination; there had never been the slightest doubt about its lack of sincerity, not even from myself.

One had to acquire training and afford paper and tools to replicate documents. So, the whereabouts of the bookbinder Svoronos had to be determined. I set my hopes on his efficiency – not only to obtain parchment, but also to teach me how to reproduce manuscripts.

Anna was sending domestics to the marketplace that day. I put on my headdress to join them. One of them attempted to object, but I berated him so shrewishly that he hushed. If the Lord wanted to converse with me and convey a message through me, who was this lowly servant to interfere in such a sacred mission? Copying would make a legitimate activity for a spinster like myself. Behind my *maphorion* – far less modest than those worn by Saracen women – I looked askance at the domestics and held my head high, as if I could never put a foot wrong. I nagged them all the way to the agora to intimidate them, all the while bearing in mind that I would need their company again when we organised our next expedition.

A buzzing throng stood watching something I could not catch sight of, while a woman let out a heart-rending shriek. As we neared, we came upon the site of three executed men – two Greeks and one Turk. The woman threw herself to the ground and began to wail. The restless horde shifted as soldiers pushed their way through, bringing with them three more men to hang. Hastily losing my haughty air, I ordered the servants to return home. Veering off on my horse, we galloped home at full tilt while I pondered the question: would we still be afraid of death if God were civil? A sly scheme is set up where happiness in the hereafter is promised us on the condition we succeed in preserving our innocence and gentleness. Yet we are subjected to baby-eating monsters and ruthless personages in perpetuity. In which deity did these hanged men believe? The one who channels bliss through poets or the one who kills them on the gallows?

19

Speak badly of us and we are vexed, see a bad dream and we are greatly frightened; an owl hoots, and we are filled with fear. Anxieties, ambitions, fancies, silly customs: all these curses men have added to Nature's ills.

Menander, *Fragment*

THEY could not dress the eldest daughter with a bridal gown because her leg was broken. Instead, her younger sister was prepared. Not used to being the centre of attention, her huge, round, plate-like face blushed, and her body puffed up when she drew breath and deflated when she breathed out; in each case she resembled a large onion.

A silver wedding crown had been placed on her head. The central panel of the crown was adorned with three gems at the front, but her head was so enormous that the crown looked tiny. Sitting with her leg supported by wooden sticks and bandaged with straps dipped in egg yolk and beeswax ointment, the elder sister appeared untroubled about not being the focus of interest at this year's festival. Conversing with all present, gushing over her sister, she giggled and complimented her guests. I was pleased about this, for I was sure I had caused it. Thank God she and the other members of the family cosseted me and gave no impression of suspecting my deed.

The mother joyfully clapped her hands and invited the youth to the table. Then, only then, I realised I should find an excuse and run home never to come back again. There was no point in causing more fatalities on such a festive day when this poor family constituted one of the few in Plekia who still treated me kindly. I decided to feign an excuse to skip out before the time came to throw objects into the bucket. Eating with them was out of the question: I could not risk being sat in front, across or next to the girl with the broken leg. A month ago, either to obtain information about Ogan and Andronicus or by reason of their deep sympathies for me, the mother and the daughters had invited me for dinner. As amicable as the welcome was, the elder daughter smacked her mouth loudly when she ate, her lips forming a grisly shape after each bite. Against my will and all etiquette, I fixated on her every morsel, the subsequent gulp and her contented expression. Unawares, she continued while I became more and more steamed up, eventually staring unblinking daggers at her. I could feel my head heating up inside, a red veil forming before my eyes. Still blind to my irritation, she licked her lips. Despondent, I averted my gaze for fear of the power of evil in my eyes, and never looked at her again until I forced a hearty "thank you" at the door as I left their home. The next day, she fell from a tree and broke her leg in two places.

I drew closer to the mistress of the house and whispered into her ear that my tummy ached, and I would go home where Anna could take care of it. The woman gave a small shriek, covering her face with her hands.

"Theia, sweety, please don't go; it must be because of hunger. If you eat, it will perhaps stop."

"Thank you, Madam Kalekas. Anna will boil aniseed in vinegar for me at home."

"Bile must have dropped into your stomach from the liver. Go to my room and lie on the bed. The servant can give you pennyroyal to drink, or even a quick cupping session. Please don't go."

"Please don't go to the bother, Madam Kalekas, take care of your other guests. If I feel better later, I'll be back."

Without giving her the opportunity to insist, I bolted. I was going to hit two birds with one stone here, for I had forgotten the thorn the Turkoman had given me for protection against Erlik which was the very object I had intended to use during the festivities.

Thirty years later, the Patriarch Michael would ban this festival alleging it was pagan. But I can tell you though – he never put an end to it. To this day, this ignoble, abominable *Bacchic* frenzy persists. The eldest daughter dons a wedding gown, and a large bucket is filled with seawater. Each person throws an object into the bucket and asks the bride a question about the future. After each question, she pulls an item from the bucket and begins to soothsay like the Virgin Delphic Oracle. The game varies by region or community, but one aspect has never changed: after the oracles, the youths pour. out of the house, leap over haystack bonfires, and sing and dance themselves silly in the streets.

When I returned, the face of Madam Kalekas glowed with joy; she held her arms out wide and hugged me as if I had newly arrived. They filled a copper bucket with water brought by one of their relatives from the Bosphorus and the kids began to toss their objects inside. Our first boy was Nike although his mother, Madam Garbas, was against this celebration, claiming it contained carnal and sensual connotations and incited blasphemy and obscenity. After each gathering, our sympathetic hostess would pay for her actions by being reprimanded by Gabras. Nike brought a wedding ring; I wondered who it belonged to. He bowed to me from afar and did not approach. His greyish hands tightly pressed on his outer thighs, his arms adhering to his body, he walked sluggishly towards the bucket. Raising his hand with effort, he threw the ring into the bucket, irritating me with his evidently unchanging simulation of some disinterred, half-alive corpse. The absence of vitality and the destitution of ardour expressed in his every gesture sickened, even offended me. That greyish colour he had brought from Constantinople still tainted his face, further rankling me. An amulet, a comb, and a bracelet were cast into the bucket next, followed by a belt buckle, a pocketknife, a miniature brass virgin and child, a nail, a gold coin, a cross, a glass bead – and then my thorn, which I tied tightly with a blue ribbon so it could be found easily.

Madam Kalekas had ornamented the parlour with scattered wreaths of leaves, and one had been placed on the head of the girl with the broken leg.

The rest of us formed a circle around her. Everyone had to hold some specific person or wish in mind, and the object drawn by the oracle would relate to it. The twelve-year-old rascal Arcadius stood up and, shouting at the top of his lungs as if we were deaf, declared he would be the first. Voices of protest rose from the group, but Arcadius dug his heels in. As though about to punch someone, he shook his fist and said, "She will read my future first! Everybody agree or I shall go and call Madam Gabras here!"

Nike did a double-take. The mother of the girl conceded: "All right Arcadius. You go first."

Arcadius shouted out: "Pick the knife, pick the knife! Take the knife out of the bucket, the knife!"

Our the plate-faced bride snapped at him: "You cannot decide that. I'll pick it randomly. Whatever comes to my hand, you must accept. And why on earth did you throw a knife into the bucket - are you crazy? What if it cuts my hand?"

Arcadius drew near and nudged the bride. Rolling up his sleeve, he plunged his hand in and began to fish around. He found the knife and took it out. With his other hand he grabbed the bride's hand and placed the knife into her palm, then, still gripping it, he submerged the girl's hand into the bucket.

"Now take out the knife."

The girl gave a harsh squint at him but complied: "Arcadius, you will go to war and not with a small knife like this but something bigger; in fact, you'll find a sword will be stabbed into your arse."

The group began to whoop and laugh. Baring his teeth like a dog and kicking a chair Arcadius protested. He fled the room, slamming the door behind him, just like Zeno and me.

I hadn't expected such courage from plate-face, so I looked right into her eyes with admiration. Encouraged by this she decided to take the lead.

"Friends, the second is Theia."

She stirred the objects and pulled out the ring Nike had brought. Stroking her chin, she got lost in thought for a few moments, which probably felt endless to Nike. His initial expression, startled with a sprightly accompanying note, coloured into a blush, then, his long neck bending, he stared frozenly at the floor. I reached out quickly and grabbed the ring.

Forged in an octagonal shape, a holy rider was being attacked on one façade by the baby-killer Gylou; flowers and scrollwork of a fruitful vine expressed the hope of fertility on another. On the bezel there was a bride and groom in frontal bust with a cross in-between. This eight-sided shape was the symbol of eternity and harmony and, besides, it was expected to impart the magical properties of what was drawn on the object, as well as enhance them. Six words were scripted on each of the remaining six surfaces: God, concord, grace, health, blessing, infinitude.

I returned the ring to the girl. "Theia," she began, "I see a marriage." Approving murmurs surrounded us. "A husband madly in love with his wife, almost blindly…" The room was quieter now. "He can even risk death for her, so profound and passionate is his love… He adores her."

In the expectant silence I clutched my arms and gave a little shriek. Nike squeezed his eyes shut and gulped down a visible lump in his throat, placing his hand on the swelling as if hiding it. Then he stood up and said to the girl, "Would you please read mine now? I must leave soon."

The girl dipped her hand into the bucket and pulled my thorn with the blue ribbon. She shook her head, tipped her lip with her thumb.

"Nike, you will marry a girl who resembles this thorn, thin and tall. However, though she will look like the thorn she will be easygoing and obedient. Blue is the colour of God's holiness, thus the girl will be a lover of God, chaste, modest and virtuous. On the other hand, the thorn also says you are in pain. But don't worry, you had a narrow escape. Your pain will soothe you."

Nike made the sign of the cross. Tears welled up behind his eyes, which he palmed away with his hands. But he recovered quickly, thanked the hostess and the bride and hastily slunk away.

I stood up and had a look at the table. There were still some almond, walnut and honey crepes and orange-blossomed honey-sesame sweets. I heaped a plate and gobbled them down till the last crumb.

20

All is flux, nothing ever stays still.

Heraclitus,
Lives of Eminent Philosophers, Diogenes Laertius

THE unpromising sky clouded over, opaque, ashen. With a shiver, I patted Pegasus, imploring him not to cast thunderbolts during our journey; he regarded me with a knowing look, as if to assure me that he wouldn't. Of our thirty mules and several donkeys, most were grey dun; a few were black, one or two brown and black, and some white-spotted. Each saddle consisted of a flat piece laid across the animal's back, with a basket attached at either end – resembling the volutes of column capitals. Stronger jennies were assigned to pull wooden carts laden with peaches and cherries. Thanks to my deep affection for him and the spurious nature of our recent deliveries, Pegasus was in charge of providing favourable weather conditions; in other words, he was exempted from heavy duty. His specific baskets, woven from white cotton ropes, not vines, willow shoots or wood splits were nearly empty, as such they were symbolic rather than functional, serving as white wings.

At every opportunity, I arranged fresh or dried fruit deliveries – none of them requested by the Caravanserai. Today, a market had been set up at the inn. I turned back and cheered three things: the sight of my dwarfish ionic pillars in tow, the promise of novelties, and my curiosity about Andronicus's presence at the marketplace. My heart fluttered at the sight of crowds bustling around the inn. We entered a busy reception in the courtyard. Leading my group to the pantry, I ordered my men to unload the peaches. Having run out of patience, I did not enquire after the pantler, and, in great haste, I joined the flock jostling to see the merchandise.

The new inspector, carrying a silver sabre, walked amid the stands, speaking various languages, one of which was a serviceable version of Greek. Now and then he intervened, reprimanding one dealer for bamboozling clients and threatened to fine him unless he reduced his asking-price. He accused another of selling poor-quality items; he commanded soldiers to collect this one's wares and expel him. Fellow vendors were rooted to the spot, a few shaking, wiping sweat beads from foreheads. A couple pleaded for mercy on behalf of their friend, addressing the inspector as Muhtasib, but their implorations came to nothing. When he approached a couple of sellers who had been sitting and drinking something, they stood hastily. He picked up one of the mugs and sniffed the liquid. At the stalls, the merchants tended to drink sour wine with rue or a combination of milk, wine and water but this time it must have been the refreshment soldiers favoured: the alcohol-free beverage of vinegar with cold stones in it, for the muhtasib put the mug back and proceeded without comment.

The inspector stopped before a Turkish trader who was exhibiting carpets with red and blue octagonal patterns and good luck charm mirrors. Speaking in broken Greek, slurring some words, the dealer was shouting out to the crowd:

"Alloyed with seven metals! Lead from Saturn to become calm and careful, tin from Jupiter to bring kindness, maturity; Mercury to purify the mind!"

He inflated his upper body, contracted his arm muscles, flaunted imaginary arms:

"Iron from Mars to gain confidence, to become tough!"

Changing his voice to a high pitch, the man made exaggerated, imaginary feminine gestures and smiled provocatively:

"Copper for beauty and amour from Venus! Silver from the moon for tender affections! And gold from…"

He suddenly staggered and fell behind his bench. Trying to stand up, he held on to the bench for support but collapsed again. The muhtasib, red with rage, swept his arm and ordered the lad to be brought forward and tied to a pole, and shouted at the top of his voice:

"Drunkards shall be punished!"

Lest I should witness a whipping scene, I scuttled away, engrossed myself in more resplendent goods, and soon forgot about the flogged man.

In competition with the great Fair of Thessalonica at the Festival of Demetria, Turks organised this market which had many of the Great Fair's makings. There were people from Babylon, Shin'ar, Persia, Medea, Egypt, the land of Canaan, Russia, Khazaria, Hungary, and from the land of Petchenegs. Merchants' booths were set up in long, parallel rows facing one another, with a broad space left between them to allow the stream of people to pass freely.

Persians sold medicines, pottery, and ceramic tiles; Armenians handled icons and jewellery. Latins brought glassware. Jews imported cinnamon, musk, aloeswood, camphor, and silk from China, and cotton fabrics from India. Greeks displayed metal jugs, oil lamps, silver-bronze goblets, silver chalices, mortars, censer cups. Arabs offered pepper, cinnamon, cumin, ginger, cloves, sherbets, pomegranate syrup, musk and fragrances. Russians brought marten skin and amber; Bulgarians, linen and honey. While I strolled among the booths and wondered about Andronicus's whereabouts, right on cue he made his swaggering entrance, closely monitored by guards. The crowd withdrew to let them through, prodding and shushing each other as he passed. But soon it was back to business as the racket built up again. Pomposity and pride screamed out loud; greed and excitement raised high voices; humbug, fraud and covetousness employed rather lower tones while following the inspector with anxious glances.

Andronicus made a first round at a slow, steady gait. I pulled the sidelap of my robe over my head to hide my face, lest he recognise me – though the odds were slim that my ordinary features would stir recall in his deluxe brain – and threaded my way through the horde, keeping just abreast of him. Andronicus halted in front of one merchant displaying items I had never seen before, exceptionally sophisticated cast gold and silver handicrafts: cock, sheep, goat-shaped trinkets. Each had a small fountain on top and when pushed they magically sprayed out rose water or perfume. Busy with a potential client was one Latin who sported a paisley-patterned dark red silk brocade. Bragging about his unique objects, the latest inventions from Constantinople, the tradesman took no heed of Andronicus. The Latin beckoned passers-by and a few other vendors to his counter and grew louder as he recounted an extraordinary performance he claimed to have seen in Constantinople, staged on the initiative of Emperor Manuel. The merchant's new topic of pride was perhaps beside the point, but he must have thought showing off would increase his chances of sales, so he sang out:

"Dogs were set upon foxes, cheetahs upon antelopes, lions upon bulls, while we drank and danced, and wrestlers wrestled! Chariot races were out, jousting was in. Nowadays, it's all Western fashions, the new Emperor likes his Frankish styles!"

All eyes and ears, Andronicus crept up to the marketer, leaned his body towards the man and crossed his arms. The man proceeded with yet more exotic delights: "a thrillingly sensational acrobatic show; a celestial organ concert; miraculously serene flute and lyre melodies; exalting drums; mysteriously melodramatic mimes; breathtaking circus turns; hilariously funny comedy pieces; diabolical illusionists; water displays; flying actors and their perplexing masks; valiant tight-rope walkers" – and, he added with a flourish – "all against life-like backdrops, and all the new fashions! Emperor Manuel's new style of clothes is a hit!"

Meanwhile by a sleight of hand, he took a roll from under the stall and presented it to the onlookers. "Here! The imperial silk… Original!"

Dumbfounded, I sneaked up. One of the princes, tall but slightly stooped and swarthy, had been attired in that very silk at the Hippodrome. He had taken part in a polo game, catching a leather ball the size of an apple. While a netted loop made of dried guts was placed on his stick he had charged on his horse at full speed towards the goal and in a matter of seconds returned, swinging his hips and spinning his horse in a circle. His game technique was extraordinary yet the physiognomy of the Komnenos brothers was not, for I had not recalled their appearance. I was certain Andronicus had not played polo that day inasmuch as neither I nor anyone else would forget his outstanding looks. Emperor John's nickname, "Beautiful," must have denoted his virtues, not his complexion, for he, too, appeared common when I had taken the chance to get closer to him. To enter into this world, the Royals too broke free from a warm, dark chamber, just like the rest of humanity. But, falling into a lilac-golden cosmos where their mothers' milk was already sweetened with ginger, cinnamon and clove sherbets, these people were anything but ordinary. The universe had its eyes on the porphyry rock room with peacock fans, gold-embroidered vermilion hangings, eagle-motived scarlet valances where empresses gave birth. The infant, a 'violet' to coddle in Constantinople, was, to the savages beyond, merely a purple plum to devour if the chance arose. Someday the son would work in an office mounted on a high platform, in a world cloaked in violet, violet in that dignitaries would follow purple inlaid stones on the flooring to come near to him. My eyes feasted as I drew closer to the purple silk and gazed upon it: bird motifs embroidered in golden thread glittered across the smooth, luxurious fabric, like lanterns hovering against a summer night. It was the most exquisite silk I had ever seen – more magnificently purple than even my Pegasus's eyes. It was as if all the molluscs of Tyre and Sidon had bled purple into this fabric. Different hues of gold were obtained not by real golden filaments but from the legendary sea silk which nobody could afford except the Emperor. Gigantic shells adhered to rocks with a tuft of thin fibres. These fibres were spun into burnished, dark golden coloured filaments that never faded.

The seller resumed: "You'll never find it elsewhere. Purple like pansies, purple like butterflies, purple like the Virgin's skein, purple like the Temple's veil, purple like Christ's blood, purple like Sappho's tiara, gold like the sun itself!"

Andronicus' face turned to stone. His usual, orange-tinted yellow stare changed to coral.

"How did you obtain that?" he growled.

Displeased, the merchant threw a sardonic glance and did not reply; his spectacle was for well-to-do clients, not for this bedraggled detainee, whoever he was. Andronicus repeated the question, venomous and loud. Giving a smirk, the fellow tilted his head and remained silent. A vein throbbed on Andronicus' forehead, his eyes were becoming incandescent, his jaw tightened. Clenching his fists, he gave a blood-curdling roar, reached out to the man's side of the bench and pounded him on the chest. The seller, a slim figure, slumped to the ground. Grabbing him again, Andronicus' forearms, corded with muscle, shook the man, slammed a fist into his face, and

I heard more than saw the nose breaking. After several more punches, the vendor's features bulged, and for a few seconds – though to me it felt like a lifetime – he was transformed into something inhuman. A mass of blood disproportionate to his small frame, obscured his face and clothes, and only when soldiers pulled Andronicus away, did he let the beaten figure drop with a thud onto the wooden floor. Agitation took over the crowd who fretted over the victim. I slipped into the yard to gather my mules.

The sky darkened, threatening a cloudburst. Cuddling Pegasus, I reminded him of his promise not to send rain. His darling, modestly purple glance comforted me, again.

21

We are the offspring of Eros;
there are thousand proofs to show it.

Aristophanes, *The Birds*

As I bubbled over with excitement at Andronicus's frenzy, I grabbed Anna's arm – busy stirring her own bubbling mix of dried myrtle berries, cumin, and honey into a sweet, pungent boil. After all, a man born in the purple was present here in Plekia, stirring excitement of a kind rarely, if ever, seen. I let loose a cascade of babble about the market, the inspector, freaky merchants, and arcane novelties. Animated, she stopped mixing the sauce, turned, and mopped sweat beads from her forehead. When she heard the description of the victim, her eyes widened.

"Really? Oh God. Is Ogan aware?"

"That's what I need to find out. I'm nearly frantic trying to locate him. Where is he, Anna?"

She stepped back to the hearth, leaned over her pan and said in a flat voice, "How am I to know?"

After fetching a fan, I sat by the stove and watched her add olive oil, grape juice and garum to her spikenard gravy, which had made her a celebrity in our village, for no other woman cooked it as well as she did. Despite her use of unexceptional seasonings, she always managed to create an exquisite relish where the fishy aroma of the garum never turned her dressing into outright sea food but instead gave a mild, salty, sourish flavour to the dish, as it should. Next, servants would bring roasted lamb, and once the condiment thickened, she would dress the meat with it, sprinkle pepper and salt over it, call for the preparation of lemonade and sweet almond syrup, and then she would set about readying sesame-honey sweets, another of her specialities. But I did not wait for all this for I heard our horses neigh, and Dog howl as the clopping of Ogan's horse echoed in the courtyard. Sprinting to the patio I yelled:

"Did you hear the news?"

Unhurried, he remained mounted on the beast, which resembled its owner, nimble and muscular, shiny, sleek and long-legged.

"Yes, I am coming from there."

"So, what did he say about hitting the pedlar?"

Holding a silken case in his hand, a wide, generous smile show-cased his dimples. He then he jumped off his horse.

"Well… he avowed that 'that pediculous, flagitious, quisquilian sod likes the colour purple… and so I gave it to him!'"

"Oh, for goodness' sake… what do those words mean? Pediculous, flagitious, and… the other one?"

He wrinkled his nose which made me focus on the lips again.

"I don't know. Maybe something like worthless, or dirty, or villainous?"

"Hmm. Probably. Nevertheless, doesn't he have a sense of humour?"

He smiled. "Indeed."

"And how did you reply?"

"By relaying to him that he'll be incarcerated in a separate cell if he doesn't control himself."

"And… how did he respond?"

"He rolled his eyes and said, 'I am already in a dungeon!'"

I chuckled. "What's in that pouch?"

"This? Something for you."

"For me?" I couldn't quite suppress a smile.

"Yes, to thank you."

"Oh. For what?"

"For your hospitality. Let me freshen up please, and I'll meet you in the drawing room."

Hospitality? Mortified, I dashed to the salon; incapable of staying still, I paced back and forth. The importance of timing should never be underestimated in matters of the heart.

Time can be your friend or your enemy. For example, if one were obligated to spend time with an undesirable suitor, an annoying parent, or a tedious friend, time would stagnate – and whatever feeling prevailed would only intensify. In that sense, time became an adversary. Naturally, exactly the opposite too was true. When one waited for a boy like this, 'time' became confounded and so did feelings. Just a few seconds induced bouts of folly, frolicking and anguish, passion and repulsion, enticement and offence. By not dawdling and coming back to the room quickly, he prevented these nasty games of time and emotions from running even wilder, for in these rare situations where a woman and a man are on their own, adoration and rancour sit cheek by jowl, like in the analogy of the fly who lands haphazardly on either a flower or a heap of excrement, which stand so close, side by side.

Slowly, he advanced and with an elegant gesture extended the case. I opened it as slowly and gracefully as possible so as to display a worldly-wise sophistication and not a vulgar enthusiasm. Chin tucked down, looking up, he inspected my reaction. The gift was a cast silver, hare-shaped perfume sprinkler from the battered merchant.

Eyes crinkling, he said, "I've been told that you took an interest in those."

In a nonchalant tone which meant to suggest a formal, if not commonplace amicability and with the detached manner of someone who receives such presents every other day, I replied, "How so very kind, thanks; you ought not…"

The idea that even beginners in courtship can apply one or two refined tricks out of necessity and keep the upper hand was one that seemed reasonable to me. I thought revelations of 'Know thyself' as in the adage of the Oracle of Delphi were emerging, and what an incredible elation the epiphany brought! Without studying the hare comprehensively, I put it on the table. And then blundered.

"I imagine you were unable to haggle much for this one's price, for the poor trader himself is all but dead."

Looking at a loss, he hesitated. Gratification at my small triumph did not last long; being a fine, able opponent, he collected himself quickly and laughed playfully:

"Oh, I did. With his business partner."

After this point, this game of trivialising had to be played to its end, so I jeered:

"So, what else did our Andronicus say?"

"Oh, he rambled endlessly about how vile and devious Latins are. His uncle Emperor Alexios apparently adjured Pope Urbanus to promote a mass movement and send Latins here to save the Romans from the Turks…"

"But it was you who kidnapped him, wasn't it, not the Latins? Why is he so bothered by them?"

He laughed. "I think he's satisfying the need to curse and swear, given the obvious fact that he cannot damn the Turks. Mind you, he uses the word barbarians to refer to them."

"He knows history, for sure. He must know that Latins helped the Romans to push the Turks from Nicea all the way to Iconium. So they weren't that useless after all."

"Andronicus pretends to consider Latin existence worse than the Turkish one. At least for now."

"What else did he say?"

"Well, he said the Pope managed to dispatch a bunch of lice-infected, yellow-teethed bandits here to the Grand Empire of Rhomanoi. Half-knight, quarter-carpenter, he called them, quarter-peasant, brainless bandits with scarlet crosses on their chests. He does like a colourful phrase." Ogan chuckled at the description. "Not a professional army made of fighters chivalrous and strong, he said, nor a folk able to swear unbreakable oaths of fealty."

"Oh my! But after all, however motley, those bandits did take Jerusalem from the Mohammedans and created the kingdom of Jerusalem and the crusader countries."

He laughed. I continued: "I personally have a few Latin clients who are not that unfriendly. There is one, burly with red hair, green eyes and freckles, so pale, so pasty that even the sun feels remorseful when he shows up."

He grinned: "Why?"

"Why remorseful? For having never showed its face to him before or for burning him now. Mind you," I added, as he listened with apparent interest, "I associate Jerusalem not with barbarians nor Hagarens, and not even Latins. I think of those yellowish green fruits that Basil brings us. I don't care about the city; I don't think Basil does either. He told me the Romans lost it a long time ago."

"Yes, you have new Jerusalem instead."

"Yes, but not the fruit. It's not dissimilar to cucumbers in shape, the colour is yellowish green, and when you peel it off heaven comes to earth!"

"Bananas!"

I chuckled. Funny word. "I don't know its name. Better than apples!"

He shook his head violently: "No, no, nothing is better than apples."

"Certainly not. If you eat the flesh of those nananas…"

"Banana."

"Ba… Right. Throw away the brown bruises. Floury, soft and sweet… Good enough reason to want to take the city that produces them. Clever Latins! Though my grandfather Zeno loathed Latins as well. He used to say the Holy Spirit and the Son both proceed from God, but these nasty people tampered with the Holy Trinity, making one superior to another. Anyway, tell me, is there nothing Andronicus admires about them?"

"Yes. He did mention one thing: that in the West, a shoe-repairing family might mend shoes for three hundred years, whereas here, anyone can accede to the throne. He gave the example of the Emperor Basil, who was born a peasant, earned his life as a groom in a wealthy household, became a noteworthy wrestler in his youth, and died an Emperor."

"What did you tell him?"

"I told him that his grandfather Alexios himself was a General who ascended to the Imperial chair with a coup masterminded by his mother. And not only her intrigues but the barbarians themselves, including some Turks, had aided him in overthrowing the previous Emperor. So, he's lucky to be born here where he is a Prince. There, the utmost he could ever have become was a soldier."

"Oh, I wish I could have seen his reaction to that!"

We chuckled. I looked him in the eye directly and did not turn away. Not to be inferior to him at repartee and as well to show off my objectivity, I added:

"And after all, why did Alexios invite the Latins? Because we Romans are an entitled lot, but also too soft, too effeminate. That must also be the best finding of your barbarian forefathers; they probably hadn't expected to come here and find such sophistication with so little martial prowess. We can talk for hours and hours. Using the sword is another matter – doubtful whether the Romans are on par with the Barbarians, much less with the Latins. Then there are skills such as archery and riding, which are even less frequently seen..."

We giggled.

"Shouldn't you seek Andronicus's guardian creature too? That way his tormented spirit might be saved."

The pupils of his eyes enlarged, as if diluted with belladonna; the irises glazed, solemn:

"I did, as a matter of fact. My wolf Asena set off to track his protective power animal but found nothing. Even if the Emperor doesn't pay, we'll allow him to flee. He'll ascribe it to his own cunning of course. Unprotected, his long-term future bodes dire, and, of course, there are other short-term concerns he is not mindful of."

Puzzled, I asked, "What are they?"

"He never learned how to be thoroughly bored, and the worst thing is that his own company is intolerably boring to him."

"An unwelcome Eureka!"

"Well, a bitter awakening, admittedly, more shocking than being kidnapped."

Anna loudly announced supper. The fragrance of lamb and spikenard filled the air. Lest he should hear my stomach rumbling, I pulled away, reaching for a honey-sesame sweet and swallowing it while Anna scowled; rejoicing, I gave her bulbous body a firm hug and a loud smooch on the cheek. Later, after dinner, when the household had withdrawn to their bedrooms, I visited Pegasus whom I had been neglecting lately. He graced me with a calm, mauve gaze. He did not budge when I held an apple to his muzzle. Sidling towards me I fondled his eggshell coat gently as if afraid to break an egg, but he remained indifferent.

"You must understand Pegasus... There is a situation..."

He shut his eyes and opened them again. That was enough.

"Good night, Pegasus."

22

Temperance is mean with regard to pleasures.

Aristotle, *The Nicomaean Ethics*

My next encounter with Andronicus occurred early one morning. He had sent out a messenger, urging a prompt visit from Ogan. Despite the unease I felt at Andronicus's proximity, I found the prospect of spending the day far away from Ogan worse, so I appealed to the boy to allow me to accompany him. Despite the unreasonableness of the request, he accepted without hesitation. I dealt with my emerging sense of unease by repelling it like a bothersome fly. This time Andronicus did not keep us waiting after we knocked on his door. Shuffling his feet forwards, he opened the door in a somewhat jaded and significantly less sinister manner than before. I even discerned a hint of humanity in his demeanour. The tension his body once borne with great flamboyance seemed to have eased.

His tone was croaky, "Has Manuel contacted you yet?"

"No."

"Are you sure you communicated my situation to him in an explicit manner?"

Ogan held his hands loosely behind his back, and said, "Most certain."

Andronicus gave a small, tight smile, and produced a sealed scroll.

"My cousin shall avenge me for this scandal in a way befitting an Emperor. However, he first must establish himself, for he is new and must get acquainted with state matters. Do not be enthused nor get disillusioned in the face of this ostensible indifference. He will save me from you villains." With the briefest of glances towards Ogan, he added, "Please dispatch my letter to the palace."

Ogan, in a manner studiedly indifferent, replied. "Sure. Anything else?"

"Well, I don't suppose you would deliver me some wine, would you?" Slightly raising an eyebrow as he looked towards me, he said: "Or perhaps a tender companion?"

Ogan's skin flushed, his lips flattened. "I brought this on myself," I thought.

Coldly, Ogan said, "I can provide you with wine, but I do not trust you will behave yourself, so I err towards not doing it. You can have fermented mare's milk instead - if you'd like? Much healthier, and slightly inebriating too."

Andronicus grinned a terse little smirk. "No, thanks. Didn't you pledge to treat me decently? Only savages can drink that horse piss." He rolled his eyes and began quoting from the Bible:

"'For there are eunuchs who were born that way, and there are eunuchs who have been made eunuchs by others – and there are those who choose to live like eunuchs.' (Mathew 19:12) … So, what about this matter?"

Ogan went red. I sighed at the boy's facial expressions as he rebuffed Andronicus, my gaze fixed on his pink mouth as his mesmerizing, deep voice boomed.

"Abstinence accords tremendous strength on the body, Andronicus. It also sharpens the mind. I recommend you take cold baths and skip one or two meals a day, which would augment the effect."

Andronicus smirked wryly: "Once castrated, a rooster becomes a capon – becoming more docile, fatter, a better bird for eating. You shall pay for my canonisation. And, as I've said before," he continued with a frown, "Your advice is most welcome; however, I'd rather not be starved on top of everything else."

"Forsooth, cherish the continence, Andronicus," Ogan urged, evidently sincerely. "Your memory's retentive power will expand, and you will be granted a magnetic quality. I deduce from your present situation that endowing yourself with these two virtues would be most beneficial when you return to Constantinople." And, indicating me with a tilt of his head, "We must leave now. Is there anything else?"

Andronicus rather forlornly rubbed the back of his neck and said, "Just make sure Manuel gets the letter soon."

We stepped out of his room and walked to the fountain. I sat on the green, stone basin, on whose rim a carved gilded hare was washing its chin. All of a sudden, he took off his shirt - spotless since his arrival as Anna had ensured - and plunged his head into the water. I looked aside at once, pretending to admire the cypress, elm and walnut trees scattered around the courtyard, and realised for the first time their robustness, vitality and beauty. In the middle of the fountain a bronze cylinder rose on which a perforated pinecone made of white stone was placed. Water spouted forth from the pinecone's seven orifices and fell over Ogan's velvety shoulders. Seven, a single number, neither divided nor dividing another single number; seven was a virgin like myself, and she too had no mother. Returning my glance to his muscular shoulders which had obviously felt harder forces than the piercing of my stare and the flow of the seven jets, I pondered, did my virginity sharpen my mind? If so, that sharpness was cutting right now. Did my chastity endow me with a magnetic quality? But how did that water work its way from the pinecone's seven holes to the basin and back again? Thus, it was no longer a virgin. I wanted to be the iron powders flooding onto the lodestone now, coating its every single cavity, pit, and pore, with no intellect of my own, in absolute oblivion. A vision of Basil's pale, bushy chest passed before my eyes – his fat belly and his thin arms… Grateful to his image for trying to spare me from an immature disclosure, I cast my eyes down, but even that act was a kind of admission, too, so I lifted my head again and stared directly into the sun, to salute him. For he too, with good reason, was struggling to draw my attention away from the boy. I looked at him so he might punish my eyes, make me blind.

My regained sight watched his fingers running through that long, luxuriant hair which turned a fawn colour when wet, and now my palms began to burn. I immersed them in water, water that produced bitterness too for it caressed him without cooling my hands.

Having regained his temper Ogan told me: "Theia, you shall not come to Andronicus anymore. I know you are curious about him, but…."

He pointed out the gilded hare statue: "Do you know that hares prefer climbing uphill rather than running downhill? And they do it faster."

Though surprised, I did not react. Without waiting for a reply he said, "Your curiosity about Andronicus by now should be sated, shouldn't it? Besides, I am afraid I will injure him physically."

A gleam seeped out of his slanting eyes, lines as though blackened by kohl. They brought black, shiny obsidian rocks to mind if one looked too long at them, a headache would strike their beholder, and if he glared back, their dazzle could cause blindness. I looked at the sun again, and when I turned to him, I was temporarily blinded. I attempted to reply, but my voice did not cooperate. When it finally returned, I asked:

"You'd hurt him for me?"

"For his being so shameless in the presence of a woman."

Disappointed, yet knowing it could not be otherwise, I forced myself to draw a deep breath and hold sway by attempting to provoke him: "Are you scared of not being able to control your anger?"

"Well, yes I am."

"So have you identified something new about yourself too?"

"Why not? Learning is infinite. Who am I to never be afraid of anything?"

"I don't know. I am the hare; you are the wolf."

"Wolves and hares fear in the same way."

I joked: "Still, you are overconfident. The man is hulking. I am not sure if you would be able to wound him. If you call your soldiers, that is something else of course."

He laughed. "You forget we barbarians master the fine art of combat before we learn to walk!"

I did not know if he knew anything about the lentils which famously quell carnal urges. We chuckled. I could not help blurting out brazenly:

"Giving Andronicus lentils would solve this problem for you. You don't need to overthink this."

He laughed but, as I had expected, did not pursue the lentil issue. I pressed on: "Shall we race?"

The kitchen was cacophonous when I got back. I pinched my cheeks to blush them. Ravenous with hunger, I quickly took a tear of Chios from my pocket and threw the enticing sap like resin which grows on the evergreen shrub in my mouth; it tasted woody, spicy and bitter, filling my eyes with tears, but of ecstasy not agony. When he arrived, I smiled. I smelled pine. I had won.

23

The dice of love are shouting and madness.

Sappho

I DREAMT of Pegasus. He lived in Donkey Paradise with Layla in a castle made of cucumbers. Layla is a cheeky black mule Pegasus is infatuated with. Their wall-hangings were carrot bunches, and the floor was coated with hay. Despite mules being infertile, Layla produced black-and-white striped colts, cachinnating, gamboling and frisking all around. I woke up when they nudged me with their noses; sadly, it was only Anna who was poking me.

"Theia, wake up. Rise and take command of the house."

"Why me, Anna? Why?"

She spoke by carefully controlling her tone though her glare had turned flinty, her characteristic manner when she had presumed conclusively that she was overwrought and overtaxed. Customarily, she would yell or bark out orders, and one could bargain with her; but, now, there was no point in negotiating for more time to sleep. I sat up in bed.

Touching her temple with her middle finger as if having a headache, she calmly said,

"I must go to the marketplace and get some fresh fish. These servants simply can't tell a trout from a carp; I've exhausted almost all non-pork alternatives to prepare for Ogan. There's a lot of work."

Immediately revived at the mention of his name, I jumped out of bed but checked my hurry for fear of her hawkish glare, making a poor parody of reluctance with yawns and stretches.

"Anna, couldn't it wait?"

"Come on Theia, the fresh ones will be sold out soon. I should get going."

"Fair enough, but I'll go, not you."

"What? Out of the question."

"I would like to go. It's not the first time, and you know very well that it won't be the last. Don't bother putting up a front. Besides, last time you begged me to go, remember? And I refused – now I agree. What's the difference between when I flee by stealth and what you're requiring now? You contradict yourself. And anyway, you woke me up. You need help, right?"

"Ah, Theia, because of you I shall burn in hell. Do not stare at Saracens and Turkomans. Do not chat with anyone, even if they understand Greek. Do you hear me, Theia?"

"Yes, yes…"

"Don't stare at vendors. I repeat, don't chat with anyone even if they understand Greek. Also buy some flat bread please, and soap too."

"Fine."

"Don't say anything to your father and do not dilly-dally."

I washed my face, and fetching a comb I parted my hair into two, coiling each end at the sides, and joined the crowd heading into the marketplace without putting on a head cover or a veil. I was welcomed by a nomad cheesemonger. Eyes wide and sparkling, greasy face shining, he let out an exclamation, cut a piece of cheese and extended it on a knife to me.

Each sporting a long, thin, black moustache akin to hyphens joining separate words that belong to one bigger word, an insignia uniting them in brotherhood, a mutual agreement and higher cognition, the nomads gave extravagant bows, prattling in Turkish, words that were probably just being used to praise their product. The monger's frenzy took, and I ate, and not in a reluctant fashion at all. The florid, robust wives hunkered down behind, scrubbing pans and bowls while their kids cavorted close by. Resembling black-headed magpies, both men and women displayed long, black hair, the blackest of all the blacks I had ever seen, so black that it became blue.

The nomad greeted a Roman soap-hawker who approached hauling a clinking and clacking box in haste. He stopped next to the cheese stand, puffing with his labour, and began to set up his merchandise, which consisted of ingredients to manufacture the soap: bottles of wine, pots of honey, oil and vinegar, and of course the essential ingredient, salt he had extracted from dried lake beds.

I summoned my attendant, indicating the stall to him, meaning he should instruct the seller to blend the crucial component with vinegar to take to Anna, and as he talked to the pedlar, the idea of demanding a salt, honey and oil concoction to place against the ghastly pores of my skin crossed my mind but I quickly silenced it. But although I promised Anna not to address anyone, I drew closer to the Roman and asked the whereabouts of Andreas the fishmonger. He scraped his hand through the air and said: "He is dead Ma'am."

"What?"

"He was killed by Turkish soldiers, Ma'am."

I could barely gasp the words: "How could this be? But why? And who?"

"They mistook him for who-knows-what and attacked him. But don't worry. He didn't suffer. He died at once." He opened his mouth to say something else but thought better of it.

I sat down on a bench and burst into tears that streamed down my face like the many heads of Hydra extending their long necks, first one, then the other, then all together, flowing and flowing. I cursed like a Constantinopolitan innkeeper too, wondering why every so often my womb insisted on migrating about my body these days, why the freewheeling octopus of hysteria captured my organs, especially the heart, and provoked these outbursts. The nomadic cheese-vendor uttered something to the women. One of them, with rasping breath, rushed to me with cool water. With her dry, cracked hands, she rapidly produced some white handkerchieves from her pocket, wetted them and placed them on my face.

An old, white-bearded Dervish, a wandering mendicant wearing a dirty woolen cloak, drew near. Taking my face in his hard, chapped hand he said, "This too shall pass, child."

And he turned his beady eyes to my servant. I blew my nose, an inadmissible act, and while wiping it, I called out to my servant. He took a Roman coin from our purse and gave it to the old man. Goggling at the generosity, the old man bowed with a hyperbolic gesture. So, we had just bought a spiritual lesson for one coin. But couldn't the Dervish reveal a little more in return for all that money? Perhaps tell me what would pass and how, for example? And also, what is happening to me? It's easy to be mystic when you give out such limited information, old man, when somebody else pays for your bread, but you didn't explain if you ever had to pass from tumult to tranquility and again from tranquility to tumult, pass and pass, indefinitely, did you? It isn't difficult to be unyielding like you are, old man, when you want nothing. Seeing your clothes, and worse yet sniffing your pungent odour, it is more than evident that you do not need anything in your existence. Happiness comes to you in small crumbs.

With great difficulty, I was able to stop weeping, but I continued to sob gently. I felt something tugging my dress from behind and turned. A Turkish girl, aged around six, fondled my cheek with her tiny hand, grabbed mine and put a minuscule white pearl in my palm. I lifted and fixated on it, realising it was a tooth she had just lost. Grinning and exposing a new gap in her smile, she pulled me toward her mother who smiled and saluted me in Turkish as I held out the tooth to her; she took it and settled it into a loaf of bread, speaking to me more. I looked at the nomad man questioningly. He said his wife would throw the bread to the crows and the kid would sing a song requesting an iron tooth from the bird to replace the one that had fallen. Unfastening our case, I gave the girl a golden coin.

I arrived home sulking. Anna met me at the door. I gave her the cleanser and told her, "There was no fish Anna, and I forgot the bread."

Her mouth half-open, she gawped at me; not waiting for a reply, I got away from her and went to the garden, where I came nose to nose with Ogan, and instantly exclaimed:

"Why, Ogan?"

"Pardon?"

"Why did you murder the fishmonger?"

"Who?"

"Andreas the fishmonger."

I could only stare at him. Eventually he shook his head. "I don't know who that is, but I swear to God, I did not kill him, Theia."

"God only knows which God you are swearing to."

His breath hitched. "What do you mean?"

"It's become a bit crowded with Gods here currently. Think about the populous Olympian Gods, where are they now? There are those who kill for their God, there are others who get killed for their God. Then there are others who trade their God for profit, and interest and power. Sound familiar?"

"I assure you…"

I interrupted him. "You have your God, and you have all your flying animals, the Sky God too. So, which God do you swear to?" I glowered at him. "The one your father traded for power?"

Standing slightly straighter, he replied: "I have never killed anybody in my life!"

"Well, somebody did!" I felt my voice rise. "Tell me, do they massacre in the name of your God? Or do they think they are martyring themselves for God? Where is their God? In fact, where is God?"

He looked at the floor. With a sigh he looked at me again. "I don't know. But I know evil is needed for the good to exist. I cannot change that. This is the way this universe is designed. This is the principle."

"They killed an innocent fish-seller! His Lordship cannot eat fish today!"

"I don't care about fish!"

"No, you don't."

"But…"

I strode away and withdrew to my room. Did the beady-eyed Dervish know the truth? If I found and paid him, would he be able to tell me why I had been so despicable to the boy? And was there a cure for this pang of conscience intermingled with a sense of satisfaction from which I was suffering from now? The Dervish perhaps had the answers, but would he give them only if his stomach agreed? After all, stomachs didn't care about truths; they wanted food, just like bodies wanted to be caressed, and wombs to reproduce. We needed refreshing air, cold water, a toothsome apple, and fatty pork – or lamb in their case. What was transcendent about all those, the stomach, the womb, the apple and the lamb? What had I done now? And what would I do next?

24

Pray for things possible.

Oracle of Delphi

On Sunday, Basil, accustomed to my usual reluctance, was surprised to find I was keen on going to church. At times, if life had been tedious the previous week, the buzz and chanting were pleasing – though most of the time I was bored, wishing I could stay in bed. Whichever the case, two things were certain: I never prayed for anything, for I did not know what to demand, and I never thought my deeds were bad enough to repent for even when the feedback from others told me otherwise.

Once there, we walked up to the front, kissed the iconostasis, and lit candles as the liturgy began. When the hymns commenced, my spirits rose, and my heart filled with joy.

"Mark 11:24: 'Whatever you ask for in prayer, believe that you have received it, and it will be yours.'"

Delicately holding my thumb and two fingers together and pressing the last two down to my palm and pushing my hand from right to left in a careful manner, I made a sanguine, slow, diligent cross, one that was very different from previous perfunctory, sloppy ones. So, I prayed: "Please let the boy be mine!"

Recoiling at the directness of my wish, lest God notice my crassness, I told him in embarrassment: "I am so sorry that I am here now in utmost appreciation of your Divinity for my own ends. Please forgive me." Then I thanked him for he had vouchsafed me with something I had never beseeched. I prayed.

The house was quiet when we came back home. Basil plonked himself down in the chair. Anna came with a plate of cherries, the first harvest of the year, firm and deep red. Basil prompted Anna to call for Ogan so he too could taste them. I did not have the heart to face any hint of aloofness or possible indifference from his side, so I left the parlour in haste and took my position at my peephole. Walking briskly, his shoulders appearing wider than usual, Ogan entered and sat, straight, his legs slightly apart. At ease and well-rested, he leaned forward and took one cherry each time Basil passed the plate to him. The droll line appeared again on his face and a warm stream of balm flew from my throat to my belly first, and then surged towards my arms and legs. I looked at that mouth, O of Omicron; O of orphan, round and tiny, kissed by a virgin nibbling a cherry, and if it kissed you back, a disc of blush would be left behind… All I had to do was take a few steps to the parlour, take that head and press it against my breast, yet the distance between us seemed impassable; my little window on the world, which I deemed infinite, became a tiny hole again, dwindling away.

I sat on the floor.

Ogan…

If there was a song sung with O's of all the Oracles ever spoken, O's of all the Odes ever written, and I whispered it in your ear, would you whisper back to me? Did you see how two tiny O's made love and gave birth to Omega? Did you hear how the Great Sage revealed: "God is a circle whose centre is everywhere and whose circumference is nowhere"?

25

It suffices to hang bells from one's penis, fetter feet with chains or hang ropes around one's neck to be honoured in Constantinople!

John Tzetzes,
Letter addressed to a sausage maker in Philippopolis

One of Nikephoros's slaves entered the courtyard, followed, at a distance, by his master. The man walked next to a mule carrying a wooden box. They halted and stood aside till Nike alighted from his horse in slow motion, his limbs straining as if toting a heavy load. He shuffled towards me with what seemed to be great effort. Depleted of energy, he saluted me with one word that sounded like the last of a finished speech – flat and final:

"Theia."

"Nike?"

"I brought the book back."

His grey eyes darted about, his thin lips curled, and, without intonation, he said:

"I see you are on the go again?"

It was a threadbare question, perhaps even mean-spirited to a slight degree as it feigned heedlessness. I saw he pretended not to expect an answer but, being gloomier than him, I had no wish to stress him by mocking his clumsy ways.

"Is the barbarian here?"

"Not at this present moment. You cannot pass by as you please, coming here unannounced and arbitrarily; it is not done. Practice what you preach. And yes, I will collect money from a sick merchant which happens to be none of your business."

His slouched posture and inert voice disappeared at once; he now stood erect, though he answered in a huff:

"Don't you think your father should go instead?"

Annoyed, I said: "He's not here. Why did you come back from Constantinople, Nike?"

Surprised, his shoulders dropped again. "They are not for me, the intrigues of the Establishment. I do not know how to play games."

"You never did."

Blushing, he averted his gaze.

Embarrassed, I added, "Sorry…"

But I resumed quickly: "I assume your lack of talent in the Latin language played a role too? After all, without having a good command of Latin, you can't possibly go that far there."

"Yes. I never managed to learn the language. I still can't speak a word. But even if I could, I wouldn't be able to survive there. We may learn the language, but we are not like the Latins. Hierarchy and fealty do not hold the same importance to us – more's the pity." He clasped his hands behind his back like a scholar lecturing a disciple on his specialized subject.

"Anyone can assume any duty there, whether of noble blood or not, wealthy or not. There's no hesitation in turning an ally into an enemy from today to tomorrow." His tone was bitter now. "Surreptitious scheming outweighs merit in Constantinople. Sycophancy and puppetry override hard work. Fidelity is nearly impossible to find in that place. To take office there, one is obliged to be involved in double-dealing plots; nothing happens without them. I would never make it through."

"Well, I felt similarly at the Bride Show. But I am female. I may be feeble. That said, your escape, well, I did think it was rather cowardly: one does not go to Constantinople to be faithful to whatever or whoever. But now that you are telling me all this, it's a good virtue that you know yourself. It is a strength and…" I paused.

"I admire your attachment to loyalty in life," I said.

Though he was evidently irked by my appraisal of him I continued: "Anyway, tell me, wasn't there anything interesting you experienced or learned there?"

"Yes, in all my studies, not one teacher could complain of my truancy. I am pleased I studied, and not everyone I met wielded influence behind the scenes within political circles. Prodromos for example is a person I am grateful I had the chance to get acquainted with. He's much older than me, but he became a friend."

"Oh? And who is this Prodromos?"

"Theodore Prodromos. He is an avant-garde writer. He is penning a romance called 'Rhodante and Dosikles'."

"Who would this pair be?" I tried not to smirk.

"Imaginary characters. Dosikles falls in love with Rhodante. He abducts her with the help of his friends, then happily finds out she too is in love with him. So, the story transforms into a mutually agreed elopement, a love story rather than that of a kidnap."

"What about the girl's family?"

"She is engaged to someone else. Her father would not approve of Dosikles, anyway."

"What happens next?"

"Prodromos is still busy writing it. The couple will come upon many adventures."

"What sort?"

"Well, they will go to a feast together, Theodore told me that much."

"Oh, but you would consider it permissible to portray a woman, not to mention she is not even married, daring to go to a banquet with her love interest?"

"Rhodante will feel uncomfortable, but Dosikles will convince her. The Mistress of the house where the banquet will be given asks for Rhodante's presence, so she joins men and other female relatives and dines with them."

"Ah, but that's unheard of!"

Stiffening his scrawny neck and with a slight smugness, as if he knew something secret, Nike replied:

"I told you Prodromos is an avant-garde artist! In his own words: there will be flights and wanderings, tempests and billows and brigands… and, erm… grievous eddies, sorrows that give rise to love. There will also be chains and indissoluble fetters, he said, and imprisonments in gloomy dungeons, grim sacrifices and bitter grief and…"

"But Nike," I interrupted, "you don't like people who are on the go like that. Why so ecstatic and in awe now? This Prodromos sounds far too innovative for you."

He lurched a step backwards as if wanting to run away and then froze.

I continued: "Ah, calm yourself. I trust the church will protest about your author friend. How does he earn his keep by composing such obscenities anyway?"

Opening those pinched lips, with a voice once more devoid of emotion, he said, "He's living off influential benefactors."

Poetry was not storytelling. Poetry was worse than curiosity – my ailment. Even more juvenile, more embarrassing. Poetry was a contrived arrangement of emotions and miracles at odds with the values of dignity, solemnity, and Godly passivity. I well-nigh pitied Gabras for having such a foolish boy as a son. It sounded like writing meant to flaunt one's superior education – to display, to impress, to please others with overly polished words, with false fervour, and flattery aimed at those Constantinopolitan patrons.

"Those patrons must be open-minded people then. I doubt if anyone will ever take Rhodante seriously. What else will happen?"

"I think it will end well but they will have suffered by that time." With a grim twist to his mouth and an unfocused stare in his eyes he added, "Don't you think it funny that sometimes love is present but is hindered by external handicaps. Hence sometimes union is impossible, or…"

"Or holy matrimony is permitted but there is no love!"

A flicker of reaction in his eyes, then: "Yes."

"Or the girl does not love the boy back." Glancing at me before looking away again, he clamped his hand over his mouth. He blushed.

I resumed: "I am sorry Nike, ours is a different situation. The one of your Rhodante and Dosikles isn't officially written yet, but nowhere could people possibly imagine a woman like Rhodante here in the countryside, even if they were shown in fiction. You seem to be in awe of this Rhodante," I gestured as though she were standing beside him, "but in our story, the young man's mother possesses a less vivid imagination, she neither needs nor wants them. With or without literature or the new fashions of moral conduct, she is strictly against this girl; so there it is, our hero has a second handicap as bad as the first one!"

Nike's features were fixed, glum.

"Besides," I went on, "our young man may be impressed by the progressiveness of a popular poet from the capital, but he will never stomach someone like Rhodante as a wife, though he does not realise it. I am sorry Nike. You should not entertain false hopes."

His shoulders slumped and he gazed downwards.

"I know," he murmured. "I've always known."

"These new literary vogues this friend Prodromos dares to pioneer in Constantinople will be temporary fads and they'll be punished by the authorities and if not, by God. Whoever is in charge of writings will have him scourged and…" I drew a deep breath. "Now, I should be going. If you would like to return the book, your slave must find Anna. He must handle it with high caution."

He gave a forced, lopsided smile. "He surely will."

"And, Nike?"

"Yes?"

"This too shall pass!"

26

Human affairs look like a circle, a turning wheel,
and no-one's happiness lasts for long.

Herodotus, *The History*

THE household was awakened at dawn by shouting and the clatter of horses. The domestics rushed to the gates as Turkoman horsemen rode in, swift and intent, seeking Ogan. He arrived almost at once, entering in haste and rendering messengers unnecessary. It was clear that something had befallen him, for, gasping, he put his hand on his chest. Basil understood what the men reported and looked rather dazed. I turned to Ogan and exclaimed: "What is wrong? Is your father dead?"

"No, my wife! She fell very ill. She is expecting."

One would think a pang would benumb the brain, but it did not happen. On the contrary, when he hurried upstairs to pack, a flash of thoughts, incompatible with the situation, sprang to my mind. The Oracle of Delphi sat on a high tripod stool on a cleft which emitted fumes, and by inhaling those she slid into a state where her spirit spoke prophecies. My premonition must have come at the marketplace the other day: my vapour was the trenchant, garlicky, salty odour of cheese and sweat, the tears had already been shed earlier, there were no more now. A part of us, a portion of our own mind which we don't know very well, always knows better. I was the sibyl of sibyls, an Oracle of flatulence, caustic miasma! So, what were the "things possible" mentioned by the Oracle, so we could pray for them? The mystery surrounding those Dervishes, our absolute acquiescence to this life's iniquities, maturity with its bag filled with excrement, the awe and the resignation, the apple tree, the onyx eyes and the blond hair, and everything else – every object, every person and their flesh, and their spoken and unspoken words – everything could all burn in Hell while this crescent-shaped Turkish dagger was stabbing me. One only had to wait for it to be pulled out, while it portended it would hurt forever more, drawn out slowly, as if preparing meat for a casserole. Just wait and see.

The Turkomans loaded the horses, Ogan bowed and thanked us in haste, and they whisked him off apace, leaving a dust cloud behind.

I retired back to bed. Nightmares showed mercy, or they must have been afraid of scaring me. He was gone. He had always been gone. Later, I sneaked into his room and buried my face in his bolster and inhaled the sweet, pink-white scent that lingered – the scent of his wife ingrained in him as he drifted off to sleep thinking of her, while I was waking to a permanent nightmare, one who was far less merciful than her nocturnal sisters. I had to resist the itch to steal the linen for fear that Anna would notice it. I scuttled back to my room and stayed in bed all day long, pretending to be unwell. God recognised the claim this time. My fever climbed, and waves of heat and cold washed over me. Only one dream stuck in my mind from these three days: my hare fled my body, travelled below ground, searching for the wolf who was nowhere to be seen. It returned, re-entering my head, and I recovered. However, I stayed in bed.

Anna brought food in the morning. She put the tray on a table and approached.

"Didn't you know, Theia?"

"Know what?"

"That he had a woman?"

"No… Why didn't you tell me? You could have saved me the shock at his departure."

"The boy is 18 years old Theia. I thought you knew from your usual eavesdropping, snooping… and still…"

"And still… Despite, you mean… Typical of me, you thought, didn't you? Yes, such foolishness… No, Anna. I never overheard anything about his wife; perhaps the Demiurge made sure I didn't so that he would have more fun with me now."

"Who?"

"Forget about it! She's not pregnant with their first child, is she?"

"No. They already have a toddler."

"What is its sex?"

"A daughter."

So, it is. Ogan had a girl made of his own flesh. She must revere him.

"When did you… notice… first?"

She sighed. "The second you set your eyes on him…"

"Well, obviously you have a higher understanding than I gave you credit for. I only wish you'd saved me from – I mean, from falling off the donkey like this. I didn't even realise it myself. It took time; I resisted it at first, and… after all, he is a barbarian, isn't he? All the more so for not telling me he's married."

"Maybe you didn't ask?"

"No, I didn't, I thought pestering guests with questions was rude… But don't you worry Anna, I'll be fine."

She patted my head.

"I am certain."

She patted my head again and left. The next visitor was Basil. He caressed my head and asked, "How are you, my Angel?"

Oh, God. What does one say? "Thank you, much better."

"I've heard Ogan's reached the summer pasture. They're camping in the highlands during summer. It is such a pity his wife is not doing well, she may have lost the baby."

"Yes," I made myself say. "A pity indeed… What is she?"

"Daughter of another Turkoman chief."

"What's her name?"

"They call her Alma. It means Apple."

Oh, that's how it was: with Alma's permission, Ogan was taking bites. Her spiritual element was penetrating into his and his into hers. The blend was breeding and continuing to breed. I lived in a garden, quite literally, but they – they lived in the Garden of Eden! – I realised I had just shouted it.

"What?" He looked with puzzlement at me.

"Nothing, Father."

The image of a rotten apple with worms crossed my mind for a second. I glanced at Christ Pantocrator but turned my eyes away from him instantly. This moment was not fitting for his stern gaze.

"And, Father…"

"Yes?"

"Have you ever seen her?"

"No."

"Father…"

"Yes?"

"You should not call me "Angel." I am not."

With a sour taste in my mouth, I reached for the silver hare bottle, the perfume I'd never had the heart to waste before. I pressed the tiny fountain, but nothing came out of it: he'd never had it filled. I threw a cloth over the icon and headed towards the door, then hurried back to lift the cloth – avoiding Christ's gaze – before leaving the room.

27

It is a general rule... that every living thing is to nothing so devoted as to its own interest.

Epictetus, *The Enchiridion & The Discourses*

A MERCHANT heralded that a sand scientist had arrived at the inn. Reading the future, the scientist saw prosperity, good health and a comely bride in the merchant's fate, his wife would give birth to three sons, and they too would prosper. After he left, I bid a servant take my horse and ride there as quickly as possible, book a séance with the fortune teller and not come back unless a date and time were fixed. The domestic appeared rather late in the evening for he had had to wait for the clairvoyant at the inn, but he had managed to schedule a meeting for me, to take place in two days. Since Ogan's departure, it was the first time in days I did not toss and turn in bed only to succumb to a dark, death-like sleep at dawn. While waiting for the diviners, I woke up early in the mornings, counted money as merchants came by, supervised the loading of mules and went to bed sooner than usual in the evenings. Aware of the improvement in my daily program, Anna did not object when I took a few servants and rode to the inn on the grand day. There was nobody around the courtyard who wore a turban with golden inscriptions as described. When I turned to leave, I came face-to-face with Andronicus, out for his routine pacing. In a fake tone of surprise, he exclaimed:

"Ah, the Fruit Lady is here! Are you here for me?" Grinning: "Come into your garden, my love; taste its finest fruits. You must learn the Song of Solomon."

The man's orange stare never failed to give me goose bumps. I recalled an Arab merchant who once told me, "Projecting arrogance onto an arrogant man is almsgiving." I never understood whether the alms in this saying were meant for the arrogant man himself or for others – but I had no intention of yielding to his audacity – purple blood or not.

"Far from it!" I responded, "my name is Theia, daughter of Basil Maleinus, Your Highness. My grandfather was Zeno Maleinus. The founder and main financier of this very monastery was my great grandfather, and as a rule I do not deliver fruit here in person unless there are special exceptions." I forced myself to fix my glare at his golden, burning auburn eyes. "Ignore the shivers," I said to myself. "Courage does not mean feeling no fear, but rather facing it. Look directly into his eyes; look and speak – speak boldly":

"Given that your presence here is not a remarkable incident, I have not brought any fruit this time."

Amused, he raised his eyebrows. Baring sharp, white canines, he grinned from ear to ear. "I see you are not accompanying your 'Sweet Barbarian'. Has he abandoned you?"

"He was here to keep an eye on you, not me. He left because his wife fell ill."

"Ah! What a tragedy! Do I discern an infatuation?" His look made me flinch.

"No, that's not true! I am not infatuated."

"No, you are not." The eyes still held me. "Have you fallen then, little lamb, a little in love maybe? Or is it just desire? Virgil puts it well: every man makes a God of his own longing. Is he your God now?"

"Absolutely not!"

He gave deep laughter from his belly and in a sing-song voice again cited the Song of Songs:

"Under the apple tree,
I aroused you;
There your mother conceived you.
There she who was in labour gave you birth.
Place me like a seal over your heart,
Like a seal on your arm;
For love is as strong as death,

Its jealousy as yielding as the grave.
It burns like blazing fire,
Like a mighty flame
Many waters cannot quench love,
Rivers cannot wash it away."

He looked pleased with himself. "This, Your Highness," I said, "was in bad taste."

"Oh, not at all." He smiled back at me. "We do not know better than Solomon, do we? Intriguing, isn't it? Your barbarian is one of us, but not quite one of us. Enticingly exotic, yet comfortably familiar, like the animals at the Palace… We keep lions, elephants, cheetahs, monkeys, you would be fascinated. Let me tell you a story."

I did not demur. He seemed used to that.

"Some hundred and seventy years ago, Otto the Great's envoy to Constantinople had been given a riding tour in the Imperial Park. Emperor Phokas questioned the arrogant emissary Liudprand whether Otto owned wild asses like he did. Liudprand vaunted with disdain, claiming his master owned all sorts of animals. Refusing to take his hat off in the presence of the Emperor, Liudprand himself was one big wild ass of course. They told him that Emperor Phokas would perhaps be persuaded to gift him a few wild asses to take to Otto, he sneered that the asses would bring Otto no small prestige, the animals had not impressed the man, he thought them nothing different from the ordinary donkeys he saw at home on the streets of Cremona. "Andronicus grinned lifting his chin up:

"Anyway… in the end the audacious bumpkin took something else home. Do you have any idea what?"

"No."

"Well, Phokas gave him goats to take back home in lieu of wild asses." He burst into laughter.

"I am not sure I get the point of your story."

He smirked. "Of course not."

"And I have not fallen, as you claim."

Andronicus clasped his chin.

"After all, what is love? But don't you worry. They can wed more than one woman, these barbarians, and divorce them whenever convenient. Their rules are for the benefit of men and Allah complies. It is a pity these practices are not legitimate – and therefore sin-free for us! You might make a good second wife, or a third? Maybe there are a bunch of ladies, like yourself, aspiring to the prospect? What number might you be?"

"None of this concerns you. Besides I've never seen a Turkoman with two wives. Still none of this concerns you."

"Tell me, is he more attractive than I am? I can satisfy you too."

Trying to remain composed, I almost succeeded: "You've got it all wrong, and you are so disrespectful!"

"Darling, you want more than to be respected. If that were a profound concern of yours, you would not be here now – you'd be confined to your house's women's quarters, wouldn't you? You are lacking what our respectable Church Fathers say is the most desirable attribute in a human being, more so in a woman, and that is a 'dearth of curiosity'. There is nothing that can immure you, apart from your own passion. You and I are cut from the same cloth, so I am trying to help you. I know you want to live. You're lucky to have found the right person to open your vistas. My name is Andronicus Komnenos."

"I do not need your succour. I know who you are. But what does it amount to here, where you are a prisoner of the Turks?"

He raised his eyebrows again and said: "There it is. You are inquisitive – my kind of woman! My name means a great deal everywhere, here and there. It was me they took hostage, not your father, right?"

"Nonsense! They will never kill my father, but they might kill you."

"Ah, don't be so sure! They can change their minds in a flash. Enemies become friends; friends become enemies. They could decide to incarcerate him tomorrow morning and subsequently welcome me to a banquet to feast upon tender lamb kebab on skewers accompanied by wine…"

Dumfounded at the prospect, I shouted: "No, they will not! We serve them well."

Shocked by my blunder, I put my hand on my mouth as he slapped his thighs: "Ah! that is what I am talking about. Do not serve the barbarians. Serve me!"

I trembled with dread and rage but showed only the latter to him: "You are outrageous!"

"I like watching you. You have ardour. You are beautiful! In Constantinople, you could fulfil your dreams, if only you would comply and please me here. Rural life is not becoming to you. Think about the life you could have there."

"I am not dreaming of anything."

Leaning in: "Ah, yes you are." I withdrew. He kept on looking steadily as I evaded his eyes. "We all do, but better to know what to dream for those dreams may come true. Don't miss what that skunk Liutprand missed. Do you know what it is?"

I huffed wearily: "I don't want to know"

"He needed those wild asses more than he knew for it is widely known both in Saracen lands and ours that staring into the eyes of a wild donkey guarantees healthy vision. Literally and figuratively of course."

"My vision is perfectly fine, thank you."

He crossed his arms.

"Domesticated donkeys cannot bestow this valuable characteristic, even though that might seem ironic. Only wild ones do, and they are found in Constantinople."

Looking at the sky, he paced back and forth:

"Despite the fact that I loathe Latins and wish to destroy the progeny of these thieves, I must admit they have some wise poets. Quintilian declared something important: "Vain hopes are like certain dreams of those who wake." As if noticing my presence for the first time, he turned:

"So, lambkin, be realistic and consider my offer. Take care of me and I shall take care of you. You will become an indispensable figure in the elite entourages of the capital or maybe even in the palace. Imagine the blue of the Bosphorus, the splendid breeze on the terraces, the company of civil friends instead of..." and he looked around dismissively, "tamed donkeys and barbarians!"

"I like donkeys!" I blurted out.

"Don't spurn what I'm offering you. I will prepare the appropriate machinations for you. I might even find you an elderly, noble husband, who knows?" The tiniest smile played on his lips. "I will ensure not only that he will never, ever touch you but that he will also be brainless enough to maintain that you are pure."

"I am pure! Why on earth should I want that?"

"At a certain stage of life, my dear, many women secretly regret having lived chaste lives, all the more so if they have had a chance not to. What I am proposing to you is worth its weight in gold. In your circumstances, and in light of your character, you'll probably end up a virgin in a convent in Constantinople. I am granting you a life that will not depend on your moral excellence and virtuousness." And now he was positively delighting in his own words: "You will be pure and safe like the Virgin who watches over Constantinople, but be stimulated, entertained and intrigued like the city she is shielding. You will be my Virgin and I shall be your capital!"

I almost recoiled: "What are you suggesting?"

He leered at me. "You are a headstrong, intrepid woman, too young yet to know what you need. I know what your type wants. By the time you know what you wanted all your life, you will be an old-fashioned banquet that has never been thrown, a temple where there had never been worshippers, a saint who had no disciples."

"Oh, stop, you scoundrel!"

He bowed his head, and sounded less playful when he spoke again: "One day, when your bloom fades, you will understand me, but by then it will be too late."

Sick in my stomach, I ran to the storeroom, not knowing which was stronger: fear of the future or disgust. I sat and tried to calm myself; after all, I had just insulted a Prince born in the purple room.

Divine Madness

(Theia Mania)

For Funda,
My Light.

Avenue Winston Churchill, 28/10
(B)1180 Uccle
www.ederneditions.com
info@ederneditions.com

1st edition

Layout and art direction: Jack Durieux
Cover llustration:
Pıtırak, Lutfiye Batukan

Printed by BOD (Germany)

Dépôt légal: D/2025/10.807/63

28

With humanity a word is an omen, you call a sneeze an omen, a meeting an omen, an unknown sound an omen, a slave or an ass an omen.

Aristophanes, *The Birds*

THE sand scientist, a short, squat man with legs like logs, scuffed his swollen, bare feet along the ground. He was followed closely by a mule from which hung his sandals, and behind the mule a rangy man I supposed was his assistant. I walked towards them, hoping Andronicus would not show up, and addressed them.

"Hello, sirs, I sent out word for this meeting. I imagine you remember? About a séance of divination?"

The scientist resembled a thick book with legs, for he wore Arabic inscriptions embroidered on long sash-like bands that draped even over the upper sleeves of his robe and his turban. The tall, scrawny man turned to his stout master and appeared to interpret my words from Greek into Arabic. Exposing chalk white teeth in a wide grin, in sharp contrast to his brown skin and black beard, the inscribed seer spoke in Arabic, which his helper translated:

"Yes, Miss, we were notified about your request. It will be one gold *hyperpyron*. Let us proceed."

Their mule carried something resembling a rectangular wooden embroidery frame, over which a thick fabric was stretched, and alongside it a bulky sack was seemingly filled with sand.

The acolyte unloaded the board, set it on the ground, then emptied the sack onto it and spread the sand smooth with a scraper.

Meanwhile the diviner, his eyes moving incessantly, recited Arabic words I took to be an incantation. Approaching the frame, he placed the tip of his middle finger of his right hand on the sand, and swiftly etched a number of furrows which appeared random. As the Greek continued his hymn, the Arab – his expression ecstatic – rolled his eyes and traced fresh jabs into the sand, creating ripples of varying lengths. Then, he wiped the lines away a pair at a time until only one or two remained. He repeated the ritual four times, ultimately producing a figure composed of four levels. His face betrayed nothing.

Though I trusted him, I sensed there was something wicked about him. He was not considerate with his helper either. Still, the dots and lines he conjured were all I had at that moment. Jesus, on my icon, had a friendly and fatherly glimmer in his eye, but he did not answer my questions. Even the beady-eyed, numinous Dervish had seemed more trustworthy than this sly diviner – but he gave too little information, always leaving too many blanks to fill in oneself. He was cheaper, yes, but one does not think about money when one is desperate in the way I was.

I could have given him the income of a whole season's apple harvest if only the man had told me something agreeable.

But he did not.

He pulled a wry face and said something to his assistant, who looked worried. Short of breath, he sat down. My heart was beating out of my chest – was this the terrible prognostication I feared? His assistant rushed over to him and opened the collar of his kaftan. Could it be something even worse than Ogan never coming back? Worse than the fact that he was married to another – and happily, at that? But what could be worse? Why did this man overreact so?

Impatient now, I exclaimed, "What does he see? Something terrible will befall me, won't it?"

The man ignored me and tended to his master who clutched the left side of his chest and began to vomit. Then he fainted, never to wake up again. Just like that. He was dead.

Perhaps it was the power of my curiosity about my foreordained fate, or my anger that it remained as obscure as ever. Perhaps it was the habit of seeing imminent or actual death now and then, or perhaps even the antipathetic appearance of the man who had just passed away. But witnessing this human tragedy did not affect me at all in that moment. I rather pitied the Greek, who looked utterly bewildered. Poor man. He had just lost the source of his income.

Burning with curiosity, I wanted to ask him if he could interpret the figures the Arab had drawn – but I saw that it would be inappropriate under the circumstances. Soon they would come to take the body, and my callousness would shock him. What those embroidered inscription bands on his clothes had meant would also remain a mystery, though illuminating the client about their meaning should have been part of the service. But one just can't expect value for money these days.

Still, I took some comfort in knowing that it was pity, not self-interest, that had prevailed in me. I was, after all, still a good and wholesome person. And in any case, the man likely couldn't read them either. I even refrained from asking for my money back, though it had been a considerable sum. His death, I suppose, was his windfall – an unexpected boon that found him. As for me, the mystery of my future was now even further shrouded in mystery.

On my way back, I pondered Andronicus. The geomancer's death had made the future feel even more distant and abstract. Most of Andronicus's remarks were preposterous – meant to frighten me, seduce me, or even insult me. But one thing he suggested did not square with the rest, and it greatly unsettled me: he had called me beautiful.

29

I know some doctors preaching to their patients self-restraint;
yet if they fail themselves, they do what they forbade.
It's different to be in pain and different to watch.

Philemon, *Fragment*

MATURED apples dangled across the path, wet like my pain – enticing, precisely how I imagined his wife Alma to be. So I saw fit to look at the quinces, twinkling against a grey background, and not the apples. Sopped by unabated rain, they evoked his golden hair and the walk we took together in the orchard.

If he had to come and go, I wished his arrival had occurred in winter and his departure in spring. But one must not cite too many *if-onlys*, or else the natural flow of things might be disturbed. It is wiser to leave fate to its own devices; in that way, it might forget us – and if the air is auspicious, what we yearn for might coincide with its wishes.

Because I had meddled in its business, fate's course ran counter to my desires. My prayers at the church were superfluous. One cannot fool God.

Now I was being punished for my audacity. I forced myself to sleep during the daytime and when I finally managed to drift off, I was glad to have a break from my own thoughts. However, the consequence was tormented hours of wakefulness at night, and dark hours only accentuate melancholy. I wanted to abandon this atrocious habit, but my system was perturbed, and so I began sleeping all the more by day.

One rainy day at noon, Anna woke me to say a beggar had come to the door. She offered him a few copper coins, but – asking for me – he refused to leave.

When I descended the stairs, I recognised the beady-eyed Dervish from the marketplace. He wore a three-layered skirt with three different hemlines and was wrapped in a cloak that once upon a time must have been white. He was thoroughly drenched, and an acrid stench of grime and wet wool drifted through the entrance.

Annoyed at being woken up, I stood at a distance, directing an enquiring stare at him. He greeted me and bowed in a showy manner, but before he could say a word, I did:

"No need old man, no need for a show. I have no desire to watch cups filling themselves now. I will give you what you want, but after that you should leave at once. No services are required from you."

I desperately probed around me in the hallway, searching for a gold coin. The idea of clambering to the upper floor to look for money felt too exhausting. However, enduring his unctuousness seemed even more of a burden, so I decided to bring not some paltry sum, but one gold *hyperpyron* from my money box in the office. That should do the trick of making him disappear quickly, I thought.

With a gentle smile and soft voice, he said, "I have no cups, child."

"What is it then?" I demanded, oblivious to his tone. "A turban that makes you invisible? A flute that brings the dead to life? Or a knife that slays man and beast at your command? Spare me please."

"None." Languid in movement, he lifted his palms above his head and sighed.

"Child, I am like fire. Vital and indigent, it shirks not from touch, but reduces all things to their constituents, seizing nothing for itself. Fire is poorer than water and wind..."

I broke in: "Wait here old man, I shall give you what you want."

His eyes looked up: "At this moment, you need my services more than ever, and they are worth more than a couple of copper coins!"

"I will bring you more than a few copper coins. Wait here."

"Halt, child!"

I turned, and he went on talking. "Whatever chagrin is pulling on your heart now will be replaced with higher graces. When you uproot the heartache, you will discover superior favours bestowed upon your soul."

I frowned. "I don't understand you. Agony? What makes you think I am in agony? Besides, it's none of your business."

"My child, sunshine all the time makes a desert. If all your wishes came true, you would never learn to develop the sense of hope. God would never cross your mind."

"Enough with these fulsome pearls of wisdom," I thought.

"I don't follow you, old man. However, no need to expound on whatever your issue is."

He lifted his wooden sceptre with three large knots on it and said,

"Your distress called me here. Whoever appears from the invisible realm out of the blue is a guest to be honoured and treated well."

"I am treating you well; I'll go to get your money now."

I attempted to leave, but he stepped forward, stopping just within arm's length.

"I am aware you are suffering, child."

I shrugged half-heartedly. "The remark you made in the marketplace was wrong. It didn't pass, it worsened."

"No, I was right. Change arises from the forceful and alternating interplay of opposites and that creates pain. We must suffer in order to learn. You were shedding blissful tears that day and now it is the contrary."

Astonished, I snapped at him to save face: "I am shedding no tears."

"Tears are God's benediction; they wash the dirt away. Where there is a river, there are also green grasses. Never be afraid of tears. God likes them."

"I know God derives pleasure from inflicting agony, but why? Why is God replete with contradictions? Doesn't He know what He wants himself?"

"Love, my child, is just a tool to reach the Holy Secret. Now you have an idea of what that secret might be. Before, you did not. You, and me, and the one you love, are all parts of a sacred mystery; now you are a step closer to God. The lover and the loved are God, they are one."

"Ha! He said the same about apples. And now he is back to his blessed apple. And tell me – how can we be 'one'? He is gone, for God's sake!"

"What you feel is only a foreshadowing of what you can feel for the Divine! You now have a taste of it."

"Well, I must tell you it is rather bitter."

"Real love, my child, has no rigour; it is not supposed to be loyal to one perishable body either. Don't mistake lust for love. Now you must look for the treasures in yourself, dig further, delve deeper beyond. There is another you hidden inside you."

"Sensuality is from God too. What you say makes no sense." I wasn't sure if I was arguing or exploring with him. "Is love divine or is it physical? Make up your mind."

"Desire is just a means to reproduce. Anything the body craves pulls you down; spirit is light, it flies."

"Why don't we procreate by flying then, Dervish Baba?"

"My child, reproduction is God's imitation of Himself in us, but He is grander."

"Oh, I've thought about that. But I couldn't work out why God should want it like that: to pursue grandness, we must be base? Really?"

"Whatever you want with all your heart and God does not bestow upon you is because either it is not good for you or because something greater will unfold." He paused and continued when I looked at him again. "Keep your faith. Relinquish desiring worldly things, strive for the virtues of the Divine World. When bad befalls us, it also is a product of his maturity. Stones and pearls lie together on the seabed. Emotions and worries are the spoils floating over the water. Know what you have learned."

"Ach, you are never clear, old man. What is love then? Am I not in love?"

"Love is a state of being and that is benevolence, occurring like any other urge of nature. There comes a time where the heart becomes too small to endure the 'perfection'; the God in us grows too immense to hold and we need to award a portion of it to someone else. That is love, wanting to give out a fragment of that elation, glee, and bliss to another." I looked away again. "Unfortunately, a recipient is needed to deliver this blessed present to, and sadly the grantee is never, ever as perfect as the feeling itself, and hardly ever merits this sacred and ideal present. It is like filling a bowl from a well, carrying it to the lakeside and feeding the lake with its water, drop by drop, with a spoon. Water back to water. I want you to give water back to water; only then, will you be carefree. Fall in love with God."

"And that is the very misfortune." I met his look, then turned away. "But enough for now. I shall fetch your money."

Not waiting for his reply, I ran upstairs, fetched some dry clothes for him, pushed my alloy *trachea* and copper *tetarteron* coins aside, and took a clean, shiny gold *hyperpyron* from the bottom of the box. Collecting bread from the kitchen, I put everything in a cotton case. When I handed him the pouch, he smiled and without opening it, said:

"Seventy-two of those can buy a slave. You are generous my child. I must come back several more times to deserve such a gift. A Dervish does not beg; a Dervish bestows life."

"Do not bother please. By all means you have deserved it. Do not worry about coming back."

He nodded elegantly and walked towards the door.

"It's still raining," I said. "Don't you want to wait in the barn until it stops?"

He indicated the sky with his finger and said: "If he sends rain, he intends to clean us from sin. We must wash ourselves then. Farewell child."

30

Disguising his looks so as to betray nothing in regard to the calamity.

Thucydides, *History of the Peloponnesian War*

THIRST woke me at night. My sleep, once deep, peaceful, and almost always uninterrupted, had transformed into the snooze of a hare: piecemeal and oversensitive to the faintest sounds: natural wood creaks, owls hooting from afar, even to the movements of my internal organs, whose existence I was not conscious of throughout the day. Strange pangs struck in the dark hours, alarming me with what I imagined were signs of a deadly malady. By morning they would vanish mysteriously, only to return the next night in a different part of my body.

I put on my slippers, opened the door, and stepped out. Shadows of trees flickered on the walls. Basil's door creaked and I could almost hear him whisper something. Rushing back to my room, I poked my head through the doorway and began to peer out. My reader might expect the ethereal being of a dainty angel to slink out of Basil's room, a delicate, heavenly silhouette sashaying away in the dead of the night, but this did not happen. Rather, a dazzling moonstone orb rolled out of it. The owl outside, who lost its own moon and wisdom, hooted. The pristine white of a pair of large buttocks and the fat layers of a broad back lit up the corridor. Blinded, the owl shrieked. The generously-formed apparition in the corridor reminded me of that legendary flower that glows at night. If any vegetal creation of God was ever bestowed with such faculty, I would imagine a melon rather than a flower within this context, for Anna was superfluous with flesh and one never knew if she would be sweet or bland, just like a melon, and her very figure here in front of my eyes, which she quickly half-enshrouded with a white sheet she had been tugging along, waddled clumsily downstairs.

I lurked behind her, tiptoeing, but halted at the stairs, hesitating about whether to go to the ground floor or back to my room. For fear of coming face-to-face with her or meeting a servant snoozing in front of the furnace, I slipped back to my room and threw myself into bed, trying to recall the scene, the image of her plentiful mass… a night flight conducted in stealth, Anna's familiar form, unable to glide through the corridor in elegance and harmony.

Basil's voice resounded in my ears.

Drowsy, my mind grew to be doubtful of the reality of the incident. Thirst could be the alibi, but it had faded in my half-awake state, and I fell into a dark, sticky sleep made from bitumen. Undisturbed in total oblivion, I came to life again only at noon.

At first, I was struck by a simple fact – not by the fury or disgust I would have expected from myself. Anna's amulet… was it an old one she had kept from the time when her husband was still alive, as she claimed, or was she aspiring to become pregnant by Basil? The second possibility caused my mind to return to its old habits of interaction when miserable: bitter and biting. But now, it felt better to embrace it rather than fight against it or feel guilty about it; now I could be *right* for once. She stood before her oven, and upon noticing my presence, uttered a small yelp. Against my usual habit I had not rushed to the hearth to ask for food and give her a good morning kiss but had sneaked up on her instead. It did not take her long to revert to her usual know-it-all posture and she even smiled at me affectionately and asked what I wanted to eat.

I gave a curt reply. "Now that Ogan is gone, I suppose I have little choice. So why ask?"

Agape, she said, "Not at all. You're lucky. I found goat's milk, so I prepared a honey rice pudding. I have fresh eggs so I can prepare you a *kaigana* and add vegetables or herbs to it. Would you like that?"

"Ah! You seem to be in a good mood today – dessert and an omelette! But no thanks, I'm not hungry."

Anna always balanced her stand-offishness, an innate indifference, with a measure of caring, a somewhat maternal amiability, the genuineness of which I never doubted. She shrugged her shoulders and withdrew to the hearth, saying, "Suit yourself."

I took a spoon and followed her. "Nonetheless I will taste the rice, now that you want to please the household so heartily."

Before dipping into her rice, I furtively scrutinized the amulet around her neck. It was of bronze and embellished with peony seeds.

I ate a spoonful of the confection. Tossing the spoon aside, I sneered.

"Nah. Basil might find your rice sweet, but I don't. Not at all. On the contrary, I think it's rather bland... Overcooked, and the milk is sour."

Her eyes darkened in astonishment; her face became reddish. I headed for the door as she folded her arms on her chest and exclaimed: "Where are you going?"

"None of your business."

I chose a few men as attendants and asked for my horse to be prepared and, to avoid attracting any attention, I tied up my hair and put on a veil. Lacking patience to send someone ahead to check whether my intended host was at home or not, I seized the chance, and we wended our way to the impoverished quarters of the town to visit Sophia, the woman who manufactured amulets. Fortunately, she was at home.

She opened the door and regarded me with a blank look. Behind her stood several rubicund children dressed in rags and tatters, their faces, arms, and legs grimy, feet black. One wiped his nose with the back of his forearm and green snot smeared his sleeve and face. Pleased with this gesture he smiled, lifting his forearm closer to see the work of art better, then stuck his tongue out and began to lick the mess on his cheeks. The one with one green and one brown eye that was born last year was walking now. Narrowing her quirky eyes she gave us a welcoming smile. My servant told Sophie we needed information about a particular amulet. She gestured me into her shack.

Attempting to pull their tails, some kids ran after two piglets that bustled about the rush-floored space. Wattle-and-daub walls were damp with stains. The stench of urine assailed my nose. Resisting the urge to flee I got straight to the subject:

"It is a round amulet, made of bronze with Peony seeds on it. What is it for?"

She did not seem to take umbrage at my directness and lack of grace. Turning to the kids, she shouted, "That's enough now!"

She spanked the eldest one and turned. "Ah, that one? That's an amulet I should have made for myself."

"What? You wanted more children?"

"Heaven forbid, no. But Leo never let me in peace. He was a potent man, needed to be satisfied sometimes three times a day. What could any amulet do?"

"I don't understand. I thought this type was used to assist getting pregnant."

"No, Madam. Are you trying to conceive? Do you want me to prepare one for you? I didn't know you were married. I had heard Madam Gabras did not find you eligible." She pinched her lips.

Outraged I bellowed at her: "No, I am not married! What on earth is Gabras saying about me?"

Her voice weakened. "Nothing My Lady, nothing. I've just…"

"That's enough already! Tell me about the amulet."

"The amulet is the womb. When the peony seeds are mixed with a mule's earwax and exposed, it acts as a contraceptive, whereas when the wax and the seeds are hidden it is to help with getting impregnated."

She ventured a small grin. "Do you want one with seeds displayed then?"

Sophia's great-grandmother, grandmother, and mother were all also amulet makers; in other words, this family had known the secrets, desires, fears and jealousies of the whole town since forever. They never used this treasure of information against anyone for their own interests. I am confident neither professional ethics nor fear of God were the reason; a certain opaqueness of mind perpetuated their virtuous practice which was transmitted from generation to generation: a head which stored an eternal variety of amulet recipes but knew nought of cunningness; these women were as stupid as lumber in life's other struggles.

Still, I stared at her threateningly. "Of course I do not want an amulet, you fool. You'd better keep this visit secret or…"

I threw her a few coins and left her putrid pigsty.

On the way back, my head felt like a casserole of boiling chickpeas: water frothed, foam raged, chickpeas rose, the lid lifted – and everything overflowed. Heat burned the empty pan, frying my brain. In an attempt to get pregnant by Basil, Anna would be appalling, but aiming to avoid pregnancy was worse.

31

An inapparent connection is stronger than an apparent one.

Heraclites, *Fragment*

I NEVER knew whether Basil's light-heartedness in the face of malaise was a calculated act of cunning or merely an awkward attempt to comfort me whenever I felt out of sorts. Either way, without fail, he would insist all was fine and swept whatever he considered dirt under the rug. And yet again, he greeted me in the barn with his usual joyful voice – perhaps slightly more spirited than usual. In response to this specific predilection of his, I mostly adopted his good humour because it was the easiest thing to do. I could not bring myself to let a suffering man suffer even more. Seeing me in better spirits, he would always rejoice in our reconciliation and our conversation would carry on in a joyous manner as if we were people who did not have a care in the world. Then he would slip back into his natural state of unmindfulness – where he felt the most at ease.

There were times I would remain grumpy and snap at him. In such cases, he would always make a second attempt, starting a never-ending prattle while ignoring my misery. In doing so, his spirits would improve even more, I would then recognise the hopelessness of the situation and finally surrender, feigning cheerfulness as I joined in the chit-chat.

Talking to Pegasus, my head inclined towards him, I noticed Basil but did not turn to look at him. Seeing me disregard his presence, Basil came closer.

"I have news!" he announced.

I turned my back to him and patted Pegasus. He walked around Pegasus and came into my sight: "Andronicus is leaving!"

An ox seemed to have sat cross-legged on my chest. I gasped for air; my legs weakened. I shouted, forgetting I was giving Basil the cold shoulder. "Why? Did the Emperor pay?"

"Not yet, he is going to Iconium. Sultan Mesud has called for him."

"I thought Ogan would take him there."

"I don't think so. He'll probably send somebody else to do it."

Tears filled my eyes. I turned away to hide them. They came to symbolise my stupidity and idiocy, and they hurt more than the disappointment. Somewhere in the back of my mind I had imagined Ogan returning without Madam Apple, and without intending to, through my wishful thinking, once again I had meddled in the business of the future, challenging what was predestined. Wasn't Andronicus' departure inevitable, eastwards, westwards or elsewhere? How could destiny engage a prince born in the Purple Room to serve my caprices? What was supposed to betide Madam Apple, anyway? I had never dared to wish her death straight out; the worst that I allowed myself to visit on her was injury or disability as had happened to the girl who broke her leg. Madam Apple was far away, and I shouldn't direct my ill thoughts towards her. Even though she was innocent, she had done something that hurt me far worse than smacking her lips while eating.

"When is he departing?"

"Soon, but I have other news."

Tired, I gawped at him as he told me: "Nike is getting married."

I kept silent. He repeated himself. "Did you hear me? Madam Gabras found a girl for Nike."

"Oh, really? So quickly?"

"Actually, Nike's aunt organises the pre-selections of the Bride shows."

"His aunt?"

"Yes, the lady who welcomed you in Constantinople. She is Madam Gabras' sister and she knows all the eligible girls. So…"

"Really? Her sister? Her real sister?"

"Yes."

"And yet…" I raised my voice: "When the village of Plekia where her sister resides sends a girl off to Constantinople for bride selections, she treats it like a mundanity – the fool can't even manage to pay attention to the name of that person. She was certain I came from Plokia, and that my name was Malalas not Maleinus. Madam Gabras must really be out of favour with that green monster in Constantinople."

"Watch your language please, Theia!"

I ignored him. "Or maybe the hag is just so immersed in her vanity that showing a tiny bit of hospitality to a hometown girl of her sister Madam Gabras was beyond her capacities… Anyway… so Nike is marrying a girl who was a candidate for the Imperial marriage? Who is she?"

"A fourteen-year-old from Cappadocia. The daughter of a Magistrate."

"Fourteen? Well, she must have already wisened up then – or should I say wizened? … How is it she wasn't taken before? Well… whatever…"

"There is one more thing, Theia."

I sighed. "I am not interested in chatting today, father, really."

"This is about you. Anna told me you left the house with some servants the other day and did not tell her where you were going. May I know your whereabouts please?"

"Ah. Now she is provoking you?"

"Nonsense. She always wishes you well. She thinks…"

I interrupted. "What does she think?"

"She thinks you could be the wife of Nike, if you didn't…"

"If I didn't…?"

"If you did not have these unusual habits. She means…"

"She would like me to leave the arena to her, that is what she means, so that she can become the official boss of the house." I realised I was glaring. "Talking about conventionality, I don't consider her to be in the right position to teach me proper manners… the rules of chastity and all, don't you think?"

"What do you mean? She always wants the best for you."

My voice boomed, "She's not my mother, is she?"

"Keep your voice down Theia. May I demand to know where you were yesterday?"

"I went to the market to find paper and the bookbinder."

"You should not do that. Ask me and I will get it for you."

"Trust me, I have no more reputation to lose. I told you I never wanted Nike or the others. I might choose myself a barbarian husband after all. Their ways are also odd, but it seems they're perfectly acceptable to you…"

Weary, he lowered his voice. "Theia, I shall give you this one piece of advice as a father and will never, ever extend any other than this one. I hope you will listen to it. Do not say whatever comes into your mind; life holds only calamities in store for such a person regardless of their age, sex, status, and wealth."

He left the room.

So, Basil, without 'saying' things, we can do whatever we fancy – like yourself. What makes the difference is transparency, then? This is good guidance, Basil. Here is a story from one of my marketplace adventures:

"They make the scavenger smell the best perfumes of the world and he finds them all repulsive. One day they make him sniff a carcass, and he says, 'Ah that is what I was looking for.'"

It is all relative, Basil, isn't it?

32

Blushing is the colour of virtue.

Diogenes of Sinope

MADAM Gabras made her entrance to the Sunday mass arm-in-arm with her new daughter-in-law. Piney, green, resinous, fresh perfume of terebinths had been wafting gently nearby, little-by-little. With her passage it somehow floated through the whole body of the church, medicine-citrus-peel like, and bitter. At once I ceased breathing. In that second, I decided to think heinous thoughts in the Lord's House, prepared to face the ramifications, ready to be cursed, acrid thoughts. Only later did I take notice of the new girl's exceptional height and slender build. As though attempting to lower herself down to her mother-in-law's stature, the girl arched her back. Bending like a young twig I thought, but she was not a fresh green offshoot; she was more a dried, stiff thorn straining herself to keep up with Gabras, a long, scrawny thorn. Gabras walked on the balls of her feet, peering around and simpering, her chest visibly heaving behind the golden spangles of her frock – a rich green, *clovis* green to be precise – identical to the one her sister wore in the capital, except that the pattern on Gabras's dalmatica was less common. Images of peahens and peachicks were sparsely aligned on Gabras's deep green frock. My Lady's dress in Constantinople, on the other hand, was embroidered with foliate medallions enclosing face-to-face panthers, arranged in solid, infrangible rows. Our Gabras's choice of asymmetrical, sprinkled peachick motifs may have seemed incidental – but only to naively well-intentioned birdbrains. This apparent randomness was either a thinly veiled attempt to present herself as a cheery, verdant, fresh spirit, or else it was intended to betoken her mother-hen-like qualities. The Village Ladies probably reckoned the latter. I, on the other hand, would not rise to the bait: I knew among all the motifs, that the lion stranglers would suit her best.

One of my merchants, a native of our own Plekia – "a ludicrous upstart" as Gabras would disparage him – explained to me that addorsed, identical lions or facing eagles were easier, thus cheaper to manufacture because the same animal motif was simply turned on the loom to produce a reverse image, whereas to weave dispersed, irregular motifs required no fewer than two draw-boys working in shifts, in addition to the weaver himself. Consequently, that bird gracing Gabras's dress, resembling Nike with its skinny throat and awkward posture, was pricey – triple the cost of her sister's in Constantinople. Not only were these fabrics valuable but also knowing where exactly to acquire them would not be obvious to our village ladies whose channels of communication were not as expansive as those of Gabras. Procuring skeleton relics to imitate Gabras was much easier for them and, while she revelled in being emulated, once again she was one step ahead. She also sported another fashion that conveyed a similar if not more arrogant message: tunics with griffin patterns. Griffin-patterned dresses were conventionally gifted by the Emperor. Thus, that figure was affirmed to be of the most noble and prestigious provenance, so representative that the Emperor never wore it himself, for no one was higher than him to be in a position to present him with this peculiarly designed fabric.

Gabras's case was odd. The year I was born, Constantine Gabras, the hereditary Governor of Trebizond, revolted against Emperor John the Beautiful – father of our new Emperor Manuel – and established a form of semi-independent rule in Trebizond. Constantine Gabras belonged to the same family as our Gabrases here in Plekia, to which that cumbersome Nike and his loathsome mother, Madam Gabras, also belonged.

Emperor John the Beautiful managed to bring the Gabrases to heel in the end, though there was never any indication that *our* Madam was in danger of falling out of his grace. The enmity between the Gabrases and the Imperial Komnenos family was so fierce that, when John's brother Isaac had to flee after plotting against him, the

Gabrases were the first to receive Isaac and his two sons before they made their way to the Turks of Germanic Mesopotamia.

One of those sons was our very own Andronicus. And yet, our Madam Gabras owned griffin-patterned dresses and never ceased to conceal her family's dark side – treachery, perfidy and other such dire and objectionable truths like holy-spear-stealing relatives and God only knew what else. With her family being kept under the imperial thumb, she either obtained the griffin fabrics from contrabandists or had connections with the most state-of-the art looms in the realm – ones unknown to our village ladies.

Today, she also sported a gigantic eye-shaped amulet, with a lapis-blue iris and a black pupil. To extinguish the gleam of jealousy emanating from brown eyes was easy, but the efflux of a beam exuding from a blue eye would draw envy upon her head; it could bring on poor health, and possibly even wreck her son's union. Thus, the airborne clash of blues, a battle in the cold to call for protection against the evil eye – the blue evil eye… my blue evil eye!

And today, Gabras's spleen opened wide, liberating black bile. It travelled first to her liver, that repository of abnormal substances – instead of housing rich, warm, deep-red blood it held a purulent, diluted liquid, pinkish-yellow, just enough to fill a small goblet and no more. Black fluid invaded the liver in no time, and from there it ascended to her heart, suffusing it, not with nourishment, but with murk instead. From there it mixed with the air the lungs had sent, and part went to her tissues, engendering a wonderful, vital new spirit in her, while another part travelled to her brain, invading its ventricles and setting the phlegm free.

Well… the new soul of Madam Gabras ran now, a pneuma that would never be digested but would surge! It would flow down to her gall bladder and finish off the yellow bile there. Three humours intertwined within her, fighting for their dear lives, like vipers coil around a pole. But not the healing, medicinal staff with those non-venomous snakes that could be found slithering freely on the floors of ancient hospitals, or healing temples – not those non-venomous Aesculapian snakes. These were more like the snakes of the Serpent Column.

Black bile itself could destroy; it could poison even the poisonous snakes; black bile was tantamount to leaving her cold and dry;

it would cause her life juice to run no more in her entrails; today all the humours struggled to operate at full power in Gabras.

Her proud, now arid womb which was once a dwelling to the perpetually drawling Nike, moved along side-by-side with the fresh uterus of the girl being primed to breed further languid Gabras offspring. I pitied the gangly girl for being obliged to put up with this puffing turkey for the rest of her life; no matter how much dowry she brought or how estimable her father was, Gabras would not even let her be tall in peace anymore. The bride-to-be's, for now, eagerly compliant docility would have to endure for a long time – a very long time – because the Doukas family, from which Madam Gabras hailed, always produced long-lived females, and the mother-in-law of this unfortunate girl would be no exception.

Besides, she would suffer chronic neck and back pain for the rest of her life. This woman would exploit to the fullest the power of her legal position as a widow in any matter concerning the family – be it the education of grandchildren or the administration of the estate. She would exercise ultimate authority, imparting no one the right to speak.

Even a diffident, unambitious widower – one who enjoyed great power and understood that life was far easier unfettered – would still wish to remarry. And many did. Their choices remained a mystery to me forever.

Also considering the size of the bronze amulet Gabras made her wear – on which Solomon was riding a horse lancing a spear into the eye of a supine demoness – it seemed to present a story of malice versus her good fortune: again, the evil eye, the blue evil eye, my blue evil eye!

The priest pronounced: "The envious do themselves much more harm than they do to those against whom they direct their envy. Aren't we afraid of making ourselves servants of a deadly demon and the enemies of a God who is good and free of all envy?"

Madam Gabras, manipulating the priest, was foisting a magical practice onto the program of the church. Fortunately, the priest did not go as far as uttering incantations against the evil eye at her behest. But why didn't he distance himself from this old wives' tale? Instead, he told Gabras, "Because Christ's hand relieves pain, he will not fear the plans of demons, or the unlawful eye of man."

Since the afflictions and banes I had entreated upon them obviously had no effect, the two women took their places in the women's quarters. Nike was in the atrium conversing with some other men. They grinned playfully and patted his shoulders, normally so stooped but today straight. At ease, he walked towards the narthex with them. Instead of nodding at me as he usually would, he turned his head away as he passed. As was proper, the bishop and the crowd proceeded to the nave in solemn fashion while Nike's face beamed out of the group. Throughout the service he never looked at me. From time-to-time he lifted his head to look at the Virgin in the conch of the main apse as if he had never seen her before; lowering his head, he caught the eyes of his fiancée and grinned while the girl blushed. Preceding each stare at the girl, he would examine a different part of the church and at one point he spuriously knit his brow and gazed upon a youthful-looking Zeno who stared back with his prominent, contemptuous eyes and cracked a cheeky smile. My grandfather being the subsidiser of all this grandeur, one could say he was entitled to the audacity of having himself portrayed below Jesus. But being Zeno, he had another message in mind. The message was stronger than his benevolence and magnanimity, as writ in the intentionally scornful expression of his central icon. It told the good folk of Plekia: "this is my garden; you are all extras here." "Here" denoted the front of the icon, the church or village, or life or the universe – whatsoever only Zeno knew. Frescoes of saints decorated the lower walls of the nave which I suspected were not chosen in consultation with the priest but were arbitrarily Zeno's own fancy. They were Theophilus of Adana, who signed a pact with the Devil in his own blood renouncing Christ and the Virgin, to get his bishopric back which he had lost due to his own humility, and Nikon the Metanoeite who struggled to return recent converts of Islam back to Christianity, converts who had been corrupted "by time and long fellowship with the Saracens," to use his own words.

A year before he died, on the lower wall of the other side of the nave, directly opposite his own, Zeno had two new frescoes painted without any objection. An unfamiliar foreign saint, not completely tonsured but with a circle of hair remaining around his head, his gray beard slightly divided into two tufts, a round pallium on his shoulders, held a book in his left arm close to his torso. When we asked Zeno who he was, he said Saint Augustine, but he did not elaborate.

Next to him was a noble man wearing a red cap trimmed with fur and a golden cross on top. When asked about this one Zeno said, "Not a Saint, but certainly worthy of the honour; he is Prince Vladimir of Rus," and would elaborate no further. It would take me years, an encounter with a Russian, and another with a Latin merchant to find out who these irrelevant men were and what they had in common, and my finding would be the verification of our Bishop's mellifluence, his malleability, and his excessively hasty acquiescence to his benefactor. Both men were belated mellowers. The Russian was notorious for his cruelty in his younger life. He was devoutly Orthodox but had selected it as if selecting a piece of fruit in a marketplace; he went out shopping for his religion. Judaism and Islam had dietary restrictions and Latin Christians' churches and rituals were not as beautiful and glorious as the Haghia Sophia, and "so be it," he declared, "the Orthodox faith it is." Had he studied its truth and merits? I doubt it. The latter of the two stole pears from an orchard when he was young, not to mention leading a dissolute life with friends he called "young menlings" as well as with the opposite sex – he was, he apparently confessed, "a slave to lust." From among all the Saints, our Zeno had chosen reformers who did things to regret, not those who had innocuous pasts. Ironically, if someone had ever robbed Zeno's orchard, he would never ever have forgiven the felon, never. I knew this from experience.

Nike's glances continued wandering over the balustrade of the bema, the mosaics, the frescoes and wind-swept acanthus leaves of the column capitals, halting on his fiancée. When we began to hum the single note to accompany the chorus, his voice came out so strident and tremulous that, instead of enhancing the melody as purposed, he wrecked it into the chanson of a cheap Constantinopolitan slapstick. The priest glared at him at first and thereafter grimaced with indignation, but Nike took no notice. At the end of the mass the face of Nike's fiancée was so reddened that Gylou would never dare to disturb her.

The service ended and the crowd dispersed. I held back to spy on Nike and the women. Madam Gabras walked along the nave in the same fashion she had entered it: arm-in-arm with her daughter-in-law. Lingering, Nike held his hands loosely behind his back. A few men approached him and exchanged handshakes with both hands. He swaggered with them past me towards the exit, ignoring my presence again.

How little it took to transform from a reptile into a high-flying eagle. How readily that sickly, sallow, flesh bloomed with promises of caresses, no matter who promised them, and now that I was letting it rile me up, what was the difference between him and me, for my rage was not what this lowly lizard merited, it should have known better.

In the afternoon, I set forth for the monastery to talk to Andronicus. Avoiding Anna, I ordered a servant to tell my father that I was looking for a papyrus dealer who was lodging at the inn, and I departed there with three male servants.

Upon my return, I found him pacing up and down in the courtyard as I had expected. To my surprise this made me pity him, though I knew that would only last until he opened his mouth. When he noticed my entrance, he leered at me from afar but didn't approach. Astonished, I scurried towards him. Underwhelmed, he gave me a weary smile.

"I knew you would come," he mumbled.

"I heard you were leaving!"

"Does that concern you?" he asked.

"Who will take you to the Sultan?"

He put his hand on his forehead and guffawed. I looked at him quizzically.

"Ah! that is it," he exclaimed. "I don't know, little apple, if it will be your Sweet Barbarian or some other one assigned by Sultan Mesud. I am sad not to be able to help you in the way you'd like. I have been trying to explain to you how I *can* help you in other ways, but you're heedless to all my pleas."

"Did you just call me an apple?"

"Erm, yes."

"Why did you call me an apple?"

He let out a loud belly laugh and began to recite:

"I awakened you under the apple tree,
there where your mother conceived you,

there where she gave birth to you.
Set me like a seal on your heart,
like a seal on your arm.
For love is as strong as death.
The flash of it is a flash of fire,
a flame of Yahweh himself.
Love no flood can quench, no torrents drown."

Looking at me he added, "Do you know that the word for evil and apple is nearly the same in Latin? 'Malum' it is."

"Really?"

"Not for your barbarian though. They trust that the snake of Eden was good, and so was the apple; both of them opened humanity's eyes to reality, saving them from a fake heaven and sending them to this hell."

I rolled my eyes. "I wish we had stayed in that heaven, fake or not..."

Smiling, he said, "This can be discussed of course whether being kicked out of heaven was a good thing or not. But you are contradicting yourself. I've been offering you heaven and you've been consistently refusing it and now you say you would have been content to remain in another fake one?"

"Not so simple. There, we would never know what hell is, therefore heaven would not sweep us off our feet. With you, I would have to choose between hells not heavens.... I prefer my own hell to the one where you would eventually take me."

He gave a booming laugh and changed the subject:

"Anyway, I had a dream last night. There was a juicy apple before me. I tried to grab it, but it ran away. Finally, I got hold of it. I unsheathed my sword and made a tiny puncture in it with the tip of the blade. A crimson juice gushed out of it." His mouth looked vaguely indecent as he said it. "I drank it slowly. I wanted to cut open the puncture to get more, but a dagger with a recurving blade flew out – like the ones these barbarian foot soldiers use, fancy-looking but of poor quality, my dear..."

He saw me arch my eyebrows.

"...Anyway, it came flying and cut the apple into small pieces... Then a bunch of dogs came and ate the pieces."

"What a nonsensical dream."

"Dreams are never nonsensical. Have they never taught you their meanings?"

"There is a dream interpretation book at home. Ataman gave it to us."

"Of course, he does not care about dreams. He sends people to their dreams."

I giggled. "So, you know about their kams?"

"I made long wanderings in Turkish lands when I was a child. I'd like to think my father and my brother John were not fugitives but rather honourable guests at Mesud's court. A kam is a dream-catcher, girl. Didn't your barbarian catch your dreams? He probably is one, as far as I can tell. One can never be sure, but I noticed his forefinger…"

"I rarely have dreams."

"We dream every night, sweet girl. One of my dreams is to give a good punch on the nose to John Komnenos when I arrive at the palace of Sultan Mesud."

"Are you insane? John is dead!"

He smiled. "Not my uncle; Emperor John, silly. This is my brother John, his namesake, who betrayed the Romans and defected to the Turks on the battlefield. He even converted to Islam and married Mesud's daughter. I must have a half-Turkish nephew or niece, like your beloved Gasmule. You see? Life is full of surprises."

"Mesud would never let you punch him. When are you leaving?"

"I don't know. I could do worse things than punching. Poisoning? Remedies are inexhaustible."

"Have you just called me a sweet girl?"

"Yes."

"Why?"

"Well… because I find you so."

"You just say this because you have an interest, something perverse to gain from me."

"So? At least I'm making the effort. The world turns around *it*, doesn't it? What are you coveting that has to do with your Sweet Barbarian? Talk about astronomy? Homer? You are craving to execute it from the evening till dawn and from dawn till evening. What is the difference?"

Feeling bewildered, I yelled:

"No, I am not, and if I was, there would certainly be a difference."

"And that is?"

"…Love."

He gave a loud hoot of laughter. "My lamb, love is only shadow puppetry. Do you really think that the hell you'd create here for yourself if you had the chance to have him would be better than the one I offer you? You are already defiled. And what would the Virgin say if she heard that you fantasised about an infidel? Not even a Latin or an Armenian but a Barbarian to make it worse. Isn't everything relative?"

"Yes, true. Everything is relative. Have you ever heard the story of the scavenger and the perfumes?"

I narrated him the story. He smiled until the end without interrupting. After I finished, he stayed silent. Uncomfortable, I exclaimed:

"But let's put this story aside… Tell me, how am I sweet, then? Now that you claim to be making an effort. Go ahead."

He grinned. "Finally, you are starting to come round."

"All right, I am waiting. But don't be cheap. I am familiar with the latest literary trends of the capital. Anything trite will be noticed; do not underestimate me."

"Wait," he laughed, "I have been out of practice for some time!"

His face became serious. Coughing, he said: "You are… relatively beautiful!"

I laughed now. "I knew you would have to force…"

"No, really you are not bad. And, in any case, there are recipes for rejuvenating unguents and special perfumes at the Palace from the last century. They were jealously hidden by Empress Zoe. She obsessively concocted them by boiling cauldrons in her apartment."

"Empress Zoe?" I groaned at his mention of another of his obscure forebears.

"Upon seeing her, flatterers fell over as if thunderstruck, more by virtue of her unfurrowed, glowing white skin at the age of seventy than by virtue of her sovereignty. Now if that is not a treasure for a woman…"

"Why is it a treasure?" I was quick to curtail his wistful meander. "My father told me beauty is dangerous. Those comely Abasgian youths stolen from their parents to be castrated and sold as eunuchs, would they have been taken if they were unsightly? And then look at the character Rodanthe that this poet Prodromos I heard about is writing. She was captured by an evil pirate on account of her beauty. She was so splendid looking that the pirate lost his mind and wanted to sacrifice her to his Gods."

"Beauty my dear is the greatest asset of a human being, more so for a woman, naturally. Both in heaven and hell. Especially in hell. Zoe took Constantine Monomachos as her third husband." Ah. Back to the kin. "Why? Because he was a marvel of beauty. Another example is Basil the First. He won favours in the first place with his handsomeness, not his horsemanship as people believe. Emperor Michael took him into his service on the merits of his exceptional looks which, ironically, set in train his own murder, but that is another subject. Beauty is power to its bearer." Did I detect a slight self-satisfied shift of posture as he said this? "If we get back to Zoe again, she was the grandest alchemist in history, for beauty is gold. Braziers blazed in winter and summer in her apartment. Servants measured herbs, boiled mixtures of myrrh, mastic, frankincense, coal tar, saffron, musk, ambergris, cinnamon, and agalloch, my dear. It can all be yours. An exquisite woman will never end up ravenous, she will always be rich. It stirs affection in men, jealousy in women."

"Well…"

But he wasn't for listening at this point. "Look at Theodora…"

"Theodora of… centuries ago?" I groaned inwardly.

"Six centuries ago, to be exact. She came from the dregs of humankind, daughter of a bear-trainer and a dancer, an accidental magic fruit of canaille breeding, beautiful, witty, and charming. She worked at a brothel prior to becoming somebody's mistress for four years. As in your story," he made a generous gesture in my direction, "the somebody was just a scavenger; he did not appreciate her, but her qualities mesmerised the Emperor Justinian. Against all odds, he married her, and she became the Queen in the Queen of Cities."

He crossed his arms as I interrupted:

"Ha! That is not the convention anymore, those were the old days… I have been to the beauty contest; trust me the chances of becoming a queen in that city are as high as Pegasus turning into a Prince and proposing to me, which I must admit would be the best among all the alternatives." His small smile encouraged me. "I have seen the vicious women ready to eat a raw chicken to become the Augusta! They will not hesitate to scratch out the eyes of others…"

He waved his hand. "One must not conform to conventional ways. Theodora was anything but conventional. She co-ruled with the Emperor and had his ultimate trust. Sadly, a woman who is good-looking when examined from all angles is a rarity, rarer than people think. As rare as gold. Sometimes women, heedless of its worth, possess beauty and trade it for nothing. Just like those Zimbabweans. Do you know how we trade with them? Through Axumite merchants. They manufacture a breast-piece made of thorns and hang it somewhere in the jungle, placing pieces of dried cattle, iron and salt on it then going into hiding. Those black men, who have also taken cover, emerge and look at the goods. They leave a pebble of gold, which they own in abundance, on each item and withdraw. Then our men come out. If they are happy, they take the gold and leave the goods, if not they hide again without touching anything. The negroes come out again and this bargaining goes on for around five days. The parties never see each other face-to-face."

We both shifted as he drew breath to continue.

"A woman cannot trade her gold in this fashion, my dear. She should display it and make a demand for it directly, even open up bidding for it. Once it is sold, the buyer might naively believe it belongs to him exclusively, but the bidding should go on. Do you understand me? Unfortunately, nature is rather miserly in granting perfect beauty. But it has provided us with tricks which can be employed to enhance ordinary looks, which could come in handy for you at the contest. Which of my cousins did you compete for anyway?"

"I don't know."

"Lucky you, you've found me here. Not that you would escape my notice had you been chosen at the Brides show. Anyhow, you didn't miss anything, trust me: two of them are dead and the remaining two are total bores."

"A bore? Well, I heard that at the battle of Neocaesarea, Manuel, when he was a mere youngster, couched his lance and charged the Turks, and that as a consequence won his father's heart." Andronicus gave the smallest of nods. "The Emperor was furious when he noticed, though, and flogged him with a whip of willow twigs for having taken such a risk. But in view of this incident your uncle preferred him to his eldest brother, Isaac. Is that right? To me Manuel does not sound like a bore."

Andronicus pressed his lips into a white slash. He narrowed his eyes.

"All the more reason for his future wife to be obliged to show piety, to the point of sainthood, while he savours life's pleasures. Anyhow, they found the right woman. As tedious, austere, and demure in disposition as you could imagine."

"Who is she?"

"King Conrad III palmed his sister-in-law Bertha of Sulzbach off on Manuel last year. Unfortunately, we need to use the Germans against the Normans, as you may know. She is still waiting to marry him. She does not use eyeliner or powder, preferring nature's flush to rouge. That is of course the least of the problems she has."

"Oh? What is her bigger problem?"

"That she is from the yellow-haired nation, a German. Unbending and opinionated. You cannot be both in life my dear, you should be either like that and painted or not like that and plain. We are hitting the nail right on the head here: you are quite a different case."

I hoped I didn't look too curious. "How so?"

"Take my hints. Let us get back to Empress Zoe of the years of yore… Zoe knew beauty mattered the most and she employed her exceptional intelligence to serve vanity. You, Zoe and Anna all suffer the same malady."

"Anna?"

"Anna Komnenos, my aunt. She is as old as the mountains; she must be around sixty nowadays… In exile, all alone, in Kecharitomene. Contrary to the name of the monastery, she is anything but 'favoured'. Destiny must be cracking up playing jokes on her – what a finishing touch! You remind me of her. You are smart like her. There is only one difference between Anna and you. She knew what she wanted; you don't."

"Oh? And what did she want?"

"The throne. She even plotted the murder of her brother, Emperor John, so her husband could take his place, but John outmanoeuvred her plotting."

"Why would you compare me to an evil person like her? Is this the way you are to inveigle me? Evidently you are out of practice."

"The Emperor has forgiven her, hence John the Beautiful, as befits the name, a beautiful soul... Love of a sister won. I personally would never pardon her; I would have had her impaled. Thus, my willingness to help you."

He expected this to endear him to me? "I don't want your help. You want something from me, not vice versa."

"In the short term, yes. Your mind is acute, it might lead you to bite off something larger than you can chew. I would not wish such a calamity to befall you; you might not be as lucky as her. I might be your salvation in the long term."

I could feel my urge to resist his line of thought again. "And how will that be?"

"Brains and passion together are a disaster for a woman. The paramount tragedy with Anna is that her knowledge of medicine, history, literature, geography and mathematics is superior to that of any well-educated man in Constantinople. So, she is doomed."

"How?"

"She was a despondent enough woman when she was young."

"How do you know; how can you be so sure of all this?"

"Anna is a morosoph, a shrew, as most educated women are."

"I do not understand you."

"I mean she has the brains but not the common sense. She is unhappy. She has a husband she is not satisfied with. This type of woman thinks they want a feeble husband, but let me assure you, my dear, they don't; it turns against them after a while."

I was prepared to demur, but his chosen example matched the tenor of his rhetoric: "When she tried to have Emperor John murdered, she received no support from her husband, Bryennios, which led to the failure of her conspiracy. She was stuck, like a caged tiger – nobody taking her roars seriously, not her husband, not her brother. Do you want to be a maddened animal like her? She was like a barbarian raining arrows, but all of them missing their target. There was a time when Anna cursed God for giving her the 'opening' and her husband the 'protrusion'. I assume, because of that, she was not exactly most amiable during the communication between these two agencies, which she believed God had wrongly distributed. Do you want that?"

I felt my face blush. "Sorry, but what is the relevance of this crassness to our subject?"

"Oh, it's all relevant. I am telling you, a woman like yourself, insightful and ambitious, is doomed to be miserable. You need freedom but you also need protection, however paradoxical it may sound. Anna is confined to writing now, locked in a monastery. That is exactly what your type does in the end."

"What? Writing?"

"Yes, she is writing history. The very little history she lived through herself and more of other people's glory and achievements, namely my Grandfather Alexios's. She hates John, so she won't write anything nice about him. Would you want your history to be on paper only? Would you want your passion, your cravings to be reduced to mere letters and ink? Surrender to me and I will give it all to you." He seemed assured of the efficacy of his logic. "Forget about the barbarian; there is no chance there. Look at Anna, she believed the weakness of her husband would help her to take over the throne, but the opposite came true. This ilk of woman lives a pathetic life riddled with paradoxes. Anna even once said she wished her husband had been born with a hollow vagina instead of a male organ, for she thought him the biggest coward on earth."

"Scurrilous! I must leave, I cannot be subjected to this…"

"Wait. I have not finished yet. You must know, you would have a pitiful life with your barbarian too. What you find most attractive in him now would bother you later. I am offering you a clean, carefree life."

"You've no idea what you're talking about. Besides, you speak as if you have the Imperial power, but you don't!"

"It is the idea of the Emperor that is not challengeable, my dear, not the Emperor himself. Our system of usurpation has always been full of vitality, hence the success of us Romans. Emperors change, they die, and they get replaced."

"What are you up to?"

"All in good time, my dear. My concubines… They are happier than Anna, Zoe or you. That is, if you do not take heed of me. So was Theodora! Do you know the only thing in life which Theodora said she missed?"

"No, I don't."

"Another orifice!"

"Ah… What do you mean?"

"She said the God-given orifices in her body were not sufficient, more would be more satisfying."

I sensed my ears warming. "Outrageous! I must leave…"

"Wait! Do you know how I know my concubines are elated?"

"I don't want to know," I said.

"I'll tell you anyway. Because I give them my undivided attention when I make love to them; their limbs stream to me like I am a mercury puddle and they are drops which were distanced from me by misfortune; slowly but surely, they trickle towards the source to reunite therewith forever; to become a whole again, that is happiness… Come with me; come to my room now."

I knew he could see my reddened cheeks. "Ogan talked about the same thing, to become whole again with God, but after that he left me behind, to become whole again with something else. Anyway, fair enough, you did your utmost to convince me, but I must leave you now; they will wonder where I am soon."

He leered and said, "Ah, you must leave – not that you want to. I shall wonder where you are too, during the daytime, and I will go on wondering at nights; you shall be in my dreams… And, Theia!…"

I had scampered towards the exit gate of the courtyard. Perplexed by hearing him utter my name for the first time, I stopped.

"Does the amulet-maker write lead curse-tablets too?" he asked.

"No, why?"

"Why doesn't she?"

"I would imagine she does not know how to write, that is why."

He squinted, grinning, and put his hand on his chin. "So, she is good?"

I hesitated. "She isn't the sharpest tool in the drawer but one cannot say she is intentionally evil. Even if she could write, I doubt if she would jinx a scourge. But why?"

"So, she is poor?"

I took a calming breath. "Yes; why?"

"For you, my sweet."

"What?"

"Someday, sooner or later you will need an amulet to prevent fecundity. At least she won't gossip behind your back."

Before I could grasp what he meant, lose my temper and use foul language he turned his back and strutted back towards his room.

A few days later, Nike and the gangly girl got married at a ceremony performed at dusk. Because the girl hailed from Cappadocia and it was impossible for the groom to fetch the bride from her house, as custom dictated, Nike approached the Gabras mansion where the girl and her family sojourned with a jovial band of musicians and brought the wedding robe to her. As the bride descended, the buoyant relatives threw flowers and apples to the happy couple, and one giant apple ended up on Nike's head – not that I witnessed this incident, for I was not invited, but so I heard. Perhaps Nike knew, since I did, that the gangly girl had received as a gift nightgowns made of the famous (and infamous) transparent linen fabric from Constantinople, because the apple accident did not spoil his fine spirits or those of the group, who burst into laughter and made merry. There were two who remained unmoved, however – if not outright morose – on account of this droll occurrence: the gangly girl and Madam Gabras.

33

May men say, 'He is far greater than his father.'

Homer, *Iliad*

HOLDING an envelope to his chest, the new visitor, an emaciated man, entered with a faded smile as if wondering whether smiling was the right thing to do. Maintaining his grin, he held a letter out to me. When I took it, he stepped back and assumed an awkward posture, as though unsure what to do with his now-empty hands. I recognised Zeno's insignia instantly, and when I spotted the word *quince* in the letter, I quickly lifted my face to look at the man. He was caught off guard, no longer smiling that clumsy smile. His expression was brooding – his lips set in a hard line, brow furrowed. The resemblance of this expression to Grandfather Zeno's made my stomach somersault.

This was the once-chubby peasant to whom Zeno had bequeathed the harvest of a single quince tree – the same man who had appeared at the funeral with the same letter. His extreme loss of weight and dark expression made the resemblance uncanny. But he was someone else entirely when he smiled, even when faking it, because Zeno never did.

My hands trembling, I pretended to continue reading the detailed description of the tree. I already knew it, but the moment gave me time to think. When I set my gaze upon him again, a flush crept across his cheeks, his ears turned red, and his chin trembled as if he might start weeping. This shattered any resemblance to Zeno: Zeno never blushed, and his facial muscles only ever trembled to indicate fury, never embarrassment.

Though tattered, the man's tunic did not stink; his hair was not greasy, and he did not sweat. He tucked his thick, bruised hands behind his elbows, where the tunic's fabric was nearly worn through – and soon would be.

Quickly I calculated what I should give him had the yield been at its best, though it had not. We had quinces that year sufficient to cheer me against the bleak setting, but not plentiful, and far from enough to sell to buy a new tunic, let alone bread. Just as I had done with the Dervish, I went upstairs to fetch money, as opposed to offering him a few bruised quinces - nobody's favourite fruit anyway. Beautiful but burdensome, it tires your teeth, hurts your gums; it is sourish, hard, a fruit whose abundance in autumn portends biting, frigid winters. Basil liked quince marmalade made with honey, but Zeno used to eat it with salt and lemon juice on it, to the astonishment of everyone at home and in Plekia, for eating the fruit raw without a goblet of water was dangerous enough; if it did not stick in your throat and make you choke or die of suffocation, it would eventually induce a persistent hiccup, like an insistent mosquito, and even constipation to crown it all.

When I came back to the staircase landing, I saw Basil, who had just arrived, holding his newel cap with one hand and touching his throat with the other. He tipped his head to one side as if to see the man better, then shook it as if to say "no."

I called from upstairs: "Father, this is…"

He raised his hand to ward me off. Squeezing his eyes shut, he took the man by the arm and led him slowly to the parlour. I descended. Leaning my ear against the door as usual would be effortless and the possibility of Anna showing up was a matter of indifference to me, but I was disinclined to eavesdrop at that moment. Instead, Grandfather Zeno's dark, unwanted clothes occupied my mind. At that moment, Anna showed up. I ordered her to fetch the parcel of clothes and give them to the man when he left. Perking up her posture, eyes wide and blinking, she gazed at me.

"I didn't notice anyone coming. Who's in there?"

"I don't know who he is but I'm sure he's in dire need of those clothes and he won't reject them because I'm also certain that he didn't know Zeno – at least not in the way we all did. Some people are better when they're not known and it's also best not to know them, you know?"

"What does that mean?"

"I mean, sometimes the absence of a father is better than having a venomous one at home."

"Whose father?"

"The one that's not known. You can envision him to be good if he's away. You can freely imagine."

"Whose good father is poisoned?" she asked, looking baffled. "Is the visitor's father poisoned? What are you on about?"

"I don't know if that man's father was poisoned himself, but I know he poisoned others."

She slapped her hands on her cheeks: "What? Is he a murderer? What has this got to do with us?"

I laughed. "Not a murderer in a hurry, a slow contaminator perhaps… And yes, it has a lot to do with us."

Moving jerkily, clearly alarmed, she gasped, "Oh my God! Where is the killer? Where is he?"

"Not here," I said, and went back upstairs to put the money back in its place. I don't know what Basil gave the man or what he did not, but the following year he didn't come back. Anna must have passed the clothes on to him for they were no longer in the house. Basil never said a word about him and whenever I attempted to broach the subject with him, the muscles of his normally relaxed face and body contracted, just like Zeno. That look did not suit him, so I gave up.

34

If you have a clean mind your body is clean.

Epicharmus of Kos, *Fragment*

ANDRONICUS entered the courtyard accompanied by at least twenty Turkish soldiers. After closing the gate, they withdrew and left him alone. His eyes met mine directly with no sign of surprise. He beckoned me closer. Being damp, his hair was darker than usual, his face glowed ruddy pink, the creases smoothed. He seemed rejuvenated. One might be deceived by this younger, all-but innocent-looking Andronicus, and hope the bath he had taken had reformed his spiteful personality, but I already knew this was just my wishful thinking ahead of the coming conversation. Thus, while I awaited some venomous or obscene remark he said, in a nonchalant tone:

"Theia, do you call this a bath?"

Nonplussed, I asked, "What?"

"This place you call a bath, it is basically an indigent hut with a hearth in the middle. The caldarium, the tepidarium and the frigidarium are all in one room. How shameful. The door doesn't close well, one shivers from the draught and then it gets too hot and cold, and hot again, and smoke fills up the room. I had to cough all the way through. Preposterous!"

"I'm sorry the bath did not meet your expectations."

"Really, are you so cynical?"

"No, really, one wants to hear good things about the facilities of one's *heimat*. You must be leaving very soon?"

"Why?"

I shrugged. “Now that you’ve taken a bath.”

“How often you provincials take a bath I do not know, but I take one twice a month as recommended by doctors. It is good for all sorts of ailments, they say. Mind you, here, it is a cause of sickness. On the other hand, I must admit that by force of this dreadful experience, I learned more than from the abstinence that your Sweet Barbarian imposes on me. Damn, we have a good life in the capital. Normally in the frigidarium, I have two concubines who keep me warm. My body still exudes a luscious, sweet smell after each bath…”

He extended his arm and indicated the door of his room. A corner of his mouth lifted.

“It’s chilly here. If you wish to talk to me, you will have to accompany me to my cell.”

He observed me with a lopsided grin, waiting. I passed in front, opened the door, and entered, while saying, “Why do you go to the frigidarium, then? It is to chill the body. Do you always have to have the ultimate comforts?”

His grin froze somewhat, and he quickly followed me into the room. Looking around, a flush of embarrassment crept into his face.

“I most certainly do, my dear,” he said. “Look at the conditions I’m forced to live under now. I’ve fallen a long way.”

“You haven’t fallen far. They take good care of you. It could be worse. They gave you a decent bed.”

His eyes lit up; he stood by the bed. “Well then, we must make the best of it. Would you wish to lie there next to me?”

I stood by the door, afraid he might touch me. He lay down on his side, observing my reaction. I averted my eyes and tried to speak in a voice without inflection:

“Anyway, is that all? You simply wanted to take a bath? You are not leaving?”

He propped his head up with the palm of his hand.

“Well, not with your Sweet Barbarian in any event, if that is what you are trying to get at. He was there with me, actually, taking a bath. I do not know if it was a coincidence. I suspect not.”

My stomach sank. “He’s here?”

He looked down as if he has been wronged.

“But my dear, it is always me answering your questions. That is to say, satisfying your curiosity. Yet I get nothing from you. Have you even thought about bringing me some sweet, dried apricots? I've had enough of those lentils they fill me up with. They hope to destroy my semen and suppress my appetite. Which is rather naïve of them."

"I promise I'll bring you dried fruits next time. But tell me now if that's what you want."

"Oh no, no. I prefer fresh fruits. I always have. I have tried the dried ones, even those Saracen ones. Hmm… how do you call them, the imported fruit, shrivelled, much too sweet? Ah yes, dates. I have even tried dates, just for the hell of it, at the risk of possible, perilous outcomes; but one must try new things, different things. One's digestive system can only grow stronger in that way. Look at yourself; you have a natural predisposition towards the exotic and you're as strong as a leopard."

"But enough with your bawdy innuendos." I had to prevent him getting into his stride. "Don't you see they are not working, only vulgarising the conversation and distancing me? What do you gain out of that? Besides, dried fruits would do you good. So why such ill-manners? Come on, tell me now. What is Ogan doing here?"

His eyes widened; his face froze.

"Is that the way to talk to a Prince?"

"You are right. I do not know how to talk to a Prince. So, I am leaving now. I shall find the information by myself."

He gave me an incredulous stare and spoke quickly. "Wait… So you did not know your barbarian was here? How so?"

"I said bad things to him before he left."

And now the self-satisfied grin returned to his face, displacing the petulant look. "Ah, now it's getting interesting. Somehow, I am not surprised you did. Still, I'd like to know – why did you do that?"

I considered a moment then replied. "I don't know. I don't know why I wanted to hurt him to draw his attention. Perhaps you can enlighten me."

"Men do not like visibly shrewish women. You should call for recognition with submissiveness, softness… but remain true to yourself stealthily…" He looked directly at me. "Which in your case is intense, too intense for a man to digest."

He lowered his eyes and simpered: "Look, even my appetite for you is a little gone today… Although after a bath I am always in a good mood."

"Will you give me a proper answer please?"

He lifted his eyes again. "What? Ah yes. Your barbarian. I am so curious about what attracts you to him. I personally see nothing special in him. But yes. Yes, he is here. He is moving into a house here."

"A house, here in Plekia?"

His laugh was more like a snort. "A normal evolution, child. That old adage says all Turkic peoples are alike, but they are not like other people. I doubt if that is true any longer. When I walked among them in the olden days, the Court members and settled Turks of Iconium despised these new incoming nomads for being savages; but the reverse was true as well. To nomads like the tribe of your Sweet Barbarian, those who no longer roamed from place to place and had to settle were dishonourable, people of the lowest provenance. These were the times when they believed sheep came directly from heaven. Now times have changed: now it's gold that comes from heaven. Even the wildest wolves must get tamed in the end."

He bent down and roughly patted Dog on the head.

"Hard to believe this too was a wolf once upon a time. This lazy, languid beast. Why do you take him everywhere with you, like Latins do?"

"I don't. He chases me everywhere."

He laughed.

"You could never do that. Loyalty is performed only by docile cowards – and only stealthily docile cowards seek it. Like Latins. Greed on the other hand is universal. Now that those bastards are even here, the place has become too small, too crowded. Your barbarian is a part of the game. You don't expect him to camp in the highlands during the summer and drive livestock anymore, do you?"

"He isn't ambitious, his Father is."

Andronicus waved his hand in dismissal.

"These things change very fast in State matters, my dear. Enemies become friends; friends become enemies. Sons can even become enemies to fathers, and vice versa."

"So, who will take you to Iconium, if not him?"

"Aha! You are genuinely wondering about me? Hmm… I don't know. I didn't ask. By the way, your Barbar mentioned that his wife is here. I have yet to see the girl. Terribly curious though…"

A pang shot through me. Sensing tears filling my eyes, I bowed my head.

He continued. "I care about what I have here at hand and how I shall deal with Manuel. That is, once he is through with parties and is sufficiently consummated, the bastard. As for your barbarian and his family here in Plekia… The Sultan needs half-breeds for they've absorbed both Roman and Barbarian qualities. The poor creatures, they're prized for the eternal curse of being a hybrid. Look, you did fall for him, didn't you?"

My face still downcast a tear dropped onto the floor, and I hastily sniffled to prevent my nose from running. I dug in vain for something to wipe it.

He held out a handkerchief and laughed.

"Lift up your face, girl! What are you sad for? That face of yours has become unmistakably beautiful now. You see? I told you – paint and rapture yield prettiness to an ordinary continence. Pain, on the other hand, surpasses them both in generosity: it imparts ultimate magnificence!"

35

Like the sweet apple which reddens upon the topmost bough,
Atop the top-most twig – which the pluckers forgot, somehow.
Forgot it no, nay, but got it not, for none could get it till now.

Sappho, *One Girl*

MADAM Apple hurried towards me. When she reached me, she grabbed me by my shoulders and then took my head between her hands and kissed both my cheeks, then enfolded me in her arms and pressed me to her bosom. This display of endearment lasted some seconds; I had barely been able to see her face. Nonplussed, I stood stock still, not because I did not enjoy her honeysuckle scent but because I did not know what to do with my body.

When she released me and withdrew, I saw a creature that brought the Dervish to my mind. He had proclaimed that love is our imitation of God, a tool to reach Him. If so, to reciprocate our favours and prayers, God must have created Madam Apple. He imitated Himself in her; He also made her the reminder of His greatness and what He is capable of.

But I've always found his actions rather coercive and, more than that, I believe he miscalculated on this occasion. Very likely, the time frame He chose to execute His operations was opportune for Him – but most of the time was inopportune for us mortals.

His compassion, served as His means of communication. Rest assured it has ends we are unaware of and soon it will be replaced with its exact opposite. We are puppets.

After all, what was there in the beauty of this woman for me? If God wanted to do something for me, I preferred him to do it more directly, no roundabouts… When I saw her waist slimmer than a wasp's, my stomach sank. So, she had had a miscarriage. But this vision did not correspond to a woman who had lost an unborn baby. That baby knew it was destined not to be born but chose to luxuriate in her at least for some days, just for the sake of it. She celebrated him; she did not kill him.

She had long raven hair, unbound, flowing past her shoulders. She did not wear the hair cover used perfunctorily by some of those nomadic women, pretending to fulfill the requirements of their new religion. Symeon the Theologian's praise of the flesh as one of the wonderful creations of the world so described this girl. Every limb in our body was Christ, according to Symeon, even the shameful parts were graceful and decent by His divine beauty and glory, and we must not be ashamed. Well, this girl certainly had nothing to be ashamed of. Nonetheless, some things did not conform.

If Aristotle had a point in affirming that all beings on earth and in the heavens are inextricably linked together in close connection – as extensions of one another, parts of a whole, in *Sympatheia* – then what was the link between myself and this lovely being? And if the ancients were correct that everything we see around us constitutes the parts of one great living organism, the universe, then I wished to know: what did this Lady represent in it – and what did I?

After all, regardless of the gentle view of Symeon, not all the components of a body hold the same importance or beauty, or nobility – do they?

And if truth complied with what heretics claimed, *"The All is mind; the Universe is Mental,"* and *"Every cause has its effect; every effect has its cause,"* then I wanted to understand: who was the trickster here? The famous trickster some heretics speak of? Even Plato suspected he existed – a malevolent second god who played jokes on people, supposedly to assist the first, the real one in implementing his plan? But who was that trickster and how did he operate? By giving "feelings" to us humans?

To me, his schemes and ruses were not welcome. I was not feeling happy here right now, and there were no guarantees that I would be any happier the other side, either.

And if some omniscient mind was arranging all these happenings, and if earth and the celestial planes corresponded and interacted, then it was perfectly possible that there was no heaven to go to – not here and not there. Some heavens were here, but only for some people. Just like that dimple on her chin, so much like her husband's – minute, pink, and plump – placed beneath a dainty, turned-up nose.

If there were deliberate causes and effects in this world, the first being altogether obscure to me here at this moment, the latter came to me as a dry, iron-like knot settling in my stomach. Madam Apple's lips displayed a half-smile which I might have understood as cynical had she not wrapped her arms around me. I would deem that smile as the mark of her grand self-assuredness, but now it made her look naïve, even well-intentioned. I knew when the likes of Madam Gabras exhibited such crooked smiles, I resented them, with an urge to smack them with the back of my hand; but this was not the mouth of any such person, nor any person at all, not even Ogan's wife... this was the entrance gate to the Promised Land, one could never go farther.

The Empress Theodora did not find her God-given orifices adequate. To have queried God's allocations, Theodora must not have been as satisfied as Andronicus claimed she was. This ethereal creature before me, on the other hand, Alma, was at peace with her body and all its parts. God made it easy for some people to be well disposed; I desired to press my lips on hers and in place of being ashamed my thoughts turned to the angel of night, Lailah. Lailah made the skin of this woman out of her own wing, translucent and sacred; not even a tiny spot or scar marred its purity, it was clean.

Alma too was clean – so much so that it was nearly offensive. Besides, she was generous and considerate because her eburnean skin radiated the colour of the moon, just like the moonstones we Romans believe solidify the moon's rays; her skin gratified us, the mere earthborn. Alma was modest too. Lailah had forgotten a piece of night on her right temple: a midnight blue vein began with her hairline and ran all the way down until her brow bone. Or perhaps Lailah had not forgotten it. Perhaps she had drawn it on purpose. In any case, it made Alma look human – fragile, even vincible.

Moonlit skin. Moonlit, dainty… This time reality was imitating the dream – not its everyday opposite. This creature had enraptured him – had enraptured me. Then she began to speak, and I did not understand anything of what that mellifluous voice poured into those unknown words – where vowels rolled trippingly off her tongue, repeating themselves over and over harmoniously, round and merry, nearly funny. The vowels ebbed melodiously, creating a sense that I understood them – then consonants flowed with many sh's and ch's as if she were hushing me – hush, hush, hush. And there I lost myself to a strange effervescence, a titillating sense in my stomach – where the knot took its leave.

I heard Andronicus's taunting, teasing laugh behind my back, but I did not turn. Apple said something I did not comprehend and walked away. I watched her pace – shoulders erect, back unbent, head upright, muscles somewhat taut, all limbs in harmony. Similar to Andronicus's, it was a gait that got along well with each organ and was on friendly terms with each muscle. I followed her with my eyes until she disappeared into her room.

"Isn't she something?"

"Is that a question or your opinion of her?"

"Oh, my opinion formed the moment the second I set eyes on her. The challenge would be hopeless – and yield nothing to me. Worse still it could endanger my well-being in Turkish hands. What was she telling you?"

"I have no idea. If you'd gotten here a little earlier, you could perhaps have translated."

"I shall. You must be really curious about what she says. You'll have to keep me pleased, though…"

"Not necessarily. I can find other interpreters here at the monastery who'll willingly help me, and at far more reasonable prices."

Andronicus guffawed and clapped me on my back. I took a step back and continued.

"In fact, we both know you would be thrilled if I gave you the chance to translate."

He chortled. "Don't bite your tongue, girl. You want to find out if the husband is here. I will quench your curiosity… Yes, he is here."

He carried on: "It would be so lovely if you would ask me now whether he is here to finally carry you away with tears in your eyes? But you say you are not interested in that, are you?"

I did not reply.

"I'm in a generous mood today, so I will proceed with delivering favours. The other day the two were sitting on the marble rim of the fountain..."

He paused and his stare focused on me. Then he chuckled again.

"Nothing lascivious was going on, girl – do not go red. They were perfectly decorous and serene. Apple played a kopuz, the horse-hair fiddle. I often heard its melodies at the court of the Sultan during my exile. They heal mad horses with its music."

"First, she kissed it three times, of course. Those lips... Too much information?"

I tossed my head back. "No... Go on."

He smiled. "The instrument is sacred to them – hence the kisses. The bottom part represents the earth; the upper part, the sky. It has two strings, two pegs. One is the sun; the other, the moon. Men are the sun; women, the moon. You see?"

"Not really," I sniffed.

Ignoring my reply: "When the fiddlestick rubs against the strings – "

"Oh, stop now!"

Surprised: "Don't be so prurient... I was going to say when the instrument is played, the wind ceases blowing, mountains stand up from where they sit, birds freeze midair, and water stops flowing."

My face burning, I replied sulkily: "Do you mean she plays it so well?"

"I am no judge of this. It is a strange contraption peculiar to these barbarians. Two strings, for example, symbolise the two opposites of this world. Music is produced by the interaction of the two polarities, like a baby produced by a man and a woman. Apple plays; her boy listens."

"So, it is some kind of lute. How does it sound? To you?"

"There is a story. A certain mathematician and musician called Al Farabi is invited to a music recital at an Emir's court. He criticises all the singers and musicians. When they ask him if he knows better, he says yes, he does. From his bag, he takes out several reeds, puts them in a certain order, and blows them. The assemblage begins to cheer and laugh. Then he changes the order of the reeds and again plays them. This time they cry. Then he moves the reeds again and plays on them one more time. Now they fall asleep.

But what begets all those states of being, do you think?"

I looked at the floor. "I don't know."

"These barbarians assign sacredness to many things one would otherwise find mundane – like rivers, mountains, and musical instruments. When there is sacredness, there is no anxiety; in my case, there is nothing sacred here, only incertitude."

"But how did you come here?"

"Didn't your father teach you to listen?"

"I was only wondering how Apple's instrument sounded to you?"

"Pythagoras thought the universe to be a monochord with its single string stretched between heaven and earth. It sounded like hell if you must know. Like hell. According to these mysterious pagans, every human has an idiosyncratic keynote, and if it is ever sounded, it will destroy him. I thought that was what was going to happen to me. To you the melody would probably be like heaven – if you found the girl attractive and shared the sense of sanctity. But you envy her, so in all likelihood, you too would find it hellish.'"

"I don't envy anyone."

"No, Theia. You certainly do not… Deceptions, my dear. Delusions. Wishful thinking. Anyway… while spying on them, I said to myself, perhaps we can draw inspiration from that old saw: 'All Turkic people are alike, but they are like no other people.'"

"How so?"

"We should instead say: 'Apple is like nobody else, nobody else is like Apple.' I also told myself… mind you, under this insidious captivity, I have developed odd habits, one of which happens to be talking to myself…

If it is true that Alexander the Great built an Iron Wall to keep the barbarian peoples Gog and Magog, from flooding into these lands, then he would also have barred the likes of Apple from entering these lands – which would be a pity. Fortunately, these people cut through iron as easily as they tear papyrus; no iron wall could stop them.

Long before Alexander, one of the last surviving Turkic tribes suffered a devastating defeat and, retreating, followed a trail worn by wild sheep until they found a narrow pass into a valley surrounded by steep mountains rich in iron ore. Centuries passed. Their numbers swelled, and the valley became too small to accommodate the tribe. However, with time, they had forgotten where the narrow passage lay. Trapped, they burned a passage – large enough for a giant – through the iron mountain and eventually made their way here. Ezekiel prophesied that the sons of Magog, a great and mighty people from the northeast, would one day invade the habitable earth and reach Jerusalem."

"These are legends."

"Only partly. Legend says the Gog and Magog people ate raw flesh, and drank human blood, and rendered their weapons invincible by smearing them with the blood of human embryos. I've never seen them doing those things."

"So?"

"Before setting off on a long journey," Andronicus continued, "they placed a piece of raw meat under their saddles, generously peppered and salted. It was pressed under the weight of the rider and dried out in time. Occasionally, they would cut a slice with a knife and eat it. They call it *pastirma* – meaning 'press' and 'pressure' in Turkish. My aunt Anna finds them arrogant, with their heads in the clouds. Lustful and addicted to wine, she says, and claims they worship Dionysius. I personally have never seen them drinking blood, though."

"Eh, you see? More legends." It was clear we'd finished with Alma for the time being.

"Legends and myths are symbols that sometimes reflect greater truths, my dear. And yet, there is more reliable evidence: Ezekiel 38: 'Son of man, set your face against Gog, of the land of Magog. You will advance, coming on like a storm. You will be like a cloud shrouding the land, you and all your hordes, and many peoples with you. You will come from your place in the far north, you and many nations with you, all of them riding on horses, a great horde, a mighty army. You will advance against my people, Israel. In days to come, O Gog, I will bring you against my land, so that the nations may know me when I show myself holy through you before their eyes.' You see? To descry His holiness, we needed to find ourselves in such dire straits."

"It seems to me that this insidious captivity redounds to your wisdom. Perhaps you too needed dire straits to appreciate God's Holiness? It is unfortunate there is no iron around for you to melt and escape your slavery."

He chuckled: "If only I could melt your heart!"

Then he began to cough. Sweat droplets formed on his forehead.

"I'm feeling very tired suddenly. I should let myself into my room."

"Is your health all right?"

I escorted him to his room. Before entering, he did not turn – as usual – for a last attempt to invite me in. Under his breath he said:

"Thank you. Let me deliver you a favour in return for this act of kindness. Here is one more piece of news for you. Your beloved will move into a vacated house in Plekia with his family."

And he gently closed the door.

36

"Stand a little out of my sun."

Diogenes to Alexander the Great

I WENT to Skleros's house on Friday. Since I had been treating Anna as if she didn't exist, I hadn't bothered to find an excuse to go out to avoid her badgering. The distress this caused her – and its proof, the look of pain I observed in her eyes – gave me great pleasure. She was proud, nevertheless; keeping silent about her woes not only because, throughout her life, she had advocated the merit of detachment, but also because she had every confidence her incuriousness would, in turn, cause pain to others, serving as a memento of her revenge. I was impervious this time, and her tribulation intensified my desire to torment her further.

The structure of Skleros's house, a singular building standing alone in the open with no exterior walls enveloping it, predictably gave me no opportunity to hide and spy on the Turkomans in the garden. Besides, I had taken Dog with me and even if there was a place to hide, these men would smell him, even if he cowered silently in some corner. The most logical thing to do was to greet the Turkomans and enter the garden directly. I recognised the grinning cheese-seller from the marketplace. Expectedly they lined up alongside each other and bowed, generously exposing their white teeth. They howled at Dog and returned to their work. Dog put his tail between his legs and hung back and did not attempt to rub up against me while we were there. He observed us from a safe distance away.

Skleros had applied for two permits, one to emigrate to Constantinople and one open a bakery there. He paid the debt that he owed Basil with his house, originally intended to accompany the oven he had planned to build in Plekia. He received a bit of extra money for it as well, though not much, since the house was small and simple. Having obtained the permits, he was ready to set off for Constantinople. Before leaving he said:

"I have lost my faith in the baking business since these nomads' flat bread baked on flat iron sheets took over the market. I have a better chance in the big city, Master Basil."

Skleros was a clever man. Bakers were exempted from all public service, and if landlords imposed arbitrary increases to the rent of a bakery, they were punished with life-long exile. The City Eparch regulated the price of grain as well as the price of salt, checking the accuracy of balances and scales regularly. The Eparch of Constantinople wore a black and white garb, symbolising justice: the separation of the illegal (black) from the lawful (white) in all professions. This symbolism served the bakeries well. In a trade fraught with uncertainty, cruel Constantinople was heaven for bakers.

Ataman bought Skleros's house from Basil for Madam Apple and Ogan. The excuse I had prepared for today, should the need arise, was that I wanted to look at the wares Skleros might have left behind. Naturally there is no point in me divulging at this point what my actual purpose was.

The men were setting up a gigantic tent next to Skleros's house. This was one of those tents they pitched in summer pastures; they were called *yurts*, meaning 'homeland' in Turkish. All five of them wore close-fitting leather caps made of hides stitched together and joining at the crown with a sharp triangular seam and brims made of fur. Each sported the usual tight leather trousers and tunics made of rough fibres. They were not particularly young, except for one with a ruddy countenance, and they had yellowish skin and slanting black eyes. They placed footings in a circular shape and apart from each other. Across the footings, they placed cut wooden beams and fastened them. Then they fastened cut strips of wood to the beams. All of this was done very efficiently; obviously they were experienced. The wall of the tent consisted of criss-crossed lattices and took them longer, for they worked on this one-by-one. Facing east, they installed a pre-prepared door and, lastly, added evenly spaced rafters. The frame was crowned with a wooden ring leaving the very centre of the of the rooftop open – allowing light to enter and smoke from the hearth within to escape. The cheesemonger, defter than I would have expected, let out a joyful cry and pointed at the hole:

"This, *changarak*!"

The plaited ends of a rope were then tied to a stake and driven both into the ground and through the *changarak*; thus, it stood in the centre of the room. One of them took out his knife and carved seven equally spaced notches onto the stake while another hung red or blue rags, pieces of cloth and ribbons on the rope, a peculiar and inexpensive home decoration, I thought.

At this point, all five sat cross-legged on the floor and opened their fardels. As he did at the marketplace, the cheesemonger cut a piece of cheese and extended it on a knife to me while chatting with the others. The ruddy faced one opened a leather bag hanging from the calf of his leg and took out a pressed, almost deformed piece of meat, which I suspected was the cured beef Andronicus mentioned once when he was talking about the Gog and Magog people. He cut a thin slice of it and also extended it to me on a knife, watching my response with curiosity. The meat was highly seasoned and smelled strange. I wasn't enchanted at the idea of eating something that had been squeezed between his leg and a horse for far too long, but I made an effort. To be sure I could spit it out without being seen, I pointed in an exaggerated motion to the plaited rope with rags and ribbons which were attached to the stake. They all turned to the stake and laughed, exposing pearly teeth. Meanwhile I chewed the strange meat and found it rather delicious. One of the men began to sing while another joined in – wordlessly. The sound that emerged made me jolt in shock. From deep in his throat, layered over his own voice, he produced a whistling, vibrating tone as though he were singing with two pitches at once. He did not form words but uttered long resonant O's and R's that hummed and buzzed, while his face slowly turned red like his friend's. The sound rang out as if from some mysterious instrument rather than a human voice, compelling me to look around, half-expecting to see someone playing one. After all, when these men went into battle, their enemy first heard the howling of wolves and were then struck by arrows before ever catching sight of their foe. One man played a long flute while the other howled like a wolf, and the other Ooo'ed and Rrrr'ed.

When the song ended, they stood up and began to spread coloured felts over the skeleton of the tent. The door, made of wood, faced east. Without bringing the felts to the side of the tent pole, they left a small round hole in the ceiling.

I held my hands up, shook my head and said: "What is that?"

They began to explain in Turkish, but I interrupted them, opening my two hands at my sides and wearing a dumb expression, signalling my ignorance of their language.

The one with the ruddy face stood up and drew a cross on the ground with his stick. Indicating the horizontal line by hitting it with the stick, he bent down and touched the soil with his other hand. Then he rose. Pointing to the sky, he stroked the vertical line. I shouted, "Christ?"

Holding his hand palm down, parallel to the ground, he rocked it slightly – meaning "so-so."

I grabbed the wooden stick from his hand and redrew a cross on the floor:

"You cannot divide the cross. It is one and whole. He cannot be half. You don't mean half-Christ, do you? In fact, what do you mean?"

Smiling, he came and sat by me. Again, pointing at the horizontal line, he touched his chest, slightly poked my shoulder, turned to his friends, and made a movement with his arm as if embracing us all together. Then, once again, he traced the vertical line with his stick and gestured to the sky. I shook my head exaggeratedly to convey that I still did not understand. He stood up and pulled down the waistband of his trousers. When he lifted the hem of his shirt I screamed. As I prepared to take flight, they burst into laughter. The man put his finger on his navel and spoke softly. After tucking his shirt back into his trousers, he made a gesture with his hands and arms as if wiping the entire sky with a huge mop. Opening his arms wide, he moved the sky along the perimeter of an imaginary circle towards the ground and then in the same way moved the ground towards the sky. He repeated the same gestures taking all of us into a large circle, the frame of the tent, himself, me, Dog, his friends and everything else. Then, looking at me, he held the pole one more time in one hand and his heart with the other. He grabbed my arm and pulled me to the tree in the garden, a resplendent juniper, standing alone. This time, he touched his heart while touching the tree and then he reached his spine on his back, moving his hand all along.

"Yes, upright. Backbone!" I shouted. "A spine, vertical. I get you. Life Tree! The stake with the rope is the Tree of Life?"

He smiled though Greek was as incomprehensible to him as Turkish was to me. One more time he touched his navel and feigned to embrace all those things around us and finally hugged the tree in a true embrace.

"In the belly button of the ground, there is a Life Tree?"

Approvingly he inclined his head. He took my arm and led me back to the stake, placing his finger on one of the seven notches he had etched, all the while making wry facial expressions. He narrowed his eyes and pursed his lips as if crying and drew imaginary tears in the air.

"Pain? The notches are pain!" I shouted.

Touching the holes within reach and pointing at the ones above while his face still showed pain, he finally indicated the hole with his thumb. His facial expression changed to one of bliss and a wide smile turned his dark, slanted eyes into one horizontal black line – reminiscent of Ogan's.

"Heaven after seven tribulations?" I shouted again.

He probably didn't understand but nodded his head anyway. If he was miming that seven agonies were needed to reach paradise, I thought the number was rather substantial, but could be achieved. The beady-eyed Dervish who had once visited me maintained, along with his benevolent God, that "sunshine all the time makes a desert". All these peculiar people were privy to secret and varied wisdom that I was not, and it seemed that this constituted one of my seven tribulations. Discussing seven possible levels of maturity with this strange nomad was out of the question without a shared language, so there was no way we could move closer to paradise in each other's company. Later I would learn that the vertical beam of the cross not only symbolised the Tree of Life but also the spine. It was the divinity in man while the horizontal beam traversed the earth, the ground of everyday experience. Sitting cross-legged on the floor they shared a meal from a large copper tray laid on a large cloth. When they finished eating, they folded the cloth and put it into a basket.

Quickly standing up, two from one side and three from the other spread a gigantic felt cover and horsehides over the tent frame, pulling them tight and securing them with braided horsehair. The Friday call to prayer sounded out from far away, from the tower of the chapel that Ataman was transforming into a mosque. The reciter was the third the Sultan had appointed from Iconium. The first muezzin had fallen from the tower and died. We had heard that when the second died after falling on a relatively smooth road and banging his head on a rock, the villagers began to pray not only to Muslim saints but also to Christian ones to guarantee the life of the third muezzin. I didn't know whether this story had come to the Muhtasib's attention, and if it had, what sort of plan he was designing to prevent another mishap.

I was still sitting cross-legged where the nomads left their basket, keenly watching them while rubbing Dog's head. Suddenly he leapt up, baying. Then stretching his front legs between his hind ones, he broke into a run, barking at full stride. I recognised the short, fat Muhtasib bouncing towards us. Obviously, his mission this time was not ensuring that the surroundings were clean and proper or that nobody was cheating. Another of his tasks was preventing any Christian's house from being higher than a Muslim citizen's house. Forcing drunks back home with or without having them whipped first was another duty, as was forcibly removing silk clothes from men, as he did at the marketplace. Muslim men were not allowed to wear silk, though wearing silver was permitted, for the fabric of a linen-cotton tunic was almost invisible under silver embroideries. Silk had various meanings. Six hundred years ago, the Emperor Justinian dispatched two secret intelligence agents disguised as monks to China and after a long, adventurous journey they managed to bring silkworms and mulberry seeds back to Constantinople, hidden in bamboo sticks. To us, silk was money and prestige founded on theft, perseverance and risk, all qualities and values quite in keeping with the spirit of the capital city. To Ogan and the Turkomans, silk contained insulating powers by its very essence, hence their wrapping mirrors into silken cloths. The kam of the tribe, like his grandmother, treated headaches and cases of paralysis with a mirror, the origin of which they believed was heavenly. It was a receiver and transmitter, a door to other worlds. They never slept in a room where there was an uncovered mirror. A mirror was the most powerful object, a dangerous and respected item maintained in the most revered part of the house: above the hearthstone.

The Muhtasib threw a menacing stare at me, and began bawling at the group, sprawling and spluttering words of which I did not understand a single one. Legs planted wide, face reddening, arm jerking sharply, he shouted for some time. The cheesemonger blushed to the roots of his hair. Then the Muhtasib turned towards me and hollered:

"Missus! Missus! What in carnation are you doing here? Off you go! Go! Go home!"

Should I say it was his expression while telling me this or was it his intonation or the inflection of his squealing voice while speaking his passable Greek? But at that moment he resembled Anna too much for my liking. My face warmed, I became short of breath and my hands began to sweat. Unwittingly, I too planted my feet apart and gave such a wild, guttural roar that the four Turkomans stopped working and turned towards us. The cheesemonger's face turned white as I took a step toward Muhtasib, lifted my hand as if I was going to hit him and shrieked:

"If my father does not interfere, it is not your concern where I am or where I go! Mind your own business!"

If there was a door around there, I would have slammed it and made a spectacular exit. The Muhtasib, his unbelieving eyes wide open, took a step backwards and held the cheese-seller's arm for balance. He held his throat with the other hand, mumbled something under his breath, turned and hastened away with the cheese man. One of the Turkomans patted me on the back, laughed heartily, and returned to the yurt, tightening the hinges of its wooden, east-facing door.

The trumpet blared from afar and drums beat, notifying us that it was the time of prayer.

I stepped up to one of the nomads and, through gestures and miming, asked why they did not join the Muhtasib for prayer. He laughed, pointed to the tree in the garden, and placed his hand on his chest again, continuing to speak words I could not understand. Turning toward the house of Skleros, I mimed an imaginary bed and pretended to sleep on it, then sketched a table in the air and mimed eating at it. Finally, I gestured toward the tent, raised my eyebrows in a questioning look, and asked:

"Why are you pitching a tent when there is already a house?"

He smiled and murmured; had he made the effort to explain, I would have perhaps understood, but he did not. He went to his buddy, who was trying to circumvent the felt laid atop of the tent with a thick rope made of braided horsehair. Faces red, jaws clenched, veins bulging, all four pulled the rope around the yurt, tightening and fastening it while they whooped with delight.

Anthemios, the great architect of Haghia Sophia, came to my mind an extraordinary mastermind who halted Atilla, the scourge of God, Atilla who had reached as far as Athyras, just outside Constantinople. The city's fortifications had been destroyed by violent earthquakes, but within three months, they were rebuilt, and the Hun – worse than cholera and the plague – was forced to retreat.

Anthemios's neighbour, the lawyer Zeno, had built a balcony which spoiled the architect's sea view. When the court ruled against him, Anthemios swore revenge. Zeno's living room stood above one of Anthemios's ground-floor chambers, where he constructed several vats for boiling water. As the water boiled, the lids of the vats, or perhaps leather tubes laid along the beams – channelled steam upward, causing Zeno's floor to shake. So terrifying was the sensation that Zeno and his guests rushed outside, convinced it was an earthquake. Another of Anthemios's contrivances involved burning mirrors: by carefully focusing an array of mirrors in certain directions, he sent beams of light into Zeno's living room, rendering his life a living hell.

Thus, a base fly can sting both a beggar and a prodigy, can't it? If the glorious Anthemios – who designed the Church of Wisdom – could not find comfort in his own house, if the mastermind of the mighty barbarian-repeller was reduced by a petty neighbour to childish contrivances, then my own fantasies hardly mattered. After all, these were tricks life played on us to bring us to our knees; the way it ridiculed us. I was ready to collaborate with it.

So, I envisioned it: burning mirrors placed before Apple's tent, catching the sun's blinding rays. At first, a tiny, invisible spark – innocent, unassuming – melded with the red felt as if it belonged there. It then grew bigger and bigger, licking upward like the tongue of a dragon, devouring the structure in greedy flames. In the end, only a gritty heap of ash remained on the earth, while faint crepuscular rays shimmered over the mirrors.

I touched my forehead with my thumb and first two fingers and held them there for a little while, then my belly, and there too rested my hand for a moment. Slowly I brought my hand across to my right shoulder and touched it and then to my left shoulder where I held my hand longer. I did it mindfully while begging the pardon of God.

I had only visualised the conflagration, merely imagined it.

37

Men who wish to know about the world
must learn about it in its particular details.

Heraclitus

I PUT my palm on his forehead, and this was our first physical contact. Andronicus was burning up. Propping his back up with a pillow, I helped him sit. He cracked a feeble smile, looking somewhat thankful. I lifted his arms and took off his soaked nightshirt.

"Do you know the story of the viper?" he asked me in a weary voice.

"No."

I slipped a clean nightshirt over his head.

"The viper bites a eunuch and dies when it gets contaminated with the eunuch's blood!"

"Here," I said, proffering a cup.

I had asked the cook of the caravanserai to prepare *kyminaton* for him, warm wine spiced with pepper, cinnamon and aniseed, fennel and caraway seeds to which mint, and cumin were also added. I put the drink to his dry, chapped lips.

"Be careful, it's very hot. What's the meaning of that story?"

"I don't know, work it out yourself."

"Our priest is also a eunuch. He is a good man."

He laughed: "His buttocks are fatty, though, aren't they?"

I frowned. "I did not examine the priest's buttocks. What are you trying to say?"

"Nothing, forget about the eunuch. I mull over the snake, the snake. The poor snake."

When he finished the *kyminaton*, I helped him lie back down in bed.

"The fever got to your head, I think; you're talking nonsense."

"Have you seen the ostrich eggs Ataman has had hung all around the courtyard?"

"No… Why?"

"He had a serious row with the Muhtasib."

"Why?"

"You will see, often the Turk will first sacrifice a ram then sack the church; but he will always respect the power of the cross. When destroying one, he will obliterate only the horizontal beam, the patibulum, not the whole cross."

"What has this to do with the fight?"

He grinned. "No patience as usual. When two Turkoman workers died in two days at the mosque work site, he took down the cross of the chapel he'd annexed to the mosque, and had it mounted right next to the crescent – to avert being jinxed. The Muhtasib got mad when he saw this, hence the fight. And so, Ataman had the eggs hung up where everyone could easily see them."

"What does that mean?"

"It means, be careful. The ostrich lays eggs, she inspects them and if there is an egg she finds unworthy, she throws it away and it snaps open; do you understand?"

"Is the cross still adjacent to the crescent?"

He swallowed and looked down. "That I do not know yet." He sighed: "Do you know? If demons have an effect on humans, then humans can also have an effect on demons. Some heretics believe humans and demons share the same material nature, and that this similarity allows demons not only to impinge on humans, but also humans to scourge demons."

With difficulty he swallowed again. His normally bright eyes were tired and watery with sickness.

"So can you dream up the life of poor demons, at the mercy of idiotic humans…?"

I approached him and touched him a second time, laying my hand on his forehead, which scorched.

"I will call a physician for you."

"There is a crazy man here. He said he has kinship to a grand, respectable philosopher called Al-Biruni. Have you seen that man? Your beloved was just talking to him."

I pulled away his duvet for I thought too much heat was rendering him crazed.

"No, Andronicus, I have not seen him."

"He is with a group of travellers all the way from Samerkand, city of crazy people. Day and night they sing and play drums here; I get headaches. They hung banners on their doors with black crescents. Everywhere they go they take these stag horns they brought from home with them. Bunch of lunatics."

"Please lie down and keep quiet. Don't tire yourself."

"This relative of the grand philosopher told me anger gives rise to my fever."

"Don't tire yourself."

"He claims the Grandest Physician on earth, from Bukhara, said anger dispels moisture in the humour regulating the heart. The decline in moisture rapidly increases the heat. You see? If you took care of my heart, I would not burn now."

"You really are talking nonsense now."

"Among all the things to think and do, this estimable Al-Biruni counted the petals on all the flowers. It is always three, four, five or six or eighteen and never ever nine. Did you know this?"

"No, I didn't know. As a matter of fact, I don't really pay attention to vegetation, or plants, unless they happen to be weeds, creeper plants and that kind of thing."

"How about apples, my dear? Do you pay attention to them?"

He grinned and, licking his dry lips, began to quote from the Song of Solomon:

"As an apple among the trees of the orchard,
so is my beloved,
I sat down under his shadow with great delight,
and his fruit was sweet to my taste.
He brought me to the banqueting house,
and the banner he raises over me is love.
Feed me with raisin cakes...."

His voice grew weaker.

"…revive me with apples
for I am sick with love."

"You don't have to be mean just because you are proud," I said. "It's all right that you have fallen sick. It's all right."

"My dear, there are worse things than getting sick. To be more precise: living vicariously here through visitors and inhabitants of this inn… Being bored is worse than being captured. I should have counted petals before that philosopher… It never occurred to me… "

I moved to the door.

"I'm going to fetch someone for you."

"Wait."

I turned. "What?"

"The petal philosopher also said light reaches destinations before sound does…"

I rushed to the courtyard and came nose-to-nose with Ogan.

I shouted at him: "He's having a fever fit in there!"

He first gave an incredulous gaze but answered on impulse: "I know; the physician is coming."

He raised his eyebrows and gave a small smile which became bigger soon enough:

"How are you, Theia?"

"Good, thank you."

I forced myself not to look at my feet. He seemed thinner and there were blue circles under his eyes; he looked less healthy than his wife, in fact. Naturally I was tempted to presume this development had occurred because he was missing me, but that was wishful thinking. The cause was probably the loss of his unborn child.

"So, you are moving into a house and a tent as well?" I was going to force a laugh but thought better of it.

"Yes, in a few days."

I turned away: "So, when are you going to take Andronicus to the Sultan in Iconium then?"

"As soon as he heals."

A strangely clad man who showed up out of the blue drew close to Ogan and said in broken Greek: "We brought your order," motioning to the boxes stacked against the cellar wall. "We unloaded them there."

Ogan grabbed the man's arm with an aggression I had never seen from him before. His face glowing red. Without saying a word to me, he strode off dragging the man along by his arm. I waited a while in the hopes of his return, but the pair disappeared into the cellar. The cargo consisted of three identical boxes, the size of a small foot stool made of iron or lead – I couldn't tell.

At once the Muhtasib flounced into the courtyard. He did not see me. I slipped off into a corner and hid behind a column. He carried one of the ostrich eggs in his hands. It had seemed an auspicious moment to leave unnoticed when suddenly he hurled the egg to the ground where it smashed open. At that moment, a door opened, and Basil appeared, neck craning forward, slightly crouched, a much smaller than usual looking Basil. He and the doctor filled a sack with bottles and small packages on the doorstep. Basil cast a wary glance around to see if there was anyone else in the vicinity, darted across the yard with the swiftness of a storm and vanished. The doctor locked the door of this chamber and headed towards Andronicus' room.

Another segment of the Song of Solomon rang in my mind:
"Under the apple tree I aroused you.
There your mother conceived you.
There she was in labour and bore you.
Set me as a seal upon your heart,
as a seal upon your arm;
for love is as strong as death,
Jealousy as cruel as the grave;
its flames are flames of fire,
a most vehement flame.
Love no flood can quench, no torrents drown."

38

Riddle:
I have nothing inside me
and everything is inside me,
and I grant the use of my virtue
to all without charge. What am I?

In the year 1143, when our Andronicus was captured, the course of policies the new Emperor Manuel would pursue regarding Turks and Latins was not yet known. His grandfather Alexios had been so determined to repel the Turks that he had even dared to have the church's gold melted down and turned into money. The synod rebelled, accusing him of profanity, though they knew money was needed. The day they had to acquiesce half-heartedly, the meaning of the word 'blasphemy' became obscure for many people, including the Emperor himself. His argument was, "If God, whom he represented on earth, wanted the Romans to spend money for the right cause rather than to show it off, who was he to say "No"?"

Desperate in his mission to drive out the Turks, Emperor Alexios invited the Latins to Rhomanoi; he anticipated receiving auxiliary troops to protect Constantinople, but received armies which instead went marching off to the Holy Land which had not even belonged to the Empire for more than four centuries. Perceiving the invitation as an excellent chance to bring east and west under Papal leadership, Pope Urban made fervent speeches to the council he summoned to meet at Piacenza, where Alexios's Ambassador was also present. God was to fight through Christians against Muslims, that is Saracens in Asia and Moors in Europe. The Pope asked for defeat of the machinations of the barbarians who had seized Christian land in the

East, where wide-scale destruction was taking place. Restoring the Holy Sepulchre, liberating the churches, and the Christians of the East – this, ostensibly, was the ultimate intention. With cries of "Deus lo volt," crowds flocked to the Pope. They were to confront a pagan or Saracen enemy of barbaric character in Asia Minor, though he did not name the Turks explicitly. There was hope, he claimed, that these foes might come to recognize the Christian truth – the lost limb was to be restored. And here the trouble began: we, Romans, did not see ourselves as a lost limb.

He also reckoned the Crusaders would enlighten the Orientals. The fallen and sinful Christians joining the cause, he said, would attain redemption by fighting against peoples alienated from God. So – was he suggesting the bald would comb the bold? We were not of the same mind. And if, under false pretences, he was dispatching these scoundrels east merely as a way of disposing of them, then once again, we would strongly disagree.

Crusaders did not call themselves "Crusaders" but "pilgrims." However, that did not engender sympathy for them nor make us take them at all seriously – who were these people, after all, that did not use actual bread in communion but preferred an unleavened wafer? Whose bishops shaved like women and depilated their bodies and yet called Romans effeminate? They were not able to control their impulses; they criticised Romans for diluting their wine and mocked them for eating lettuce? Our aversions were mutual. They found us to be lacking in martial prowess, effeminate, perfidious, supercilious. We thought them arrogant, greedy, contentious, boorish, gluttonous, and violent. Our aversion to the Latins was not a novel affair. Two centuries before, one particular ambassador of theirs, Liudprand of Cremona, belittled us Romans:

"On their table one finds only rusks and they drink or rather sip bath water from tiny glasses."

Two hundred years later, it did not take long for Alexios to put Crusaders on the same footing as Turks, other barbarians, and Patzinaks. Though originally, he had been the one expecting troops to come to his assistance, he now felt obliged to supply troops to accompany them. He provided no more than a few squads who he determined would go no further than Asia Minor. There was even an incident where he sicced his fierce lions on them. A rowdy, obstreperous group of Lombardians camping outside the city walls clamoured for provisions and refused to move on. Seeing they persisted in their efforts, Alexios commanded that three fierce lions and seven leopards be driven between the first and second walls surrounding the city. Unaware and with no experience of confronting wild animals, the Crusaders sent their javelins and spears. Some were savaged. In the end they climbed on the walls to save their lives.

The Seljuks, the Turkish governors of Iconium, showed little interest in the passage of these rapacious Latins – nor did the nomadic Turkomans. Neither, however, had any intention of forfeiting land. Heavy Latin armour was moved in wagons or on packhorses or mules – they only put the armour on when they anticipated danger or battle. When these sluggish, poorly-equipped luggage wagons and vulnerable cavalrymen and infantry squadrons crossed Turkoman territory, by mistake or by design, notwithstanding the first sonic assault by howling wolves that couldn't be seen, the Latins would then be charged at by riders at a velocity they could hardly imagine existed and then the riders would storm, then vanish, then all of a sudden strike forward again, leaving blindsiding and dumbfounding the trespassers. From personal experience with Ataman, though bloodless, I reckon at such moments one could doubt if the encounter was real or not. The time elapsing between the soldiers realising their powerlessness and the sight of real bloodshed and resounding war cries would be so brief and the confrontation so intense that biblical curiosities and divine, unearthly thoughts would swarm at once into the minds of the victims. They might seem unpractical in the face of the disaster befalling them. Their benumbing, quiescent effect, however, is unmistakable. God is not always cruel: when one's leg breaks suddenly in an accident, there is a certain moment of vacuity, and no pain; the pain ensues only afterwards. A good, correct mixture of Socrates's murderer's hemlock, the scary-man-shaped mandrake root, chicken-killing stinky henbane, and wild opium poppy help to numb the hurt, but here in the eye of the onslaught, the Latins had no time. Before they died, they wondered: which of the sheep of Luke 15:4 were they – the ninety-nine in the open country or the one that was lost? And where was hell? Here or hereafter?

The Turk was hands-on. To him, hell and heaven were here in this life, on earth. He freely chose his hell and heaven operating on some sort of self-rule resembling what Plato had described as: "A charming form of government, full of variety and disorder; and dispensing a sort of equality to equals and unequals alike."

So profoundly was this principle embedded into his nature that even the order of Caliph Umar, the most powerful and influential Muslim caliph in history, was ignored. To our acidic Muhtasib's frustration, the precept that non-Muslim *dhimmi* must wear vestimentary distinctions was dismissed, not only in our village Plekia but also in Iconium, where the Sultan and his sophisticated governing class lived. Occupying their own consulate, Genoan and Venetian alum dealers also lived there, and there were Christian Turks speaking Greek and Muslim Greeks speaking Turkish. There were Armenians and Jews, too, dwelling in the capital. After all, with such a motley population, not being a *dhimmi* was the exception. Let us not forget the hybrids. The question of what hybrid persons should wear – which many Seljuk Princes were – did not arise, and if it did, the challenges would be greater here in Plekia, for our Muhtasib was fervently adherent to the orders which the Sultan himself was probably unaware of or unconcerned about. Failing to grasp the nuances, the Muhtasib divided rather than united – nor did he hesitate to use his whip…

As for the Latin, allegedly he undertook this arduous project for salvation and heaven. One of aims of the ordeal was to enlighten the ignorant barbarian to the truth of this life so that the Latin himself would go to paradise. And if the barbarians refused to see the light, the Latin was to remove them, irrespective of the fact they were the indigenous population. Thus, only the celestial boons mattered to the Latin, but ironically almost all the songs the Latin sang alluded to money, gems and silver, palaces crested with gold, and filled with strange beasts or exotic foods of the Orient.

Jerusalem was a city of depredations, conquered at the very least on three, possibly four occasions by Turks, Fatimids and local factions. It had passed from Seljuk Turks to a powerful Caliph of Egypt of the Fatimid Dynasty, when, after a violent siege on 15 July 1099, the Crusaders took it by storm and affected a terrible slaughter there. Godfrey of Bouillon accepted the title of King of Jerusalem. A certain Baldwin took Edessa and established a Principality there, a bulwark against Turkish attacks from Asia. Following him, Bohemond of Tarentum became the ruling Prince of Antioch. None of them took the vassal oath to our Emperor Alexios. Distrust gradually increased. Turks became essential friends and optional enemies in the same facile course; chivalry became tyranny and hubris became humility. Thus, the well-known axiom of the Turkic Dervishes came true for Emperor Alexios:

"Seasons pass; branches of trees that used to give shade dry up; whatever you say won't happen, happens; you say you'll never fall but you fall; the beloved becomes a stranger; your friend becomes your enemy; your enemy becomes your friend – so strange is this world."

Alexios's son, Emperor John, spent his life on expeditions and battlefields, exerting himself both to finally drive back the Turks and to bring the Prince of Antioch, and the Count of Edessa to heel. John demanded oaths of allegiance and fealty from them, as well as the rights to their lands; in return, he promised them fiefdoms and the hereditary rights to the Muslim towns.

The Latins pretended to submit, but the reality was different. Their disdain for the authority of a so-called schismatic Greek Emperor was the real cause; the Papacy's claims to universality was their ostensible justification.

On his last expedition in 1143, John died without entering Antioch, having achieved nothing new. The same year, the King of Jerusalem also died, in a hunting accident, and left the throne to the headstrong Queen Melisende and her son.

To depict the state in which we Romans found ourselves, I found the Turkoman saying, although rough and obscene, somewhat applicable:

'A stick with its two ends plunged in shit.'

This was an adage Basil was particularly fond of, and I'm certain he would use it if asked the question, "Were the fruits of the orchard a fortune or a curse to Theia?" I am sure nobody asked him this question, though. The reply from the likes of Madam Gabras would obviously be the latter.

The bliss of ignorance resembles a luxurious sofa. Surely "there's a bum for each saddle," but after a while, when one begins to take its comfort for granted and fails to appreciate those properties which make it special, obtuseness grows as far as the butt sitting on it does.

There were moments in my life when I too yearned for the fool's paradise, but it was too late – since happy ignorance also resembles virginity: once it's gone, it's gone. Even so, thanks to the fruits of the orchard, I led a slightly more enchanting life than that of my peers, not to mention the occasional entertaining epiphanies that transpired. Some could be regarded as exhilarating – that is of course if you are the type of person who relishes the cut and thrust of life. Others prefer tranquillity.

My revelatory moments occurred among the fruit baskets and except in my arrangement of the early ones, when I was still naïve, and by extension interested only in the fruit and the basket, not the client, later, I had a hand in the setting up of each of those transactions, regardless of the variety of the client. When the conversation came to pass, I certainly was not questioning the particular man's faith, though: one might query the creed of one's enemy but not one's client. So, I took credit for the amity and trust this man placed in me by sharing his peculiar views. The idea that Latins were heretics with whom spiritual communion was simply not possible had prevailed in Rhomanoi for as long as anyone could recall, and it is still predominant to this day. The person in question here, on the other hand, was not a Latin, or a Barbarian, or any other foreigner, but a perfectly run-of-the-mill Roman – one of us – who did not even bother to pretend to be a God-fearing Orthodox Christian, as if his discourse was the most commonplace truth. Optimistic and self-assured, he said to me in the flat, knowing tone of a physician:

"The Tree of life in the Garden of Eden was the secret of immortality, the emblem of bliss, no worries, no vainglory, no desire, no cowardice, no jealousy, no envy, no resentment, ultimate ecstasy. This was the life promised Adam and Eve. They tasted from the Tree of Knowledge the secret of mortality. And the secret of mortality is life: life with good and bad, pain and pleasure."

And black and white, I thought… And love and hatred… So, if these two idiots had never touched the Tree of Knowledge, would we all still be in Paradise, indulging in endless delights? Some heretics here in Roman Lands claimed the snake was the knowledge, the mind, the wisdom and the salvation. The snake was Christ. In those days, it did not crawl upon the earth, but stood upright, coiled around the tree. Just as Moses lifted up the serpent in the wilderness, so too the Son of Man had to be lifted up. The forbidden Apple was the light – understanding, awareness, and the knowledge of reproduction – a symbol of the divine light of the Creative God within our very bodies. But whether the snake was good or evil, what did it matter? I did not care who said what.

I would prefer not to know the God within my body here on earth but dwell with the God in the heavens, knowing nothing at all.

This hand of mine that puts this infidel balderdash on paper, should tremble, should it not? Daring to question God? Instead of uniting with him, it is breaking his sacred creation into fragments and scrutinising it like a vulgar merchant auditing his accounts or an architect inspecting his construction or even a physician examining the pus. Even a Geniza should fear to contain it if it be discarded. It is true that my pen is shaking slightly as I write this, but only because I am old. Neither then, nor now, does that Roman's conviction strike me as being all together outrageous; notwithstanding, I contemplated it, and I still do. Why was the light kidnapped and introduced into the body of Man? What was the interest in doing this? Why did they want to keep Adam and Eve in the Garden in the first place? And if Jesus was a snake who tempted man to 'knowledge,' why was the earth the place to get this knowledge? At the time, the naturalness of the heathen client's comportment, his confidence, and his maverick ideas corrupted my young mind and contaminated it, but after forty and some years have passed, the questions remain. By then, I had mastered the art of extracting not-so-innocent information from innocent chatter about fruits.

There were allusions here to our 'magnificent capital' as well, Bosphorus and Phosporus. Lucifer meant phosphorus. In the guise of a serpent, Lucifer revolted against men living and dying without light, without understanding his servitude to the mandates of the Demiurge, God's assistant. Lucifer was comparable to the Goddess Phosphorus lighting the sky of the Bosphorus to warn the citizens against invaders: Lucifer was the angel of Light. Like Prometheus he brought light to humanity. Lucifer was Jesus fighting against the dark authority, the bright Morning Star spoken of in Revelation, thus the same as Jesus, not satanic.

Then there was another one, who said the opposite: "Until Lucifer, the material world did not exist. Naughty Lucifer wanted to perform Alchemy and misused the ingredients." He resembled our cook Anna, though she rarely ends up with a cooking mishap. "Lucifer was the Demiurge!"

If I had deliberated with Andronicus about these idolatrous opinions, I'm positive he would not have trembled. He would probably whoop loudly and say, "All heretics are alike, but all heresies are different."

Or perhaps the other way around: "All heresies are alike, but all heretics are different."

Anyway, I didn't ask him. The conundrum of the serpent, the legitimacy of other dimensions, the sacrilegious tenets – of which Lucifer was one – all still persist.

As for light, the Latins' dreamt of banishing darkness – enlightening non-Christians, illuminating first the Turks, then the Saracens. I was not acquainted with the lives of the latter, but for the former, Jerusalem was a portable Tree of Life in the shape of a tent pole, and he could take it with him everywhere. Any type of Tree was transportable – whether from Eden or from earth, it made no difference. Light, too, could be delivered conveniently to one's doorstep.

Resourceful Ogan had already worked out how. In those iron boxes he had imported mercury from Andalusia. At the time, I hadn't the faintest idea that Al Biruni, the very philosopher Andronicus envied for discerning the immutable number of petals, had also claimed that light travelled faster than sound. Mind you, I had reflected on that matter for quite some time. The sound of Ogan's light reached me rather swiftly, carried by the whispers of my informants.

He had a large tray built – an iron platform – and had it filled to the brim with mercury forming a flat gleaming, resplendent pool not dissimilar to that in which Narcissus saw his beauty reflected, but this was not for Ogan's beauty; it was for that of his Apple. Every day, Apple sat beside the artificial pond, as the sun's rays struck its surface. I've heard that sometimes for hours on end he would sit by the liquid mirror and observe her in awe. The reflection of light on the mercury frisked and gamboled, over her face, and he kept on watching her, his stare intense, his heart ablaze. They would laugh together, growing giddy. Sometimes, in his joy, he would stand up, do a handstand or perform somersaults… And yet, the indulgence of Ataman in allowing the couple to fool around in this fashion remained a mystery.

Had I asked Andronicus to conceal my true intention – my desire to know more about them – under the guise of curiosity about hereticism, I was certain he would see through it at once and mock me: he would reenact the scene of Apple playing the strange instrument and then, cracking up, say something like:

"Ah the good Apple, mystery of regeneration, my dear, of germination, Jesus's gift to humanity. Once tasted, no longer immortal, but engulfed in ultimate delectation. Do you think the fire I saw in your Sweet Barbarian's eyes and the very glow that illuminated her face sprang from within? Might those be the alleged Godly Sparks trapped in the human body, traces of the good God? And, my dear, the very copulation itself is the work of the bad one."

But I did not ask Andronicus.

In 1143, while the new Emperor was getting acclimatised to the throne, the Synod had brought charges against several bishops relating to the Bogomil heresy, and Manuel, who had not cared to save his cousin, did not take an interest in looking into the Synod's investigations. This rather foreshadowed his pursuit of different policies from his grandfather Alexios, who burned Bogomils' leader at the stake, and his father Emperor John, who persisted in condemning and executing them. Manuel must have either prioritised other challenges or have secretly agreed with the Bogomils who contended that since this world was replete with crimes, wars, epidemics, oppression, pain and suffering, it could not be the creation of the Supreme God but a fabrication by some other one, an evil one. The Godly Spark along with the spirit trapped in it, also resided in the body of man. All of this, they could have kept secret, avoiding attention, and living their lives in relative peace, but they refused to honour the cross – and that brought unwanted attention. They defied:

"If any man slew the son of a king with a bit of wood, how could this piece of wood be dear to the king?"

To them, the church was the body of man where the light was ensnared. My repository of blasphemy expanded over the years thanks to their teaching too. While building it, I learned something else: every single person, from mundane merchants to banal or sanctimonious priests alike has an idea. Fruitmongers, cheese-and fish-sellers, wanton women, market women, respectable ladies, dervishes, savants and shepherds, Jews, Mohameddans, pagans and barbarians all have an opinion. Everybody is entitled to some sort of conviction. People think – that is what they do. They cannot help it. Very rarely in the course of my long life have I met a person who claimed to be too stupid to have an opinion. Decided idiots, on the other hand, never claim anything and remain the wisest and happiest, away from the anarchy of the deliberations of smart alecks. As for me, I arrived at an idea – one that teetered on the edge of a blasphemy, for, ironically, it concerned the very nature of thought itself:

"There exists a Supreme Universe, a great depository from which we draw when we think, bringing what we select into our reality here. Thoughts have substance, they are invisible forces with weight and form, not mere wisps of the mind. What we think, we become; what we think becomes."

Thus, my picture, inspired by the Great Architect Anthemios's blinding mirrors, had somewhat come to pass. I had imagined mirrors and blazes nearby the tent, and I welcomed them. The blasphemy did not claim we would get exactly what we envisage – apparently, even the Supreme Universe was not exempt from imperfections. A mirror made of mercury casting the rays of the shining sun on the already naturally sunny face of Apple: Apple shone with sunshine. A liquid mirror of delight and entertainment, mirth and merriment, unlike Grandmother kam's mirror, swathed with silk in fear. Instead, a perilous gateway between this world and others, a mirror that is not a working tool to travel between worlds but to celebrate this one. Not glowing for revenge like Anthemios's blazing mirrors but one that burns for love. So, the answer to the riddle was 'a mirror' for it had nothing inside and everything was inside it, and it granted the use of its virtue to all without charge. But to me, this was "life telling a lie," for nothing was free of charge. Perhaps heretics were right, life was an impersonal tool in the hands of invisible entities, evil powers who fed on us. And yet when they were asked, "But why? Why all this?" they would declare: "Because we must taste matter."

But why did it taste sweet to some and bitter to others? Who was feeding on the pain of jealousy? Who benefitted?

There was no response. All was everything and nothing. But now that I had discovered that thought influences the way some things materialised one way or another, could I think up other things?

39

Sour milk and dried bread are enough,
and enough is as good as a feast.

Epicurus

THE fragrances of flowers and spices suffused the kitchen. I could make out pennyroyal, artemisia, mandrake root, wormwood, calamint, peony, garlic, myrrh, ginger, aloe, saffron, cinnamon, violet, iris. I noticed none of these were being added to the food. Were they being boiled for Basil as a remedy against flatulence, or some sort of internal obstruction, a bowel ailment or a liver complaint? Perhaps.

My Lady Anna had not been getting out of bed and had been avoiding her domestic responsibilities. Basil, too, had been lying low. All day long he had been staying in his room concocting excuses, or he would leave the house, speaking neither to me nor to Anna. Anna did not bother to hide her discomfort about my visits to the kitchen.

Sometime later, I began to hear her retching, gurgling, even vomiting. When I asked her what was wrong, she brushed me off, saying she was unwell but would soon get better. The following week, Anna got herself to her feet and washed her bed linen which she had dumped in a corner. She was dumb enough to think that she was doing the laundry surreptitiously but naturally the blood stains on the sheets had not escaped my notice. I caught her when she returned to the kitchen after hanging them.

"Prepare a honey rice pudding for me, will you?" I said.

Anna shrugged her shoulders and turned away.

"Turn round Anna!"

"Why?" she hissed but obeyed. Hands on hips she stood, puffed up, squeaking:

"Last time you said my milk was sour, the honey was crystallised. You said my pudding wasn't edible."

I waved my hand: "Yes, I did. But I need one. Hopefully this time you won't use sour milk."

"Why?"

"Why what?"

Squinting her black eyes she continued her reluctance: "I don't feel like cooking right now. I feel extremely fatigued."

"Fatigued by doing what? Washing sheets? Perhaps you got sick because you don't sleep the night through. Not getting enough sleep or not sleeping deeply enough might be the cause, don't you think? But now you're fine, my dear."

"Why should you need a pudding anyway?"

I sighed: "What a stupid question. Besides, obviously you aren't tired enough to not stick your nose into things that don't concern you, but if you really insist on knowing, I'll tell you: I will take the pudding to Ogan's wife, Apple, to congratulate her on their new house and convey my best wishes for their future."

"You shouldn't do that. Anyway, since when did you care about their happiness?" I dug my nails into my palms.

"Don't start preaching. And, just so you know, I do care very much care about their happiness."

"Yes, but not like that… Don't twist things around. Don't get involved."

"It's called being friendly. And we have already got involved. No, I mean when he came and stayed here. Don't you think sometimes fate draws us into unexpected things? Take yourself, haven't you ever found yourself involved in something you could never have foreseen or dreamed of."

"Never."

"Never?" I cocked my head. "You sure?"

With firm voice: "Yes, I'm sure. Never."

"Ah! As the Grand Sage said, 'Know thyself!'"

"Keep away from them. It's not decent."

"Since when have you been the measure of decency, Anna?"

"What do you mean?"

"Ah, just leave it. You know in the end I'll do what I want to do."

"Just don't. For once do nothing. Nothing, for your father's sake. Do nothing, Theia."

"Anna, I don't need your advice. Besides, Apple likes me. She hugged me."

She was about to take that famous pose of hers with her arms akimbo and on impulse I jumped towards her. Holding her arm, I prevented the triangle that her elbow would form outwards. Shocked, she liberated her arm from my clutch and took a step backwards. I let her loose and, more perturbed than her, backed off. I sensed my head getting hot and my temples throbbed.

"How dare you!" she growled.

"I know myself."

"What the hell does that mean?"

"I'm protecting you from me. I don't like you standing like that – all akimbo."

"You impertinent child! Your manners are becoming atrocious."

As she looked me up and down indignantly, I laughed. "And who is to blame? Me? You? Madam Gabras? Nike? I would take soup to *his* new wife too, if she were not so bony. Apple, on the other hand, seems to be someone who has a zest for living. She has a small waist, but the rest of her body is voluptuous."

"Where did you learn to speak like this? So insolently? And your father…"

Fury never failed to rejuvenate Anna. She was long past the age where certain expressions, or the right angle, might lend a woman a fleeting semblance of youth. Her white hair had already begun to overtake the jet black. But she had bright black eyes which glimmered incessantly and shapely rouge and plum lips so her teeth seemed very white, and she could blush at will. She could tense all her muscles so tight that it looked as if she were not fat anymore but knowingly, happily and consciously overweight – not unlike Andronicus, who carried his body with the same self-assured ease, though his flesh was in prime condition. Her assuredness made me fly into a rage and I hollered like never before:

"Leave my father. Leave him!"

I pounded my fist on the countertop.

"Now, will you or will you not prepare the pudding?"

"Not on your life!"

"Very well… I shall take a soup then. That too will be fine."

At the end of every summer she prepared *trachana*, a dried mixture of sour milk, crushed wheat, mint, fenugreek seeds, and onions. The gruelling process consisted of mixing sour milk with new sour milk every day and fermenting it for a minimum of two weeks. The top was shielded using branches of wild thyme to ward off flies as well as work the smell into the mixture; it was stirred twice a day. It would then be poured into the copper kettle and heated until hot, but not boiling. Then cracked wheat and the rest of the ingredients would be added. The mixture would be stirred for at least three hours. When cooled, the sticky dough would be kneaded and dried in the sun for a week. Later, in winter – or even in summer, if one preferred – these pieces would be re-boiled in chicken broth with beaten eggs and lemon juice, transforming into a delicious soup.

"I'll boil some water myself."

When I headed towards the cellar to bring dried strips of trachana, she snarled:

"*Trachana* is sour milk too; sour, sour milk! So, you should know!"

She waved her hand and walked away. I turned and screamed:

"You always think I know less than you, Anna, always less than you! What would you understand about diplomacy anyway? You're such a sour puss!"

As a token of my good intentions, tact, and – last but not least – my artfulness, I took my *trachana* and, true to form, slammed the door behind me. After all, wasn't this the essence of finesse and diplomacy? The first-ever Roman ambassador, too, had to follow unconventional methods to win the trust of those he was sent to communicate with. He had been greeted with an opulent welcome by the tribe known as the Sky Turks, but before he was truly accepted, he first had to prove himself by undergoing a ritual cleansing by fire. To them, none of what the unknown poet had said seemed to hold true:

"Sea, Women and Fire are three of the greatest devils."

They paid no heed to the sea, and their women seemed not to be at variance with men but in harmony with everyone in the community – men and women alike – like the left arm and the right arm working together. These women acted like potash alum in dyeing: they brightened and fixed each other's colours rather than darkening them. They existed together in the same way as the squares of a round Zatrikion board. Here the women walked ahead, not behind. They ate first and did not wait on men. And while the tribe held archery and horse-racing activities in high regard, those pursuits paled in comparison to the mission the matriarch bore within the family.

She was the chief of the sacred fire, through which the souls of the family ancestors were manifested and transfigured, sustaining the happiness and continuity of the family. A flame was always lit by her and nobody else, she oversaw keeping the fire alive. Taking it out of the home or giving a piece of it to someone else was strictly forbidden. She protected it and prevented the greatest crime from transpiring: putting a knife or an axe into it or pouring something nasty over it. Only she, the commander of the house, fathomed the secrets of fire. She was what Euripides described:

"Over against fire, another fire was born much greater, woman, even more unconquerable."

If there was any devil and he was out there, she indubitably knew where to find and finish him off without a hitch; after all, she could gallop and shoot arrows and more. In keeping with her race, where Alma was an exception with her diaphanous complexion and her fairy-like demeanour, benefaction came from God, malice from the earth. So, with her powerful torso relatively longer than her legs, her broad shoulders, and solid arms, she could take care of anything.

As they rang bells and beat drums above the aghast Roman ambassador, his retinue, and their baggage, they ran around them in a circular pattern, frenetically chanting cryptic songs and burning flaming, snapping incense. Ultimately, they had him and his party pass through a fire whereby all the evil spirits he had brought from Constantinople were expelled. They placed the stupefied, but also purified, ambassador on the right side, and the place of honour was given to the Khan's golden, two-wheeled throne pulled by two horses. Officers of the court squatted in two long rows on felt mats. Sitting on the floor, covered with beech bark and foal pelts, other members of the tribe formed a semi-circle around a fire, with females on the right and males on the left. The men, their faces smoothly shaved, sported either long, braided hair like their women or a long strip of hair in the centre, with both sides completely shaven. This allowed the kam to grab them to save them from the boiling cauldron of the evil god

Erlik. Hair on the scalp, not the face manifested the growth of the spirit, and they cut it only when a loved one had died. This symbolised the separation from past actions and thoughts, and so they did it to their enemies too. Each person passed his or her right hand through the fire and touched fingers to lips. A woman brought a silver tray bearing drinks. The ambassador's drink was in a silver goblet and the Khan's, to the ambassador's astonishment, was in a wooden cup. The ambassador had anticipated that he and the Khan would drink from a goblet made out of a skull, for that was the idea they had of the Turks. In due course, he would learn that Khans always drank from wooden cups. I've heard tell that hundreds of years later even Atilla did so.

The Khan stood up and stepped to the fire. Holding his cup in his left hand, he poured some liquid into the palm of his right hand, and with that hand he sprinkled a generous amount of the drink onto the flames. The right hand was the apt one for the right represented the spirit and the self, the goodness and the future, while the left belonged to Erlik and the material – the left is where they kept the dirty dish water in *yurts*. Holding the cup aloft, he performed what was likely a welcome speech to the ambassador, and then began to drink. The same woman who had brought the silver tray scattered drink all around while another served the beverage to the company, beginning with the female members.

The ambassador noticed the drink, which was obviously not made of raisins for they had no raisins in Central Asia. When asked, they explained that it was made of soured milk, re-soured and preserved for a long, very long time. The alcohol began to take its effect, mellowing the atmosphere and rendering the Khan even more amicable and emotional, so much so that tears flooded his eyes, to the shock of the ambassador. Asked why he was weeping, the Khan said, "Now that we and the Romans are exchanging ambassadors, we will also have to go to war against each other, sooner or later."

Andronicus must have known this story. I changed my mind abruptly and steered my horse to the Caravanserai, not to Apple's house. At first, the beast was surprised but he quickly complied.

The courtyard was quiet. The cellarer awoke with a start from a deep, snoring sleep when he heard my voice. I extended the bowl of soup and demanded he re-heat it. While he obeyed, I knocked on Andronicus' door, but nobody replied. Returning to the cellar, I ordered the man to find someone to open it. He complied without objection or question, and without casting one of those mocking, enquiring stares that I was becoming used to. He found the key in haste. Seeing no soldier guarding Andronicus's door gave me the impression that they were beginning to neglect security measures. Probably, the soldiers, too, were snoring somewhere. Andronicus was sleeping soundly. I turned to the cellarer and, putting my fingers to my lips, motioned for him to be quiet. Once more acquiescing, he cleared away.

Intending to sit and wait, I was turning towards the armchair when a hand grabbed hold of my arm. Andronicus was smiling. I recoiled and liberated my arm from his clutch. He reclined his pillow against the wall and straightened up.

"I brought you trachana soup."

"Ah, so I smell."

"Are you hungry?"

Heaving a sigh, he answered: "For so many things… It is a pity I am so weak."

I took a spoon of soup to his lips but before that I blew the smoke because the cellarer had boiled it. Resembling an obedient child or cat, he swallowed it up. When he took the second spoonful in his mouth, his eyes became wet. I thought the soup was too hot, rather than that he was feeling emotional. He licked his chapped lips and then the broad curve of a smile covered his face.

"This is even more delicious than what we have at the Palace. Neither too sour nor too mild. Perfect balanced."

"But of course. Anna made it."

"We should take her into the Imperial service, this is a *trachana* worthy of an emperor."

By all means, I thought. I shouldn't ask, who is going to cook for us then?

"Oh, take her," I said, "she can have her. Please, take her with you when your cousin saves you." I rolled my eyes.

He burst out laughing. "So, we don't like Anna?"

"Well, I do. But…"

"What?"

I stared at the floor, drawing in breath.

"I prefer not to talk about it."

As he knows everything, he is going to guess this one too. Let's see what he will say, I told myself, and he spoke:

"Do you know why Jesus cursed the fig tree?"

"Eh?"

"Do you know why Jesus cursed the fig tree?"

In a flat tone: "Because it had no figs? Although he would never be so mean…"

"No. He cursed it because the tree had put forth leaves out of season. When a fig tree has leaves, it must yield figs as a matter of fact and that one did not."

"I take it there's a lesson here?"

"So, he damned it. For promising but not delivering."

"And the relevance of this? I mean I understand the moral. But what does that mean here?"

"Oh, don't pretend. You know very well what I mean… You know the story of Tantalus?"

"Yes. He was a titan who mocked the gods, and they became very angry and punished him."

"He was the half-mortal son of Zeus and did two very nasty things. While he was dining with the gods, which they did with first generation mortals, he stole the nectar and ambrosia that was served and gave it to his friends down below. And second, to test whether gods are omniscient, he killed, cut up and stewed his own son and served him to all the gods at dinner." Relishing the gruesome even while ill, I thought. "All but one of them realised the trick. Demeter was distracted and ate the meat. The gods flew into a rage. They brought the dead boy back to life, replaced his shoulder with ivory and punished Tantalus. Any idea how?"

"No."

"He was made to stand in a pool, under the branches of an apple tree. When he tried to reach for a succulent apple that hung above, the bough would ascend out of his reach; when he bent down to drink from the pool, the waters would recede… You are that apple, my tantalising Theia… You are my apple!"

He sighed, let his head fall back and closed his eyes. Then he flattened his body. I tucked him in and left.

40

It seems I am adding fuel to the fire.

Aristophanes, *Fragment*

His fabric was brought to the caravanserai by a Turk who had just returned from Central Asia. Greyish-white in colour, and robust in construction, it was rough and plainly woven with no floating yarns; it seemed impossible to snag. Its back and front were the same. The seller wore a double-breasted crossover-style coat, long leather boots, and tight trousers, and sported a fur cap. His skin was much yellower than that of his fellow Turkoman denizens of Romanoi, with swarthy undertones, which made him utterly more alien to me than the others, perhaps wildly so. He had exceptional sharp, green slanting eyes. Speaking Turkish to the cellar man, he briskly took a pitcher the man had handed to him. I immediately took my place at the front of the crowd of around forty curious villagers and closely observed his chapped fingers. He did not resort to the usual unctuous, exaggerated sales pitch of market hawkers and street pedlars; quietly he poured fruit sherbet from his carafe onto the fabric. The liquid diffused rapidly, and a pinkish red stain emerged, precisely in the shape of an apple. Since the fabric didn't absorb the liquid uniformly, the resultant blot was made up of varying tones that gave it the impression of length, breadth and depth. I shrugged my shoulders at this coincidence, certain that it had nothing to do with Ogan's wife, and that, in all likelihood, my mind was playing tricks on me by manifesting my *Theia mania* in images of apples here and there.

The Turkoman seller took a piece of iron and drew it firmly across the edge of a flint rock. Flakes of metal sheared off from the rock, in a shower of sparks. He directed them into a bunch of shredded cotton which he had taken out of his pocket and placed in a tin bowl. When the pieces of cotton caught fire, he hastily grabbed them by their not yet burning ends and threw them onto his own fabric. Those of us at the front involuntarily stepped backwards, for fear of the leaping flames. But the pieces of burning cotton which fell on his merchandise instead were reduced to ashes while also erasing the red apple stain entirely from the fabric. The cloth remained intact, as clean as before. It was nonflammable. The crowd cheered while the Turkoman's expression did not change – as if the phenomenon he had performed was the most mundane in the world. Impassive, he made a sign to the spectators and summoned them to the kitchen which was not large enough to accommodate everyone. Around thirty of us barged in behind him, jostling, pushing, and elbowing each other to get a better view, while the rest were left outside, damning and cursing. The pantryman announced loudly in Greek and Turkish that the Turkoman would repeat his spectacle a second time for those who could not see, and that placated the malcontents.

The second demonstration consisted of slowly folding the fabric and casting it into the hearth. After a while, the Turkoman took it out with tongs and placed it on a stone counter. The audience cried out words of shock and admiration for once again the cloth remained intact, though the flames had licked it aggressively. I pushed my way forward and touched it. It was undamaged and warm, not hot.

While the seller was repeating his spectacle we approached the cellarman, who I suspected would receive an agreeable commission for his translation services, to pose him some questions about the fabric. He raised his hand to ward us off and gave a dazed look at the gate. At once there was a hush, and I turned my head in the direction everyone else was looking. An unusual visitor was making her entrance, with servants.

She was dressed in monochrome, as was the vogue in those days, and had chosen tones of green for that purpose. Neither the cuffs and fringes of her inner tunic nor the open chlamys displayed ornaments; no gold or silver bands decorated the arms, although to the discerning eye, the unsymmetrical motifs that ornamented her dress, made it clear that she was wealthy. Her headcloth was wrapped in Islamic fashion, much tighter than our vernacular style and her veil hid even her eyes. Yet somehow, one could tell she was not a Saracen. As they approached, I recognised one of the servants. The lady was Madam Gabras. The head-covering she sported made her stand out instead of blending in as she had obviously aspired to, but there were no Saracens in the courtyard that day, only a few nomadic Turkish women, and she didn't resemble them at all. They too were looking at Gabras with surprised expressions. We stepped back as she walked up to the cellarman. She gave a quick, impersonal bow to the crowd without meeting my eyes, thus I was uncertain whether she noticed my presence or not. Remaining detached from him, angling away from the crowd and stooping slightly, she asked him about the fabric. Her voice lost its usual husky and aggressive pitch, though it didn't sound friendly either. The neutrality of her tone – which, for her, signalled modesty – as well as the clear effort she was making to blend in with the barbarians, only left her looking more awkward. The sight of it filled me with a sudden sense of power. She was not mingling, she appeared lost and odd. A few Turkish women sneered at her which added a great deal to my amusement. I felt as if I belonged there, and she did not. With an excessive bow of salute, the pantryman ushered her into the kitchen where the others were.

The crowd began to mutter and complain to each other.

The old butcher Demitrios said, "If she intends to buy some magical fabric, it'll certainly cause this barbarian to increase the price."

"Could she not have come later?" asked the Armenian, Bardas. "Why did she not send a servant instead of showing up herself?"

"Perhaps she's here to spy on us?" mused Svoronos the bookbinder.

Sophia the amulet-maker chipped in with her thoughts too: "Yes, for sure! She'll write to her sister in Constantinople and let the Emperor know that Plekia folk are involved in magic, purchasing heretical items!"

Pardos the eunuch priest's pale face turned ashen. He looked around as if searching for someone.

The new fishmonger turned to Sophie and spoke sharply: "Nonsense. That fabric isn't under a spell any more than your scarlet threaded amulets are. She never protested your infidel amulets, did she?"

Sophie opened her mouth, but nothing came out. Her chest caved; her chin began to tremble. She rubbed those extremely wide-set, down-turned eyes in an attempt to wipe away tears but didn't succeed. The power of tears when they want to spill is insurmountable, and so she surrendered. Face bright red, ears darker, she burst into a lamentable crying fit, theatrically loud. My own fits came to my mind, which, too, were likewise inordinately frantic in relation to their cause and the context in which they took place. And I knew how ashamed she would soon feel. I stepped in and pulled her into a side hug.

"Come on now, it's nothing. Gabras is only here to buy fabrics for her sister in Constantinople, not to denounce us. Relax. I know the woman."

Another man who seemed impressed by Sophie's tears added, "Bullshit. Amulets are not sinful. And anyway, now this is the territory of Ataman or some Sultan in Iconium, not the Emperor. Look, his cousin is sleeping next door, and nobody gives a damn."

Another yelled: "No, no. Amulets are blasphemous. They are, yes!"

"No, they're not."

"You don't even fast properly. Is that not sinful?"

"That's right! And besides he always snoozes at the church when the priest speaks. Supplicate Pardos; go on, ask him – he'll tell you."

They stopped talking and looked about. A few continued with raised voices.

"Pardos, where are you?"

"Where's the priest?"

But Priest Pardos was nowhere to be seen. Demitrios turned to the amulet-hater and said:

"In fact, you, speaking in such a fashion, really, that's what's sinful."

"So, you know what is sinful, right? Well, then why are you here to buy this product of wizardry? Get lost, you double-faced idiot!"

The arguments were heating up, and a brawl was about to break out when, as luck would have it, right on cue, the cellarman reappeared. The fight was swiftly forgotten, and, as if they were children, the group huddled around him. I spoke up to demanded, "Is this magic?"

He lowered his brow, shaking his head and wagging a finger. "Of course not. It is made of wool but not sheep's wool. Come. See, touch."

He summoned us to the room where the sales would of course be conducted; we took a glance inside where rolls of fabric were piled up neatly. He picked up a piece and handed it to Demitrios.

"Here, examine it and pass it on. It's made of salamander wool. Just like the lizard, it, too, is incombustible. Immerse it in fire; it'll not just stay unburnt – it'll be cleansed."

I saw Madam Gabras' footmen preparing her sedan chair. I assumed she would leave shortly and revert from her subdued state back to the usual smug one. I didn't wish to lose the taste of my newly found eminence, even if it was illusory. Discreetly, I drew away from the group and headed towards Andronicus's room.

The door of his cell was ajar. I pushed it open without knocking. Seated with his back turned to the door, he was wearing a geranium and petunia wreath on his head and quietly murmuring to himself. I burst into laughter at the sight. He turned slowly, undazed, as if expecting me.

"Arrant twaddle, my dear, tantalising Theia," he said. "That fabric is not made of salamander wool."

Wiping my eyes and nose, I had to ask: "What's with the wreath?"

Leaning back in his chair, he held his hands to the nape of his neck and grinned.

"I stole some wine yesterday, or rather, the guard let me pass to go and fetch it. Of course I convinced him."

"Really. You have nothing to offer. How did you inveigle him? You might as well have him bring some vinegar today to treat your headache."

"I did. It did not help, hence the wreath. When you do not drink every day, the aftereffect is more severe. I don't mix wine with resin nor dilute it though, even when it is of lower quality, which it was. As for how to persuade people, that is my specialism, my dear. It's easy when you have something to offer. The trick is to manage it when you have nothing to give but your name and a few promises. Naturally he'll be compensated in factual indemnities when I return home. I never forget kindnesses and favours shown to me."

I laughed. "You couldn't persuade me!"

He sneered. “We’ll see about that…”

“So, what about this fabric?”

“Ah yes, a salamander has no wool but moist skin only, so that fabric can’t be made of its wool.”

“That’s what I thought.”

“You clever girl!”

He leaned back in his chair, placing his hands behind his head again.

“For once Aristotle and Pliny were wrong. They both thought salamanders would put out fire by contact because they’re cold like ice. Jews believe that too. You smear the blood of a salamander on your skin, and it doesn’t burn. All unfounded stories, my dear.”

“So, what is it made of then? It is indeed incombustible. I saw it with my own eyes.”

He gave a lopsided grin. “A stone.”

“A stone?”

“Yes. A rock, fibrous in composition, common to their lands in Central Asia, but its origin is Saturn – cold, taxing, rigorous, exacting, and trying. They separate the fibres from the stone and then they pound and crush them. They blend, comb, and clean them, make them into little slivers, and spin and twist them into yarns. As simple as that. Saturn induces trials, imposes difficulties, the fabric being from Saturn endures as befits.”

“I’ve heard about sea silk, or the famous purple dye taken from sea snails but never that. It doesn’t sound that simple. But how do you know all this?”

“I told you: I lived with them for years. Purple is from Tyre. You need thousands and thousands of snails to colour one garment. And the sea silk, it’s made by us Romans.”

“Really?”

“Yes. Clams adhere to rocks with a tuft of strong filaments. Fine artisans spin and treat these fibres, they sing over them too, because vibrations have a bearing upon their finesse and textures. My mother had gloves made of sea silk, her hands were always warm. They had the colour of gold, shone like gold too and it never faded. You could fold three pairs and fit them into one walnut shell. It’s a creation that fits our Roman disposition like a glove, fine and sophisticated, and theirs conforms to theirs too, harsh and invincible.”

"Your mother..."

He interrupted me, "But if we get back to the lizards, my dear... There is another type that is much, much more interesting than those salamanders."

He stood up. Despite his sickness causing great weight loss resulting in hollowed cheeks, pale skin, a sluggish posture and a languid quality to his limbs, he was still a very beautiful man, imposingly tall, with broad shoulders. Now that he was no longer tanned, that yellowish amber colour in his eyes seemed less frightening and salient, and his hair was longer, deep brown and unkempt.

"That one is coated with dry scales. Good old Pliny mentioned it and was right about it. I've been in search of those but to no avail. They grow in Egypt, skinks, fat ones. You soak them in wine with rocket seeds and satyrion root and eat them."

Covering my mouth, I exclaimed, "Disgusting! Why would you eat a lizard?"

Jokingly he jerked away then quickly turned and swooped down on me, seizing me around my waist with an iron grip. Lifting me up he forcefully pressed his lips on mine. Off guard, I could not react for a second and a strange, tingling thrill suffused my whole body, flooding up my legs. I pushed and kicked him violently but could not scream, knowing it would be heard. Fearing the worst I began to kick and hit him even more fiercely; he stopped at once and put me down. I snapped at him:

"How dare you! Never attempt something like that again. Never. Ever!"

As if the scene had not happened at all he turned his back, strode to the table, lifted the carafe and poured himself a cup of water.

My head still hot, but the tingling nibbling away at me, I hissed at him again, intending to say, 'Do not do that ever again, never ever, ever. Do not make me regret my presence here.' Instead, what came out was, "I asked you something. Answer. Answer why one should eat a lizard? I order you to answer me now."

He stroked his neck, then touched his mouth. "How much money does the barbarian ask for the fabric?"

"I don't know yet, but..."

"Ah! The mighty *hyperpyron*... In the hands of all nations today, together with the barbarian *dinar,* and yet at one time only we possessed the purest golden coin, and no one else. I loved to visit the minting facilities when I was a kid. To his great pain and regret, Grandfather Alexios had to debase the currency, so he introduced the *hyperpyron*. There was no other way, no other choice. These barbarians were unravelling us like doilies. Normans, Pechenegs, nasty Latins and what have you. Do you know what *hyperpyron* means?"

"Refined over fire?"

Tipping his head to one side: "Bravo, girl. Fire purifies metal. Fire is the test of gold; adversity the test for strong men – just like Seneca said."

"The lizard I was enquiring about…"

He waved his arm. "To not burn in fire, one must possess great will, intransigent determination, unyielding perseverance, iron stamina, and sharp, agile intellect. When the King of Babylon threw Shadrach, Meshach, and Abednego into a fiery furnace, heated seven times hotter than normal, they came out unharmed. Flames had licked them like a loving dog licks his owner. King Nebuchadnezzar had to promote them to high office."

"The lizard…"

"The lizard… Yes, the lizard… Perhaps your Sweet Barbarian was not altogether wrong when he alleged that abstinence accords tremendous strength to the body and sharpens the mind. It might, in effect, be imparting better benefits than the reptilian. You must know, abstinence and chastity work in opposite ways. The first may enhance the mind, but the latter certainly stupefies it. Beyond doubt. Manuel, on the other hand… He is spoiled and will pay for this."

As it became evident the subject of the lizard had been dropped, it was also high time to leave. His wandering monologue provided the right moment to slink off, so I did, gently closing the door behind me.

I saw Ogan in the courtyard loading two fat batches of the fabric onto his horse. He blushed again to his ears, just as he had when the boxes containing the mercury had arrived. Without giving me the opportunity to blush too, he ducked his head, got on his horse, and was gone.

41

Before death catches up with me,
I shall play and laugh and dance.

Anacreonta, *Fragment*

THE Muhtasib turned his head with deliberate affectation, purposefully ignoring a number of guffawing girls who were competing with boys at archery on the lawn. Another band, made up of both boys and girls raced horses further afield. The Muhtasib carrying a velvet case with silver Arabic letters on it, walked a step ahead of the circumciser who had been sent by the Sultan in Iconium – a small stooping man hauling his paraphernalia in a leather bag. The Muhtasib seemed in a better mood than when he had strolled among the market booths inspecting vendors and drunks. His fierce reputation followed him though most of the nomads were entirely uncurious about his antics. They were in the habit of showing interest only in what was at hand, and, in this case, these were sweets that the children's mothers hid in their palms – flour roasted in butter with honey or molasses.

Five centuries ago, Emperor Heraclius received a foreboding message in a nightmare: "Verily, there shall come against thee a circumcised nation and they shall vanquish thee and take possession of your land." When he woke the next day, he began searching for this "circumcised nation" so that he might take precautions, and given that in those days Turkic men were not circumcised (and had even provided much-needed auxiliaries for him in his struggle against the Persians), he naturally found the Jews. All Jews were to be baptised in all the provinces under his dominion, or else they would be beheaded. A few days after the issue of the edict, a messenger from Bursa brought a Bedouin to Heraclius's court. He reported that a prophet named Mohammed had appeared in their midst, calling idol-worshippers to the knowledge of the one God. Some believed and followed him, declaring him their prophet, and others did not, and wars broke out between them. More concerned about the impending danger than the tenets of the new Arab Prince's teaching, Heraclius ordered the Bedouin to be stripped and found that he was circumcised.

During the following ten years, Heraclius kept paying tribute to the Muslims, adherents of the new creed. Then the Prince of the Arabs sent an army into Egypt, defeating the Romans, first at Memphis, then at Alexandria. Since then, the Arabs have twice laid siege to Constantinople, failing each time – thanks to the superiority of the Roman navy, the deadly power of Greek fire, and the formidable strength of the city's fortifications.

Heraclius's nightmare had been proved wrong until now. But Turkic boys are still circumcised, even nomads. In front of each kid's bed, the circumciser flamboyantly whetted his razor on a whetstone. I didn't know if this was necessary or if it was part of the ritual. Unaware of the nuisance about to befall them, the moon-faced children laughed at first. Mothers caressed the long strip of hair left in the centre of their boys' shaven heads. This warrior's lock left upon a boy's shaven head was his tether to the living world, a safeguard against the boiling cauldrons of Erlik. Should the devil steal his spirit, the tribe's kam would seize that sacred tress and pull him back out of the cauldron.

In fact, a number of their horses sported the same hairstyle which began to seem rather endearing, bringing to mind my own Pegasus. Pegasus boasted an unusually long, upright mane which grew long enough to comb down between his two ears and lavender eyes. Unfortunately, it was coarse, somewhat felty, and when compared to the lofty forelocks of the Turkish horses, it succumbed to the same pitiful predicament of his tail which was practically a cow's tail. But then we already know: "Things will never be as we want them to be."

The Muhtasib strongly disapproved of the nomads' manner of wearing their hair, citing the Prophet's guidance: 'Either shave all of it or leave all of it.'He noted that freely flowing, long locks, and braids were for Jews, tuft befitted Magians. However, in his high spirits today, he ignored this pesky detail.

Besides, all the fathers were present. A handful wore braids, many had long, loose tresses, while the majority shaved their heads, leaving some sections intentionally longer, creating a strange contrast. Yet, they matched the horses spectacularly. The Muhtasib dared not hassle the men – not that day. However, he never stopped nagging the boys' mothers in private about their sons' hair. Still his efforts were wasted: the foreskin could go, but not the hair.

Among the portable beds, he walked; the moon-faced nomadic Turkic boys smiled so widely that their eyes narrowed to the same horizontal black line as Ogan's eyes.

He did not understand. Braided hair signified something crucial to these nomads – a belief deeply engrained. Hair had a vital function; it was one of the seats of the spirit. When braided, it embodied the unity with the infinite. Free-flowing hair flowed as life itself flowed; that which wants to flow must flow. Hair allowed unearthly perceptions, exactly in the same way a jellyfish utilised its tentacles or a cat its whiskers.

As I write these notes in the year 1143, women no longer shave their heads when they lose their husband, but in those days, they still did. When he died, the growth of her spirit died, too. Her vitality departed; animation halted. Ah! Olden days knew greater love stories....

The crook-backed circumciser bent down in front of the children one-by-one. He cut surprisingly rapidly and by the time he lifted his head, the smile from each boy was just beginning to turn into shocked tears and giggles into a heart-wrenching bellow as the flame of pain burned them, and this was the very second the mothers shoved the hidden sweets into the mouths of their moon-faced boys. The Muhtasib shouted:

"Allahu Ekber!"

And when several public servants who were also sent from Iconium chanted Quranic quotes the Muhtasib would yell again:

"Allahu Ekber!"

And then another foreskin was cut. The stooping man bent down in front of the boy and spread a red cloth over his lap so the boy couldn't see. Each scream was followed by another from the Muhtasib: "Allahu Ekber!"

He opened his velvet case and flauntingly handed a large piece of gold to the nomad, posturing to the degree that his double chin became even more prominent, stacking in great folds beneath his face and protruding as he pushed his head backwards in a bid to appear even more lofty. The gold was gifted from the Caliph Al Muqtafi in Baghdad, not that the origin of the gift mattered to the nomads. I don't doubt though that the Muhtasib, from his position as Consul of the Sultan in Plekia, made this information widely known.

For Turks, the coins were to buy sheep or goats in the future. The boys fretted and wailed, and mothers stuffed more sweets into their snot-and tear-smeared faces.

The curious tune of a *kopuz* reached my ear. It had three strings along which the player's long-nailed right hand moved, engendering a high pitch from the upper parts of the finger board, and lower pitches from the gourd-shaped body of the instrument. The musician held it over his shoulder, then between his knees. I couldn't decide if the tune would still be happy to my ears if it was not accompanied by the appetising smell of whole lambs being roasted on a spit. I decided the music was joyful, somehow homely, and I was sure it would sound even better as soon as I approached the nomad who was in charge of the grilling. He smiled much like the moon-faced children and cut a piece of lamb, wrapped it in flat bread and handed it to me without saying a word. The music was decidedly happy as I took a bite of the wrap. I felt as though my insides were also melting as the succulent meat melted in my mouth.

Next to us was a woman who was boiling something in a cauldron. With an exaggeratedly questioning expression I indicated the cauldron.

Another moon-face smiled and told me: "*Tagan*!"

I didn't know if this was the name of the meal or the cauldron, and I did not have the opportunity to ask, for the sound of another *kopuz* joined the first one, and then another one, and then another. Within a few seconds, at least a dozen of the instruments began to weave melodies in unison when suddenly Apple sprang forth from nowhere. Raising her arms into the air, she began to wave them from side to side. She bowed, turned around, arched her elegant white neck and kicked up her legs; her small feet were bare, white, and dainty. Petrified by this boldness I swallowed my meat the wrong way and began to cough. Tears filled my eyes as I tried to push the meat down and catch my breath. A woman made her hand into a fist and pummelled my back to open the airway as drums began to beat forcefully. Much embarrassed, I deployed many gestures to thank her and urge her to stop. She smiled and joined Apple with another bunch of dancers forming a moving ring. The drums gradually slowed and quieted.

When I had pulled myself together, I looked around for Ogan but didn't spot him. After that, all I could see was Apple. The crowd disappeared. The *kopuzes* were silent. All the other girls became shadows.

She lifted her arms again, imitating the movements of a bird, her slender waist begirded with a silver belt, bending and squirming... Her figure fluctuated between corporeal and immaterial as she leaped and descended. Since I know nothing finer than a diamond, I must employ that platitude, for she truly shone like a one. When you turn a diamond towards the light, it dazzles your eyes, turned away, it no longer glows, but it is still a diamond, is it not? Where does the gleam go?

Boiled water evaporates into steam, which vanishes. Rainbows fade into the light. The sun departs; storms end. Wherever they all went, she did too – only to return with all her bliss, oscillating between the celestial and terrestrial.

But where was Ataman during this disgraceful display of unrestrained abandon?

Dressed in red, she became a bird, flying higher and higher as the girls whooped in unison, their whirling growing faster and faster. The wheel of life turned and turned. The drums beat faster. The girls, all barefoot, bounding upward, revolving on their own axes, circling with arms still raised, swaying from side to side. Apple whirled and whirled to the sonorous vibrations, surrendering her body to their power.

I felt queasy but kept my eyes upon her, and so did Muhtasib, with his dark, scary eyes, and lips curled as he stroked his throat. Would he not disperse this unabashed, immodest group, I wondered? But he maintained his distance.

Pouring the last drops of their liquor onto the ground, men began to join the dancers, mimicking the graceful movements of a bird. Men and women faced each other but kept a certain distance between them.

"Theia, dance with them!"

I lifted my head and there stood Ogan, readying to join Apple, licking his lips like a child, his eyes squinting. I lifted my hand up and blocked the compulsion to flee. Smiling widely, like an idiot, he repeated: "Come and dance with us."

I attempted to turn away, but he grabbed my forearm: "Come!"

His fingers burnt. I shivered and felt I must faint soon; he had never touched me before. I yelled:

"I don't know this bird dance; I should not dance."

"It doesn't matter. Just fly! Fly like a crane!"

"I can't fly," I protested. "I'm no crane, I'm a hare."

He stroked my forearm which he had not released.

"I know you're a hare. Alma is a crane. She'll teach you. Come!"

I pulled my arm away harshly. His fingers felt hard and sore.

"The hare can't fly. I cannot!" I snapped at him. "It's made to climb up hills, it can't dance, it can't even go downhill fast. It's built to endure."

He let out a heavy sigh and moved back, unhurriedly joining the dance.

The hare is an animal whose head resembles a cat's, its ears are a donkey's, its nose a mouse's, and its feet a dog's. An animal all blood, with no flesh – not to be eaten. These nomadic Turks did not eat it; the Armenians did not eat it. The hare: melancholic, unwholesome, unclean, unlucky, portending evil to any man who should meet one. If one were to cross your path, you would undoubtedly turn back. The wicked Caliph Yazid who in his power struggle, killed Mohammed's grandchildren Hasan and Husein turned into a hare. Mohammed's cat turned into a hare. The prophet Ali kept a hare, not a cat. The hare was both beloved and hated. It could never fly. It was all contradictions. Pliny observed that hare meat cured sterility and enhanced sexual attraction for nine days. And what was traditionally recommended to promote fertility? Rabbit blood.

Ogan danced. His fine hands and nimble fingers – no longer flexing bows and pulling strings – moved sinuously now. He raised those fine, shapely arms into the air, flying from the sensible, serious, wise son of the Bible to the prodigal one, the son who returns home after squandering his fortune. And instead of punishment, his father prepares a feast.

Where was Ataman?

Luke 15:11-32 described the parable. In his honour, the father even has the fatted calf killed, and when the older, hard-working son hears the music and the dancing, he rightfully becomes angry:

"I've been slaving for you and never disobeyed your orders. Yet you never gave me even a young goat so I could celebrate with my friends."

And what is the answer of the father?

"This brother of yours was dead and now is alive again; so we must celebrate."

Muhtasib shouted out again: "Allahu Ekber!"

The *kopuz* went silent again. With bated breath the dancers waited. He shouted yet again:

"Allahu Ekber!"

And they picked up where they had left off.

42

These grapes be sour.
A fox looked and beheld the grapes that grew upon a high vine which he much desired. And when he saw that he might get none, he turned his sorrow into joy and said these grapes be sour and if I had some, I would not eat them. And therefore he is wise not to desire that thing he may not have.

Aesopus, *Fables*

We may not realise it, but when something good befalls us, or when calamity strikes, it may be the result of a whim – or even the humiliation – of someone we have never met. If that person is an emperor, the links can be traced easily, and if it is a woman, not so easily. Everything in this world unfolds in chain reactions, one event setting another into motion. Sit, take a breath, and assess. No matter how elusive, that chain is always present. One strand of hair can cause a war to erupt and lead to the deaths of thousands. Mull over the fragility of life. I assure you, it has happened many times in history, and will happen again and again.

The demure and austere German, Bertha of Sulzbach, came to Constantinople in 1142 to marry Manuel. Our Nike's famous friend, the court poet Prodromos, knew full well the fickleness of destiny, especially when one works for the royal court. If you wanted to entertain personal fantasies such as writing a bold romance like *Rodanthe and Dosikles*, you had to keep on kissing important derrières. He welcomed the lacklustre Bertha with a poem comparing her to a "Western vinestock to be planted in the imperial garden of the East."

Being the youngest, Manuel was not intended to replace his father as Emperor; he had three elder brothers, two of them still alive. Emperor John had intended him to marry Constance, the only child of Bohemond II, heiress to the Principality of Antioch. John's idea was to establish Manuel as the ruler of the Latin States, the bleeding wound of Byzantium in the east. Constance's mother agreed, but the Latins connived with the King of Jerusalem, and the girl ended up married to the prince of Antioch. Emperor John's pride was hurt.

He embarked upon his own death-bound expedition to the Latin Principality of Antioch, accompanied by his bravest son, Manuel to enforce a treaty wherein the Latins had been rendered a vassal state of the Byzantine Empire during the reign of his father, Emperor Alexios.

Armenians – a learned people, craftsmen, artists, merchants – dwelt there. Where Arabs had evacuated, Romans had resettled with Armenians, yet they were poorly protected against the Turks or any other foe. Loyalties shifted easily. John had to wield a big stick to keep the Armenians, Latins, and Muslims in check otherwise they could form alliances with each other, or anyone else for that matter. Getting a bit of revenge for the Latins' marriage insult was also a big objective of John's military campaign. John died on that notorious expedition; yes, emperors too can die under such nondescript circumstances, far from frenzy and festivity. Two of his elder brothers having already died, Manuel became the new emperor. The remaining one, Isaac, had been ostracised by Emperor John for his recklessness and irascibility. On his deathbed at the camp, John declared:

"Even though my two sons were begotten of the same father, excelling in robustness of body, nobility of form, and profundity of intellect, they both differ in temperament. It is perfectly obvious to me that my last-born Manuel would be the better administrator. There is palpable evidence that God wishes none other than Manuel to be awarded the sceptre of the Romans."

Your nickname might be John the Beautiful but one cannot remain 'beautiful' under all circumstances, not to everyone, not even your own children. Everyone has an Achilles› heel, even the beautiful ones. But I digress, normally it was considered an immutable custom that the elder son would become the emperor, and to his shock and dejection, his father had promoted Isaac's younger brother over his head as the emperor. I personally have never known the predilection for one child rather than another, for I was an only child. But not only emperors have this foible. Even my affectionate Basil could be loving towards some of our animals and not others, for no obvious reason. Emperor John also said of his son:

"Provoked by some cause, Isaac flies into a towering rage, a fault which ruins the wise, and leads the majority of men to act irrationally. I have chosen Manuel to be emperor."

Isaac's pride, too, was hurt. The most significant things in his world did not unfold in a neat succession of cause and effect – indeed they often did not happen at all. Perhaps he acted as he did to ingratiate himself with his imperial father, to reaffirm his own worthiness, his deservingness. Yet, unwittingly, he provoked the opposite reaction.

Bertha, meanwhile, still waited in Constantinople. Manuel kept her waiting until 1146. God knows how much longer he would have delayed the wedding had events not intervened. When Melisende, Queen of Jerusalem, sent word to Pope Eugenius of the fall of Edessa to Zengi, he issued his papal bull, *Quantum predecessores*. In response, Bertha's brother-in-law, King Conrad III of Germany, took the cross at Speyer, and began his preparations. The Second Crusade was off and running. Manuel panicked because now a double-disaster was inevitable, one being his imminent marriage to the tedious Bertha. Crafty Manuel demanded an improved dowry from the German King before he married her. He received, or rather 'extorted' former Byzantine Apulia from Conrad. Thus, both the 'Western vinestock,' as our inventive writer Prodromos had likened Bertha, was planted and the price she paid to become an empress, along with her own worth, increased. However ironic this may sound, so too was the poor woman's position.

One must wonder what she did during those four years of her life, having to skulk around in permanent uncertainty. As a wedding present, she gave a golden plate to Manuel probably without rumination – after all an empty plate is an empty plate. But sometimes objects come first, and their meaning manifests afterwards – hence the irony of her marriage, shiny but empty. Bertha's pride, too, was hurt. And at other times, what is taken for granted as the conventional comes to nothing – hence the predicament of Isaac.

Remember the chain I mentioned? The link between causes and effects remains mysterious. Our minds are more powerful than we know. If life is here to teach lessons, here is another: if you do not take your own anger too seriously, your fantasies may come true. If Isaac had slain a few barbarians on the battlefield instead of just raging in his own head, it would have been he who became the emperor, not his brother. Those who turn their rage inward rather than unleashing it upon others do not make good emperors.

Yet another lesson provided by Andronicus:

"If Bertha had been comely and alluring, in spite of her typically Nordic saturnine demeanour, Manuel would have taken her within the first week of her arrival. For beauty comes above all."

I replied, "She probably doesn't even know who she is anymore, waiting for years in suspense in a foreign country away from her family."

Scratching his belly, a vulgar act which did not befit that equipoised body of his, he shrugged. "She was to marry a prince, and if Manuel does not dump her, she will marry an emperor instead. Not a bad deal if she learns to become more flexible, less stiff."

"What a lamentable fate; it depends entirely on the whims of a man, or rather two men…"

Supporting his chin with his thumb and placing his forefinger vertically on his cheek he scrutinised me as if he had never seen me before, pursing his lips he said:

"But so is yours, darling. The only way to change it is to change the men in question."

Shrugging, I turned away.

"I have no wish to discuss my fate with you."

He grinned.

"So, you prefer to converse about other women whose plights are worse than your own? What for, sweetie? Does that alleviate your agony?"

I stood with one leg crossed over the other and sized him up as if I intended to attack him. This amused him; he covered his mouth with a closed fist, which scared me slightly, and then burst out laughing, I raised my own voice to drown out his boisterous one:

"I am not in agony! I was only trying to tell you that here in Plekia even your incertitude is better than Bertha's situation in

Constantinople. At least you understand their language, and by now you know that they don't want to kill you. Poor Bertha, how awful…"

"Girl, get this into your head" He was animated: "God did not forge this universe so that the natural course of things would be benign, even if we comply word for word with what we are told. The device God made resembles the automata at the Palace. The roaring of the lions and chirping of the birds are not real. It's an imperfect illusion."

Raising his voice, he went on: "If this were not an illusion, there would be no you, no me, no Ogan, no village of Plekia, no Constantinople and no life as you know it. There would be only nothingness."

"Have you met a bunch of heretics here and talked to them? You sound just like one."

"I do not give a damn for their conjectures. Just beware – humans are not naturally inclined toward goodness; it is evil, wickedness that creates, not virtue. Good is only a lucky by-product of what will inevitably come to pass. Good is a potential force; it does not govern this world. It's cowardly, even passive, malleable. Evil knows what it wants. It does not care about hurt pride; it has no expectations. It acts. It solves problems. It is *ponēria* that wins, not *agathōsynē*."

The amber shade of his eyes turned dark, almost black as he said this: "Goodness has a wicked appendage, it always causes pain. Look – if one is happy, there is always some sort of unhappiness accompanying it. Learn this, and do not question things simply because they seem 'wrong' Learn to capitalise on what exists. And that oppressively boring German cow should do the same."

He took a drew breath and smiled. "Like the Turks say, 'Eat the grape, do not question which vineyard it comes from.'"

"Now that you are cooped up here, how will you turn things to your advantage?"

A wary smile flickered on his lips, but his voice still sounded hard: "You'll just have to wait and see, won't you?"

As I walked to the door to leave, he spoke with a different cadence, slightly more hesitant, looking down at his feet: "By the way, Ogan is not taking me to Iconium, his father is. Ataman."

When I got back home, an intensely brewed scent wafted towards me. I could make out wine, mint, cinnamon, fennel, aniseed and caraway, and perhaps some cumin, as well.

Instead of Anna serving Basil his *Eukration* in a glass in the living room where he mostly drank it alone, I found them both sitting in the kitchen on chairs with a table between them, sipping from everyday earthenware cups. A moist nimbus of mutual understanding hung over their heads. In the languor of the ambience, Anna clambered sluggishly to her feet. Before Basil gathered himself up – which I had no doubt would also be in a slothful fashion – I turned my back and closed the door gently behind me. Deciding to eat the grape and not question the vineyard, I returned to Andronicus. I could tell he had half expected my return. Leaning back at ease and in control, never losing eye contact, he gave a small smile which spread into a grin. On my part, there was no surprise; I knew him by then.

It occurred but once, by my sanction and authority – for indeed, I was a hare, as Ogan had stated. A hare, you see, moves swifter uphill than down, which was the very essence of my action, and the particular disposition of my collaborator.

43

The road to Hades is easy to travel.

Bion, from Diogenes Laertius's
Lives of Eminent Philosophers

AT a tavern in the city of Philippopolis in Thrace, when a snake extended its head from the basket of a local Atzinganoi – a gypsy (still a Greek, hence Eastern Roman) – German King Conrad III's soldiers were lost for words. Reputedly devoted to spirit liqueurs, they were taking a break during their expedition to Asia Minor to save Edessa from the siege of the Turkoman Atabeg Zengi. When the snake reared up and spread its distinctive hood, flicked out its forked tongue, and rotated wherever the charmer turned as if spellbound, the Germans were aghast. Terrified but also furious, one took his sword and murdered the snake charmer right there.

To the crude dispositions and imbecilic minds of these soldiers, the snake charmer – capable of the unusual feat of commanding a serpent – would likely have been seen as a practitioner of black arts, a votary of Satan, exhibiting the evil intent of the Greeks and mesmerising them to undermine their Crusade. Knowing their character and anticipating the likelihood of their rampages, Emperor Manuel had previously requested their good conduct while passing through Byzantine lands, requiring that should they conquer any Turk-held territories, the provision of supplies would be contingent upon their being restored to him. Manuel's grand design was to re-conquer the occupied western lands from the Latins and end the schism between the Eastern and Western churches, which had befallen the empire in 1054 when Pope Leo and Patriarch Cerularius had ex-communicated each other. He was bent on bringing the separate churches of the West and the East under one Patriarch, in Constantinople naturally, and becoming the Holy Roman Emperor of both East and West, recapturing the lost lands from the Turks. He had at his disposal a grand treasure accumulated by his father, the austere, prudent John the Beautiful, and was never any more willing to grant autonomy to the troublesome Latin States in the east than his father had been.

After the murder of the snake charmer, a brawl ensued between the resentful Greeks and the drunken Germans, escalating into a major riot. The Bishop of Philippopolis endeavoured to repress and allay the Greek indignation while King Conrad III and his princes attempted to appease the agitated Crusaders in vain. At Adrianople where an ill German noble was taken to a monastery to rest, a group of angry Greek foot soldiers took the opportunity to retaliate, by robbing and killing the nobleman. Conrad III ordered a halt to his march at once and commanded his nephew Frederic to return to Adrianople and punish the assassins. This young Frederic would go on to become the legendary Barbarossa, or Red Beard. He was a man of indomitable courage, boundless ambition, and unwavering self-assurance, so much so that he would consider even the Pope his inferior and answer only to the authority of God once he succeeded his uncle as emperor. But unlike Conrad III, who had the tact to address Manuel as "Emperor", though he did so grudgingly due to the contentiousness of the issue, Red Beard would impudently deploy only the honorific "Rex" in the future for our Emperor. This man was to remain perpetually hostile towards the Romans and, in the throes of his arrogance, he would pledge to permanently expel the Eastern Romans from Italy.

Young Frederic hanged the murderers of the German magnate and burned down the monastery. Some said a "great slaughter" occurred, while others called it "a genial brokering of a peaceful outcome" between the Germans and Byzantines. Either way, the man who imposed a final resolution was Porsuk – no less dauntless and crafty than Frederic himself. He was Emperor Manuel's senior commander – a Turkoman, to the surprise of many – who had converted, and whose name the Byzantines altered from Porsuk, to Prosuch. To protect the natives, his troops were advancing parallel with the line of Conrad III's march, just about restraining their foraging inclinations. Apt to the meaning of his name, 'badger', Porsuk was bold, determined, and ferocious when cornered. He always saw challenges through to completion. To the Crusaders, a Turkoman General and troops of a Christian King employed as guards against Christians was as bizarre as the dancing snake; these feats demonstrated Manuel's ungodly connections and deceitful objectives.

Byzantine merchants continued to cheat the German troops relentlessly. In response, the Germans, and others who followed, raided and pillaged poorly defended Byzantine towns for supplies. Conrad III wrote a letter to Manuel acknowledging the unruly conduct of his men, indicating that such challenges though regrettable were inevitable when an army of such size was on the move. Manuel thanked Conrad III sardonically in reply and suggested that, in the future, he too might find it difficult to restrain his impulsive followers. Porsuk, the badger, wanted to respond with force but had to be repeatedly placated by Manuel. These new Crusaders were indeed obvious intruders, brazen interlopers, but Manuel did not want quarrels with them.

Andronicus was certain that his grandfather, Emperor Alexios, had only asked for help from the Westerners once – when he wrote a letter to Pope Urbanus. All other letters circulating around Europe that were attributed to Alexios – especially the one written to the Count of Flanders, appealing for support – were counterfeits, penned by that crook Pope Urbanus himself.

But why? Andronicus would grin his typical complacent grin. "To raise a big stink, that snake!!!"

It was Andronicus who also told me that, although Pope Urbanus was entirely unaware of it, grandad Alexios even wrote to the King of Northern China, urging him to initiate a military operation in the west against the Turkish Grand Seljuks.

Waving the index finger of his large, veiny hand, he spat on the floor, and with an equally imposing voice he bellowed:

"The hoggish Latins likened my grandfather to a scorpion: nothing to fear from his face, but be careful with his tail. Let me tell you, girl: a scorpion surrounded by fire does not commit suicide; fire only provokes convulsions in it. That's the long and short of it."

The specific colour that furore always brought into his eyes – that of stolen gold and wildfires – slowly changed into a coagulated blood tint as he narrowed them. Calmer now he uttered:

"The scorpion dies though; in any case it dies when encircled by fire.... And do you know, Theia that the venom of the scorpion is less dangerous than that of a snake?"

Byzantine messengers to the West challenging the motives of this second wave of Westerners had enquired as to why they had wished to wage war. Did they really consider that the present threat embraced the Church as a whole, that the events in the Levant were relevant to Christians everywhere? Were they really undertaking such a gruelling, perilous, and costly operation for no personal gain, but uniquely to protect the Church of God and Christianity that was under attack in Edessa?

"As a great token of nobility and uprightness," their Pope had pronounced, "those things acquired by the efforts of your fathers will be defended by you, their good sons."

The overconfident, rowdy ways of these barbarians were foreign to Emperor Manuel. Their alleged sense of honour and chivalry in the field came across as exaggerated, their passion for feats of arms strange, if not more outlandish, more bizarre than the dancing snake. To us Romans, our diplomacy and our down-to-earth nature went hand-in-hand. Manuel resembled an alchemical adept, knowing when to apply each of these traits. His messengers attempted to convince Conrad III to take the route via the Hellespont and the Dardanelles, and thereby steering clear of Constantinople. Their suggestion fell on deaf ears.

The Germans' slaying of the gypsy snake charmer in Philippopolis foreshadowed their hazard and misfortune. Had he used his juggling skills instead of making his snake dance, would he have kept his life? Who knows? Among all the twists, just one twist may change one's destiny. The snake coils up, undulates, and squeezes, so does life. One twist, that of nature, hit the yellow haired Germans badly. To the west of Constantinople, on the plains, the River Melas, swollen with the deluge of seasonal rains, poured over their camp. Every brook and rill turned into wild torrents that swept away baggage, tents, horses, weapons and men. Showing the abilities that would make him the Red Beard, Frederic had wisely pitched camp on the highest ground available and many of his soldiers escaped the full devastation on his hill. But the loss was immense, and a division of Crusaders following behind had to come to their aid. Their arrival in Constantinople was yet another diplomatic disaster. The snake throttles, and hisses. Manuel, who in fact wished them all dead, became the snake. Did you know? In the Saracen language the word 'hayyaat' means 'snake', and ironically also 'life'. Turkoman kams milked snake venom to make medicine and antidotes; a profusely bleeding cut when staunched with the correct amount of the right venom, coagulated the blood. The crystallized venom of steppe vipers occluded wounds. Manuel sent envoys to Conrad III offering help after the flood, his tone was relatively conciliatory – it was of course driven by 'malicious glee, a gloating delight of evil' not sympathy. Both Manuel and Conrad III were claiming to be the Holy Roman Emperor – although Conrad III had not been crowned by the Pope yet – and neither acknowledged any superior to himself.

Each detested the Count of Sicily, Roger. The Greeks saw him as a bandit who had stolen their former lands in Southern Italy, and the Germans opposed him because they believed Roger supported a false Pope. Aware of the imminent arrival of the Crusaders in Constantinople, Roger began to seize Byzantine lands and plundered large quantities of gold, precious metals, and icons. The nadir was when he captured two thousand Byzantine Jewish silk workers from Thebes. These were no ordinary labourers but the most skilled artificers of purple cloth throughout the Eastern Roman Empire. He put to work in Palermo, thus plundering all the secrets of their trade – a veritable pirate he was.

Having the same arch-enemy did not really help alleviate the distrust between Manuel and Conrad III when they met. In addition to the hostile correspondence between them, there was the matter of the non-existent position of Bertha at the Byzantine court. Although the men were brothers-in-law and common courtesy required the emperor to receive another sovereign and entertain him at the palace, this did not happen.

Conrad III's ordinary foot soldiers were stationed in front of the moat of the grand wall as well as along the inner walls, while the Crusaders moved across the Golden Horn and camped in the Pera district opposite. Conrad III obstinately demanded that Manuel meet him outside Constantinople. Offended by what he saw as the King's arrogance, Manuel naturally refused. Tension rose and the Germans pillaged and destroyed many beautiful villas around the city. Manuel's navy rapidly transported some of the Germans into Asia and supplied them with guides so they could get rid of this uninvited, belligerent guest as soon as possible.

A second army followed the Germans, marching a few days behind: that of the Franks. Their King Louis VII had requested the Germans await his forces, but Conrad declared, "I intend to complete the expedition with due haste."

Accompanied by his daredevil nephew, Conrad chose the shortest, yet most perilous route, leading directly across Anatolia via Iconium, towards Antioch. His journey entailed famine, lack of water, harsh, sterile landscapes, some horrible wilderness and constant harassment by lightning-fast Turkish raids. Once the Turks loosed their arrows, they could wheel their speedy horses and vanish beyond the reach of exhausted German swords. The border between the Greeks and the Seljuk Turks was porous and ill-defined, much like their relations. In some places, they were allies whilst in others the Turks acted autonomously. For the most part, the vast Byzantine lands were freely roamed by the Turks. Castles would often change hands – sometimes being taken and held by the Greeks, and sometimes by the Turks. Yet, oddly, the two peoples divided the revenues.

To their astonishment, the Crusaders found that there had a been a twelve-year truce between the Greeks and the Turks. However, when the journey was announced in letters addressed to the Westerners, Emperor Manuel professed his intent to fight against the Seljuk Turks and expressed great joy at the advent of this Crusade. Could he be dissembling? And now the guides Manuel had assigned to Conrad III were sent to help Louis. Were they instructed to mislead them, or were they being bribed by the Turks – or both? Who could presume to say? The snake entwined and hissed, and should the need arise, it would bite…

The snake had to curl and turn; we Romans called this 'Statecraft' and have imparted this skill to others, both Barbarians and Latins alike. Mind you, one can respond to trouble like a brutal butcher or like an artful maker of delicate jewellery. Take the Latins, for instance: as expounded by the grandest of Physicians from Bukhara, and as witnessed with Conrad III and his soldiers, these Nordic peoples display wild manners due to the excessive innate heat of their hearts, where they are missing an external agent to balance the warmth – namely the cold weather of their homelands. What we Romans undertake is to tame the wild and educate these nations in statesmanship and artfulness; this is what we teach them, to help them overcome their inadequacies.

The impetuous Conrad III was critically wounded by an arrow along the way and subsequently fell ill. In light of the calamity, these Crusaders decided to withdraw to Nicaea to rest and recover. Manuel sent his boats to Ephesus, where he collected the King and brought him to Constantinople to be treated by Imperial physicians. At last, poor Bertha of Sulzbach could finally meet someone of her kin and fulfil her yearning to speak in her mother-tongue again and receive news of her sister. In this convivial atmosphere, Conrad III naturally enjoyed many receptions, outings to sumptuous recreations, and, of course, the Hippodrome chariot races. Constantinople could kill, but also heal, much like snake venom.

Upon Conrad's arrival in Jerusalem and Louis's in Antioch, to the profound disappointment of their rulers, their focus shifted from the fates of Edessa and Antioch to attacking Damascus. The city had once been an ally of Jerusalem but had since shifted its fealty to the Turkic Zengids. Contemporary witnesses described the attack on Damascus as madness. Bribed, yet again, this time by the ruler of Damascus, the guides misled the Crusaders, and instead of assailing the city from the west where there were orchards for sustenance, they led them into approaching the city from a plain on the eastern side. Although this side was less strongly buttressed, there was also much less food and water at hand. Consequently, the siege was a debacle, and plans went awry. The story went that some of the wretched foot soldiers were pitied by the Turks and given food and money; others were enslaved by the Greeks.

The King of France did not know that he, too, was walking to the twist of his destiny, but in his case, he followed a snake that ate its own tail. Eleanor of Aquitaine was said to accompany him during the Crusade because he feared her infidelity. The thousands and thousands of paces they had marched together brought them into the heart of betrayal rather than distancing them from it. She walked into an incestuous amour to boot, in her famous golden boots. She fell in love with her own uncle Raymond of Poitiers at Antioch, who reciprocated.

"So strange this world is," said the Dervish.

And so, the mysterious snake meandered, El Haya', Life's antidote and poison was life itself, was it not?

44

Great Heavens! How did he find time to die
when there was so much going on?

Epaminondas,
Plutarch, *Moralia. Advice about Keeping Well*

OGAN's efforts had not amounted to much in making Alma pregnant again. The girl was lifeless nowadays, against her nature. When we tagged along with their group – consisting of nomadic women and a mule loaded with a large can of milk and large-breasted rag dolls – none threw me the "What are you doing here?" look I was used to getting from other people. Alma gently rubbed my back and cheek and winked at the group of Greek children following along with their mother, the amulet-maker Sophie. Sophie had joined us not out of professional interest, but primarily to keep an eye on her children. That said, there was another reason, one which her mind could not quite grasp, but her heart did. The memory of the latter is always stronger than that of the former. And thus, the heart she took when I had comforted her at the caravanserai on the day of the fireproof fabric sales led her to me. Poor Sophie was troubled by the accusation that her amulet-making was sinful, unable to comprehend the delicate, devious agencies of human duplicity. How could her trade be so in demand in the village yet constitute a crime at the same time? She did not understand, nor is it likely she understood that she did not understand. Nevertheless, she followed us. Dog was also present, ululating at the girls who saluted him by howling.

Something about Alma was amiss. That eburnean skin which once gleamed with the soft radiance of the moon, like moonstones, now resembled parchment rubbed with chalk or pumice. The darkness of her raven hair stood in stark contrast to her countenance, yet she was no paler than usual. Andronicus was right – beauty had to generate either perfect harmony or striking contrast, though the latter required a certain bias: sympathy. The first was a guarantee, given with or without love. But a disingenuous intelligence and acute ingenuity could transmute an ordinary face without impeccable proportions into something extraordinary, or even make the extreme lack of perfection appear beautiful. With Alma none of these speculations mattered. The girl was as perfect as the imperfect Cherry Pie flower. People thought this was a flower that turned to the sun in the manner of a sunflower, but it didn't. Painted the colour of night, it was either complementary to the sun or in utter contrast to it, thus beautiful in a very particular way. Sorcerers used it as an 'invisibility cloak' at rituals, for the rays of the sun turned away from it.

If the life force which flew within us, vibrated inside us, should escape, we could appear ordinary even if we were beautiful, and that is what Andronicus was conveying. According to Ogan, diseases emerged when feelings were ignored or they contradicted the outside reality of nature, but what would they be in this case, with such a girl who lived in ultimate concord with the world and herself? Not everything Ogan or Andronicus said, or even the kam attempted to do, was valid. This girl had had a child before. She was one of those shiny objects in the wild that dazzled birds and enticed them to steal – a gold coin, a mirror, perhaps the mercury pool, a diamond, or a crystal; she sparkled. I thought the girl had a problem that did not originate from inside, something that didn't concern her soul, only her flesh. In the eye of a kam, all troubles were generated by the soul and reflected in the flesh later. And so now we were taking the road to pray for the destruction of whatever was impeding the smooth outflow of her life force. Our kam was the spirit guide, telling us what to do to bring the stream back.

He walked to the front of the group. I couldn't help but notice his eyes moving incessantly. While an eye-roll could signal boredom or disdain when done once, the constant movements were unsettling. I had already been struck by his strange vestment: copious eagle feathers hung from his belt, while bundles of owl feathers draped from his shoulders. In fact, the man resembled a large bird. It called to mind the recent but still vivid dream in which I saw that old woman beating a drum, pricking needles into my body, and breathing a wolf into being, a hare riding upon on its back. When that hare entered my head, I was healed. Now that she was no longer alive and neither her son Ataman nor his son Ogan could talk to that Divine Intelligence, they had imported this kam from a neighboring tribe. Much like his cloak, hers, too, was densely feathered. The more feathers one bore, the wiser one was thought to be – analogous to the earliest humans, who were said to have been covered in hair. When Adam and Eve were stripped of theirs as punishment, they were left completely nude, defenseless against the trials of the earth where they were cast down with neither wit nor wits. It goes without saying that the kam was neither bored nor disdainful, and was probably following unearthly beings thrashing about on some other plane. The idea of being within their grip was maybe commonplace to these Turkish women but it wasn't to me or Sophie, despite our steady contact with foreign visitors, outlandish interlopers, and our peculiar invaders. To bring what we, as naked children of Adam, missed – the wit, wits, wisdom, the celestial, the benedictions, and the boons, this crazy man was assigned by the very same power. How cunning and pitiless this mighty force was for confounding us in such a way. But, on second thought, we were all in the same boat, or at least they were. For all his unsettling presence, the purpose for which he was employed was simple: to deliver tangible, palpable results – or nothing at all. Nothing, in its purest form, clean and clear.

Sophie and I exchanged glances – not exactly in fear, but guilt. At that moment, we both knew that, whatever happened, both my fiery curiosity and her inveterate doltishness would triumph over fear – mine, invariably. What I sensed then would later grow into guilt, while what she felt would turn into an even greater sheepishness, which too would evolve into guilt. The villagers would blame her for whatever transpired between her and this lot.

The kam wore a conical head-dress made of white lambskin embroidered with golden wire threads, with owl feathers attached to its top. Behind the conical headpiece three bands dangled and a bird motif was embroidered with golden wire threads. Iron jingle cones and dried snake tassels, leather plaits, and ribbons sewn onto birds' tails and wings were suspended from the costume. An eagle talon and a bear claw also hung from his belt. On his left side, two dark-coloured fabric braids drooped. In front of his costume there was a red stripe starting from the neckline, going to the floor. Nine knots were placed along it. Its hemline was adorned with seven straps, four made of goatskin, three from a red fabric. His accoutrements tinkled and jangled while he walked.

The man's whirling pupils froze on my Dog. He whispered something and the animal's fur stood up across the shoulders and down its back. Shifting his weight forward, Dog held his tail and head high and began to howl. The man murmured unintelligible words, and from that moment on, Dog stayed by his side, following him closely. With the rest of the group trailing behind and my Dog beside him, we headed towards the cave where Basil and I kept seasonal grapes that were not of high enough quality for winemaking. Our workers would prepare the clusters and hang them on its ceiling in September, ensuring they would not touch each other, otherwise they would rot. The cold and dark would preserve the freshness of the product and by springtime, the now semi-dried and sweetened molasses would be sold to wealthy clients.

Each carrying a torch, Alma's friends nested the busty rag dolls in the alcoves of the cave. In a bowl, sage or sweet grass burned. Upon the kam's signal, a girl began to walk about the cave with the bowl and a feather, diffusing the smoke. The cavern walls and the rocky floor which were normally arid and cool felt warm and moist that day, and a translucent shaft of light shone from the cave's mouth. Pulsating flashes of fire painted the walls pink and transformed the black veinings into dark red. With a commanding gesture, the kam gathered us to a part of the cave where the floor gleamed a lustrous black; the reflection of red undulated across it, and pulsating flames nearly brought it to life. They had Alma sit on a felt cushion placed in the middle. Staring at the children, the kam screwed up his face. There were no other children around except our Greek ones; all the Turkish women had come without theirs. I felt mortified. However, the man did not utter a word of objection. Nudging us towards the left side, which was west, he aligned the group, and with exaggerated gestures sprinkled wine all around from a flask one of the girls had brought. Upon a second command, the girl brought another wine flask; the contents of that one were also poured on the ground. After the third one, making sure the ground of the cave was saturated with the drink, he began to walk around Alma from left to right, that is moving from west to east, emitting a twanging sound from his throat which resembled the rattling or clinking of metals. As he sang, he beat his drum. I learned only afterwards that west was the direction of the dead, the ancestors and the spirits of those who were getting ready to come to this world; east was the direction of the sun and birth, hence the reason why they always have the entrances of their tents face in that direction.

All at once, the kam began running around erratically like a lunatic, made three quick, close laps around the girl, and then held her face between his two hands, bending it backwards with force. Alma's face was no longer pale but pink; she was watching the man with unwavering attention and didn't seem bothered by the prods and pushes. The man threw himself to the ground and began to make violent movements, strange contortions, then became calmer. He barked a frightful, guttural scream as he stood up, then blew on her temples and belly. Making a sign to one of the girls, the kam indicated the milk can on the mule. He grabbed the can violently from the girl and put it on Alma's head. Her eyes glittered in the candlelight. Her face was now red, and her previous frailty appeared to have vanished. She was once again beautiful. Naturally Alma did not topple the milk can: tightening her neck muscles, she kept it balanced. The kam beat his drum three times and shouted something I did not understand:

"*Kut, kut olsun*!"

He motioned as if pouring a liquid from his drum and said something to Alma. Without moving her head, and with unexpected force from her thin arms, she grasped the can and began to drink from it thirstily. Upon the kam's cue, another girl came and removed the can from Alma who held her two hands tightly on her ears as if attempting to prevent the escape of something. The milk can was once again loaded on to the mule. One of Sophie's children drew close to the mule and tugged at it while Sophie, screaming in embarrassment, leapt towards them; the remaining milk slopped onto her.

Her sloping eyes, which rather accentuated her silly expression, wept tears as she yanked the child away from mule and can. Luckily the kam was in a trance and did not notice any of this.

Wouldn't it have been more practical to go to the church and simply pray to God for a baby rather than journeying from pillar to post and back, all this yawping and milk cans, buxom puppets and strange rituals? Clearly the powers above that the kam was speaking to, and their expectations, differed from our God's. These people believed they came back until they learned the lessons of their lives; they had been reborn many times and would reincarnate again and again. So, while our God was vain and proud and could never put a foot wrong, theirs tolerated their whims and demands, feeling indebted to them, even collaborating with them.

Now the soul of the baby was supposed to descend to Alma's womb from the fourth stratum of the sky, where children's souls resided, in Milk White Lake. The bird-man was supposed to fetch it, and by closing her ears with her hands, Alma forestalled its escape. The ritual ended, and we left the cave, the womb of Mother Earth. Turks called her Umay, the owner of the milk lake. She would take one baby's soul and implant it into the womb of the mother in the shape of a red wolf and drip a single drop of milk into its mouth, thus giving it a soul. If the baby wanted to become a boy, she made him a girl. If the baby wanted to be a girl, she made him a boy. And from then on, the naughty Umay protects the mother and the baby. But be careful, she gives 'life' but also takes it; in fact, she shares 'life' with Erlik from under the ground. Regardless, the soul crawling on the dark soil eternally pines for a return to the milk lake. The blue-grey marks which typically appear on the buttocks or lower backs of babies are the spots where she has touched them; the more there are, the more auspicious they are. However, luck is only manufactured in limited quantities.

Our weary but animated convoy walked unhurriedly on its way back. No longer in raptures, the bird man now resembled a deflated pig bladder. Significantly older than I had first thought, his skin was notably rugged and wrinkled, but his bright eyes flashed and flickered with a youthful spark. My Dog carried on walking by his side. We stopped before a single, resplendent tree. Alma took out a red silk scarf from her pocket and tied it to a branch with elegant movements of her delicate fingers, and others followed suit draping mainly blue fabrics across the branches.

Sophie's cow-eyes bulged. She gasped and turned towards me, waiting for a command. At that moment, a thought struck me, one which I had not considered in the heat of the ritual, and a pang of anxiety gripped my stomach. The ceremony had been designed exclusively for Alma, yet here were all the women hanging their own pieces of cloth on the tree. Were they all trying to get pregnant, or was this act about consolidating Alma's enchantment? Despite everything, I too was a woman. Fear and shock zipped through my heart. No matter what, my probable pregnancy had to be impeded, even if I appeared haughty to Alma and others for not participating.

I gave Sophie a fake 'knowing' grin and bid her:

"Go, do the same."

"But…" Holding back my anxiety I said, "Do as I say."

She looked to see if she had a handkerchief on her but couldn't find one. Desperate, she darted towards one of her children and took one – crusty with saliva and snot – from his sleeve. She pressed her hand on her blushed cheek and tried to open the rigid folds while yellow, dried pieces fell on the ground. She hurtled to the tree and knotted it around a branch with clumsy movements.

A few days after our convoy returned to the village, Nike's gangly wife – who still hadn't pleased an impatient Madam Gabras with news of her pregnancy, despite availing herself of Sophie's amulets – wondered aloud if the bird man kam could arrange a ritual at the cave for her too. You must know, somebody like Madam Gabras – a scourge who could drive the devout to resort to sorcery, and vice versa – was a force to be reckoned with. Affliction, like Gabras's resembles Greek fire: pumped at the enemy through great tubes or hurled at them from portable siphons, it couldn't be extinguished by water. If you asked the Romans how it worked, they would tell you "The Angels" gave it to them. Gabras, too, was skilful in lending credence to the "angelic" nature of whatever she was up to. There was one form of relief from the Greek fire though: hanging clothes soaked in vinegar over the gun-holes of boats impaired its effect. However, Nike's gawky bride was far too young and naïve to contrive elaborate methods to counteract Gabras and her incendiary tongue. The monsters, freaks, and spirits we dealt with were far more prosaic and benign than her contrivances, if not all together affable.

As for me, the prospect of becoming pregnant occupied my mind for a while – a valid distress, regardless of my participation in the eccentric ritual we had been present for. However, either due to the nature of my intercourse with Andronicus or my own disposition, in which I doubted my womanhood, the anxiety quickly faded.

I experienced no guilt or shame for having attended the ceremony of the bird man, and Gabras's daughter-in-law, too, turned it to good account. By seeking remedy with him, which was not a product of a brave heart but an ignorant bliss, she crowned the experience, inadvertently contributing to the inventory of my arms against Gabras.

The kam was nowhere to be found. A day later, his flogged, dead body was unearthed, alongside his drum and jingly cloak. An abominable sight, I assume.

And then in the early hours, one day after that shock, the Muhtasib's dead body was found in the courtyard of the inn. The Muhtasib, who was strictly opposed to transcendental visits, to mortals crossing the borders of the real and unreal; now he had himself traversed to the beyond. He had been brutally stabbed through the heart with a knife that could have belonged to anyone – cellarer, cook, Iconian officials, heretic clients, Romans, a random passer-by, or even Andronicus, for I knew he had one. An ordinary knife but not an ordinary death, for the Muhtasib's face, usually red with rage, appeared blank, unperturbed. On the off chance a person sympathetic to the victim observed its expression, that person might even deem it a face of bliss, as if it had been a quick, peaceful death, and yet there was blood splattered widely around the courtyard as if it had been anything but.

The killer was not Ataman, he respected life far too much to murder in such a fashion; we had never witnessed him spilling blood. He preferred to execute people by hanging or strangling them with a bowstring, a lasso, or a cord – which would be silk in the noble Muhtasib's case. But perhaps they didn't respect the Muhtasib? Now that his blood, his life-force had touched the ground and been contaminated, he was losing the chance to watch over whatever tribe he belonged to as an ancestor. His spirit was leaking out of the sacred entity. Now that the sacred verve of animation was violated, there was no more ancestor ghost to watch over the poor Muhtasib's offspring. From that morning on, he was to join the plane of eternal non-existence, not the celestial plane of Divine Intelligence where all these nomads were to go after death. And just as his faith compelled, no help would be demanded from his dead self, for praying was only done to God and no-one else, and the Muhtasib was not a part of God.

I remembered the expression on Ataman's child-like, plump-lipped, circumspect son's face when I had accused their tribe of killing the fishmonger, Andreas. Murder was an inconceivable, far-fetched, implausible prospect. He stood in utter shock and awe at the grisliness of the concept, resembling a girl who discovers a cockroach on the kitchen floor. His sorcerress grandmother, who Ogan claimed was not a sorcerress, could speak to that Divine Intelligence and relay its messages to her offspring. Ogan, enmeshed in these fabulous stories, surrounded by flying guide animals and magical drums, lived and let life live itself – with Alma by his side. And, given the circumstances of the Muhtasib's murder, perhaps he also killed for Alma.

The Muhtasib's notorious whip was not found with the dead body. Unlike the knife that killed him, the whip with its gem encrusted silver handle was no quotidian object, and although he had quite liked brandishing it around, he had never resorted to utilising it, and in the end, it never was found. Assigned by the Sultan in Iconium, the Imam of Plekia performed a funeral prayer at the mosque, attended only by the government officers from Iconium. A new Muhtasib was never stationed in Plekia, and no soldiers of the Sultan ever came to investigate the murder.

I am not aware of what befell the Turkish girls, but exactly nine and a half months after the ritual of the bird man, Mother Earth who brings and protects life, delivered another baby to this world – not to Alma and Ogan but to Sophie, her eleventh. A Turkish girl gave Sophie a red ribbon to tie her hair with. She told her to keep it tied for forty days to protect herself and her baby from a she-devil called Alkiz, who enjoyed gorging on the livers of newborn babies and their mothers. If she wasn't hungry, under the command of the underground God Erlik, she could cause severe childbed fever or extreme gloom to the new mother during these critical days. Wearing the colour red was essential, for the she-devil was terrified of it, and the ribbon would protect both mother and baby. Though undoubtedly a kind gesture by the nomadic girl, it was perhaps a little redundant in light of our Sophie's experiences. The she-devil and Sophie had surely met head on already ten times. Sophie must have already subjugated the devil by now despite her seemingly dull ways. Besides, she must have received several scarlet threads from acquaintances and family hitherto, for we too tied them by tradition, though the church denounced it. Obviously, we and the Turks had faith in different Gods but identical evil powers. I couldn't help wondering how it was that our baby-eating Gylou and their Alkiz seemed to be the same witch.

What is more pertinent to our story is that the mule that carried the milk can got pregnant too, and carried it to term, producing a foal which became a tourist attraction. People from neighbouring villages flocked to Plekia to see it, even a few adventurers from Constantinople who probably came all the way to find out how to reproduce its like or to see if there was a way to commercialise the case of Plekia in the capital. However, no matter how they strove to convince the foal's owner to sell it, blandishing him, begging him, even threatening him, it did not work. The owner refused, and the shrewd citizens of the capital returned home disgruntled. The story entertained Pegasus considerably. When I told him about it, he peeled his lips away from his gums, and that mischievous grin lit up his face.

Many believed the foal to be similar to an ill-omen described by Herodotus. A mare gave birth to a hare when Xerxes traversed the Hellespont to conduct his ill-fated expedition against Greece. It wasn't just the oddity of a mare bearing an animal that wasn't a horse, but the fact that it was a hare. After all, had the mare given birth to a lion cub, would Xerxes take this as the harbinger of a disaster? Indeed, he was defeated and returned to his country to save his neck. But Herodotus also recounted another hare incident in history and this time Xerxes's celebrated, phenomenal father Darius was in command. The Persian and the Scythian armies were encamped on a partly wooded plain with a moderate distance between them. While the two forces were about to face off in battle, the Scythians broke ranks to the shock of the Persians. They surged across the plain, a dense, shouting mob, their laughter rending the air – all in pursuit of a hare that had bolted from a thicket between the armies. Thereupon, brought low, Darius declared:

"They do indeed despise us."

The paths taken by the hare were not straight, but, aye, it figured them out – even through a mare when necessary. Life did not come to entertain, it did not bring death to heal, nor heal to stop death. Goddess Umay and Erlik wisely shared the duality, subjecting people to life's tricks: good and bad, day and night, pain and pleasure.

The very hare whose meat was prescribed as a cure for sterility, the lustful animal men offered to their lover as a token of their passion, the fecund beast who enchanted carnal desirability, that sensuous, amorous creature, cursed and sacred just like virginity itself, was under the auspices of no other God or Goddess but Artemis, the virgin nonpareil.

Alma never conceived again. I did not fall pregnant to Andronicus.

Abundance and scarcity are never far apart.

45

There are many more non-lovers than lovers, and if you choose the best of lovers, you will not have many to choose from, but if from the non-lovers, the choice will be larger, and you will be far more likely to find among them a person who is worthy of your friendship.

Plato, *Phaedrus*

My little one,

Ataman and I are setting off now. Naturally I am planning to turn this delay caused by my seemingly endless sojourn here in Plekia into a business trip to Sultan Mesud which will consolidate mutual interests and profits. I am considering this not as a kidnap and ransom case but rather a diplomatic visitation.

The reason I have been detained in Plekia for such an extended period and that Sultan Mesud had to be deprived of the honour of my presence at his court is the coddled, effeminate, epicene, lady-likeness of that boy and how hard it was for Ataman to accept the bitter truth.

You must know that all the things that a person might secretly know about himself or his son, but is too afraid to face, will eventually come and meet him eyeball-to-eyeball sooner or later – either through his own actions or those of his son. No amount of evasion or distraction can keep them at bay forever.

That molly-coddled boy of yours does not have his father's capacity to capitalise on the Sultan's fief policy: "give me soldiers and get land taxes as income in return." As for the nerve and the heart that are essential for someone to be able to travel for days and days with a man like me, he does not possess it in the slightest, darling. He is a freshwater fish. I wish he were brave; it would suit my book; I would conveniently slip away. History is replete with flight stories which contain equal amounts of stinking ignominy and outstanding bravery, for example, the notorious Bohemond. His name means the *Protector of the Ruler*, and it also corresponds to *Behemoth*, the horrible monster of the Bible whose bones are like tubes of bronze, and limbs like bars of iron. That dog Bohemond left the governance of Antioch and Edessa temporarily to his nephew and ran away from my grandfather, Emperor Alexios and the Turks. To accomplish this, he resorted to a ruse that had never been implemented before. First, he had word spread that he was dead, then he had himself put into a coffin with secret holes in it, together with a strangled cock. With his men in tears, the coffin was shipped on a boat, and exposed to people at every harbour, reeking of rotten corpse. The stinkard rascal reached Corfu in this way and wrote a threatening letter from there to Emperor Alexios. My ingenious plan would be to feign extreme diarrhoea and weakness and persuade him and his guards to make frequent stops. Then one evening, in a woodland, I would retire a short distance from the path, take my walking stick (which I would badly need to walk), stab it into the ground, dress it with my cloak, cap it with my hat, and take flight into the forest.

As you know, when I was here, that uxorious scoundrel did not give me wine or the other minor luxuries I requested, claiming, "Abstinence accords tremendous strength to the body, Andronicus; it also sharpens the mind."

I am certain he would be most understanding about my extreme bowel movements. To control them, he would even give me some medicine. Under these new conditions, it would be impossible for that milksop to take to the road. He would be crying his eyes out in his house, pardon, in his tent. You can turn this into happiness, if you regard this as happiness, for after me, nothing will ever satisfy you. Still, I never forget favours or evil done to me, therefore, listen to the advice I shall give you. This is the ideal time for extending your sympathies with a cordial condolatory visit. When men mourn, they become rather receptive and susceptible, also compliant. You might have a chance. I repeat, there is no guarantee, but before abstinence highly sharpens his mind, you should take your chance. It is, however, only a chance.

I never agreed with the ossified principle of these barbarians: *Eline, diline, beline, sahip ol*, that is: ‹Curb your tongue, hands and loins.' I firmly agree with their conviction that hell and heaven are here on this earth, not elsewhere. But by controlling your tongue, hands and loins at all times, you may turn life here into hell. If one assumes that they imply this principle should be practised in moderation, then rest assured that what they might think of as moderation would be hell for someone like me. You must have heard about those pillar-dwelling saints. Mind you, that was in the olden days! Did they actually think living on top of a pillar was a route to heaven? Imagine, forty cubits high and scarcely two cubits in circumference for decades until death, with an iron collar about their neck and leg, hardly eating, exposed to wind, rain, snow and heat, relieving themselves in a pail and hanging it from a rope? Simeon, to ensure he would not fall in his sleep had his thigh tied to a rock, and it was so gravely afflicted with an ulcer that maggots emerged from it. He allegedly treated them kindly, pushing them back into his flesh and instructing them to eat what God gave them. Even Emperor Theodosyius demanded the 'aerial' martyr pray for him.

In some ways, it is a pity that this type of 'Fools for Christ' no longer exists in our modern times. If they did, I would certainly be the first and most devoted among the multitudes of pilgrims flocking to them from afar, hearing their sermons, seeking their benediction, guaranteeing a good deed, and acquiring merit. Unfortunately, times have changed. Things aren't so simple anymore. It's not so easy to go to heaven these days. One must take responsibility to display the unshakeable commitment to the spirit over the flesh. People have become selfish and lazy – not unlike a kam. By raising themselves to dwell in the upper air and resisting nature which weighs down on those worldly things below, these 'Fools' passed the messages of humans to God and God's messages to humans. There is no-one like them anymore. You are on your own.

There is a Turkic divinity called Burkut Baba, God of thunderbolts, a ruthless achiever, an unremitting optimist, and a gallant spirit. He even had the audacity to fight with God, much like myself, and unlike your precious, epicene half-breed. Burkut Baba chases about the clouds with a whip in his hand. Burkut knows the future and therefore now and then becomes embroiled in a clash with God.

One day, he requests God to resurrect the only son of an old man who had come to him. God refuses. Burkut decides to see to it himself. He rises up into the sky where there are seven bottles containing seven souls. He finds the one that belongs to the boy and breaks it, so the boy comes back to life. The grim reaper gets very angry and complains to God. God says, "Burkut is crazy, when he asks for one spirit to be resurrected, we should do it."

The belligerent Burkut even writes a book where he describes methods of reviving dead people. He tries to bring a dead friend back to life. This time, God loses patience and sends the Angel Gabriel. Gabriel and Burkut fight on the banks of a river. Gabriel throws the book into the water. In the end, Burkut doesn't win his victory over death.

The epitome of his bravery is when he reprimands God for not eradicating people's belief in hell and keeping them in fear. God refuses, of course, claiming no-one would work for him unless they were afraid of being punished in hell on the other side.

So, my dear, times have changed. God might be an average to mildly successful night-time procurer, but he is the best daytime merchant you will ever meet. If his prosperity has bedazzled you and you want to seize a piece of it, you need to bargain with him. If only we knew what exactly he was interested in buying. Who knows, perhaps we human beings, too, are just automata he invented, like the ones in the Palace that we utilise to impress, awe, and even scare the visiting kings or ambassadors, maybe God, too, made us as machines to shock his other, more important creations on other planes or to intimidate his competitors while haggling with them. I am almost certain that while reading this you are not sputtering and screaming "Sacrilege!" By now, you know me. You also know God better than before, and you know that shouting can't change the fact that everything is out of order in this life.

And I, my little one, I don't mind suffering a little of hell for the sake of enjoying a little of heaven. One must live and not be afraid of living. Some die only great death, and that is their final one; others die small deaths every day, in addition to the ultimate one that is yet to come. This is the fear of death – or 'fear' in and of itself. Even emperors are not exempt from dying small deaths; in fact, they might have more justified reasons. Remember Heraclius of olden days, the majesty who became distressed every so often. Frightened of traversing the Bosphorus, afraid of Arabs, scared of Jews. His almost-namesake philosopher Heraclitus thought that immortals were mortal, and mortals were immortal, living in their death and dying in their life: "Fire lives in the death of earth, air lives in the death of fire, water lives in the death of air, and earth in the death of water."

So, live, my little one. Your life should be more, much more than wondering which passer-by is at the door now. The cricket cracks its belly wide open when it stridulates too fervently, but being an old, invalid, hungry cricket is worse than blowing oneself up.

After me, you will only be disappointed by that milksop, but it's unquestionably what you want, and therefore will be better for your peace of mind. And who knows? With such frustration, you might decide to come to visit me in the big city and join the ranks of my admirers. My little one, you can come whenever you want, even if you get fat and ugly. In which case, I shall naturally not devote much tender loving care to you, if you understand what I mean. However, I shall take care of you, for you will always have a special place in

my heart. Without you, time would never have passed here in Plekia.
Enclosed you will find a second letter which will allow you to enter the gate of the Palace no matter the conditions. Needless to say, it has my signature on it. Do not forget to tip Svoronos who will bring you these letters; he procured the paper, the *kalamos* and the seal. He understood he would not be remunerated immediately. But he should know that because he paid the obeisance and showed the respect due a Prince born in Purple, I will make sure he's repaid many times over, when I return to the city. Sending Svoronos a reward will be my first deed in the capital, although there are many matters I must attend to urgently. Carrying out a tax revolution to relieve the peasants is the most significant of those. I must draw my dazzled cousin Manuel's attention to this issue. Developing a rural economy is essential; keeping these folk content here is what matters, not those dandies in Constantinople. When I become emperor, this policy will be a nod to you. Heed it, and remain well informed.
You can believe all the gossip you will hear about me in the future but do not take it too seriously. Know that I am not exactly a 'Fallen' but a 'Moving Angel.'
You know what Saint Dionysus the Areopagite says: If 'Fallen Angels' are to be called evil, it is not in respect of their being, since they owe their origin to the Good and were the recipients of a good being, but rather because of their inability, as Scripture puts it, "to keep their first place." Thus, they were good beings that lacked the ability to keep their first place in Heaven. They moved. So have I. I have been moving, and I shall continue to move.
Everybody applies the concept of 'benevolence' towards themselves as if stretching the mastic gum of Chios Island. Have you ever heard of someone who said: "Yes, I am bad. I did evil"? Everybody is loyal, kind, honest, considerate, charitable, generous, fair, conscientious, if you ask, so much so that evil should not exist at all. But evil is a hard worker; evil is discreet, toiling in secret. Evil sacrifices a lot and perseveres. Without the pain and drudgery of evil, how can all these

> sermonising, virtuous people be good? Being good comes at a price, that price is paid by evil's hard labour. To me, my little one, if one's virtues are hindering one's redemption, then they are not good, they are evil. Don't forget that even Jesus cursed the fig tree.
>
> Areopagite demands, "For I ask you, in what way are the demons evil except in the fact that they have put an end to the habit and the activity of divine good things? Their evil consists in the lack of angelic virtues! So, if Fallen Angels are declared evil, the reason lies within them, their move away from what befits them. What has happened to them is that they have fallen away from the complete goodness granted to them. They are called evil because of their deprivation, their abandonment, their rejection of the virtues which are appropriate to them."
> Yours,
> Andronicus Komnenos

In truth, I had wished death upon Alma at times – not out of malice but always with a light heart, which I admit could itself be considered evil. But somehow, I knew my jaunty and fatuous kind of doom could never injure a being such as her. I maintained the adamant belief that Alma would never die, neither the small deaths Andronicus mentioned, nor the big one. Yet, she did. An arrow once released, cannot fall straight to the ground. Instead, as if propelled by borrowed power, it follows a sweeping arc before finally curving down to meet the earth. Much like the mysterious power that sustains the growth of a baby, that force, too, must be borrowed, for in the end, all people must die. Death is merely the return of what was lent. We are debtors.

I thought Alma was special. I believed that she had not borrowed that force, that she owned that divine vigour of spirit that made arrows keep going or babies keep growing. I felt her lifeline wouldn't even follow the arc; her arrow would move forever. Never did I imagine that it would fall prematurely. And yet it happened. Alma died.

The communication the kam had established between this world and the world that is not visible to our eyes did not prevent the calamity that befell Alma. The kam failed as God's ambassador here on earth, his cleaner, organiser, and doctor. As Turks believed, God kept all in fragments upon those celestial planes and we were their embodiments in this world; He reconstituted them within our very bodies and it was the kam's job to restore their harmony when disorder arose, but he had not succeeded this time. The veil of illusion lifted. Alma returned to the source; Alma went back to God. She went back to reality. Here was not reality. Or maybe… she was so divine that he felt compelled to take her. Maybe once there, she became something even more vivid and attractive than she ever was here.

As the mourner bustled around the tent, hauling chests, bushels, and objects wrapped in canvas or goatskin hither and thither, he muttered incomprehensible words in a croaking tone, not in his usual assertive voice, and, still not noticing my presence, he cut the ropes of several of the packages, revealing several ceramic vessels, a gourd-shaped still, a few lutes, a bellow, several mortars and retorts.

These tools, many of which had passed from Plekia in the cargo of Muslim merchants, were to transmute metals into gold. Allegedly, if you mixed cold and moist mercury and hot and dry sulphur in the correct proportions and under the right conditions you could produce gold. In the secret underground chambers of Constantinople, even patriarchs were known to pursue this art – most famously Patriarch Keroularios. Though people professed an interest in the practical aspects of this science, *khymeia*, in truth, the gold sought by this blasphemous, ancient teaching was not merely the precious metal per se. Rather, it alluded to the 'secret knowledge' of those mysterious planes one enters after death – like Alma had. Gold symbolised the mystery.

When he finally noticed me, Ogan stood still and curled one arm over his head for a moment before returning to staggering aimlessly about. That lissome, sculpted body of his was now emaciated and jittery. His eyes were feverishly bright with blue circles underneath, his face was red and blotchy, and those habitually sleek and neat locks were greasy and tangled. I could have taken the gesture he made as a sign of me being unwelcome there, but it was not. In fact, I soon understood there was no meaning behind the gesture at all; he had simply gone mad.

He was going to attempt to bring the girl back, setting up a system to boil, evaporate, distillate and transmute her body, quasi-emulating Burkut Baba. I had seen a half-built furnace and stacked wood outside, and now these apparatuses explained it all.

Clearing my throat, I spoke. "I wish to offer my condolences. May God give her soul eternal rest."

Ogan barely reacted. On impulse, I began to poke about his items, blurting out: "and give her body peace… and rest with our Heavenly Father."

A fat teardrop streamed down his face, and he made no effort to hide it.

Had you not told me, Ogan, that deep inside, our souls yearn for what they have lost: their connection to the sacred? That a living thing shall never die unless it agrees to? If the apple wants to be eaten, it will let you know, but you still have to ask for its permission first. If you are not afraid of dying, you are not afraid of living. Yet now, you seem so afraid – so unlike yourself. However hard it might be for you, you must now accept that she agreed to die. She gave her permission. I don't understand how anyone could ever accept leaving you though…

His voice trembling, he said, "The first woman that was ever created was named Ay Va. Ay means moon. She, the Moon Face and the first man, Ay Atam, Father Moon had many children, many children, and lived happily ever after."

"After?"

"After being created, excessive rain inundated the ground with floods. When it stopped and the waters withdrew, streams of mud filled a human-shaped furrow in a cave. The sun, when it was at its zenith in the hottest season, baked the cave. For nine months, winds cooled the mud and the first man emerged." His voice was listless. "He was made of water, fire, earth. He was called 'Ay Atam'. He lived for a hundred and twenty years; his entrails and intelligence developed over the first forty years of his life."

He drew a deep breath. "And a woman was begot the same way when he turned forty. Only this time, late summer, the sun was not at its strongest. It did not fully bake the furrow as before…"

I interrupted: "But why not? Why was it not fully baked?"

He laughed bitterly.

"But tell me, why?"

This time dejected: "They had long lives. They had forty children and lived happily ever after."

He stared down at his hands. Another fat tear rolled down his cheek and fell to the floor.

Swiftly I bent down and rubbed the wetness with my thumb. When I stood up his head was still lowered. I wanted to reach out and touch his dirty hair. I wanted to support his back with my two hands, pull his face towards mine and put my lips onto his.

To touch and be touched were no longer strange things to me; feeling a lump growing heavy in my throat was not new either, but the sensation that teardrop on the floor left on my thumb was new, tingling, mysterious – the entire universe on a tiny fingertip. I could reach out and touch him, first the scalp, then the nape of his neck, and then the whole surface of his body, and see if that divine mystery would spread throughout and overwhelm me. Why not? But if I did, he was going to feel what I felt when Andronicus touched me: queasily vacant. It was obvious that I was not destined to learn the mystery of the universe, no more than a finger-tip's worth. The situation was all wrong. All that flowed, flowed in the wrong directions, except sadness. Sadness was steady, unchanging this time and yet in time, it too would change.

So, I stayed still.

Pressing his palms to his eyes and wiping away the tears, he let out a deep sigh. He then slowly pulled himself together, brushed the dust from the gadgets off his shirt, and then began to stack them about the tent haphazardly.

"I see you're venturing upon an extraordinary enterprise. You're squaring the circle. Perhaps… maybe… you should let things be. God doesn't always help those who help themselves."

He had been slowly dragging Alma's emptied mercury pool inside the tent from outside. He stood still on the spot and gave me a dazed look.

I continued: "You must know what the Bible says, Ogan. The Fallen Angels became enamoured with the daughters of men." Was he even listening? I pressed on. "They descended to earth to be with them, and they taught humans this science of magic – how things work in nature, and how nature itself works, and what powers we possess to shape it. What lies beyond our perception? It is not clear though whether they fell because they had fallen in love with the earthlings or if they were already fallen before falling in love. Either way, I've never heard anyone who managed to produce anything remarkable with this stuff." I indicated the equipment around us. Ogan didn't react.

Indeed, Patriarch Keroularios had not been able to produce real gold either. However, taken by mystical reveries, he did maintain frequent encounters with all kinds of miracle workers and mediums. The Patriarch's nemesis and good friend Psellos, the Consul of philosophers, deemed 'alchemy' to be nonsense, saying that its only tangible results were imitations. But in truth there was no other option but to renounce it. It was better to be a crook, a mountebank painting copper coins with gold dye than to be an infidel. By damning alchemy, the *khymeia*, and breaking his relationship with Patriarch Keroularios by accusing him of being an adept of mysticism, the Grand scholar Psellos was acquitting himself of any suspicion. In fact, they both knew, as did the kams of the Turkic tribes, what this whole matter pertained to. One could drift into slumber only to wake up on another plane, as real as this one, but unless you were outright crazy or, like Saint George, the Dragon-Slayer, you felt nothing when being boiled alive or having nails hammered into your skull, it was better to keep your mouth shut, considering the ideas professed by this bizarre lore.

There was an underlying unity to all things in this world. The original source was undivided, the past and future were already inherent in it, in the form of potentiality. Man carried within him the spark of the source. All things bore this animated essence – everything vibrated, all beings partook of it. That essence was spirit. Man was the same as the universe. Everything was interdependent. Yet man lived in oblivion, in deficiency, he did not know 'himself'. Man did not realise he was spirit here on earth manifested in form; he did not know his life was the expression of the spirit's intent. Man's soul could be divided, present in more than one place at once, or it could be hurt. When it was not hurt and could sense the sacred, joy and awe filled him, sparks of its essence leapt outward, spreading in every direction, faster and faster. The universe created and recreated itself infinitely, driven by urges, desiring to manifest itself in form to the fullest.

The kams, Psellos, Patriarch Keroularios and many others had mastered this knowledge, but attempting to describe it had to be avoided, even surreptitiously. Obviously, the very flesh, regarded as solidified spirit, the crudest stratum of being, could be deficient, imperfect, and could cause pain – a lot of pain.

The lonely mission of Psellos… He had dug himself out and found the Ancient Wisdom of ancient civilisations which revealed a secret. But how could you find out such things and keep your mouth shut? Or take the risk and explain what you're up to. He had found that like produced like, that there were sympathies and antipathies between stars, men, animals, and things, all things. And by manipulating them here on earth, their archetypes could be influenced on other planes; even the future could be affected. There was a law of similarity, sometimes things were drawn to things that were similar to them, but one could not know. The very opposites could be complimentary too; one thing could be affected by the power of another thing with opposite characteristics. In both cases, the distance between did not matter; distance did not prevent them acting upon each other. Everything had a cause and a paradigm, but it was not obvious to us – *invisible forces and ineffable powers* were at work. All was connected. But how to elucidate these things while keeping your neck intact? Fortunately, Psellos had possessed sophisticated words to save his respectability, career, and skin. He claimed his interest was merely intellectual curiosity: those mystical reveries presaged the advent of Christianity and directed the mind towards it, being entirely coherent with it. Just as poets ranked above painters, and doctors above surgeons in the Eastern Roman realm, so knowledge and philosophy were inherently superior to any practical applications. Did not physicians delve into astrology on the grounds that man was the same as the stars? The common folk naturally neither understood nor employed these fancy utterances; they labelled these matters 'magic'. And neither Christian nor Islamic divine wisdom would suffer such a servant.

The kam was aware of the composition of waters, the motion, and growth of all things, and their embodiment and disembodiment.

He discerned the arrows flight. He, the alchemist, and the magician knew nigh as much as God, but not everything. The Source remained incomprehensible. God was a metallurgist, a craftsman, a skilful artisan, but the mysteries of matter, how we came into being, where we went, why we were here, were probably half-known to Him as well. The ironsmith after all has always been sacred to the Turks.

The alchemist was aware that tincturing vapours of mercury and sulphur were the purifying waters of baptism. Here, water meant profound knowledge. The study concerned the purification and salvation of the divine soul bound within the elements, liberating the divine spirit from its fleshly lodging and thus enabling its ascent through heavens and transcendent realms. Thus, being born again, rebirth in the real Kingdom of Heaven. And yet, the greed and pursuit of gold – though perhaps a vulgar endeavour – offered a safer façade for keeping one's mortal coil intact, regardless of the mysteries and spirits involved. And if the vaunted 'boon' of the lore, the 'gold' of which alchemists spoke, referred not to secret knowledge but to actual gold, glimmering and precious, well then, so be it. To many, gold mattered more than the secrets of existence.

Jabbing my finger at Ogan, I said, "I'm just telling you all these things as a friend, you know… For your own good."

Nodding understandingly, he said, in a soothing tone, "I'm to manufacture paint."

"What?"

"I have mercury here. I heard if mercury and sulphur are rubbed together for a considerable time a black powder results. And when that is heated in a closed vessel, it yields a crystalline sublimate of cinnabar. Once pulverised, you get vermillion, a beautiful red colour."

Red-hot blood flushed to my face, burning as it spread. Ay Va being baked in lesser heat at the end of summer – that is, not as fully baked as Ay Atam had been – was what he was referring to, the missing member, phallus. I could feel my neck and ears scarlet, sweltering. Fleeing was out of the question, so I closed my eyes, covering my face with my hands. The blindness was also red. I opened my eyes behind my hands and my fingers filtering the sunshine were sanguine red. I gave a small squeal:

"If you need red paint, we could ask Svoronos – you know, the bookbinder. He could find that!"

He smiled. "Thank you. I prefer to make my own red, with my own mercury."

"But what will you do with red paint?"

"I shall paint apples." I sensed a weakening in my knees rather than a pang of jealousy for this was simply too absurd. Was he certain or was he bewildered?

"But since when have you been a painter?"

"I shall be one from now on… I shall be taught."

"But what about other colours? You cannot produce colours and paint."

"I will make only red and its shades and paint only apples. I will learn."

His expression went blank, his eyes staring dully into the distance. He remained standing there, arms limp. When he eventually exhaled, I realised it was time to leave. There was no place for a second heart there, not even a cow's. So, instead of parchment made from hides, he would need paper from Baghdad, made of linen and cotton. The cost of the utensils and access to the artisanal milieu were obviously no issue.

Like a good friend, I thought, I must acknowledge the burden that his insanity placed on him. So I said, "I'll find Svoronos and insist he procure some paper for you. That way, I'll have helped lighten the workload you'll face."

On my way back home, I cursed the Fallen Angels. Yes, flesh was only solidified spirit, the crudest level of being – so why had they lusted for it? If they had come to teach us redemption and purification from it, why had they failed to achieve these themselves?

46

What I do not know I do not think I know either.

Socrates, attributed to Plato

NOWADAYS, apostasy from Islam or Christianity – and re-conversion back – is not uncommon. However, it once was because the process of converting from Islam to Christianity was considered a significant deterrent: the Church required Muslims to renounce Muhammad's God, and many found this unacceptable.

One day, a messenger from Iconium delivered a letter to Emperor Manuel. It apprised him that, if he wanted to win back those he had already lost to Islam – or gain new converts to holy Christianity – he needed to be aware of a disturbing fact prevalent in the Turkic Seljuk realm: people were unwilling to abjure Mohammed's God in order to return to Christianity. They needed support and guidance to make the 'correct' choice.

The author of the letter was Iktiyar ad-Din Hasan ibn Gabras, one of the many members of the Gabras family who had defected to the Sultan in Iconium for political reasons. Iktiyar himself, having risen to prominence as a leading courtier of the Turkish Sultan, was now contemplating apostatizing back to Christianity.

Had I possessed this information regarding the Gabras family when I was still young – angry, unwordly, and cantankerous about being 'so unworldly' – I, for one, would have viewed Ibn Gabras's grand career as a Vizier as decadence, his religious vacillation as ignominy. Or at the very least, I would have pretended so. And I certainly would have wielded it as a weapon against Madam Gabras, especially in a moment of rage…

Of course I would not dare be as explicit as: "Shady, isn't it? Neither fully Muslim, nor Christian – too bad Nike is the progeny of such a lineage! What a family seat…"

No, I would not have the nerve. Instead, I would say something more oblique, yet equally incendiary:

"Crepuscular, isn't it? Neither fish nor flesh, not head nor tail, alas!"

She would flush red, burn, fume, and seethe – for this was not exactly what she was peddling – but she would not lose her temper with me. No, she would keep her composure. Then, in no time flat, she would turn up at our courtyard boiling and steaming, and her scourge would inevitably spill out upon poor Basil.

At the time, I had taken her conduct as an inveterate lack of respect for my persona. But today, looking back with a smile, I wonder if, perhaps, she feared me. Fortunately, that harangue of blame and accusation never came to pass.

Mystics thought that only by having your mirror rubbed could it shine. I did not grasp the concept at the time, so I never appreciated her contributions to rubbing my mirror – that is to say, turning my life into hell. But I was happy whenever Basil narrowly escaped her badgering. I was the exclusive shiner of his mirror.

Emperor Manuel, ever the master negotiator, suggested expunging the curses against Mohammed from all books – an idea that, needless to say, scandalised the clergy and the scholars, whose position on Islam was as follows:

"Their God is without Logos and without the Spirit, thus it is only material."

As had happened many a time, Manuel, outwitted them all:

"There is only one God, and we all worship the very same one. To deny theirs is to deny this fact."

Of course, he also threatened them – that was an intrinsic part of the procedure. Speak softly, but carry a big stick… In the years to come, the urgency of the big stick would evolve. For instance, in an effort to ingratiate themselves with the wealthy native Muslim elites, some heads of Crusader States would declare themselves *Malik* or refer to himself as *Sultan*. In Palermo, they would even strike new coins devoid of Christian imagery – one side inscribed in Arabic with, *"There is no god but Allah, and Mohammed is His Messenger,"* and the other bearing, *"King of Sicily."* This sort of civil machination would never have occurred to the hoggish brothers had it not been for us Romans, their enemy, who taught them how to set up a proper bureaucracy.

And thus, Manuel suggested expunging all curses against Mohammed from the books.

Yet Manuel was never one to shy away scandal. In 1161, he dared to welcome the Turkish Sultan Kilic Aslan, son of Sultan Mesud, to Constantinople. Seated in the palace hall upon a golden, elevated throne encrusted with precious stones, he received the Sultan. Andronicus was present as well, for this was one of those intermittent periods of friendship between the two men. Ever quick to notice any shortcoming, our ever-immaculate Andronicus privately mocked the Sultan's ungainly, misshapen limbs, nicknaming him *Cripple Aslan* – though, of course, never to his face.

Nearly fifteen years after Conrad's passing, Manuel made this Sultan his adopted son. They pledged to share the same friends and enemies, ushering in a peace between Turks and Romans which lasted for over a decade. This truce allowed the Sultan to concentrate on rival Turks, while Manuel turned his attention to other enemies. However, the peace was fragile.

For eighty days, the Sultan was entertained with elaborate court ceremonies, grand processions, and guided tours of the city's most splendid landmarks. Were it left to Manuel, the Sultan's visit to the holy monument of Haghia Sophia would have been beyond question. However, the Patriarch became incandescent with rage upon hearing of the Emperor's intent to bring a non-believer into the sacred space. He protested, vehemently, arguing that a non-believer should never set foot among the consecrated relics. Ordinarily, such objections would have fallen on stony ground – covered with silk, of course, as this was Manuel – but that very night, a violent earthquake shook the city. It was swiftly interpreted as a sign of divine wrath, proof of the Patriarch's righteous indignation. For once, Manuel – always a step ahead, no matter how much the fusty minds of Constantinople objected – chose to recant.

Years later, our Andronicus would work against his cousin from a castle on the Black Sea coast given to him by the same man whom he had mocked as "*Cripple*." He would loot from there and carry off Roman prisoners. Christian mercenaries were always employed by Turks but a noble like Andronicus was rare; I am certain he was filled with gratitude when the "*Cripple*" presented him with this opportunity, and I'm sure his heart was filled with genuine sympathy for it resembled a small cupboard: when one item entered, the other had to exit.

And years later during the Myriokephalon campaign in 1176 which was, as you can guess, directed against Kilic the Cripple, Constantine Gabras would serve as the Turkish ambassador to Manuel. Ambushed when moving through a mountain pass, the Roman forces suffered such a crushing defeat at the hands of the Turks that the impossibility of recovering land from the Turks became evident to Manuel. After the defeat, it was the same Gabras who initiated peace overtures to him; precisely the sort of career Papa Gabras would envision for his son Nike.

Does a maverick emerge because his environment provides him the freedom and fosters his rebellious nature, or is the trait of defiance ingrained in certain bloodlines, destined to surface no matter the circumstances?

I do not know the answer.

According to our traditional Roman view, one must remain where one is born. The restlessness that demands constant movement from place to place is judged evil, hence our assumptions about nomads: unpredictable, dangerous, foolhardy.

Nomads on the other hand deemed sickle and scythe a form of thraldom – the gravest of calamities – while horse, sword, and bow represented the ultimate liberty. The great Turkic ancestor Oghuz Khan commanded his people:

"Move about. Do not be sedentary. Roam across spring, summer, and winter pastures and by the sea, and you shall want for nothing. Let not your supplies of milk, yoghurt, and *kumis* dwindle."

What makes some creatures of God content themselves with only milk and yoghurt, while others burn with ambition and vigour?

I do not know.

Why are some of us compelled to remain still, and unable to flow freely despite being ablaze and molten within, while others, born as free as wild horses, choose to sit as still as tortoises?

I do not know.

And Andronicus? Can fire and brimstone added to hellfire intensify it? Or can fire extracted from hellfire diminish it? Manuel did not know. He had no inkling of the devils of nuisance Andronicus would unleash upon him for the rest of his life – and even thereafter.

His failure to rescue Andronicus promptly from his year-long captivity at the hands of the Turks seemed to have sown the seeds of a lifelong enmity. And yet, Manuel never had Andronicus put to death.

He fled so often that the notorious escape plot he had once fantasised about – slipping away from Ataman's custody en route to Iconium – actually came to pass. Only it wasn't Ataman's jail, but one of his many incarcerations in a prison Manuel had confined him to. Captured by some Vlachs who planned to return him to the emperor, he seized his chance on the road. Claiming the urgent need for a bowel movement, he absconded.

Andronicus was ever shifting his whereabouts; his ceaseless movements drew more censure from the learned men of the court than even his licentiousness. A fugitive at one time or another in the courts of the Prince of Antioch, the King of Jerusalem, and the Sultan of Damascus, Andronicus conspired with each of them to overthrow Manuel. Had a court existed in Kadesh, or amongst the Ethiopians, or Babylonians, or even in the Underworld itself, he would surely have sought sanctuary there too.

Andronicus had a wife but maintained an incestuous relation with Eudokia, his cousin's daughter. This incensed not only the family of Andronicus's wife but also Eudokia's side of the family. When faced with accusations, Andronicus laughed them off, saying he and Manuel were cast in the same mould. At least he was with his cousin's daughter; Manuel was betraying his German wife with Theodora, the daughter of his *own* brother. That, he insisted, was a far graver offense.

As you see, no one could surpass Andronicus in wits when it came to making light of sexual perversions, not even Manuel himself, who, in matters of the bed, was not, as the Turks say,

"As white as a spoon taken out of a bowl of milk."

One night, as he lay in the arms of Eudokia in his tent, armed troops accompanying her brothers surrounded it, intent to cut him down on the spot. Alarmed, Andronicus jumped out of bed not knowing what to do. Eudokia suggested he disguise himself as a woman, a chambermaid whom she would command loudly to go and fetch a lantern. In this way, he could make his exit. But Andronicus refused to don women's clothing. He unsheathed his sword, cut through the tent on the diagonal, leapt out and vaulted the barrier where the ambushers awaited, and vanished like lightning – leaving them agape.

Whenever he returned to Constantinople, Andronicus was met with forgiveness and new military commands from Manuel, partly as a mark of respect and affection for his mischievous cousin, and partly to keep him conveniently busy.

When extreme zeal swells up within a mediocre character, it often grows too volatile to contain. In such cases, as the Turkish maxim warns:

"Harsh vinegar corrodes its jar over time."

But what happens when the character in question is Andronicus?

I know what happened to Andronicus, but could something else have happened to him had the conditions been different? That I do not know.

An Armenian Prince whose father, the King, had died, and whose brother had been blinded in Constantinople at the hands of the Komnenos family, managed to escape his own captivity in the city. With the help of the Latins, he reclaimed his lost crown, but later betrayed the Latins by seizing a castle that belonged to the Knights Templar.

This outraged the Latins, who in turn attacked the Armenians – naturally, Emperor Manuel also had a hand in this attack. The prince then, rather humiliatingly for both parties, repelled both Latins and Romans. Eventually the Latins joined forces with him to invade the Roman island of Cyprus. And what did our Andronicus, a gifted military engineer stationed there do? He devoted himself not to the defence of the island, but to sports and other amusements.

When he returned, Manuel once again forgave him for the defeat and sent him to Hungary, where he conspired with the King of

Hungary and the illustrious Roman Emperor Barbarossa to overthrow Manuel.

Manuel, monitoring his correspondence in secret yet still bound by love for his cousin, cast him into prison – along with his wife, who was made to suffer for her wifely affections for him. She was locked in a separate cell. No one knows how he found her – for he was in fetters – yet somehow, he did, and he was so moved that his eyes filled with tears, which I am certain were sincere while they were being shed. He began lamenting the predicament, though not too loudly, for fear of being heard by the guards. And then – he somehow found time to impregnate her before escaping yet again. Neither door pivots, nor jambs or ceilings or thresholds were ever pierced or broken through at any point, which makes one wonder if he could not have taken flight from the Turks in Plekia as well if he had really wanted to. In both his flights and captivities, he could be capricious and prickly; one could never know the depths of his mind where his wiles lurked.

Andronicus resembled an audacious and greedy horsefly. When it attacks, the horse's power is limited by the length of its tail and mane, not more. Manuel at times let his blood be sucked voluntarily; at other times, he reacted savagely to his cousin's fomenting intrigues and secret affairs. This horsefly always persisted in coming back after being shooed off. After his myriad misdeeds he would throw himself at the feet of Emperor Manuel, asking forgiveness. Hiding chains wrapped around his body under his cloak, he would shed tears. Manuel, deeply moved by this cleverly engineered pathos, would command his attendants to raise him up, but Andronicus would refuse. Revealing his chains, he would conspicuously remain on the floor, asking to be dragged to the throne and dashed against it.

So compassionate and humane was Manuel that imagining this same man as someone who would not hesitate to advance himself through outright hostility and even cold brutality was genuinely difficult for him.

How does a person overcome his feelings which follow the route of a swinging censer or a lamp that occasionally strikes the wall, rebounding wildly from side to side until it finally settles at a stable point – bruised, mangled?

I do not know.

Can pure, atrocious evil emerge from harmless causes, or even benevolent ones?

I do not know.

When a horrible divination comes true, is it because it is envisaged in the mind of the predictor? Or is it not the prediction itself, but the fear of it – and belief in it – that sets the idea into action? Must we be careful of the thoughts we think?

The prophecy began to circulate in the 1160s. The diviner saw four letters – A, J, M, A – written in blood and which together formed the word for blood. These letters were also the initials of the succession of Komnenian emperors: Alexios, John, Manuel, and then an 'A'. Someone whose name began with the 'A' of Alpha was destined to succeed Manuel. But would there be blood shed if this sequence – A, J, M, A were broken? Or would blood come only if it remained intact? Nobody knew. Certainly not Manuel. Do you remember the splendid King Heraclius who was afraid of the waters of the Bosphorus? In Manuel's case, this fear became that letter, 'A'. It haunted him incessantly, making him wonder who it would be.

Bertha, his Nordic wife, had not produced a son. As the grandest of physicians from Bukhara asserted, Nordic women do not fully bleed and cleanse during menses due to the constriction of their veins and lack of liquefaction and softness, and this might cause sterility. The wombs of the women of cold areas are contracted, their milk is reduced and thickened due to the lack of external heat. Here, where we are, there are external agents facilitating the processes, namely the warm weather. So, Bertha's vessels were probably frozen before she arrived here, much like my great-grandfather Ivar's blood. Yet, despite being an old bride in her thirties, she conceived a daughter, Maria, and later bore a second child, Anna, who died at the age of four. Now perhaps she could have given birth to a boy, but Manuel wronged her in matters of the bed. In addition to her homely looks, fire was missing from Bertha's Nordic heart. Homer said the principal part of the soul is located in the heart. The Divine Scripture supports this when it says: "Wherefore do arguments arise in your hearts?" Perhaps for Nordics the seat of the soul was the brain, not the heart?

Upon Bertha's arrival in Constantinople, the city's most famous poet and grammarian, John Tzetzes, was commissioned to teach her Homer. Tzetzes acted too hastily when he dubbed her "the most Homeric of the Queens," for she paid him only a trifling sum and when he later requested a more generous fee, he was met with silence. He complained bitterly that he had used large sheets of paper to write the *Allegories of the Iliad* for Bertha's instruction, sizable leaves of paper were the most difficult to find and thus the most expensive, and, therefore, he believed himself entitled to a more generous honorarium from the Empress. Tzetzes's lamentations, however, fell on deaf ears. At last, he broke off his work altogether. For all I know, just as excessive adulation and blind attachment ill-suit the Nordic temperament, so too does the reckless splurging of money. My great-grandfather Ivar, too, was known to be utterly spellbound by his coins, treating his copper *tetarterons* with the same reverence as golden *dirhams* or *hyperpyrons*.

The verve that the Nordics lack, we Romans possess in abundance. You see, the sun and the heat fill us with ardour and vigour – whether those qualities make our lives easier remains up for debate for I am certain more murders are committed in the heat of passion here than in Nordic lands. It is well known that the two Komnenos cousins, were also fervid, but their passions were whimsical and self-serving. Manuel arranged the marriage of every single member of his family and close entourage. Sometimes mothers or daughters would protest an unsuitable groom, or an ugly bride but it goes without saying their grievances invariably went in one ear and out the other; Manuel selected them all with his political interests foremost in mind. He betrothed his daughter Maria to Béla of Hungary, the presumed heir to the Hungarian throne, yet kept the prospective couple waiting, just as he had once held up Bertha. He did, however, change the Hungarian boy's name to Alexios and elevated him to despotes – a form of dynastic insurance to fulfil the notorious 'A' of the prophecy.

When Bertha died at the beginning of 1160, Manuel roared like a lion, lamenting woefully. He said it felt as though a limb had been torn from his body. I felt the same when Pegasus and Dog died. He honoured Bertha with a burial ceremony at Pantokrator, a place considered more magnificent than the Tower of Babel or even the Temple of Solomon, where spread-out wings of cherubim touched the walls and each other. Half-alive myself, I buried Pegasus and Dog. If I could have, I too would have entombed them in Pantokrator, between the wings of cherubim.

After proper lamentation, he began to search for a new wife who would give him a son. He found one: Maria, nicknamed Xene, a beautiful Latin princess from the Crusader state of Antioch. She provided him with the necessary 'A' by giving birth to a boy in 1169 – Alexios. Now that the beseeched letter was obtained, Manuel broke off his daughter's betrothal to the Hungarian despotes and began to explore the supply of better, more useful and strategically important candidates. By the time he came upon the teenage son of a Frank Marquis and married him to Maria, poor Maria was an old, long-waiting bride in her thirties, re-enacting the destiny of her predecessor, Bertha.

Speaking of the strange ways of destiny, in fact, that much-coveted 'A' had come into existence earlier, out of wedlock, to Bertha. Sometimes, you receive what you have dreamed of all your life – but in the wrong way, in the wrong context and timing – and you realise you cannot make any use of it. Its un-usefulness replaces all previous longings and affections for it with exasperation. Manuel had gotten this bastard son from his late brother's daughter, his niece Theodora. Their shared Komnenos fervour had produced a certain Alexios, who was kept behind doors, as expected. Real life, in its strange and arbitrary turns, can be more bizarre than dreams or fantasies or even heresies. Andronicus's Komnenos frenzy would also produce a bastard child, a girl, Irene, the fruit of his incestuous union with another Theodora Komnenos, the Emperor Manuel's brother's daughter.

When the time came, Andronicus wanted these two bastards to be united in marriage. After all, where could one place them? Naturally, the Patriarch was seized with an apoplectic fit and refused to administer the ritual of this "unlawful, unholy" matrimony. Andronicus's rantings would not persuade him. Andronicus's creativity with notes of extreme cruelty was common knowledge. One particular example is worth citing: while once repressing a revolt in Nicaea, he contrived a devious stratagem in which he had an enemy's mother brought from Constantinople to the battlefield and tied as a human shield to a battering ram, which was then moved to the walls of the city. I am certain that when he came up with this idea, he marvelled at his own genius, and when he envisaged the shock and horror of his opponent, his amusement was genuine. His barbarous cruelty, his serene lack of empathy for this noble woman's terror, was as authentic as the tears he had shed in jail when he noticed his wife's presence. His affection for her at that moment had also been sincere, very sincere.

The Patriarch fled to the Island of Terebinthos, seeking refuge to avoid the sin of marrying these two offspring born of incest. Unperturbed by his flight, Andronicus had the union solemnised by the Archbishop of Bulgaria, who happened to be visiting Constantinople at the time. Years later, he would have the eyes of this illegitimate, hidden Alexios gouged out despite the outcries of his own daughter Irene, who, by chance, loved her husband. But this Alexios, too, carried Manuel's blood and was therefore a potential claimant to the throne. Irene's words meant nothing to her father. Andronicus would indeed stain the prophesied 'A' with blood.

With Manuel dead, Andronicus feigned protective intent as the boy's uncle, claiming that young Alexios – the rightful heir, whose beard had not yet grown – was unable to govern on his own, and that his own white beard and profound experience made him a more suitable choice. Andronicus secured a decree, and from then on acted as guardian and custodian of Alexios, the son Manuel had waited for so many years to have and at long last had found and then doted on. Andronicus and Alexios were to be co-emperors henceforth. While he raised his arms during the coronation rite, holding the chalice filled with precious and life-giving blood, he swore that the only reason he agreed to reign was to assist little Alexios in his rule. A few days later, Andronicus had the boy strangled, at barely six years of age. When the body was brought to him, he kicked it and growled: "Liar Manuel and whore Xene's son!"

He had one of the corpse's ears pierced and threaded into it a wax impression of his signet ring. They beheaded little Alexios, placed his body in a lead coffin, and cast it into the depths of the sea. His head was buried in a hole in the Katabate district. I don't know if the dead watch us here from wherever they find themselves, but if so, their desperation must be unbearable. If not, it was highly likely that Manuel would never know the truth about his son's fate. Just before executing the boy, Andronicus had used trickery and deceit to convince him of the boy's mother's betrayal, getting him to sign her death decree. Empress Xene, whom Andronicus detested with all his heart, was flung into a dungeon with no food and water and then strangled.

What unfolded after Andronicus finally seized the throne is an account I shall give you in proper time, but let me warn you, its colour is blood red… For now, let me pose to you a question whose answer I do not know:

Might the future have already been created and can we truly foresee it?

He would tell me: "When two feelings run counter to each other, wear the vicious one as an undergarment and the gracious one as a tunic over it. Always remember it is the undershirt that protects the body from the cold, not the mantle."

He used to claim he would never allow himself to become "a puppet of antitheses." Those "feeble voices from a faraway kingdom" he brushed aside with contempt and maintained that "it is meekness in its primitive form that is barbaric, not disdain that has been devised carefully, a repulsion that has created its own mind. An alert, mindful impulse for survival is superior to anything. Hesitation makes people into lambs. And sooner or later," he would sternly intone while wagging a finger at me, "it brings you to book; it makes you pay."

Prior to his usurpation of the throne, in the early days while he was still playing the role of Manuel's young orphan's white-haired, munificent protector, Andronicus wanted to visit Manuel's tomb at the monastery of Pantokrator. Standing in front of the sepulchre he began to weep and wail so much that they had to tear him away from it. Ignoring his attendants he demanded to be allowed to stay longer; he raised his hands with palms turned outwards, and, as rumour would have it, he said:

"You have been the cause of my endless meanderings, you have made me the subject of universal gossip, and now this marble with its seven clusters of ivy holds you in a prison from which you cannot escape. You're sleeping now and from that sleep there is no awakening till the last trumpet sounds. I shall assail your family like a lion lunging upon large prey; I shall get revenge for the injuries I suffered at your hands every time I entered that splendid seven-hilled megapolis."

His slaughter continued with the elimination of Maria, Manuel's daughter by his first wife, the German, Bertha. The girl possessed the iron resolve of her Germanic heritage and the Roman vision and ingenuity she had inherited from her father, Manuel – a paragon of both. Before Andronicus arrived at the capital, she had dispatched letters to him pledging to come and assist in overthrowing her step-mother Empress Xene, whom she also loathed. She even succeeded in gathering her own troops to rally against the Imperial soldiers. She failed and withdrew, but her very existence remained a threat, and hence her assassination by a eunuch, who used a poison that would kill slowly, not instantly – by special request of Andronicus, naturally.

None escaped his scourge: not the Latins of Constantinople whom he had massacred in great numbers by inciting mobs to pour into their homes along the Golden Horn; not the Papal legate, whose severed head was tied to a dog's tail; not the nobles he expelled from their families' native cities and imprisoned without charge, and not even vagrants. One a poor wretched lunatic named Iros was caught wandering near Andronicus's pavilion one night. Despite his madness and nakedness, they accused him of sorcery and burned him alive on a pyre of dry wood in the theatre. Secret informers denounced family members for scoffing at Andronicus. Most denunciations were likely born of private grudges. Young or old, it made no difference, he had them maimed, placed on asses, and banished beyond the Roman borders into the savage lands, where, at times, the Turks would take pity on victims and tend their wounds.

The Dervish had purported that in this life, "Enemies may become friends and friends may become enemies." With Andronicus, this came to pass so rapidly that both his victims and those who were witness to his transformation began to doubt their own sanity. One day he would include you in his most intimate circle of friends, welcome you "to the finest wheat, the fattest calf, and the strongest drink" – and the next, he would have you executed.

He resembled Xerxes, whose ship encountered a storm on its journey back to Persia. The helmsman advised Xerxes to order his marines to jump overboard in their heavy armour to lighten the ship's load. Initially reluctant, Xerxes eventually gave the command, and the ship was brought safely to land. For saving his life, the King rewarded the helmsman with a gold crown. However, shortly thereafter, in a sharp twist, Xerxes ordered the helmsman's decapitation for leading so many fine Persian soldiers to their deaths.

How did Andronicus become so consistent in his inconsistency? Why did he not direct his fury against his enemies instead of at the Constantinopolitans?

I do not know.

When the people had finally tired of his cruelty and judged it time to topple him, the mob jeered at the mighty Emperor Andronicus's shaved scalp, red like Mary Magdalene's egg. They bludgeoned him with clubs, jabbed him with roasting spits, and plucked out his beard. A prostitute poured a jug of boiling water over his face and crammed his mouth with excrement. Then they cut off his right hand with an axe.

The next day, he was still alive, suspended upside down from a stone lintel between two short columns – which stood beside a hyena and a wolf – at the Hippodrome, when they mutilated his genitals. He cried, "Lord, have mercy! Why do you further bruise the broken reed?" But can a torturer – be it God himself or the mob of Constantinople – ever torture mercifully? Notwithstanding, his question was understandable, one might even say 'honourable', for Andronicus was a man who had always harboured these stark contrasts in his soul.

In death, at least, he appeared naked before God – no underwear, no mantle, not even rags. Do you know that Turks never execute their princes in this fashion? They strangle them. Their last princely tears of fear are not meant to mix with their blood and flow through the gutters. This is not what a highborn person deserves, even if his death must be savage – the same sort of destruction he would have inflicted on his own victims. His blood is not to be splashed onto rough streets, sprinkled on damp earth, for it carries his soul and spirit. Thus, when the body decomposes the blood must decay together with it, into oblivion. If blood is shed prematurely, misery follows. The restless soul and spirit, unmoored, will wander aimlessly in this world for eternity.

It may be that last winter, Constantinopolitans mixed their wine with lukewarm water imbued with Andronicus's soul. And in the heat of the summer, they refreshed themselves with vinegar diluted with water infused with his essence. They may still be garnishing their meat with garum sauce containing Andronicus, even cleaning their sinful body parts with him – though of this, I'm sure, he would be most delighted, provided the ladies were to his liking. He would have relished being part of any concoction professing to enhance sensuality.

When far from home, in moments of extreme yearning, he would trace the currents of the Bosphorus in the air and murmur, "Flowing waters… I must be dead, living in the Paradise of the Saracens by the strait. Those things promised to them in their Bible – I possess them already."

"There are pretty virgin maidens with large, lovely eyes, their swelling bosoms guarding delicate eggs, and immortal youths serving fruits on trays of gold, and golden goblets filled with clear milk and honey. I am being waited on hand and foot by damsels in silk garments wearing bracelets of gold and pearls and drinking wine with them. Oh, the joy."

Suddenly he would screw his handsome face into a frown and continue, "Only the high-raised throne encrusted with gold and precious stones which used to belong to Uncle John is missing…" His thin lips would curl with an ugly twist, and he would give a bark of laughter: "Now God damned Manuel's… Oh, I must be indeed dead, but I shall arise…"

And arise he did – always. In fact, after losing his Saracen paradise and his youth, his life became an ongoing tale of constant de-camping, random deaths, and revivals, but also a never-ending arousal. If he ever had the chance to settle, to finally heave a sigh of relief, he never hesitated to appeal to ancient wisdom for remedies or to take inspiration from the elixirs and philosophy of the ancients.

For example, he took *Natural History* under advisement. According to Pliny the Elder, the muzzle and the fat of an Egyptian lizard soaked in wine with rocket seeds and satyrion root was an excellent recipe for better erotic performance. Alternatively, the flesh from the flanks, with myrrh and pepper, could produce a similar effect. But how to eat the lizard? Boiled? Raw? To further ensure its efficacy, Andronicus decided the best way was to have the entire animal roasted with myrrh, pepper, satyrion root, and rocket seeds. That day, he had both a lizard and a man roasted – the lizard in the palace kitchen, the man, who had insulted him, on a skewer at the Hippodrome. Thus, two birds were killed with one stone.

What remained of the man's incinerated body was taken from the execution site and hurled into one of the vaults of the Hippodrome. Only later did people show the good sense to remove his remains and lay them to rest in the district near the monastery of Ephoros.

Years later, with a bitter-sweet smile on my face, I mused… What if, by the dispensation of divine providence or simply by the banal vagaries of fate, or the whim of a vindictive deity, Andronicus ended up in the Saracen 'hell'? Their prophet had stated that "women will make up the majority of its inhabitants." I am certain those would not be the "houris with large lustrous eyes" that Andronicus used to harp on about, the ones who restrained their wide glances, nor those girls "built with a new creation: non-menstruating, not urinating or defecating, and childfree," nor those who would be so beautiful, pure, and transparent that the marrow of their legs could be seen through their bones and flesh. Instead, they would be the simple, miserable, fat, ugly, old, or handicapped remnants of this sorry world.

What would Andronicus do there?

47

I must eat, but I have no hands;
I must walk, but I have no feet;
I must endure pain, and then
I find I have both feet and hands.

Marcus Antonius Polemon
Philostratus of Athens, *Lives of the Sophists*

We heard the father and the daughter had come from Transoxiana, but I found out later that they had moved here from even farther away, from an oasis city named Turpan. In their home, too – which happened to be Skleros's former house, the one Ataman bought from Basil for Ogan – there was no mother. Their arrival had been sudden, but it was clear that behind the curtains, something had been simmering for a while, with the beady-eyed dervish playing some role in their appearance. Who knows? Maybe they were his relatives. Not just the beady-eyed one, either; other dervishes also frequented the house so often that the place began resembling a dervish lodge. The young ones had fully shaven heads and wore white conical hats; the older men sported white beards or just a white moustache, and a few wore a large iron ring on their right earlobes. Some wore long necklaces adorned with octagonal stones.

The house was illuminated day and night. Even though Muhtasib's remonstrations had long faded into the wind, a steady stream of men, albeit dervishes, frequenting a house inhabited by a single lady still raised eyebrows; nothing worthy of gossip transpired though. Ogan married the girl, and they settled down to life in their tent.

Just as when one's body hurts in two different places and one focuses on the pain closer to the head, I directed my attention to different pain, a larger one: that of Basil. He had given up the habit of taking a catnap after meals, complaining about dreadful back pain that racked his body whenever he lay down. He began to criticise Anna's cooking – something he had never done before – wandering about the house restlessly complaining that her food gave him dyspepsia. We swapped our olive oil with our neighbours in the hope that theirs would perhaps upset his stomach less. We diluted our vinegar. Pennyroyal and rose oil helped sooth the pain in his belly, so I made it my task to hunt them down at the market, and while I was at it, to pick up some gossip about the newcomers. Anna said if I couldn't find pennyroyal, I should bring aniseed instead. At the marketplace, I learned that the father of Ogan's new bride was not a dervish at all, but a miniaturist. The man was manufacturing his own paint using an ingenious, elaborate method: melting earth dyes in hot water, and adding powders from ground stones and insect shells. For a shinier raised effect, he used egg yolks – but only after treating his paper first, dipping it in melted resin, starch glue, and egg whites, drying them on a walnut-wood board and later smoothing and polishing them with a giant cowrie shell. The shell probably wasn't from our sea, for nobody had ever seen one that size before. His brush was made from hair taken from the nape of a baby cat. How sophisticated.

"So, what does the man draw?" I asked the merchants at the marketplace. One of them laughed and said, "Certainly not the Virgin and Child, nor the Resurrection."

Another added, "Nor Christ or the Last Judgement."

Frowning, I reprimanded them. "I could have guessed that much. I'm asking you what he *does* paint. Apples?"

The peasant with whom I was to exchange olive oil answered:

"He paints landscapes. For rivers, he uses silver powder, and for the sun, gold. In the foreground, there are people, or horses, and many, many birds. Lots of birds."

"People?"

"Yes – women, men. But between the people, all the empty spaces are filled with little animals or plants. Busy. Very busy."

"And apples?"

"I don't recall seeing an apple. I did see a double-headed eagle. It had copper nails. Its left wing covered the moon, and its right wing covered the sun. Oh – and I also saw a very ugly black monster under the ground."

"Ah, Erlik," I said.

"Who?" He raised an eyebrow.

"Nothing."

Time-thieves, I thought – stealing from the universe. Time-eluders, escaping it by freezing it on paper. Precisely what I had yearned to become, to be, and to do – rather than gossiping while shopping in the marketplace – to be a bird, an eagle, a horse, or even Erlik in a drawing where existence would be silent, where there would be no 'time,' no endurance – just being.

Does an image hold a secret power, or is it merely a poor rendering, corrupting the senses?

Andronicus had believed in both. Later when he became the emperor, he would commission an artist to paint him on the gate panels of the Church of the Forty Martyrs. He would especially request to be depicted not in the usual imperial vestments, but in the costume of a labourer holding a sickle in his hand, posing as the champion of the poor and their interests. He trusted not only the power of beauty but also its effect on painting and vice versa. After ordering the strangling of Manuel's widow, Xene Maria of Antioch, who was a beautiful woman, he ordered all her portraits be altered. Lovely Xene, changed into a haggard old woman so that she would elicit neither pity nor admiration from passers-by. Ironically, Andronicus remained ravishingly handsome even in his old age. Perhaps the paintings that depicted him in all his beauty influenced reality itself.

When the subject matter of an icon was Christ, controversy was sure to follow. Three centuries ago, painting was denounced as idolatry. Iconoclasts demanded that the veneration of icons be persecuted. They condemned them as idolaters, arguing that Jesus was both human and divine so artists could never depict him in an image. God, they argued, was invisible and infinite; to represent Him was beyond our capacity and our rightful place. The military success of the Arabs and the rise of their faith, which forbade sacred images, added to the concern that God was on their side, that the Arabs must be right. Images were unsuitable ways to refer to the divine; essences were imperceptible to humans; material images were not conducive to the attainment of true piety. God and the Holy Trinity resided in the soul, not in a painting. *The Book of Exodus* declared: "You shall not make for yourself an idol, whether in the form of anything that is in heaven above, or that is on the earth beneath, or that is in the water under the earth. You shall not bow down to them or worship them."

Yet the counter-argument maintained that the art belonged to the painter, but the idea and the inspiration belonged to the Holy Father, and that the art was a beneficial means of expressing the divine idea. Images could prevent confusion and ambiguity. For example, when the image of the emperor was venerated, it was the emperor in person that was being venerated, not the painting, for there was only one emperor. The image represented the prototype, not in essence but in 'name'. Names themselves were like icons. Written names were representations of sounds, and the sounds were representations of ideas, and ideas were representations of things. When an artist of meagre talent paints Paul, the poorly rendered figure of Paul still signifies the real Paul – the 'preacher and teacher of the Gentiles'. Icons were points of access to the divine. Exodus affirmed: "You shall make two cherubim of gold; you shall make them of hammered work, at the two ends of the mercy seat."

The iconophiles won the argument, but the crucial question remained: to what extent were we free? How and when did we decide where divine powers would intervene in our human affairs? What was the exact cause of Basil's bellyache, for example? His already large potbelly had swollen even further, and that is why I hadn't noticed that he had been losing weight. Only when his turnip-shaped nose grew more magnificent did I realise the rest of his facial fat was melting away.

In the face of his agony, Anna unharnessed a great vitality, forgetting her inveterate rheumatism which was the favourite scapegoat for her perpetual sloth. The weaker Basil became, the more invigorated she grew, rolling left and right, resembling a fat but surprisingly nimble ball. She suggested using cupping to his stomach. I grabbed the copper alloy cups while she took a bunch of wicks out of a glass candle holder. I helped her to strip off Basil's gown. She dipped small pieces of the wicks in oil, lit them and threw one piece into each cup. After the wicks turned into ash, she placed the cups onto his belly. As the hot air inside the cups cooled, the vacuum created sucked the flesh upwards, drawing the blood with it.

We waited for a while. Then she removed the cups, each leaving behind a vivid red, circular mark. Basil's eyes rolled upward. Looking at the ceiling, he let out a huge breath, whispered thanks to God and fell asleep with his mouth agape. This feeling of relief, however, was not due to the efficiency of the treatment, but rather to the fact that it introduced heat, hence a new kind of ache in the immediate area which distracted him from the throes of the original pain – but only temporarily. The effect didn't last long; among the aches, only the strongest prevails.

The next morning, he woke up with yellow skin – yellower even than the barbarians. Oddly, this brought a measure of relief to Anna and me. Now we were selecting between a host of ailments, and jaundice, no matter how bad it was, was still the better one as there were several widely known remedies.

Instead of sending someone out, Anna, her deep black eyes shining with a new light, first ran to Svoronos, for he owned a golden oriole, and from there she rushed to the marketplace to grab some chicory roots. Roasting them first, she added honey and vinegar and prepared an infusion. Scrunching up his face, Basil protested, whining interminably after drinking it. Anna still appeared full of hope, never complaining or answering back. Even to me she seemed friendlier than usual. Svoronos brought his bird in person. I ushered the shy soul in as he hesitated at the door, almost pushing him into Basil's room. When he saw Basil, he gasped. Basil had lost a lot of weight but now that we knew the culprit was jaundice, we were hopeful we would later fatten him up again like a duck. We had to make him take a purgative to get rid of the excess yellow bile in his body, but, before this, he had to watch the bird. While Svoronos stood in front of the bed with his cage, Anna and I held Basil under his armpits and helped him sit up straight so that he could see it well. A fluting whistle came out of the creature's incandescent-yellow body; turning its black wings and tail, it tweeted and twittered. Its eyes, reddish with black stripes extending behind, focused on Basil;

its long, pale red bill opened and closed as he made sounds as if singing. Basil opened his eyes slightly, and a faint but delectable smile lit his face, which made my heart leap. The bird being so obliging, I asked Svoronos what we should give it to eat. With a nervous hand gesture, and in a slightly tearful voice, he said he had already fed it.

"Oh, by the way, Svoronos, I'll be needing some paper. Find me some, would you, please?"

Hearing this, he gave me a quizzical look, but it seemed to cheer him a little. He nodded seriously, pledging his commitment to the assignment.

After he and the golden oriole had left, Basil's expression went back to its former agonised state. In this situation, it was imperative that he throw up, so we attempted to feed him greasy food. It did not go well. Gagging and making choking noises in his throat, he was not able to swallow the root vegetable puree. Anna had added no honey and ginger but lots of olive oil instead to make it easily consumable, but he jerked away. When she insisted, he pressed his fist against his mouth like a child and refused.

It was hard to recognise the new Basil; the merry, chubby man had departed, replaced by a new one, perhaps still not as gaunt and scrawny as Zeno, but at least as cranky. The resemblances between the new Basil and his father were unsettling, but both Anna and I were determined to bring the old Basil back. We kept on searching for him. We persevered.

Anna moved to Basil's room officially. She laid her bedding on the floor beside his and remained a constant presence at his side. Due to my connections in the marketplace, we found dried squirting cucumbers and resin of Morning Glory flower roots. The first was to add into his bath water and the latter to induce vomiting. It came as no great surprise, however, that he retched up nothing but a few drops of slimy mucus.

In view of this set back, I sent word out that we were in great need of Lemnian tablets. These were known to have miraculous powers against poisoning, especially venomous reptile bites, but they were also excellent at inducing vomiting. I didn't know if they would help Basil's specific condition, but a villager who was bitten by a snake several years ago had vomited copiously when given one with wine and he had survived. They were made of a specific type of soil where water dried up and a thick scum was left behind; this was skimmed off and mixed with goat's blood, and then formed into round pellets with the seal of a goat on them. Unfortunately, they were also supposed to function as an aphrodisiac, but that was a price I was willing to pay – if only Basil would recover.

When a camel dies of hunger even when surrounded by rich pastures, it is said to crave a single thorn from the savage desert. Let it have both, I thought – and spread word that we were seeking Lemnian tablets, the pasture, and the thorn alike – casting a sharp glance at Anna as I did. But my peevishness quickly faded for it was bath time. I helped Anna with the preparations and left the room just before she began. Spying on them crossed my mind but I didn't. What was the sense? She had washed him in better times without a doubt. Those little hands were now licitly massaging his body with emollient ointments to cure him. Despite these massages, Basil's skin turned itchy, so much so that Anna scratched him day and night to give him relief, for he was too tired to do it himself.

In our house, too, as in Ogan's, the candles and lamps burned day and night, so that we might better see Basil. Anna's struggle resembled mine: she had to decide which pain deserved her attention most. Basil wailed when she scratched his swollen, red legs and so she understood he needed something to stop the pain first. We washed his legs with cold water, but this was insufficient. When his belly too swelled and he began to groan in agony, especially at nights, we sent out for the Turkish physician of the caravanserai who had looked after Andronicus at that time. The man bowed at the entrance to the house. He was dressed in a tunic similar to Muhtasib's, but much more demure. He folded his hands, palms together, fingers straight, and placed them on his chest to salute us without directly looking into our eyes, although he smiled. He was clearly not a nomad, but someone sent from Iconium – much younger and more eager than I had expected. Almost bouncing on his toes, he followed Anna into Basil's room as I trailed behind them.

When he stepped up to Basil's bed, the smile on his face faded. He held Basil's head with one hand and artfully opened one eye with the tip of his finger, examining the pupil, then repeated the procedure with the other eye. Even the browns had gone yellow. He held his hand on the swollen belly and asked Anna to take Basil's clothes off. Unexpectedly for one of his young age, his Greek was flawless. Before Anna had a chance to nod and wink, I stepped out of the room. I thanked God that I did not have to be confronted by Basil's sick, naked body. As a matter of fact, I did not want anything to do with any ailing body. A sick body and Basil did not belong together. Basil in my eyes was not even supposed to have a body. I expressed my gratitude again to God for having made Anna and her hands familiar and deft in dealing with it.

When I returned to the room, I found the physician's countenance and posture changed. His eyes looked darker, there was a grim twist to his mouth, and he appeared somehow deflated. Basil was dressed once more in his night gown, and Anna stood beside him, staring into space, having forgotten the presence of the stranger. I turned to him and asked:

"Will he get better?… Oh… He won't recover, will he?"

The physician quickly averted his gaze, cleared his throat, but then turned back to look at me once more. Biting his lip, he shook his head and asked:

"Do you have a clean sponge at home, My Lady?"

Heavy-footed, we walked together towards the door.

A few hours after I had seen him off, a man arrived at the door with a package from the physician. As he handed it to me, he cautioned me to keep the liquid out of the reach of any children. "There is a considerable amount of opium in it," he said, "and also some mulberry juice, lettuce seed, mandrake, ivy, and a touch of hemlock too."

"Don't worry," I said. "There's no-one to take care of a child here anymore, hence no child."

He extended an unused sea sponge to me as well and left. I stood aghast staring at it, turning it over in my hand, inspecting its gigantic cavities. Were Basil to use it, I thought, those cavities would suck up too much opium, too much for his poor parched lips and throat to bear. I understood why the physician had left. Now was the time to cry. I hadn't in a long time; the urge was overwhelming, but few tears came. In the face of the magnitude of the situation, weeping seemed embarrassing, inadequate, absurd. Andronicus's great talent for trivialising life would have been so soothing right now – he would even have made light of death. He would say: "Is it hard, my little one, to understand what God wants?"

As a last-ditch effort, I sent out for the rolling-eyed kam. I had heard he alleviated, or even ended, the continual pain of patients by inserting slender metal needles through the skin. This logic-defying remedy horrified Anna. Was this the time to let a crazy pagan into the house? She protested, but this time I could not bring myself to tell her, "It's none of your business." She, for her part, did not have the heart to insist either; she did not launch into one of her endless tirades of complaint. Pressing her lips tightly, she sat by Basil and did not utter a word but kept praying to Basil's namesake saint, Saint Basil of Caesarea. Saint Basil was the one who established the first hospital in Cappadocia. It was so vast that physicians and nurses lived in the complex where the lepers were treated gratis. Perhaps Saint Basil could intercede on our Basil's behalf regardless of whether his illness was a punishment or the devil's doing.

When the partly pagan Emperor Valens called upon Saint Basil to pray for his sick son, the Saint agreed – on condition that the boy be baptised as an Orthodox Christian. The Emperor complied, and the boy recovered. If it were truly the case that disease was either the work of Satan or a penance that the Almighty saw fit to make some undergo, then in our Basil's case it surely must have been the work of the devil. Yes, our Basil had flaws, but what could he have done to deserve such chastisement? For that reason, Anna placed great hope in Saint Basil.

Dog must have sensed the man's presence before he even stepped into the courtyard for he stiffened like a bow and fixed his gaze on the door. Tail raised and growling, he pawed at it furiously. I scolded him for his claws were scratching the door and suddenly realised how much I was starting to resemble Anna.

When I opened the door, I saw one of my men accompanying the rolling-eyed kam and Ogan. I did not know how Ogan had found out; I hadn't invited him. As the kam drew closer, Dog went crazy, barking and yelping. As before, the kam said something to the animal and straightaway he tucked his tail between his legs and cringed. With a sound like a low howl, he slunk off to a corner. Still walking upright with his typical flowing gait, Ogan had evidently lost a lot of weight – and looked nearly as thin as a teenager. Today, the kam's eyes were not rolling. Bowing, he greeted me. He was not sporting his professional garb, the jingly, feathery *manyak*, but ordinary clothes like any nomadic Turkoman. Though this irritated me, it still suited my book for it prevented one of Anna's hysterical reactions. One could never be sure how she would react to the man. The bells, charms, painted sigils, and wild animal teeth that dangled from his apparel could strike horror into Anna throwing her into a panic, and instead of observing discretion she might have groaned, griped, or worse – insulted the man outright. On the other hand, what did it mean that he had come in ordinary clothes instead of in his *manyak*, which I knew to hold magical, secret powers?

The physical changes in Basil startled Ogan. Even for us, who had watched the decline unfold gradually, they were difficult to accept. For him, the sight of this, broken-down vestige of the once jolly, fat man, barely conscious in this moment, must have been a shock. Though Ogan's face showed his distress he was quick to mask it. Still, a shadow lingered, making me wonder how much was his sadness about Basil and how much was his ongoing grief over Alma's death. Losing weight sharpened his features and darkened his onyx eyes; his hair now reached his jawline, and his chapped lips took on a dark maroon colour, probably from persistently licking them to sooth the cracked skin. The violet that induced pride and excitement when recognised in emperors' ink or on flags or led to surprise and admiration when detected in the eyes of a donkey like Pegasus, now evoked a different sensation when seen in the thick rings under Ogan's eyes, stark against his pallid skin. This felt like the impulse to treat a drenched puppy with tenderness, a yearning to deeply inhale the smell of the greasy hair and sweaty skin.

The kam strode swiftly up to Basil. Without altering his expression, he opened a pouch and gave a sharp command in Turkish.

"He wants fire," Ogan said.

Anna's small, graceful feet and fine ankles that normally clumsily conveyed her pudgy body and thick, wobbling thighs to where there was work to do, hastened her to fetch it for him in the twinkling of an eye. The kam took out a piece of fabric soaked in an oily substance, tied it around an iron rod and ignited it. Spinning around Basil's bed he intoned incomprehensible charms as smoke and a strange smell diffused throughout the room. Poor Basil, not fully in his senses, coughed lightly.

The kam did not sit in front of Basil, play a lute, sing or scream, nor did he contort himself to expel evil, whip the patient, slap his face or brandish a knife, none of the theatrics I might have expected. And those excitable eyes of his lacked their usual strange light today. I was almost inclined to take it amiss and conclude he was being lazy or having a bad day at work, but then he said something that made Ogan do a double-take – his face momentarily aghast, then grim. Just then, Dog began barking again and bolted towards the door. There stood one of my men with the beady-eyed dervish.

"I couldn't stop him," said my man, bowing slightly.

The grinning dervish looked at me, standing a little too close on the threshold, clearly waiting to be invited in.

"Dervish Baba, it's not the right time now," I said pulling a long face. "Go now and come back another time. I'll give you coins again, but not now."

Persisting with the grin, he took a step inside. "I don't want money. Last time you gave me more than I deserved. Let me come in and see your father. I know that kam is here. Perhaps I can help."

Eyeing him from head to foot, I realised his woollen tunic had been washed and wasn't that grimy greyish colour anymore, but either it had shrunk, or the man had grown fatter. He didn't stink, at least. After all, he'd been hobnobbing with others at Ogan's Lodge, I thought, he must be eating well. I stood aside and let him enter.

Neither Ogan nor the kam reacted to his presence. The kam bent down to the floor in front of Basil and spoke softly.

Ogan sulked.

"What did he say?" I asked Ogan.

"He said, 'sometimes a patient cannot be cured, but he can be healed.'" He frowned.

"What?"

".... and that nobody dies unless he consents to."

Alma yes, not Basil, I thought in desperate recklessness. Not Basil. There must be some mistake, some misunderstanding. Basil might be foggy; Basil might be murky; Basil might be lax. But complacent? No. He would never leave. He would never abandon me.

"What the hell does that mean?" I snapped.

He heaved a deep sigh. "I don't really know."

"Ask him, then. What sort of nonsense is this?"

Turning towards the kam he spoke in a murmur. The kam's reply was short and sharp. The dervish smiled as Ogan responded to the kam. The kam's tone shifted from harsh and shrill to meek. At once, he turned to me, bowed brusquely, and made a hasty exit, Dog trailing behind him.

"Come here, Dog," I called.

The animal ignored my command. I went after him to the courtyard and ordered my man to make sure Dog wouldn't leave the premises with the kam. Breathless after running back, I asked:

"Tell me, did he say anything else about my father? What's that drivel about not dying unless one agrees?"

"Man is not yet finished," Ogan said, in a reluctant tone: "We go and come back until we understand. So, he said…"

"Understand what?" I was in no mood for abstract rhetoric. "Is this man out of his mind? Speak up Ogan!"

"We ascend to the first floor," the dervish interjected. "There are seven floors in the cosmos. When we are in the here and now, on the first, we do not know. We are looking at only one page of the whole book. All other pages, however, have already been written – by us." He glanced at me before continuing. Pointing the ceiling with his thumb, he said, "We write the book while we are above. One makes sense of it only after one finishes the book. The meaning of each page is revealed in its completeness. Only then. Until then, we go, and we come back." He made small back-and-forth gestures with one hand. "Until we grasp the whole book."

"Where do we go, Dervish Baba? Where is Basil going? What are you saying?"

"Dream of a big loaf of bread. You are one slice here on earth. When you die, you go back to the loaf. Your slice is remixed into the leavened dough, re-baked, a new slice is cut from it, and sent back here; you are reborn. You are the same person but also not the same person."

"Oh, that bread stuff again. What nonsense."

"But Jesus being resurrected – you believe that? And that he will come again with glory to judge the living and the dead?"

"That is something else. Besides, he hasn't come back yet. So…"

"The loaf experiences itself via its slices. Do you understand?"

"No. Not really. Why does it do that?"

"To learn the lessons. You can always invoke aid and guidance from your loaf. If you cannot, the kam can help you. Do you understand this?"

"No. No, I don't. I never will! What is it I'm learning here and now, then?"

"You shall find it, child."

This time I shouted: "And look, the crazy kam did nothing to help! He did nothing!"

"Perhaps there was nothing to do, child."

My eyes filled with tears, and so did my throat. I gritted my teeth to control them.

The dervish put his hand on my shoulder.

"Don't be afraid of crying, child."

Ogan's eyes brimmed with tears. This was for Alma. Maybe a little bit for Basil too. The dervish took him by the arm, and they walked slowly towards the front door. I did not cry. I was determined. I called out sternly to Ogan:

"Ogan, what is the name of your new wife?"

He turned back, his eyes still wet and dazed. With a low, shaky voice he said, "Bige."

"What does it mean?"

He blushed and dropped his eyes.

"A respectable lady."

The dervish quickly came back in and whispered in my ear:

"It means pure, virginal, a respectable maiden."

Once they'd gone Anna pounded her fists on her thighs. Glaring, tense, she yelled:

"Send a message. The priest! The priest should come immediately."

Christ had not separated the righteous from the sinners yet. Until Parousia, his second arrival, both the dead and the living would have to wait, whether sinner or not. Until then, the only punishment would be personal regrets, shame, and the memory of sins, nothing external. Purgatory was for the Latins. But praying would help by offering relief to Basil's departing soul, even if it couldn't change the end result. Paradise or Hades? 'Service for He who is at the Point of Death.' An urgent necessity, for Anna, a pressing want.

"*Tamam*, ok, I said."

Basil had been wriggling on his bed, now stretching his arms and legs, now contracting them. Anna soaked the sponge in the liquid sent by the physician of the caravanserai and dripped it into his mouth whenever he moaned in pain. He grunted and groaned and later lapsed into unconsciousness. Some hours later he died. Pardos the Priest had still not come. The Lemnian tablets from Lemnos arrived two months later.

48

It was in my mouth sweet as honey:
and as soon as I had eaten it, my belly was bitter.

Revelation, 10:10

An oxcart with a driver waited at the gate early in the morning. Anna had successfully evaded notice, for I had not seen her packing. Being a 'Lady of the Night,' she must have been busy while I slept, I thought. Had she decided while Basil was sick, or after his death, that I no longer required her services? She was blatantly attempting to keep communication to a minimum. Giving me a sidelong glance, she darted out to see the cart, then rushed back inside. She returned with a burlap satchel slung over one shoulder, seemingly so heavy that it pulled her shoulder downwards, almost toppling her over. Her other hand gripped another bag, of rough leather. She wore a belt-bag slung round her rotund waist, long enough to attach several drawstring pouches with jute loops to it. Quite a few bites in the pouches, I thought, not without spite – and no doubt the money she had saved is tucked safely in the central pocket, cushioned beneath the fat. She stood before me and took a very deep breath. Face glistening with sweat, she spoke in a shaky voice:

"I'm going back to my village, Theia."

I widened my eyes in feigned surprise and gave a quick, false smile. "So I see."

"Take care of yourself, Theia."

"Oh, I shall, don't you worry."

Anna's chin quivered and she held back her sobs with some force. After a moment of silence and hesitation, she laboriously dragged herself and her hefty load away. I stood still until I could hear the servant close the gate behind her, then I stepped into the kitchen, her dominion. Three bowls of honey rice pudding were sitting on the counter, still warm. This was the very moment I decided that Pegasus and Dog would live with me inside the house rather than in the barn.

The second I put one bowl on the floor, Dog devoured his pudding. Licking his lips, he placed his two front paws on the bench, wanting more. I shooed him away: the second plate was for Pegasus. While Dog continued to lick his muzzle and look at me imploringly, the ever prudent Pegasus drew his muzzle towards the pudding but then turned his head away as if in disgust.

"Come on Pegasus, this is a treat you've never had… How can you say no to a sweet? Come on, Pegasus!"

I attempted to help him eat with a spoon rather than from the dish, but he remained unconvinced. He preferred cucumbers. I divided his share between Dog and myself. We both gobbled down all that remained of Anna's outstanding pudding – probably the best she'd ever made.

Some days later, the three of us were dozing in the living room when a servant announced the arrival of a visitor. The room had not been aired for a long time. The treats I was feeding the animals were generating unsavoury odours, and besides I was not always prompt in letting them out when nature called. I was living just like the Latins. It could be the unsympathetic dervish come to visit, I thought, or Svoronos, who had found paper. Maybe it was the priest, or somebody had brought the Lemnian tablets I had ordered. It couldn't be Ataman; he had already come by to offer fleeting condolences. He brought an ample supply of that salted meat they press and cure between horse and rider and announced that on the fortieth day after Basil's death, he would throw a banquet for the people of Plekia to celebrate the departure of his spirit. Had I not known what lay behind this tradition, I might have taken it the wrong way, but I did know. Feeding spirits, throwing oil into a fire, spilling wine onto the ground, or pouring araki on graves all meant something to the Turks. He believed Basil's spirit would linger for forty days if it were the sort that refused to accept the idea of its own death. Therefore, leading up to the fortieth day, a kam would perform a series of rituals to help it move on. Then, on the day itself, the spirit would ascend to the sky. That day's banquet was both a farewell and a gesture of nourishment – for the living and the dead – to ease any ongoing confusion in the soul and hasten its adaptation to its new plane of existence. Ataman hadn't suggested any of those rituals, though, but he did insist that I should attend the banquet and, of vital importance, eat the food prepared in Basil's honour and memory. The more people ate, the better it would be. He had done the same for his daughter-in-law Alma, but I had been unable to bring myself to join that meal.

If what he claimed were true, then Basil's spirit would be hovering about us, and if he were watching me now, he would undoubtedly be displeased with my current living arrangements. In life, he would never confront me directly, he preferred to utilise Anna as his intermediary, setting us at odds with one another. He would only intervene if the quarrelling escalated to the shouting stage or if Anna complained to him about me behind my back. But now that Anna was no longer here, I was the boss and free to accommodate my animals wherever I pleased.

Still, the thought that it could be Ogan at the door made me jump, for my habitat really was unpleasant. I roused myself, opened the windows and shoved my domestic companions outside. Pegasus, who had never been keen on residing indoors with me in the first place, left without a word. Dog, however, protested.

Half-gently, half-forcefully I jostled him out the door. While he stood out there barking, Madam Gabras entered, along with her buck-toothed, gangly daughter-in-law, and some servants carrying food on trays. Before I could recover from my astonishment, she bounced towards me and hugged me tightly. Dog slipped back in through the door they'd left open. When she released me, her face was moist and red.

The gangly girl stood watching us. Her protruding teeth and moon-eyed expression inspired a flicker of pity in me – and yet it was I who was the object of pity in the room. Who could have guessed that my misery could engender such a gush of compassion – and bodily fluids – from Madam Gabras?

Between loud sobs she told me, "I brought you several dishes, Theia, and honey rice pudding as dessert. How… are you, my child? How…?"

"I'm very well," I informed her, without conspicuously emoting. "Thank you."

Not convinced, she cocked her head and raised her eyebrows: "Do you need anything, child?"

"I need nothing, thank you very much."

Looking around, she ignored the viscous mist and the generous scattering of dog hair. "Where is Anna? She should take the trays we brought to the kitchen…"

When I told her Anna had left, she let out a small "Oh" in a cracked voice and lightly hit her chest with her fist.

The gangly girl did not speak a word. I ordered a male servant to take the trays to the kitchen. Madam Gabras's shoulders were still quaking when she left, the hand that was not on her chest digging under her belt for a handkerchief.

After they had gone, I went to the kitchen to have a look at her honey rice puddings, with Dog trailing behind. We dealt with them as we had Anna's puddings. He devoured his share in no time. Gabras's dessert was no match for Anna's, being both flavourless and sludgy. I tried a spoonful but spat it out immediately. No wonder they were all thin as sticks, the gangly girl, Nike and Gabras herself.

But I had to change things at home – that much she helped me recognise. That was when I decided to *"Give to Caesar what is Caesar's and to God what is God's."* I took in my Grandfather Zeno's illegitimate son, his wife, and their son and his wife to share with them my wealth and homestead. I did so with the optimistic anticipation that the women of the family could cook a decent honey rice pudding, and they did not let me down. Across the veranda, stood a gigantic cellar built back in grandfather Zeno's time, long since obsolete. By erecting partition walls and restoring the interior, we converted it into an agreeable abode for the family. Zeno's illegitimate son Zeno, my uncle, was much younger than Basil. In the beginning, he resembled Grandfather Zeno a bit too much for my taste and comfort especially in his build and sharp facial features. I nearly got cold feet about the project and considered funding a separate dwelling for them elsewhere. But this passed quickly. I had mistaken the new Zeno's extreme reticence as an unhappy likeness to his father. In truth, both he and his wife, an easy-going character, were hard-working peasants – guarded, circumspect and maybe a little afraid too – and so was their son. I found their boy's similarity to Basil poignant but also endearing, with his cow-brown eyes and bulbous nose, and a hearty laugh from deep inside which he exhibited in those rare moments he overcame his timidity. Not once did they fail to show me respect. It is true that, though we belonged to the same bloodline, our upbringings were worlds apart. I attempted to provide education on a par with my own for their grandchild, another Zeno, who joined the family later, and later still for little Basil. With the adults, however, I never managed to achieve any sense of equality. No matter how friendly and informal I tried to be with them they clung fast to the knowledge that they were different – that they knew 'their place.'

I came to accept this fact and over the course of the years, their apparent contentment made me relinquish the idea of changing them into something they were not. I was their benefactress, patroness, and rescuer from extreme destitution. The jealous God of Exodus 20:5 who would punish children for the sins of their parents was showing mercy this time, which he had not done for the child of Emperor Manuel, who was broken into pieces at the hands of Andronicus.

While, once upon a time, Uncle Zeno's grandchildren went hungry, having been born out of wedlock, little Zeno and Basil would go on to enjoy security – and savour Homer – in the future.

49

I would fain grow old learning many things.

Plato, *The Dialogues*

THE courier hailed from the East, not the West, evidently, for he sported a turban tied with floating ends on the back of the neck. The rounded neckline of his tunic revealed an opening in the centre, and the biceps were embellished with a decorative band. This band would typically display words written in Arabic script, signifying the wearer's status as a prestigious person or an Islamic authority, and indicating loyalty to the Caliphate or to the ruler whose name was inscribed on the sleeve. But in this case, they were knit-work patterns: he was, after all, a mailman – sufficiently distinguished to be trusted with precious cargo, but not distinguished enough to wear a long tunic, for he was always on the go, riding a horse. Not looking directly into my eyes and bowing as low as possible, he extended a silken case to me; along with a small, carved wooden box, and a sealed letter.

"The case is for a bookbinder whose name is Svoronos, and the box with the letter is for you, My Lady."

"From?"

"His Imperial Majesty Andronicus Komnenos."

I couldn't resist a chuckle. "But he's not the emperor!"

Appearing unwilling to let me ask further questions, he took a step back, still bowing, still looking at the ground, and then turned hastily toward his horse.

"Stop! Where is he?" I shouted.

Reluctantly, he turned. "In Iconium."

"Still?"

He shook his head. "Still." As he vanished from sight, I opened the case. Inside were three dinars, slightly more than an ordinary family could survive on for one month. Not too bad, I thought… Andronicus compensating Svoronos's favour with money borrowed from Sultan Mesud. How was he supposed to reimburse the Turks, though? What was he promising?

The box was made of applewood, with stars interlocked through rabbetting and mortising – typical Turkish work, assembled without glue. Not unlike Ogan's chest – beautiful, perfect. However, it didn't invoke adulation but only a yearning, so imperfect in its excellence, so nearby and far away at the same time. Inside lay a golden apple. I took it in my hand and turned it about. It couldn't be a simple figure. It was pleasant enough to look at, but the shape was imperfect, its lines were clumsily sketched from certain angles, uneven. If he had sent it, then surely it must hold something more, I thought. The stem and the upper part of the fruit looked like a lid. I tried to open it but couldn't. I twisted it slowly and a jolly-looking worm hidden in its flesh wriggled out: the object, then, served no purpose but amusement.

I flinched when I opened the letter for it was written in purple ink derived from sea whelks. How on earth had he obtained the emperor's ink in Iconium, let alone dared to write with it? What sort of deluded fantasy was he suffering from now? What type of cunning wile was he formulating? I forgot about these questions the moment I read the message:

> My little one,
> The Sultan and I share similar feelings about Manuel's incompetent foreign policy and sense of loyalty to his blood and family. The Sultan knows that on a personal level he owes this grand Prince born in Purple a great debt for having deprived him of his freedom. These things he is bestowing upon me are paltry nothings, trifles weighed against the enormity of his crime, and because of this he is not loaning funds to me, he is merely settling a nominal debt.
> After that silver perfume-bottle shaped like a hare – did you think I did not know? – this becomes the second gift you

receive from a man. The first was from an epicene mongrel, the second from a manful man. The first was from that fop-doodle who fed you false hopes and used it to weave pain within you; the latter, by virtue of which you shall be brightened, taught a lesson, and shown the ultimate reality of this world, is from me, darling, your Andronicus. I trust, of course, in your astuteness to discern the difference at once and fathom the "truth."

With greatest sympathies,
Yours,
Andronicus.

It takes time for a young emperor to learn when to appear incapable and when not to, and how to project power while, in truth, being weak. It takes many instances of being taken in before one learns to conduct oneself with circumspection: what to say and what to withhold, how to present oneself to others; and it takes years of foolish denial, which we call 'love' – before we acknowledge the wickedness in others. By the time we truly learn what real love is, the body – the chief culprit which has deceived and misled us hitherto with its caprices, cravings, and complaints – has grown foul. There is little time left to relish our new discovery. It is nature's cruel decree: no soul may return to inhabit a fresh body once it has ceased to feel shame for the flesh and has at last forgiven it. By the time the spirit wants to enjoy carnal blessings, the body has become decrepit.

Once the young Emperor Manuel had acclimatised to his station and its demands, he saved Andronicus from Sultan Mesud without paying a ransom. He also came to the rescue of the city of Prakana that was besieged by the Turks. In youth, one tends to judge things at face value. The most dangerous rulers are young ones, but every emperor must be young once. Some people remain young forever. It is very difficult and painful, at times inconceivable, for that specific breed – the eternally young – to envision the workings of canting, unctuous heads and their token gestures honed over years and years of living. This "everlastingly childlike" ilk, however, does not become 'seasoned'; even if father time pressures him to, he resists. To such a man, "the other person" he encounters is ever pure by default, he sculpts his statue from pure marble, not from terracotta or common stone. And if while working on it, misfortune strikes – say, the marble is flawed within, or he ends up crafting a hideous sculpture – this naïve artist, his hands bruised and cut, is dumbfounded, yet undeterred. Still doubtless, he will carve his next statue from a pristine stone again, pristine like his heart; and so it goes, with every new statue. If our guileless artist is not a sculptor but a writer, his parchment is endless, spotless, benevolent, almost sacred. Not the smudgy, tainted pieces that you find in times of scarcity, where words must be erased, and the parchment re-used. In Constantinople, this sort of artlessness tends to be labelled as gullibility or simply stupidity. In Plekia, we are not so practised, we consider ingenuousness as a bellyache to be dealt with; we tolerate it with a cynical smile on our faces. Plekia is more forgiving than Constantinople of the naïve.

There are others, doomsaying sculptors, who are ill intentioned by nature. If they should create beauty and virtue, it happens by accident. Beauty and goodness must prove themselves to such men. They have a critical eye. They trust neither the marble, nor the parchment, nor their own hearts. Inadvertently, they expect that by design, the ugliness will settle piece by piece as portions are shed, time after time, forever.

Naturally, a young emperor resembles the gullible artist; he must learn to temper his optimism, and curb the lenience and trust he extends to others. His dignitaries, luminaries, and eminences are all, a priori, tainted parchments – perhaps even his cousin. Had Andronicus been kidnapped twenty years later, Manuel would have never made it known to his cousin that, after one year, he was being liberated without any pay-off. He would have pretended to pay a sum so vast that even the Caliph would struggle to amass it, and a docile, gleeful Andronicus would grandly, resplendently believe it; he would not feel insulted. An emperor must learn. He must change. It is no easy task. It hurts. It hurts to discover nothing is pristine.

As for the apple automaton with the worm inside – its meaning shifted over the years, depending on my mood or the latest news of Andronicus's exploits. In truth, the interpretation changed constantly. Perhaps that was the very moral he wanted to convey. Or he was simply trying to say that life is not impeccable and that one day we must all rot. Then again it could have been as vulgar and plain as an attempt on his part to console me: *Madam Apple was not so perfect, you know?* I doubted if it referred to himself for he would never consider himself a golden apple with a worm inside. Whatever its meaning, it was mature, clever in its being Delphic, and yet one cannot help but wonder how a man of such sagacity fell victim to his own misjudgement, his own ill-fated misunderstanding? He was an apple who did not even know he had a worm inside. One may see the whole world clearly but remain blind to oneself.

50

Will years ne'er make thee wise? Must thou live on to cast a slur on age?

Sophocles, *Oedipus at Colonus*

THE few people I knew who had come within a decade of my age all succumbed and never rose again. Their vim vanished for good. The only one to reach my present age was Ataman. He didn't die a particularly painful death, though that had been one of the fates foretold for rejecting his ancestor spirits' call to become a kam. Nor did he end up disabled, as the second prophecy had foreseen. The third possibility was madness and I'm still uncertain whether he truly escaped that one since the definition of 'mad' shifts with time. Should you live as long as he and I have, you might begin to suspect that longevity is itself a sort of madness. In his later years, he began to lose his words, or so witnesses said. At times, he forgot where he was; later, he could no longer place people he had once known. He ceased speaking altogether, and when addressed, he either didn't hear or feigned to understand nothing. This decline precipitated a life of isolation for him, sealed in hermetic stupor. Nobody knew what was going on in his head. There were no expectations, no decisions, no obligations, only a daze akin to the trances the kams plunged into.

When I was younger, I fell many times, but nowadays I do not even stumble despite the twinges. My bones have begun to ache lately. For one second of bliss like Ataman's, I could give my whole life without flinching. Now I wait restively for the fateful second that will bring my death. It will last exactly as long as every other second, no longer, no shorter, but will be one solitary moment which carries off a whole life that was spent waiting for bliss.

Having lived this long, I expected to one day find the Lampedona flower or the magic mushrooms. Both were purported to glow in the dark and illuminate their surroundings like a real lamp. Do they exist or not? Do they truly shine in the dark? *The Apocalypse* was written in Patmos, and the seven churches destined to receive its message were also located on this very ground: Ephesus, Smyrna, Pergamum, Thyatira, Sardis, Philadelphia, and Laodicea – the seven lamps of wisdom. Jesus spoke: "The mystery of the seven stars that you saw in my right hand and of the seven golden lampstands is this: the seven stars are the angels of the seven churches, and the seven lampstands are the seven churches."

He said: "Do not be afraid of anything that you are going to suffer. Indeed, the devil will throw some of you into prison, that you may be tested, and you will face an ordeal for ten days."

One must give this land, Rhomanoi, its due: Indeed, it was here that *the Apocalypse* was written, and here, too, flowed the river of the Garden of Eden. I would like to believe that the luminous plants, too, are here, though I have yet to encounter them. In this land, marvels and catastrophes both cross the threshold from idea to reality. They say that soon, on the fifteenth or sixteenth of September this year, 1186, seven stars will align under the sign of the Balance and a catastrophe will manifest. People are shielding their windows, digging bolt-holes underground, and stock-piling food in cave shelters. Look now, how these mature, good people are so distraught. They're burrowing holes underground – one or two as grey as I am – yet none of us has the answers: not the moles, nor the chivalrous Latins, nor the undaunted Turks. I only ask that you to be kind to the few old folk still about, even when they seem to act acrimoniously. And do not be afraid of anything that you are going to suffer.

And did I not tell you, that it was an old Saracen who prophesied that Jerusalem would not stay in Christian hands for long?

EDERN Publishing stands out from traditional publishing houses with an approach that breaks with the "book chain" in which literary life has become entrenched.

To find out more, we invite you to read the presentation on the website www.ederneditions.com, and in particular the Charter, which defines the commitments and responsibilities of the various players involved in this project.

We compare ourselves to a corsair ship where everyone contributes to the success of the publishing adventure and reaps a fair share of the profits.

On this ship, there are Wings and Feathers. The Feathers are authors, whether established or not, novice or seasoned. The Wings are seasoned Writers who accompany the Writers and their manuscripts through to publication. With the exception of reissues, there is always a Wing to accompany a text, and the "copyright" is shared between the Wing and the Writer, depending on the amount of work the former has had to do.

Divine Madness, by Esin Özmen, benefited from the support of a Wing, Éric Brogniet.